JERUSALEM
PRAYER TEAM
✡

"Pray for the Peace of Jerusalem..."
www.jerusalemprayerteam.org

DR. MICHAEL D. EVANS

PRESIDENTS
in
PROPHECY

#1 *NEW YORK TIMES* BESTSELLING AUTHOR
MIKE EVANS

P.O. BOX 30000, PHOENIX, AZ 85046

This book is respectfully dedicated
to a true friend of Israel:
The forty-third President of the United States,
George W. Bush.

BIBLE & SCRIPTURE PASSAGES *from*
PRESIDENTIAL INNAUGURATIONS 6

PREFACE.. 9

PART I

(1) IS AMERICA *in* PROPHECY? 19

(2) THE JOLT *of* JIHAD 33

(3) THE UNITED STATES: SPIRITUAL *or* SECULAR?......................... 45

(4) A LAND DIVIDED 53

(5) EXPORTING HATE 65

(6) THE HIGH COST *of* APPEASEMENT 73

(7) LUNATICS, LIBERALS, *and* LIARS 81

(8) BATTLE LINES ARE DRAWN
     through the HEART *of* JERUSALEM 91

(9) THE CITY *of the* GREAT KING....................................... 101

(10) WINNING THE WAR *on* TERROR 111

(11) TENACITY *to* THWART TERRORISM 117

(12) THE NEW ANTI-SEMITISM 125

(13) CONSEQUENCES *of* ANTI-SEMITISM 135

PART II

(14) PRESIDENTS *and* PROPHECY 147

(15) GEORGE WASHINGTON *and* HAYM SALOMON.............. 157

(16) JOHN ADAMS, THOMAS JEFFERSON
     and THEODORE ROOSEVELT....................................... 165

(17) PRESIDENT WILLIAM TAFT *vs.* HENRY FORD 173

(18) WOODROW WILSON APPOINTS *the*
FIRST JEWISH SUPREME COURT JUSTICE..................................179

(19) WARREN G. HARDING, CALVIN COOLIDGE,
and HERBERT HOOVER 187

(20) FRANKLIN D. ROOSEVELT AVOIDS *the* JEWISH ISSUE..............197

(21) FDR'S TRAGIC DECISIONS 207

(22) FDR FINALLY ACTS 215

(23) FDR'S IDEA *for a* JEWISH HOMELAND 221

(24) HARRY TRUMAN DECISIVELY MOVES FORWARD......................231

(25) TRUMAN *and the* JEWISH DELEGATION................................239

(26) TRUMAN VERSUS *the* STATE DEPARTMENT 249

(27) TRUMAN RECOGNIZES THE STATE *of* ISRAEL...........................261

(28) EISENHOWER'S IMMEASURABLE
CONTRIBUTION *to* HISTORY 271

(29) JOHN F. KENNEDY–LYNDON B. JOHNSON ERA.........................281

(30) RICHARD M. NIXON *and*
GERALD FORD ACT *on* ISRAEL'S BEHALF 295

(31) JAMES EARL (JIMMY) CARTER:
PALESTINIAN CHAMPION... 305

(32) RONALD REAGAN: *a* FAITHFUL FRIEND................................ 315

(33) GEORGE H.W. BUSH (41) 325

(34) WILLIAM JEFFERSON CLINTON 329

(35) BILL CLINTON–REDUX 345

(36) GEORGE W. BUSH BREAKS RANK 355

(37) BARACK OBAMA: NO MIXED MESSAGE..................................367

(38) THE FIG TREE BLOSSOMS 377

APPENDIX A: AN INDEX *of* ANCIENT PROPHECIES 391

ENDNOTES 397

BIBLE & SCRIPTURE PASSAGES—
PRESIDENTIAL INAUGURATIONS[1]

Each President of the United States, when sworn into office, has had the option of using the Bible of his choice open to a particular portion of scripture. Both the Bible and the scripture chosen were of special significance to the men who have served in the White House. The table below lists the known selections:

George Washington	1789	Genesis 49:13[2] (Masonic Bible); opened at random due to haste
George Washington	1793	Not known
John Adams	1797	Not known
Thomas Jefferson	1801, 1805	Not known
James Madison	1809, 1813	Not known
James Monroe	1817, 1821	Not known
John Q. Adams	1825	Not known
Andrew Jackson	1829, 1833	Not known
Martin Van Buren	1837	Proverbs 3:17[3]
William H. Harrison	1841	Not known
John Tyler	1841	Not known
James K. Polk	1845	Not known
Zachary Taylor	1849	Not known
Millard Fillmore	1850	Not known
Franklin Pierce	1853	Affirmed instead of swearing the oath; did not kiss Bible
James Buchanan	1857	Not known
Abraham Lincoln	1861	Opened at random

Abraham Lincoln	1865	Matthew 7:1; 18:7; Revelations 16:7[4]
Andrew Johnson	1865	Proverbs 21
Ulysses S. Grant	1869	Not known
Ulysses S. Grant	1873	Isaiah 11:1-3[5]
Rutherford B. Hayes	1877	Privately, no Bible; publicly, Psalm 118:11-135
James A. Garfield	1881	Proverbs 21:1[5, 6]
Chester A. Arthur	1881	Privately, no Bible; Psalm 31:1-3[5, 6]
Grover Cleveland	1885	Psalm 112:4-10; Bible opened by Chief Justice and by chance it fell to this Psalm[7]
Benjamin Harrison	1889	Psalm 121:1-6[5]
Grover Cleveland	1893	Psalm 91:12-16[5]
William McKinley	1897	2 Chronicles 1:10; Bible given to him by Methodist church congregation[8]
William McKinley	1901	Proverbs 16[5]
Theodore Roosevelt	1901	No Bible
Theodore Roosevelt	1905	James 1:22-23[5]
William Howard Taft	1909	1 Kings 3:9-11[5]
Woodrow Wilson	1913	Psalm 119[5]
Woodrow Wilson	1917	Privately, not known; publicly, Psalm 46[9]
Warren G. Harding	1921	Micah 6:8 (Washington Bible)[5]
Calvin Coolidge	1923	Not known
Calvin Coolidge	1925	John 1
Herbert C. Hoover	1929	Proverbs 29:18[5]
Franklin D. Roosevelt	1933, '37, '41, '45	1 Corinthians 13[5]
Harry S. Truman	1945	Closed Bible held in left hand; right hand on upper cover[10]

Harry S. Truman	1949	Matthew 5:3-11 and Exodus 20:3-17[11]
Dwight D. Eisenhower	1953	Psalm 127:1 (Washington Bible) and 2 Chronicles 7:14 (West Point Bible)[12]
Dwight D. Eisenhower	1957	Privately, not known; publicly, Psalm 33:12 (West Point Bible)[13]
John F. Kennedy	1961	Closed Bible[14]
Lyndon B. Johnson	1963	Missal[15]
Lyndon B. Johnson	1965	Closed family Bible[16]
Richard M. Nixon	1969, 1973	Two family Bibles, both open to Isaiah 2:4[17]
Gerald R. Ford	1974	Proverbs 3:5-6[18]
James E. Carter	1977	Family Bible open to Micah 6:8[19]
Ronald W. Reagan	1981, 1985	Mother's Bible open to 2 Chronicles 7:14 (Both privately and publicly in 1985)[20]
George H. W. Bush	1989	Washington's Masonic Bible opened at random in the center; family Bible on top opened to Matthew 5
William J. Clinton	1993	King James Bible, given to him by grandmother, open to Galatians 6:8
William J. Clinton	1997	King James Bible, given to him by grandmother, open to Isaiah 58:12[21]
George W. Bush	2001	Closed family Bible[22]

PREFACE

As an advocate for Israel, I have for the last four decades stood in defense of the Jewish people and their homeland. In the 1970s, God opened a door for me to become a confidant to Menachem Begin. When I arrived in Israel and met him for the first time, he asked me why I had come. I had no answer for him. We talked for ten minutes in his office, and the prime minister asked me again why I had come. Again, I had no reply. We discussed his having had two heart attacks and the fact that one of his grandchildren had attempted suicide. He opened up to me as if I were his pastor.

At the end of our thirty minutes together, he asked me the question a third time. I replied, "I know God sent me."

"What? God sent you to meet with me; did He tell you why?"

"No sir," I responded.

Mr. Begin turned to his secretary, Yechiel Kadashi, and shouted, "Shake this man's hand. You have met an honest man. He flies 8,000 miles to meet with the prime minister; he says God sent him, but he doesn't know why!" He turned to me, "When God tells you why would you come back and tell me? I'm very curious." I assured him that I would.

Two days later, I met again with Prime Minister Begin to tell him that God had sent me to Israel to build a bridge—a bridge of love between Bible-believing Christians and Jews."

Mr. Begin's eyes lit up. He stuck out his hand and said, "We will build this bridge of love together."

In December 1988, I flew to Geneva, Switzerland, and checked into the Hilton Hotel. I believed that God would open doors with leaders of nations, and to my amazement, I was allowed into the facility where the General Assembly meetings were being held. It looked as if I would only be allowed upstairs in the nosebleed section. After PLO Chairman Yasser Arafat had delivered his speech, it was concluded that he had not clearly stated that he would denounce terrorism as had been expected. He was forced to hold a press conference, which was predominantly peopled by the PLO executive council and organization members. The location had not been divulged to the general public.

The moment I heard of the meeting, I walked the halls of the building and prayed. The Spirit of God spoke to me and directed me to go to room 401. Once inside, He sent me to the second row of seats next to a long table. There I was told to put my locked briefcase on the center chair and then leave the room.

Hours later, as Arafat's minions filled the room strict security was in place to keep out those who were unwanted. When the room was completely filled, I approached one of the terrorists acting as a security guard and requested that I be allowed to find my seat.

"What seat? You have no seat here. You cannot enter," he snapped.

My reply was: "Go to the front row of chairs. You will see my briefcase on the second row, middle seat. Open it; the combination is 0001. Inside you will see my passport and several other things."

He reluctantly turned and stalked up the aisle. Shortly he came back and escorted me to the chair that held my briefcase. Minutes later, Arafat entered. I was directly in front of him in the middle seat. The camera crews had been assigned row three—just behind me. Not even the PLO executive council had been permitted to sit in rows one and two. The cameramen were screaming because my head was in the way.

Before me was a table where Arafat and the few men who would accompany him were to sit. They entered the room, and the PLO chairman delivered his speech. Afterwards, he said, "I shall allow three of you to speak. You may choose among yourselves."

Knowing I would not be chosen, I clutched my Bible, stood to my feet, and held aloft a copy of the PLO charter. "Mr. Arafat, if you denounce terrorism, then denounce this covenant that calls for the destruction of Israel." Raising my Bible in the other hand, I began to recount the biblical position of the Jewish people.

Arafat screamed: "Shut up, shut up! What must I do to make you shut up?" When he paused in his rant, I turned and was met by eyes filled with murderous hatred because of what I had said. Suddenly, it was as if a carpet had been rolled out. I saw a path I could navigate. I walked quickly through the midst of the gathering into the dark hallway, climbed into a taxi and was taken back to the hotel.

In October 1991, at the conclusion of the first Gulf War—Operation Desert Storm—Israel was again forced to the bargaining table at the Madrid Peace Conference. Viewing the richly appointed royal palace, I realized the beautiful interior was all glitter and no substance, a disguise for its actual purpose: the place where even more land-for-peace would be demanded of the Jews.

The ceiling in the grand Hall of Columns was ornately embellished with the images of false gods: Apollo, Aurora, Zephyrus, Ceres, Bacchus, Diana, Pan and Galatea. From their lofty perch, these bogus gods looked down on the official proceedings to elicit a counterfeit peace. Like the apostle Paul at Mars Hill, I found myself praying to the one true God while under that canopy of idolatry. How ironic that Israel had been forced there, of all places, for an international peace conference—to Spain, where one-third of the Jewish population of its day had been massacred during the Inquisition. Representatives of nation after nation mounted the podium to insult and accuse Israel, and to demand that her leaders relinquish the majority of her land.

I can still hear their voices reverberating through the marble halls: "We will accept your land in exchange for peace." What they were really saying was: "This is a stick-up. Give me all your land and you won't get hurt—much." Muggings usually happen on the streets of major cities, yet the Madrid Peace Conference, by any measure, was an international mugging. And the world was the silent witness too intimidated to report it to the police. Most of the nations represented pretended not to see the "gun" pointed at Israel's head.

As I left one of the meetings, the Syrian foreign minister stopped me, pulled a picture of Yitzhak Shamir from his pocket and told me he intended to accuse the prime minister of being a terrorist. Shamir had been a member of the *Irgun* (an early Israeli paramilitary organization). I borrowed a cell phone and called Benjamin Netanyahu to relate to him what I had been told. The next morning before the beginning of Shabbat and in the presence of President George H.W. Bush, President Gorbachev, and other world leaders, Mr. Shamir stood and said, "I have to leave now. I am an Orthodox Jew, and I leave these proceedings to my able delegation." Thirty minutes after he departed, the Syrian foreign minister stood to speak but faced only an empty chair where Shamir had sat.

In March 2009 I was in The Hague, Netherlands, at the International Conference on Afghanistan. It didn't take long to discover just what Secretary of State Hillary Clinton would deliver to Iran, whose Islamic Revolutionary flag was flying just a few feet from the U.S. flag on the dais. The only flag not in evidence at the convention was Israel's. But then, why should they have been invited when the majority of Arab states still refuse to recognize their basic right to exist?

I stood and spoke boldly against Secretary Clinton's assurance to those in attendance that the majority of the Taliban were "moderates" and the U.S. would accept them if they wanted to join forces. What? The Taliban are the extremists who decapitate Jews and Christians. Its adherents throw acid in the faces of young girls or shoot them at point-blank range just for going to school. There is no such thing as a moderate Taliban.

I was outraged to realize that the terrorist nation whose proxies are killing Jews and wants to wipe Israel off the map with an atomic bomb would be invited to "help" the US win the terror war in Afghanistan.

On July 19, 2013, Secretary of State John Kerry announced President Obama's new peace plan that had the support of the Arab League. The pressure on Israel is and has always been to divide Jerusalem from east to west, making East Jerusalem—the home of Christianity—the capital of an Islamic state. Most of Judea and Samaria would be included.

During the same week, the European Union announced sanctions to exclude all Israeli settlements in the "occupied territory" from European cooperation—an economic declaration of war against Israel. Such a move would cost the Jewish state tens of billions of dollars in lost trade.

It took the US government six months of shuttle diplomacy and six trips to the region to accomplish this feat. Stunningly, at the same time, almost one hundred Syrians have been killed in a civil war; the Muslim Brotherhood has torn Egypt apart; Iran is but the turn of a screwdriver away from going nuclear, and Hamas and Hezbollah terror organizations are plotting every conceivable act to kill Jews. No, none of those issues were on the U.S. diplomatic radar screen.

For too long, God-fearing Americans have been silent. The prophet Zechariah, in chapter 12, verses 2 and 3 declared:

> "I am going to make Jerusalem a cup that sends all the surrounding peoples reeling. Judah will be besieged as well as Jerusalem. On that day, when all the nations of the earth are gathered against her, I will make Jerusalem an immovable rock for all the nations. All who try to move it will injure themselves."

The United States is in prophecy. Since the inauguration of George Washington, who on April 30, 1789, placed his hands on Genesis 49:10, NKJV, which reads:

> "The scepter shall not depart from Judah . . . Until Shiloh comes."

From that day forward, America has been blessed because she has blessed the Jewish people and Israel. Genesis 12:3, NKJV, says, "I will bless those that bless thee, and curse him that curses you."

Now, rather than confronting the radical Islamic virus that is rampant in the Middle East, the U.S. seems determined to antagonize the State of Israel, America's greatest ally in the region. If God-fearing Americans do not take a stand, a curse will fall upon this country. The United States must not touch prophecy by leading the nations of the world to divide Jerusalem, or by taking Judea and Samaria from the Jewish people.

Throughout history, the nations that came against Jerusalem were cursed by God and ended up in dust and ashes. The Roman Empire collapsed after destroying the Temple and leveling Jerusalem. Israel was God's dream; the title deed belongs to God Almighty. When he gave Jerusalem D.C. (David's capital) to the Jewish people, there was no Washington, D.C. or even a United Nations—only pagan nations. The prophetic spotlight of heaven is on Israel. It all began there, and it will all end there. If America touches God's prophetic plan and people, she will be sticking a finger in the eye of God:

> "For he who touches you, touches the apple [pupil] of His eye," (Zechariah 2:8, NKJV.)
>
> "I have set watchmen on your walls, O Jerusalem; They shall never hold their peace day or night. You who make mention of the LORD, do not keep silent," (Isaiah 62:6, NKJV.)

Presidents of the United States have played a sometimes major role in determining whether Israel survived and thrived or was overrun by the enemy outside the gate. Some have compromised the relationship between the U.S. and Israel; others have proven to be staunch friends. Those who desired the blessings of God upon themselves and this nation stood strong in the face of intimidation and terror. The U.S. has one reliable ally in the Middle East—Israel—and must defend her right to exist in Palestine—the Jews' God-given homeland.

PART I

PROPHECY

(1)

IS AMERICA *in* PROPHECY?

"Their horsemen come from afar; they fly like an eagle . . . "
(Habakkuk 1:8b.)

Is America in prophecy? While skeptical of attempts by many to link the United States to prophetic interpretations, after many hours of research I am totally convinced that the US can be found in prophetic scriptures, though not mentioned directly by name.

The thread began in the Old Testament with Abraham and his offspring, Isaac and Ishmael. The US has tried to join hands both with Israel, a descendant of Isaac, and Arab countries, descendants of Ishmael:

> The LORD had said to Abram, "Leave your country, your people and your father's household and go to the land I will show you. I will make you into a great nation and I will bless you; I will make your name great, and you will be a blessing. I will bless those who bless you, and whoever curses you I will curse; and all peoples on earth will be blessed through you," (Genesis 12:1-3 NKJV.)

The United States has endeavored to employ Israel, the tiny democratic state in the midst of a sea of instability in the Middle East, as a firewall in deterring communism, fascism, and terrorism. Its liaison with Arab countries is one of convenience and economics: The mortal enemy of Israel brought a dowry of black gold (oil) to the marriage and uses it still today to intimidate the United States.

The Middle East is home to two-thirds of the world's global oil reserves. OPEC presently accounts for forty percent of the world's oil imports. According to the International Energy Agency, by 2030 that figure is on course to rise to sixty percent. By that time, it is projected the Middle East will supply fifty percent of US oil imports, fifty percent of European imports, eighty percent of China's imports, and ninety percent of Japan's imports.

As Middle Eastern oil flows to the West, arms are shipped in their direction. In fact, the Middle East region is currently the United States' number one client for weapons of war. Even after 9/11, petrodollars earned by countries such as Saudi Arabia, Iran, and Libya have been utilized to sponsor terrorism, produce weapons of mass destruction, and finance a gospel of hatred that is employed to brainwash millions of Islamic youth. America has been unwilling to admit that it is being blackmailed, let alone drawing a firm line in the sand against it. It's time for the US to stand up to these bullies and stop capitulating to blackmail; our future depends on it.

Knowing Islamic fundamentalists are hell-bent on annihilating the tiny country, Israel has developed the fourth largest nuclear arsenal in the world. Israeli leaders are determined that what happened in the Holocaust will never happen again. Israel has reportedly opened her nuclear silos during three Middle East wars, and has targeted cities such as Baghdad, Damascus, Cairo, and even some in the former Soviet Union.

It has long been known that Israel has had nuclear strike capabilities since at least the late '1960s. Today Islamic nations are very close to having a finger poised over the red button as well. It appears at least one of these nations may have obtained suitcase nuclear bombs paid for by money from oil sales to America. In addition to this, the *Washington Post* reported the following on December 21, 2003:

> Documents provided by Iran to UN nuclear inspectors since early November have exposed the outlines of a vast, secret procurement network that successfully acquired thousands of sensitive parts and tools from numerous countries over a 17-year period. . . . While American presidents since Ronald Reagan worried that Iran might seek nuclear weapons, US and allied intelligence agencies were unable to halt Iran's most significant nuclear acquisitions, or even to spot a major nuclear facility under construction until it was essentially completed . . . . Iran's pilot facility, which is now functional, and a much larger uranium-enrichment plant under construction next door are designed to produce enough fissile material to make at least two dozen nuclear bombs each year.[23]

Through these two political—and spiritual—liaisons, the US has stepped into the center of a prophetic storm. She now finds herself trying to accommodate Jew-haters who have refused even to acknowledge the very existence of the State of Israel. The US now has to appease with both bombs and baksheesh (bribes): more than $400 billion in military equipment and over $100 billion in aid have been dispatched to various Arab countries.

Liberal politicians and special interest groups continue to propagate a myth that Islam is a peaceful religion, but think about this for a moment: Islam has approximately one billion adherents worldwide. The actual number is probably higher, but one billion is a nice, round number for the sake of argument. Even if 99.9 percent of the Islamic world is completely nonviolent, grave danger still exists. If only one-tenth of one percent of all Muslims were radical Islamists, that is still a staggering number: it means that one million people are intent on murder and destruction. It took only nineteen hijackers to wreak massive destruction on the United States on September 11th. Each one of those men believed he was on a divine assignment from Allah.

The terrorists' war against the US and Israel is rooted in a radical religious doctrine called Islamic fundamentalism, a distorted belief very difficult to comprehend. One reason is that our modern secular world is still conflicted by the relationship between science and religion—which most assume was won by secular science. Suddenly, a religious adversary is attacking secular America. It's no longer just the streets of Jerusalem that are threatened, but those of New York, Washington, Boston, and who knows how many other cities.

In April 2003, while the US was in the midst of the Persian Gulf War, I wrote a book that ultimately became a *New York Times* bestseller, *Beyond Iraq: The Next Move.* In the book, I stated my belief that weapons of mass destruction were in Syria. It took the US almost a year to be willing to admit that. I also stated that compliments of the Syrian government and the Iraqi Embassy in Damascus, money and key Iraqi leaders were being moved through Syria.

It is possible the US may soon have to go to war against Syria, a proxy of Iran and a much more dangerous terrorist-harboring state than Iraq. Hopefully that war can be fought through economic and diplomatic means without the loss of American lives. If not, the US—and Israel—will still be forced to shut down the engine of terror in Syria.

Untold numbers of free world troops died because Syria allowed Islamic martyrs to use their country as a pipeline from other Arab states into Iraq to attack the US "infidels." There is little doubt that Israel will have to go into Iran and take out its nuclear reactor in the same way it did in Iraq. It appears likely, too, that the US will turn a blind eye while Israel does so, and then deny any involvement, as it did in the 1981 attack on Iraq's nuclear reactor.

Israel must be allowed to fight the war against terrorism that it has never fought. Sadly, it will undoubtedly be forced to do so alone. Israel is surrounded by enemies and must be allowed to root out the terrorist organizations that threaten. The war on terrorism will never be won as long as Syria, Lebanon, Gaza, and the Palestinian territories remain points of exportation for suicide bombers. The dissemination of media propaganda that enrages the masses from adjoining Arab countries must also be stopped.

True hope for peace lies in discerning truth and acting on it, not in believing myths propagated by liberal power brokers that incite Jew-hatred. Too many people in the US view the real enemy as "narrow-minded, right-wing, Bible-thumping Christians" who believe in black and white, right and wrong. The same people who see conservative Christians as the enemy often legitimize the acts of cold-blooded murderers as a means to obtain freedom and peace. These apostles of appeasement have raised the hopes of the Islamic fanatics so high that the national security of the United States is now at stake, and equally important, our very freedoms are at risk.

The question is often asked: Why do Islamic fanatics hate us? The answer: They just do! The more important question is this: What is fueling that hatred, and how can the engine of hate be derailed? Bigotry is at the root of it all. It is no coincidence that the World Conference on Racism in Durban, South Africa, turned into a "World Conference on Jew-hatred," and ended three days before September 11, 2001. Was there a correlation between the US and Israel walking out of the conference, and the events on 9/11?

Many believe the current Palestinian crisis has much to do with the issue of Jew-hatred, and it does. The entire Palestinian crisis can be attributed to two things—refugees and terrorism.

Is there another refugee crisis anywhere on earth that has drawn the world into such a mess? The answer clearly is, "No." Civilized countries solve refugee crises on their own; conversely, the Arab world has fueled and fed the Palestinian refugee crisis to exploit Jew-hatred. The attitude is: "Blame the Jews for all problems, just as Hitler did, and we will not be held accountable for our brutality." Since these "thug-ocracies" are run by the bullet, and not the ballot, someone needs to bear the blame . . . why not the Jews and so-called crusaders. The Liberal Left media contributes mightily to the problem.

The US has done little, if anything, to address this danger that must be stopped. Every possible means available must be used to shut down the Islamic fundamentalists who kill in the name of Allah. Some have even recruited children and used them as suicide bombers, mine sweepers, and decoys.

How did Israel solve its refugee crisis in Europe at the end of the Holocaust? How did it resolve the crisis in Arab countries where Jewish citizens were being killed? It simply took care of its own.

Why did the Arab League turn its back on the very refugees it created? Why did it initiate the myth that Israeli Arabs must have a separate state inside Israel, even though a Palestinian state has never existed? These refugees were told that Egyptian-born billionaire terrorist Yasser Arafat was their "George Washington." Why?

There is, I believe, a direct correlation between current events in the Middle East and prophecy. I am firmly convinced that President Jimmy Carter unlocked Pandora's Box in the Middle East; then President Bill Clinton stepped into the ensuing maelstrom. The US began to tolerate subtle anti-Semitism perpetrated in the name of Islam. It is a bigotry presently polluting and poisoning the peace of the world. The war on terrorism cannot be won without a war against such prejudice.

Had the US maintained moral clarity, Iran might have continued to be pro-Western. Iraq might never have gone to war against Ayatollah Khomeini and Iran's Revolutionary Guard, a war which took the lives of 1.2 million Arabs. The USSR might not have invaded Afghanistan, and America would not have armed and trained thousands of terrorists throughout the Middle East to battle the Soviets. These same US-trained and armed terrorists—Osama bin Laden's *al Qaeda* being the most infamous example—have now turned on America. The truth is: America might never have ended up in this mess had it maintained a conservative policy of not negotiating with terrorists.

Rev. W. O. Vaught, Clinton's pastor while he was governor of Arkansas, and who made more than forty trips to Israel during his lifetime, told Clinton that God would forgive him for mistakes he made while in office:

> "Bill, I think you're going to be President someday. I think you'll do a good job, but there's one thing above all you must remember: God will never forgive you if you don't stand by Israel."[24]

That quote turned out to be as prophetic for the Clinton presidency as Galatians 6:8:

> "For he who sows to his flesh will of the flesh reap corruption, but he who sows to the Spirit will of the Spirit reap everlasting life,: (Galatians 6:8, NKJV.)

Barely a month into his first term, President Clinton received a wake-up call from bin Laden's organization. On February 26, 1993, a truck bomb exploded in the underground parking garage of the World Trade Center in New York City. While this first WTC attack went relatively unnoticed, in it were seeds of the eventual September 11 attacks, and not only at the same location. The actual aim of the bombing was to topple the towers and kill as many as 250,000 people—seven individuals died.[25] If the attack had been successful, we would be commemorating February 26, 1993, rather than September 11, 2001. But, because our president at the time was more occupied with implementing his economic program than keeping Americans safe, US security forces paid little attention to the bombing.

As the author of *Losing bin Laden*, Richard Miniter, said about Clinton's inability to deal with bin Laden throughout his presidency:

> In 1993, bin Laden was a small-time funder of militant Muslim terrorists in Sudan, Yemen, and Afghanistan. By the end of 2000, Clinton's last year in office, bin Laden's network was operating in more than fifty-five countries and already responsible for the deaths of thousands (including fifty-five Americans)....
>
> Clinton was tested by historic, global conflict, the first phase of America's war on terror. He was president when bin Laden declared war on America. He had many chances to defeat bin Laden; he simply did not take them. If, in the wake of the 1998 embassy bombings, Clinton had rallied the public and the Congress to fight bin Laden and smash terrorism, he might have been the Winston Churchill of his generation. But, instead, he chose the role of Neville Chamberlain (whose appeasements of Hitler in Munich in 1938 are credited with paving the way to the Nazi invasion of Poland that began World War II the next year).[26]

The 1993 WTC bombing had been planned and organized by Sheikh Omar Abdel Rahman who said:

> The obligation of Allah is upon us to wage Jihad for the sake of Allah. It is one of the obligations which we must undoubtedly fulfill... and we conquer the lands of the infidels and we spread Islam by calling the infidels to Allah and if they stand in our way, then we wage Jihad for the sake of Allah.[27]

The FBI eventually found forty-seven boxes of Rahman's terrorist literature. In an unbelievable fit of moral blindness, the agents marked the tops of the boxes, "Irrelevant religious stuff." It seems the very reason for the attacks and failing to connect them to the worldwide Islamic fundamentalist movement that had fueled it was totally dismissed.

In October 1993, the same year as the first World Trade Center attack, US troops had been sent on a humanitarian mission to Mogadishu, Somalia. Two Blackhawk helicopters were shot down and a roughly twenty-hour firefight ensued in which nineteen US soldiers and over a thousand Somalis were killed. Shortly after the massacre, President Clinton made the decision to pull out of Somalia. Evidence was later found that the Somalis who shot down the helicopters had received training from bin Laden's forces. Those same mercenaries had become adept at bringing down advance Soviet helicopters in Afghanistan with rocket-propelled grenades. Bin Laden eventually admitted his significant involvement in Somalia, although in a supporting role, and considered it a glorious victory for Islamists.[28]

The United States is still the mightiest nation on earth and has long been a partaker of God's blessings. During the past few decades, America has seen her culture polluted, attempted to dethrone God, and defiled her heroes. Bible-believing Americans have been demonized as bigots and extremists. God has been taken out of schools, courts, and town squares, and some have even tried to remove Him from the Pledge of Allegiance— "one nation, under God." The same moral compromise infecting our domestic policy has also tainted our foreign policy: the US sends foreign aid annually to such terrorist-harboring countries as Egypt, Iraq, Jordan, Pakistan, West Bank/Gaza, Indonesia, and Somalia.

If Americans do not wake up to the truth, the US political machine will continue on a collision course with prophecy. Many believe there is nothing we can do about it; that if it is foretold, it must come to pass. However, we could be missing the true point of prophecy. The Bible doesn't tell us what the future holds so that we can sit back and let disaster strike; but rather so that we can take any necessary actions to make sure we are on the prophetic side of blessing. In the Old Testament God often warned His people of impending disaster—not just so they would know it was coming, but to give an opportunity for repentance and restoration. It is up to God-fearing Americans willing to step out and make a difference to keep our country headed in the right direction in both domestic and foreign policy.

This is also why in 1981 I accepted an invitation from President Reagan's staff to attend a high-level briefing with US generals and admirals over the sale of AWAC planes to Saudi Arabia. I challenged them regarding that decision, warning that those planes could eventually end up in the hands of Islamic fundamentalists thereby posing a major threat to US and Israeli security. When I inserted a scripture into my short speech, I was asked, "What does God know about foreign policy?"

I replied, "He *is* foreign policy!"

Do we truly think we can move our government forward without His guidance? Our forefathers certainly didn't!

Several months later, as part of a small US delegation, I was invited to have lunch with President Reagan and his Cabinet. Sitting next to me was the late Chuck Colson who was making his first visit back to the White House since his Nixon days. I said to Mr. Colson, "I imagine you're thinking all about the White House strategy that's going on in this room." He smiled and said, "Not at all. I'm thinking about one thing . . . eternity!"

His statement really struck me. Sooner or later everyone on this planet—rich and poor; skeptic and religious; president and pauper—will be forced to think about eternity. Can we really plan for the future—of our nation, our world—without considering it? While democracy may have been conceived in Greece, it was not until Bible-believing, God-fearing people joined together to form the United States of America that it has risen to the ideal it has become today. Our governmental structure may not be perfect, but it is the best our world has seen, and all because it was founded as a system defined by moral clarity, and based upon biblical principles.

Dr. Martin Luther King Jr. said, "Nothing in the world is more dangerous than sincere ignorance and conscientious stupidity."[29] The US entered the twenty-first century with a terminal case of both. Our nation is in this position primarily because of its alliance with both Israel and the Arab nations. The descendants of Abraham, Isaac and Ishmael, are still in a struggle for dominion; the US has stepped right into the middle of it.

Ancient scriptures have a great deal to say about the two spirits behind this battle. Ishmael was not the son of promise, but the son of a man trying to work the will of God in his own way. God had promised Abraham a son, but his wife Sarah was barren. At her insistence, Abraham took Hagar, her maidservant, and impregnated her. Ishmael was the result of that liaison. A man of faith, Abraham acted in his own wisdom and lust rather than following God's direction. He justified a foolish action through moral relativism, tradition, and human reasoning. He was trying to secure God's blessing on his own terms. It was not until some years later when the son of promise, Isaac, was born that Abraham fully realized the gravity of his mistake. Rejecting the "son of human reasoning," God made a covenant with Isaac, the "son of faith." Ishmael became the father of the Arab race, and Isaac a patriarch of the Hebrews. The battle continues even today. The Quran teaches conversely that Ishmael, not Isaac, was the son of promise, and that he inherited the land and the title deed to Jerusalem.

The United States today is caught in the same moral dilemma: wanting to "do good" without God, but only making our halls of government secular, amoral, and blind. Instead of looking to God for blessings and prosperity, we look to our own reasoning and logic. For this reason we are willing to trade almost anything to get the black gold—oil—that keeps our economy lubricated.

The majority of Arab countries have believed the same lies spoken by Hitler to twist the minds of the Germans: that the Jews are the reason for the ills of the world at large. If they were simply annihilated, everyone worldwide would sleep easier. Yet, the US has done little to counteract this vile doctrine. Instead we label as diplomats those who preach hatred and anti-Semitism—terrorist organizations such as the PLO, Hamas, Hezbollah, Islamic Jihad, and others. Through negotiations, Israel is forced to make concessions to an implacably angry Arab world that will never be appeased with a Palestinian state. Only possession of all of Israel will suffice.

While terrorists may wave the Palestinian Authority flag with the cry of "Death to Americans," we cannot believe that it will suddenly begin to love the US and Israel if statehood is granted.

Dr. Yossef Bodansky and I spent considerable time in Jerusalem discussing this matter. In his book, *The High Cost of Peace*, he states that the Palestinian step-by-step plan to retake Palestine actually came from the experience of the Vietnamese in dealing with the US:

> Abu-Iyad detailed how he brought up the question of why the Palestinian armed struggle was considered terrorism whereas the Vietnamese struggle was lauded and supported throughout the West [to the Khmer Rouge]. His host attributed this phenomenon to the different ways the two liberation movements had packaged their goals. The Vietnamese team agreed to sit with the PLO delegation and help them develop a program that would appear flexible and moderate, especially in dealing with the United States, the Vietnamese explained, one must "sacrifice the unimportant if only in order to preserve the essential."[30]

The book emphasized that the Palestinian Authority must remain committed to its ultimate objective—namely, "the establishment of a unified democratic state in the entire Palestine"—in the near term, and that it would be politically advantageous to accept transient phases and even short-term solutions. The Vietnamese suggested accepting "the division of the land between two independent states," without making it clear that this was only an interim phase.

The Hanoi team also introduced the Palestinians to such issues as dealing with the US media and with liberal political circles and institutions. It also provided insight into the power of the Jewish community. Experts in disinformation and psychological warfare assisted the Palestinians in formulating a "moderate political program accepting the establishment of a small Palestine in the Territories." The result was the "Phase Plan" adopted as the resolution of the twelfth Palestinian National Council in Cairo on June 19, 1974.

We can never win the war on terrorism by appeasing terrorists on the one hand while trying to dislodge them with the other. This is a sure guarantee for another 9/11—or worse. This tide will never be turned without getting to the root of Palestinian hatred for Israel and for the US, and exposing it at the source.

(2)

THE JOLT *of* JIHAD

In righteousness shalt thou be established: thou shalt be
far from oppression; for thou shalt not fear: and from terror;
for it shall not come near thee,
(Isaiah 54:14, KJV.)

The teaching of jihad must be unearthed and outlawed in America. Islamic fundamentalists use religion to recruit *shahids*—martyrs—men or women willing to kill themselves. When the late Yasser Arafat delivered a speech calling for one million martyrs to liberate Jerusalem, he was not simply humoring the crowds. Jerusalem has experienced more terrorist attacks than any city in the world. When Islamic fundamentalist clerics in mosques across the nation of Islam call for jihad, it is not just religious jargon: Islamic fundamentalists kill.

It's not only critical that we understand why they hate Westerners, it is absolutely vital that we understand why they act on that hatred. The *shahids* believe they are performing a holy ritual for Allah. From childhood, Muslims are taught that to be a martyr one must be chosen by Allah, the greatest honor in life. They are taught that when a martyr dies, there is no memorial, but rather a wedding. This is the reason Muslim families forego a funeral when a child commits an act of martyrdom; instead, a wedding celebration is held.

The prospective *shahid* is told that when the holy and religious act is performed:

» He will feel no pain or fear. In essence, the sting of death is removed.

» He will not die, but will go directly to paradise; his own personal and immediate resurrection.

» He will be honored when he arrives in paradise with a crown of glory with a jewel of the wealth of the world in the center of it. (In Christianity, saints lay their crowns at the feet of Jesus.)

» He will attend the wedding accompanied by seventy-two black-eyed virgins. The word "black-eyed" does not denote eye color; it denotes that they are incorruptible–an interesting word. This belief is so strong that before the act of martyr-dom, the *shahid* shaves all pubic hair, and tapes his private parts, symbolic of what is to come.

» He will pave the way to paradise for seventy rela-tives, and will be exempt from the horrors of hell. In essence, the blood of the *shahid* atones for sin.

The insane aspect of this belief is that a diabolical battle for the minds of children begins in kindergarten. Cartoon characters similar to Mickey Mouse or Donald Duck are combined with a message to seduce and recruit small children as *shahids*. Kindergarten camps teach the principles of *jihad*. Bridges, roads, parks and buildings are named after the suicide bombers. Posters with photos of the martyrs are everywhere.

(Thousands of children were forced to clear minefields during the Iran/Iraq war. Red plastic "keys to heaven" were hung around their necks and a martyr's badge pinned to their clothing as they were sent out to die a horrible death.)

Today's war on terrorism is fueled by stone-age hatred—the same as Cain had for Abel, Ishmael for Isaac, and Satan has for Jesus. Terrorists wage a spiritual war of fear and bigotry beyond understanding; such a war cannot be won with tactical weapons alone.

Islamic fundamentalists are the reason for the September 11 attack that launched the United States into a war against terrorism. The ideology is as lethal as fascism or Nazism. As long as godless liberals attempt to dull the senses of God-fearing Americans with a steady stream of political correctness, the war on terrorism will not only survive, but thrive. In order to win this battle, Americans must speak out against moral decay, bigotry, and anti-Semitism as Abraham Lincoln, Martin Luther King, and other brave men and women have done.

Yet Americans hide their collective heads and do little to counteract the vile doctrines embraced by Islamic fanatics. Instead, in order to appease Arab allies, Israel is often denied its rightful place as full partner and democratic ally in the Middle East. For instance, following the first Gulf War, Israel was forced to bear the attacks of Saddam Hussein without being allowed to retaliate. The US aligned herself with Islamic terrorist-funding regimes and armed Islamic terrorist-harboring states. This is a certain guarantee for another 9/11—or worse. Bigotry is an equal opportunity employer: Extremists murder Christians with the same justification used to kill Jews. Someone needs to shout out, "It's about prejudice, intolerance, and narrow-mindedness!"

The war on terrorism being waged today is a spiritual war of fear and hatred. There has never been a more urgent time for Americans to act with moral clarity than today. Despite the danger, we seem more complacent than ever. The future of our nation, as well as our world, hangs in the balance between apathy and action.

The US has rejected the foundation that has traditionally held it together (God and the Holy Scriptures) and as it drifts away from that center, we no longer hear His voice. As a nation our innocence has perished. Those who would declare the Words of God—in the political arena, the pulpit, and the halls of justice—no longer possess that conviction in order to be effective. They are being systematically silenced because of a perverted interpretation of "separation of church and state." First Amendment rights are denied to those who would speak for God; meanwhile those who fight for self, special interests, and immorality are passionately intense as the spirit of the world takes over. This spirit can be seen in the "isms" that have plagued us: fascism, Nazism, communism, and now twenty-first century terrorism—one of the greatest threats to human liberty the world has ever faced.

The final battle will one day take place in Israel. The line will be drawn through the heart of the city of Jerusalem, whose disposition has continually thwarted peace efforts in the Middle East. Palestinians have been offered their own state time and again—first in 1947 by the United Nations, then in 1991 at the Madrid Conference after the Gulf War, then at the Wye River talks, and again during a desperate President Bill Clinton's final days in office. The major stumbling block on the way to peace has always been control of East Jerusalem, the historic city of David where the Temple Mount rests—the very spot where heaven and earth met, and will meet again. Many of the most dangerous prophecies concerning the nations of the world are written in its stones. It all began with, "But now I have chosen Jerusalem for my Name to be there, and I have chosen David to rule my people Israel," (2 Chronicles 6:6, NIV.)

With the dawn of the first decade of the twenty-first century, the United States continued to stand prominently as a buffer between the Arab nations and Israel. From the time of Israel's declaration of statehood on May 14, 1948, providing military materiel during the Yom Kippur war of 1973, and the defense aid we have given since, no nation has championed Israel as has the US. On the other hand, since 1945, when

President Franklin Delano Roosevelt met with Hitler-supporting King ibn Saud of Saudi Arabia and promised that no decision regarding the Middle East would be made without first consulting the Arabs, the US has also been closely linked to the Muslim nations in that region.

US influence on both sides goes even farther back. What these relationships have done is make the United States a broker accepted by both Arab and Jew to attempt to barter peace between them. This position has placed the United States squarely in the eye of the storm of biblical prophecy.

Caught in the tug of war between oil, political expedience, and conscience, decisions and policies concerning the Middle East will determine whether the United States survives or goes the way of the Roman Empire. Only the People of the Book—and I mean the Bible—can tip the scales in the right direction.

Though many warnings have sounded, America remains too complacent. As examples:

» 1983 - Beirut barracks bombing, October 23, 1983; 305 people, including 241 US servicemen, killed by 2 suicide bombers.

» 1985 - TWA Flight 847 hijacked; US Navy diver Robert Dean Stethem killed by Hezbollah terrorists.

» 1985 - *Achille Lauro* hijacking, wheel-chair bound Leon Klinghoffer, an American killed by Palestinian militants.

» 1988 - Pan Am Flight 103, outbound from London for New York with 259 people aboard, destroyed by a Libyan bomb on December 21, 1988 while over Lockerbie, Scotland. All aboard the aircraft were killed as were eleven persons on the ground.

» 1988 - 1990 - Marine Col. Rich Higgins kidnapped, tortured and murdered by Hezbollah terrorists.

» 1993—First World Trade Center bombing, February 26: 6 killed, 1,042 injured.

» 1995 - Killing of two US Diplomats in Pakistan, March 8.

» 1996 - Khobar Towers bombing: 19 American servicemen killed.

» 2000 - USS *Cole* attacked in Aden, Yemen; 17 Navy sailors killed, 39 injured.

» 2001 - September 11, 2001 World Trade Center attacks, 2,997 killed;

» 2003 - Three American diplomats killed by a roadside bomb targeting their convoy in Gaza. Palestine Resistance Committees, an umbrella organization has taken responsibility for the attack.

» 2004 - Civilians Nick Berg, Jack Hensley, and Eugene Armstrong kidnapped and beheaded in Iraq.

» 2004 - Paul Marshall Johnson, Jr., civilian working in Saudi Arabia, kidnapped and beheaded; five other Americans died in attacks in Saudi Arabia.

» 2008 - John Granville, US diplomat, assassinated in Khartoum, Sudan.

» 2012 - US Embassy in Libya attacked. The ambassador and three other Americans killed.

» 2013 - Boston Marathon bombings, 3 killed, 183 injured.

The spirit driving Hitler and Stalin is the same one driving terrorists today. It is the spirit of hatred that always begins in the same way: first with Jew-hatred and then graduating to hating Bible-believing Christians. If you read some of the Islamic papers today, many are eerily reminiscent of newspapers from the early years of Nazi Germany. Hitler's gospel has resurfaced.

The United States can ill afford to ignore signs that another world war could soon be upon us. The first is the increase of rabid anti-Semitism again spreading throughout Europe and which has never ceased in Arab countries. Do not doubt the US can be destroyed by terrorists despite it being a mighty nation. If Americans were to experience an equivalent number of suicide attacks in malls, movie theaters, restaurants, churches and synagogues per capita as does Israel—and that would mean hundreds of attacks weekly—would it not be better to declare all-out war on terrorism now, before all-out war is declared on US cities?

Arab leaders are at the tip of a pyramid whose base rests on the blood-lust of millions of fanatics, sympathizers, and potential terrorists who lionize the bin Ladens of the world.

Kesser.org, a literary repository yielded the following opinion:

Joseph Goebbels was Hitler's master propagandist. Using the medium of radio and motion pictures, he crafted some of the most compelling propaganda theater of all time. Weaving together myths about the German Teutonic past, as well as exploiting traditional German xenophobia and anti-Semitism, he must be seen as one of the major fertilizing agents [manure] in allowing Nazism to take hold. Similarly, Adolph Hitler, who was one of the most charismatic German speakers, used his oratorical strengths to both vilify Jews, as well as to play on feelings of lost German pride after the "disaster" of WWI. It was this combination of negative propaganda (anti-Semitism, anti-west, anti-communist) as well as "positive" propaganda . . . that was the key to toppling the forces of humanity, civility, and democracy in Germany.

Similar parallels exist in modern Arab and Muslim nationalism. Arab propagandists have a rich soil for spreading their lies. There are fears in the Arab and Muslim world about being swallowed in permissive secular western culture and about loss of identity. This is coupled with a deep sense of history and awareness of the fall of the Arab/Muslim world from its dominant position to one of subservience to the West. The Arab world, like the pre-war German world, is searching for a banner and champion to restore its lost pride and identity.[31]

Why would the US then turn a blind eye and even fund anti-Semitic, terrorist-harboring regimes? Have we learned nothing from 9/11? Have we forgotten the screaming mobs chanting, "Death to Israel" and "Death to America?" The goal of an Arab conquest of Israel is to launch another Holocaust. As for the United States, Islamic extremists hate everything about us, but their greatest hatred is our Christian majority and biblical principles upon which our nation was founded—the emancipation of women, freedom, wealth, power, and culture. They want to kill Americans because of all we represent in their oppressed and twisted minds.

While researching this book both in America and the Middle East, I experienced some eye-opening revelations about America's role in prophecy—past, present, and future. Below are some of the questions I have had answered:

» Why does America continue to feed and fuel Islamic regimes that are more racist than the Nazi Party and whose population is taught terrorists-breeding ideologies?

» Why was America afraid to arrest a terrorist/ murderer, Yasser Arafat, who killed dozens of Americans, including diplomats; a terrorist who kept on his desk one of Hitler's best-loved books, *The Protocols of the Elders of Zion*, and proudly quoted from it?

» Why has America not allowed Israel to fight a real war against terrorism?

» Why did the US State Department keep FBI agents from arresting three terrorists traveling with the Saudi entourage that met with President Bush in Crawford, Texas seven and a half months after the 9/11 attacks?

» Why did leaders of nations call for a 2001 conference on racism and the attendees work themselves into a rage against the Jews? Why was the United States attacked just seven days after joining representatives from Israel in walking out of the conference in protest?

» Why is Hitler's *Mein Kampf* still a bestselling book throughout the Muslim world over sixty years after Hitler's death?

» Why is the US promising a terrorist regime for half of Jerusalem when prophecy pronounces a curse on those who divide this city?

Our nation's fate will be determined in a final test. Will the US choose God's side of the prophetic battle, or will she fight against God? If America chooses the latter, she will end up on the ash heap of history.

The war against such apocalyptic hatred, I believe, can never be won without first dealing with four key issues:

1. America must not ignore the virus spreading the plague of Jew-hatred throughout the Middle East. The flood of billions of dollars of war materiel flowing into Jew-hating Arab regimes must be stopped, and the recruitment of a new generation of suicide bombers must be deterred.

2. The events on September 11, 2001, would never have happened had the US fought bigotry in the 1990s rather than appeasing those who spread it. Millions of Jews would be living today if anti-Semitism had not been ignored in the 1920s and 30s.

3. The war on terrorism has been fueled by US support for Islamic terrorists surrounding Israel. The Arab world also feeds that war to save its own "thug-ocracies." These leaders have refused to take care of their own so-called refugees as the rest of the world has done. This mind-set has infected world leaders (as evidenced by the Durban Anti-Racism Conference of 2001.) Should that support continue, the war on terror will never be won.

4. America is under a biblical curse—one that can be reversed. Jerusalem is to be the final compromise. Should the US support dividing Jerusalem, there will be no forgiveness.

This nation has been "weighed in the balances and found wanting" (see Daniel 5:27, NKJV.) The graveyard of history testifies that God rejects nations that reject Him and His Word. Is God preparing to reject America, or will God-fearing Americans stand in the gap and speak the truth? These words are etched into the wall in the lobby of the original CIA headquarters building in Washington, DC, to characterize the intelligence mission of a free society: "And ye shall know the Truth and the Truth shall make you free," (John 8:32.)

I believe we are closer than ever to the coming of Christ. America's fate will be determined in a final test. It is time to repent and return to the God of our fathers, and to our Judeo-Christian beliefs!

Many who speak on the subject of prophecy give a sense that circumstances are accelerating toward some unknown event. Prime Minister Benjamin Netanyahu, speaking before the US House of Representatives Government Reform Committee on September 20, 2001, said: "September 11 was a wake-up call from hell that has opened our eyes to the horrors that await us tomorrow if we fail to act today."

In Deuteronomy 30:13, Moses warns:

Today I have given you the choice between life and death, between blessings and curses. Now I call on heaven and earth to witness the choice you make. Oh, that you would choose life, so that you and your descendants might live!

(3)

THE UNITED STATES: SPIRITUAL *or* SECULAR?

"Where the Spirit of the Lord is, there is liberty,"
(2 Corinthians 3:17, NKJV.)

From the charters drafted by the Pilgrims who first colonized what would one day become the United States of America, our forefathers purposed to be a force for good on the earth as defined by the Bible and its prophecies. As stated in the Declaration of Independence, they believed these truths to be "self-evident, that all Men are created equal, that they arc endowed by their Creator with certain unalienable Rights that among these are Life, Liberty and the Pursuit of Happiness." Thomas Jefferson, one of the writers of that Declaration, further said: "Can the liberties of a nation be secure when we have removed a conviction that these liberties are the gift of God? That they are not to be violated but with his wrath?"[32] From this first declaration and by invoking the blessings of God in its foundation, our forefathers placed the United States of America into the hands of God for its existence and its future.

Bible prophecy begins and ends with the nation of Israel. By founding the nation and its values on these same scriptures, the framers of our Constitution forged an alliance with God's chosen people. This decision would eventually lead America to be a key player in bringing about the most significant prophetic event in nearly two millennia—the rebirth of the nation of Israel.

Though some scholars debate whether or not the United States was founded as a Christian nation, it is difficult to look at the writings of the founding fathers and not see their faith. There are many writers who do a better job of proving this than I can here, but suffice to say that up until the latter half of the twentieth century this debate would never have been raised. In fact, in 1892, in the case of *Church of the Holy Trinity vs. United States* the Supreme Court ruled that the Church has precedence over state and federal law, because "This is a Christian nation." In the court opinion written by Mr. Justice David J. Brewer, the court felt that:

> No purpose of action against religion can be imputed to any legislation, state or national, because this is a religious people. This is historically true. From the discovery of this continent to the present hour, there is a single voice making this affirmation. . . . [33]

From there the Justice went on to give various examples of America's connection to Christianity in documents ranging from the foundational principles set forth for the colonies to the constitutions of several of the states to a myriad of court cases supporting biblical principles, all of which supported Christianity as the basis of our laws and government. One argument from the state of Pennsylvania even went so far as to say that the defense of Christianity was a necessity, while the defense of the religions of the "imposters" Muhammad and the Dalai Lama were not. From these precedents, Mr. Justice Brewer had this to say in his concluding remarks:

These and many other matters, which might be noticed,
add a volume of unofficial declarations to the mass of
organic utterances that this is a Christian nation.[34]

If the Supreme Court found this to be "a Christian nation" even 116
years after the Declaration of Independence, then it is odd we should find
otherwise today. Somewhere along the way we have lost connection with
our roots—our moral compass was replaced by moral relativism and the
ship of our great nation began to drift off course.

Considering these roots, it is not surprising to see that Christian
men setting the foundations of our nation felt an ingrained bond with the
dispersed Children of Israel in their day. They were the other people of
the Bible, the descendants of Isaac, with whom we felt a kinship from the
beginning, and with good reason.

American history textbooks once carried a story revealing
Washington's heart concerning how God's hand was upon him. On July
9, 1755, during a battle of the French and Indian War near Fort Duquesne
in Pennsylvania, Washington was the sole mounted officer to survive
uninjured, despite the fact that he had four bullet holes in his coat and
two horses were shot out from under him. On that day over half of the
nearly 1,300 American and British troops with him had been killed or
wounded, including the British commanding officer, General Edward
Braddock. History eventually dubbed Washington "bulletproof" because
of this incident and his never having been wounded in battle.[35] A godly
man was needed to chart the course of the United States as its first
president, so it appears His hand of protection rested upon Washington
throughout his lifetime.

While America was a Christian nation at its inception and throughout
the Civil War, can the same be said about us today? If we are not following
godly principles, has the hand of God that protected George Washington
and the United States during earlier years and conflicts been removed
today? After the attacks of 9/11, we should answer a definite "Yes."

The United States adopted the Ten Commandments and laws of the Bible as the basis for its own laws. The newly-born nation rejected tyranny, creating a constitution of checks and balances to control government power, and also declined to embrace old world struggles, i.e., that of Christian against Jew, as part of its culture. The fledgling government took literally the Scripture, "old things are passed away; behold, all things are become new," (II Corinthians 5:17, KJV.) This admonition was the basis of "separation between church and state"—that all faiths would have the right to freedom of religious gatherings, worship, expression, and that the State would not dictate which church one attends, nor would it deter anyone from expressing their faith in public office or halls of government.

The writings of Georg Hegel were not then available to our forefathers when the US constitution was forged. Hegel, born in 1770, conceived the dialectical philosophy that would inspire Karl Marx who preached that the State was actually "God walking on earth . . . and had the foremost right against the individual." [36]

The founding fathers saw no conflict between these freedoms and an outward demonstration of their religious beliefs as they went about daily, nor would they silence any religion at the behest of those who chose not to believe in God at all. The government was not to be anti-religious, amoral, or secular as the courts seem to think today—but rather impregnated with the Judeo-Christian virtues of love and a dedication to pray for others rather than try to force change upon them.

This kindred spirit between Jews and early American founders would be taken to a deeper and more active loyalty in just a few decades. In 1814, at a dire point in the midst of the War of 1812, the United States caught a glimpse of what it would grow to be just over a century later: a nation integral to the rebirth of Israel. A Presbyterian pastor in Albany, New York, John McDonald made a startling discovery while teaching on Old Testament prophecy to his congregation. He had been preaching on the subject for some time, especially focusing on the prophecies in the book of Isaiah, which spoke of the restoration of the nation of Israel and the subsequent redemption of humankind. One day, while pouring over Isaiah 18, he read a challenge to "the land shadowing with wings, which is beyond the rivers of Ethiopia: That sendeth ambassadors by the sea," (Isaiah 18:1-2.) In this he believed that "beyond Ethiopia" meant a nation far to the west of Israel, which was where Isaiah spoke these words. It was a nation shadowed by wings—a nation whose symbol was a great bird—like the bald eagle, perhaps—one that sent its ambassadors by sea. He pondered: what other nations were forced to send their ambassadors by sea besides those on the continent of America? In MacDonald's eyes a prophetic notion took shape—it had to be the United States! And what was the challenge to this nation? "Go, ye swift messengers, to a nation scattered and peeled, to a people terrible from their beginning hitherto; a nation meted out and trodden down, whose land the rivers have spoiled!... In that time shall the present be brought unto the Lord of hosts . . . to the place of the name of the Lord of hosts, the mount Zion" (Isaiah 18:2, 7.) In that chapter, MacDonald heard a clarion call from God for the great nation of the United States to send ambassadors to help reestablish a kingdom for the Jewish people upon Mount Zion—the city of Jerusalem![37]

While Washington and other founding fathers had called the Jews friends and allies of our nation and seen the founding of America as a parallel to the Jews coming to possess their promised land of Canaan, MacDonald had seen a divine call to champion the Jews. It was a call to help them regain their own nation, in the Holy Land with Jerusalem as its capital. In his eyes, America was the nation of prophecy that would "send their sons and employ their substance in his heaven-planned expedition"[38] to reestablish the nation of Israel.

Thus MacDonald sounded a prophetic trumpet: "Jehovah . . . dispatched American messengers to the relief of his prodigal children. Rise, American ambassadors, and prepare to carry the tidings of joy and salvation to your Savior's kinsmen in disgrace!"[39]

It was not long thereafter that a flamboyant New York Jew by the name of Mordecai Manuel Noah stepped behind the lectern of New York's Shearith Israel synagogue on April 17, 1818 and struck a similar note, one that would resonate for over a century and a quarter. In his address that day, he stated that the Jews:

> . . . will march in triumphant numbers, and possess themselves once more of Syria, and take their ranks among the governments of the world . . . This is not fancy . . . [Jews] hold the purse strings, and can wield the sword; they can bring 100,000 men into the field. Let us then hope that the day is not far distant when, from the operation of liberal and enlightened measures, we may look towards that country where our people have established a mild, just, and honorable government, accredited by the world, and admired by all good men.[40]

This image of 100,000 Jews marching to Palestine was of note: in April 1948 diplomats discussed returning to Palestine *this exact number* of European Jewish refugees displaced by the Holocaust.

The murders of Jews in Damascus in 1840 had apparently opened the eyes and ears of America's leaders to the need for a Jewish homeland within whose borders Jews worldwide could find security from persecution. The incident was the epitome of old-world prejudices from which the United States had been struggling to escape. It was the first and only time the State Department acted on behalf of Jews without first being prodded by the American people.

The affair was brought to the attention of President Martin Van Buren and Secretary of State John Forsyth in a dispatch from the American consul in Beirut. The document described the massacre of Jewish men, women, and children in Damascus who had been accused of "blood libel," a perceived ritual murder to obtain blood from Christian children to be used in Passover services. Ultimately, it was discovered that French agents had initiated the rumor to incite Muslims in that region against the Jews and to enhance France's position as protector of Christians in the area. While the issue was undeniably a gross violation of basic human rights, the end result placed the United States unequivocally and officially on the side of the Jews. It forced the US to communicate through formal diplomatic channels in support of the Jews. US action was so swift, that by the time the public raised the issue to the government, formal protests had already been lodged.[41]

The British Foreign Secretary, Lord Henry John Temple Palmerston also supported the Jews, being one of the first government officials to endorse Jews in Palestine by extending consular protection to them. Another Englishman, Sir Moses Montefiore took a series of trips to the region and became a new "Nehemiah" with charitable works conceived to help Jews living in Palestine.

In the 1830s and 1840s, a great number of Jews entered the United States from Central Europe. The unrest inciting these families to seek new hope in America was also a precursor of what would happen over the next century. "The Jewish Problem"—i.e., the displaced people of Israel scattered among the nations without a land to call their own—would fuel the Zionist movement and eventually lead to Hitler's abominable "final solution to the Jewish problem" in the death camps.

Even as a young man Adolf Hitler was convinced that he had been anointed to rid the world of "undesirables", and to establish a super race that would rule the world. At the age of 25, he volunteered for military service. He later told an acquaintance that he was so overcome with emotion he fell to his knees, "and thanked heaven from an overflowing heart for granting me the good fortune of being allowed to live at this time."[42] When Austria was swiftly and successfully conquered, Hitler addressed jubilant German crowds:

> I believe that it was God's will to send a youth from
> here to the Reich, to raise him to be the leader of the

nation . . . I felt the call of Providence. And that which took place was only conceivable as the fulfillment of the wish and will of this Providence.[43]

Following an early failure in his rise to power, Hitler affirmed, "We knew we were carrying out the will of Providence, and we were being guided by a higher power...Fate meant well with us."[44] To Italian dictator Benito Mussolini, he stated: "It is obvious that nothing is going to happen to me; undoubtedly it is my Fate to continue on my way and bring my task to completion."[45] And following an assassination attempt, Hitler opined, "I regard this as a confirmation of the task imposed upon me by Providence."[46]

In 1937, five years into his campaign to obliterate the Jews, Hitler was still convinced of his calling and his invincibility:

> . . . yet at the moment when [the individual] acts as Providence would have him act he becomes immeasurably strong . . . When I look back only on the five years which lie behind us, then I feel justified in saying: this has not been the work of man alone.[47]

Fortunately for the Jewish people, biblical prophecy triumphed over Hitler's "Providence."

(4)

A LAND DIVIDED

"God heard the lad crying; and the angel of God called to Hagar
from heaven and said to her, "What is the matter with you, Hagar?
Do not fear, for God has heard the voice of the lad where he is,"
(Genesis 21:17.)

It may seem strange that no one seemed to be concerned about
Arab reaction to a Jewish homeland in Palestine when the Balfour
Declaration was written; at that point, there was little cause for
concern. The Turks, not the Arabs, controlled the region, and Britain
hoped to liberate it by the end of World War I. The Arabs, on the other
hand were scattered throughout Palestine with no central leadership or
apparent nationalistic leanings. In 1917, few, if any, foresaw the war that
would erupt at almost the same hour a Jewish state was declared three
decades later. The reason for this is that while the Jews were struggling
for statehood, Arabs were recovering from having been removed from
long-held control in the Middle East.

The Muslim world was at its zenith in the early part of the second
millennium, excelling all others in arts and sciences. Islam was expanding

into Northern Africa, Europe, and the Near East. Believing non-Muslims to be infidels and barbarians, Arabs cut themselves off from the rest of the world and savored their glory days. Because of this isolationism, the kingdoms of Islam failed to notice when Europe emerged from the Dark Ages into the Renaissance, the Reformation, and then the technological revolution of the early industrial age in the West. Until the late eighteenth century, only one Western book had been translated into a Middle Eastern language—a medical book on syphilis. It was allowed entry because most Muslims felt the disease had come from the West.[48] Earlier in the rise of Islam, Christianity had been the greatest threat to its spread, but as it seemed to be fading with the crumbling of the Roman and Byzantine Empires, Arabs had little trouble thwarting the Crusaders. In their view, Christians would eventually fall by the sword of Allah as all other religions had at the time. China was too remote to be a concern; Africans were too easily made into slaves; India and the Near East were slowly being converted to Islam. The followers of Allah grew content to conquer the world little by little. After all, they felt their eventual dominance was inevitable.

For the Muslims, Judaism and Christianity were thought to be brought to completion by Muhammad in much the same way Christians believe Jesus fulfilled Old Testament prophecy. Thus the threat of Christianity was not one of conversion, but of power, technology, and conquest. Buddhism, Confucianism, and other religions of the East had not fared as well as Christianity, so they posed a much smaller threat. Muslims were not afraid of ideas at this point—for their culture was so much more advanced—but of Europe's military might. Over time, many Muslims developed a tolerance for Christians and Jews as monotheists, or "People of the Book," because they were mentioned in the Quran.

Western culture and ideas soon eclipsed those of the Islamic empires as Arabs and Persians went to war. Author and Islamic history expert Bernard Lewis notes that, had it not been for the Ottoman Empire's differences with Persia, Europe may well have become part of their empire in the mid-1500s.[49] However, the Ottomans fought with the East instead of the West and the struggle went on for centuries, taking attention away from Europe. The Ottoman Turks were Sunni Moslems and the majority of those in Persia and the Arabic Peninsula were Shi'ites. In response to the Shi'ites converting those in the extreme eastern portion of the Ottoman, Ottoman Sultan Selim I (and subsequent Ottoman rulers) invaded the region. At its height in the late 1600s, the Ottoman Empire stretched east to the Caspian Sea engulfing the westernmost parts of Persia (Iran), south to the base of the Red Sea and along the Asir Mountains thus controlling Lebanon, Syria, Palestine, Egypt, Iraq, Kuwait, and edges of the Arabian Peninsula. To the west it reached into North Africa nearly to Morocco, and then north to Hungary and the provinces on the northern shores of the Black Sea. The bulk of the center and southern edges of the Arabian Peninsula however, a vast desert at the time remained free, and the Arabs of that region became tribal, nomadic, and divided during the centuries prior to World War I.

In 1744 Muhammad ibn Abd al-Wahhab had formed the fundamentalist Wahhabi sect and spread it to the Saudis by making an alliance with Muhammad ibn Saud. It appears that al-Wahhab's daughter married ibn Saud, and thus became an ancestor of the Saudi royal family. He preached that Islam was deteriorating because it was being infected with heresy from outside religions—a form of polytheism. Things such as the veneration of the early Islamic disciples, worship of sacred trees and the like were all forms of idolatry—and, again, polytheism. In his *Book of Tawhid*, ibn Abd al-Wahhab wrote, "*Shirk* [polytheism] is evil, no matter the object, be it king or prophet, saint or tree or tomb."[50]

Since there was not a large enough Christian or Jewish population in the Middle East to turn his attention to, he attacked other Arabs who had become apostates. To justify this, al-Wahhab reinterpreted the ideal of *jihad*. For most Muslims of his day, particularly Shi'ites, *jihād* (meaning "struggle"), was described as the spiritual struggle towards holiness. It included missionary outreach, but no longer necessarily called for battles.

However, al-Wahhab taught his followers that for the prophet Muhammad *jihad* had been a "holy war upon the infidels" and had never changed. Those of false faiths—including Muslims who had perverted their religion with outside influences—were deemed acceptable only for either conversion or death. Conversion was definitely the secondary goal. So polytheists, called *mushrikun*, were considered less than human, cattle to be slaughtered in sacrifice to Allah, the one true god, and women, children, the elderly, and the defenseless were no exception. The Spanish Inquisition had nothing on Wahhabism. Under al-Wahhab's doctrines, committing mass murder became a way of drawing closer to God.

With the strength of the Saudi armies, al-Wahhab soon established a nationalist Arab state in Najd, the region in the central Arabian Peninsula around Riyadh. From there a war was waged to purify Islam, including sacking the Shi'ite holy city of Karbala in 1802, part of Iraq today. Its religious shrines and temples were destroyed and the Shi'ites ruthlessly slaughtered infidel polytheists. Al-Wahhab even destroyed the tombs of the first disciples of Muhammad because they were being venerated in a similar fashion to those of Christian saints. During the raids, thousands of men, women, and children were cold-bloodedly murdered—the youngest, the eldest, and the pregnant were all mercilessly executed.[51] In 1803 the Wahhabis captured Mecca and even threatened Damascus from 1803-1805. Eventually though, the marauders were pushed back and retreated to Riyadh, where in 1824 they established their capital and recaptured much of the previously occupied land. However, the dynasty fell into civil war after 1865, with the kingdom divided among the Ottomans and various clans. The Saudi royal family fled to Kuwait for safety.

The House of Saud would, however, rise again. In 1902, a young Abdul Aziz ibn Saud retook Riyadh, and by 1906 his forces controlled the Najd region and were establishing themselves as a fighting force, although a small one. Ibn Saud's forces showed the same brutality in their warfare that their Wahhabis predecessors had a century earlier.[52]

For ibn Saud, the extreme fundamentalism of Wahhabism was an incredible tool for religious and political control. Defined by isolationism and nostalgia, it engendered a longing in its followers to return Islam to its former greatness. It created an aura of romance around the Bedouin lifestyle and the glory of ancient Arabic royal courts. One thing to note about this Muslim fundamentalism is that culture, government, and religion are inseparable for them.

As Zionism began to rise in the West and Britain, Jews were encouraged to look to Palestine as a possible new homeland. Men such as T.E. Lawrence (of *Lawrence of Arabia* fame) and Harry St. John Bridger Philby were organizing Bedouin Arabs to help Britain oust the Turks from the Middle East. While the bulk of this was structured by Lawrence with Sharif Hussein as the puppet leader of the Arabs, the British sent Philby to clean up a bit of muck hampering that cause. A small group of dissident Moslems from an extremist sect were making terrorist raids on Hussein's forces. Philby tried to dissuade their leader, Abdul Aziz ibn Saud, a ruler of the extremist Wahhabi sect, to stop the raids and join the British cause. Ibn Saud, as he became known in the West, eventually went on to establish the nation of Saudi Arabia. Its leaders today are direct descendants.

The idea of separation of Church and state was introduced neither by our forefathers nor modern liberals; it was done by Jesus who said that we were to "Render to Caesar the things that are Caesar's, and to God the things that are God's," (Mark 12:17, KJV.) Christianity was a spiritual kingdom that brought about change in people's hearts; Islam was founded on secular laws of government and culture that then determine one's spiritual status. Thus Christian fundamentalists can deal with the heart issues of the Bible through a more literal interpretation of it and apply them to any culture. They do not demand a return to the dress and cultural practices of Jesus and the disciples.

Wahhabists, however, not only return to a more literal interpretation of the Quran, but also to the culture and practices of the time those scriptures were written. Both progress and modernization are viewed with great suspicion as temptations and corruption. Al-Wahhab preached an ascetic and legalistic doctrine that rejected all luxury: dancing, gambling, music, and the use of tobacco among other things. Such a belief system could not co-exist within another, but must pervade and dominate. Its objective is to take the entire world back to the ninth and tenth centuries. All that is modern is seen as perversion—except modern weapons that can lead to the ascendancy of Wahhabism. Anyone seen as forward-thinking is simply characterized as a follower of the Evil One.

Government and conduct in most Muslim countries today is based upon *Shariah* Law, which consists of four principal sources:

1. the Quran;

2. the Sunnah, a collection of actions and sayings of the prophet Muhammad;

3. *ijma*, meaning "consensus," which refers to the consensus over the centuries of the schools of law, but can also refer to the consensus of the Muslim community;

4. *qiyas,* reasoning by analogy, in which jurists and scholars formulate new laws based on the Quran or the Sunnah. Wahhabists, however, reject *ijma*—there is no room for consensus or other opinions.

Law is thus handed down from the Quran by cleric/judge/leaders, called *ulema,* or scholars, called *muftis,* or in decrees, called *fatwas.* Such declarations are binding and not debatable. The populace needs no education besides these *fatwas,* and, as a result, over half those in most fundamentalist Muslim countries today cannot even read the Quran for themselves. Ibn Saud and his descendants could rule without opposition backed by a religion that enforced his absolute authority.

Outsiders, especially modern Westerners, were viewed quite dogmatically as infidels and contact with them was seen as risking contamination. Thus when European Jews reached the shores of Palestine to build homes and set up shop, they were an incredible threat to the Wahhabist way of life. And with no great love for ruling by consensus, democracy was no welcome neighbor either. The British and their Balfour Declaration were nothing ibn Saud wanted to see in his domain.

Despite this, however, Philby and Saud became friendly—probably because they could be mutually beneficial. It appears that Philby helped make ibn Saud king of Saudi Arabia and Saud helped make Philby rich. Perhaps part of it was also that Philby had an equally strong contempt for the Jews. The two formed a lasting partnership that would empower the Arabs with both hope and the means to return Islam to greatness. What ibn Saud and Philby began in World War I marked a straight and clear path to 9/11 and today's ongoing war against terrorism.

During World War I, both T.E. Lawrence and Philby embraced the Arab culture and ways, and adopted a native lifestyle with Philby assuming the name Sheikh Abdullah. Philby felt that Britain was assuring independence to Arabia if it helped defeat the Turks and Germans. The two promised Arab counterparts everything they wanted in exchange for loyalty. As a result, each of them took it as a slight betrayal when Britain adopted the Balfour Declaration and a full betrayal when Britain refused to move significantly toward Arab independence. Those in power in Great Britain saw the Arabs as a rag-tag lot that couldn't hold a government together if it were handed to them on a silver platter. They weren't worth the effort or expenditure to support, and so they refused to let go of the cords that bound Arab leaders.

Lawrence took this as an affront, yet remained loyal to the crown; Philby decided to turn traitor. He preferred the Arab lifestyle to returning to England, though he did make the trek from time to time to keep up appearances. Philby, an excellent spy, produced a son, Kim Philby, who became the most infamous Soviet double-agent in British history. After the First World War, ibn Saud began to call for the overthrow of British puppet leaders in the region. Philby, who had actually been fired for his outlandish attitudes and outspokenness on behalf of the Arabs, managed with the help of Lawrence to stay on in the Middle East as a chief British representative in Amman, Transjordan. Thus he was in the perfect position to feed ibn Saud intelligence needed to overthrow the British. Ibn Saud took the cities of Jebel Shammar in 1921, Mecca in 1924, Medina in 1925, and Asîr in 1926 with remarkable swiftness. Ibn Saud then proclaimed himself king of Al Hijâz. In 1932, after unifying the conquered territories, he declared Saudi Arabia a nation. It remained a backwater state however, until oil deposits were discovered in 1938. Saudi Arabia played both sides during World War II until it was obvious the Allies would win and then declared war on Germany and Japan in March of 1945. By the time Israel declared statehood, ibn Saud had collected a decade of oil money, and US companies had paid $53 million in royalties, which quadrupled to $212 million by 1952.[53]

This might be laid at the feet of Philby and the British had it not been for the partnership they had with two American brothers, John Foster and Allen Dulles. The two lawyers had connections with Germany between the world wars that ultimately helped to fund the Nazi Party. Their connections with the oil companies delivered power to Saudi Arabia and wrested Middle Eastern oil rights from the British in order to give them to US companies. The Dulles brothers' political careers blossomed under President Eisenhower as John Foster was appointed Secretary of State and Allen Director of the Central Intelligence Agency. Washington's Dulles International Airport was named in honor of John Foster. According to Supreme Court Justice Arthur Goldberg who had served in US intelligence during the Second World War, "The Dulles brothers were traitors," because they had given aid and comfort to US enemies before and after World War II.[54]

As a member of the Wall Street legal firm of Sullivan and Cromwell, John Foster Dulles represented a number of large German corporations, one of which was IG Farben. He also represented wealthy American clients whom he persuaded to invest in German industry. These were some of the same clients who were involved in the round-robin of reparation payments known as the "Dawes Plan" whereby loans were made to Germany to pay reparations to Britain and France. The medium of exchange was gold. The plan was devised by the Dulles Brothers, who incidentally sat on the boards of German banks and IG Farben, which later manufactured *Zyklon B*, the poison gas used in the extermination of Jews.

During the 1920's one of Hitler's ploys was to attack the industrial corporate structure of Germany as part of the Jewish international conspiracy to destroy the country. Dulles' client IG Farben was at the top of the list.

After WWI, US companies were encouraged by the Dulles brothers through the Wall Street firm of Sullivan and Cromwell to invest heavily in German industry. German companies likewise invested in US companies. IG Farben owned large blocks of stock in American oil companies. Owners, in return for gold payments, exchanged important industrial information with German industrialists including technological patents. John Foster Dulles in 1934 drafted an agreement between Standard Oil of New Jersey (Rockefeller) and IG Farben to provide the Nazi war machine with synthetic oil and rubber patents. Farben manufactured the products using slave labor at Auschwitz, the notorious death camp. So while Dulles sat on the board of directors of IG Farben, the company contributed to the genocidal policies of the German government by working slave laborers to death for profit.

In the 1930's the Dulles brothers continued their duplicitous projects by encouraging their Western clients to contribute to the Nazi Party as well as the Nazi war machine in return for financial favors.

According to some sources, the Dulles brothers used legal technicalities and their personal connections to impede the prosecution of German corporations that had used slave labor to produce war materiel. In addition, they were able to prevent the prosecution of Nazis who were known mass killers. The brothers personally interceded on their behalf and were instrumental in arranging Nazi escapes from Germany and southeast Europe to the US, to our Allies and to South America. Under the Freedom of Information Act the supportive documents for these statements of fact are filed in the historical archives of this country and are now available.[55]

John Foster died in 1959. Allen was eventually forced to resign as director of the CIA by President Kennedy because of the Bay of Pigs debacle, but was appointed by President Johnson as a member of the commission that investigated Kennedy's assassination.

Despite all of this, however, the Middle East of the 1950's became a chessboard of the Cold War. Independence was wrested from imperial powers and Arabs began to adopt self-rule rather than British protectorate status. Two trends began in the Middle East, one toward Arab nationalism and modernization following the vision of Egyptian President Gamal Abdel Nasser, and the other towards the nostalgic Wahhabist vision of the monarchies of the region. Saudi Arabia, of course, was the leader of this latter group. The monarchies of Saudi Arabia, Iraq, Iran, and Kuwait also had a legitimate edge over the nationalists because they controlled the oil. The Cold War further polarized the region. Because of the influence of American oil companies, the US supported the monarchies, and though Presidents Eisenhower and Kennedy both made solid efforts to court Nasser, Egypt and Syria moved to the Soviet side of the table having received most of their military technology from them.

Thus the chess pieces began to be moved across the board as East and West played their game: Britain signed the Baghdad Pact in 1955 with Iraq, Iran, Turkey, and Pakistan in an attempt to keep these nations pro-Western. In 1956, Britain moved with France and Israel to invade the Sinai Peninsula which precipitated the Suez Crisis. In response to these maneuvers, Egypt and Syria formed the United Arab Republic in 1958. It would eventually be the alliance that initiated the 1967 Six-Day War and the 1973 Yom Kippur War. In response, Jordan and Iraq formed the Arab

Union of Jordan and Iraq that same year, joining together their Hashemite kingdoms. Former premier of Iraq, Nuri as-Said, was named leader of the new venture. Nasser responded by calling upon the people, police, and military of Iraq to overthrow their pro-Western government. This resulted in the July 14, 1958 *coup d'état* that put the military in control of the country and dissolved the Arab Union. Iraq withdrew from its own Baghdad Pact in 1959.

An odd trend developed: the US began to favor the regressive regimes over the progressive ones. While both were dictatorships and repressive, America was supporting the faction that would produce terrorism and continue to return the region to the Middle Ages, not the side that would move towards modernization and a better standard of living. As the US had depleted its own oil reserves in Oklahoma and Texas to win the Second World War, Middle Eastern oil, and particularly that from Saudi Arabia, Iran, Iraq, and Kuwait had become of great interest, if not a necessity to keep the US economy prospering. As Americans paid richly to pump the crude to keep its economy thriving, they were unknowingly funding a growing underground movement against Israel and stability in the region.

Through it all, Saudi Arabia maintained the neutrality ibn Saud had exhibited during World War II. After Ibn Saud died in 1943, his second son who became King Saud waited to see what would transpire before taking a stand. Though Saudi Arabia had no love for the fledgling Jewish state, it was more concerned at that time with its aggressive neighbors, particularly the Hashemite kingdoms of Jordan and Iraq on the northern border. Under King Saud, and despite the continual flow of oil money into the region, Saudi Arabia was plunged into financial chaos. King Saud was eventually deposed and replaced by his younger brother, Faisal bin Abdul Aziz, in 1964. The Wahhabi *ulemas* (Muslim scholars trained in Islamic law) had much to do with this change in leadership, and Faisal wouldn't forget it. Saud's government had grown soft and more open; Faisal would return the country to its ultra-conservative Wahhabist roots. Faisal, whose mother died when he was six years old, was raised by his maternal grandfather. He advised the future king, "Saudi Arabia should lead the Arab world and the ideology of Wahhabism should be exported."[56]

Though Faisal's grandfather died not long after giving him this advice, apparently it was never forgotten. It also appears Faisal was more like his father, ibn Saud, than his older brother had been. But it was the clever, behind-the-scenes ibn Saud that came out in Faisal rather than the cutthroat invader who had retaken Mecca and Medina. He would use his influence and the power of Wahhabism, not military might, to promote Saudi interests. Just as Saud had supplied only two Saudi brigades to help fight the Jews in their war for independence in 1948-1949, so Faisal would only supply one for the Six-Day War in 1967. The division would see no action. Saudi Arabia ultimately benefitted from Israel's victory in many ways. With Egypt embarrassed and weakened, Nasser pulled his troops from Yemen where he had hoped a coup would deliver the Arabia Peninsula into Pan-Arab Nationalist control. With Nasser's withdrawal, Saudi Arabia's southern border was again secure.

King Faisal showed no gratitude for Nasser's move and soon found another way to undermine Israel and those Arab states that might rival Saudi in the Middle East. He began to financially support an upstart organization called *Fatah* (The Movement for the National Liberation of Palestine), headed by an Egyptian who adopted the name Yasser Arafat. *Fatah* and brother organizations used Saudi money to destabilize Jordan, eventually forcing the country to apply its full military might to oust them during Black September—the Jordanian civil war—of 1968. However, *Fatah* would still manage to take full control of the Nasser-created Palestine Liberation Organization (PLO) in 1969, combining several terrorist groups under one umbrella.

All the while, Saudi Arabia continued to maintain solid relations with the US as oil money flowed into Faisal's coffers. Indirectly, US dollars promoted and exported Wahhabism—the doctrine hatred for Israel and the West.

(5)

EXPORTING HATE

As for Ishmael, I have heard thee: Behold, I have blessed him,
and will make him fruitful, and will multiply him exceedingly;
twelve princes shall he beget, and I will make him a great nation.
But my covenant will I establish with Isaac.
(Genesis 17:20-21)

The Six-Day war of 1967 and the Yom Kippur War of 1973 not only preserved Israel, but also turned the tide in the Arabic world toward regressive, pro-western monarchies. As the Arab nationalists following Nasser failed repeatedly to defeat the small sliver of a state that is Israel, Saudi Arabia sat back quietly and paid thugs to ensure its interests. This money assured that targets such as the TAPLINE—the Trans Arabian Pipeline—stayed off terrorists lists. The pipeline ran from Sidon in Lebanon, through the Golan Heights, and into Saudi Arabia. The protection money failed to achieve the desired result though when Lebanon collapsed in 1983 and the oil stopped flowing. As the PLO took control over terrorism in the region, Saudi Arabian princes and kings became Arafat's most faithful backers.

While King Faisal suspended oil exports to the US and Great Britain during the Six-Day War, the results were minimal and Faisal hadn't fully discovered that oil could be used as a weapon. However, the world changed greatly from 1967 to 1973. By that time, both Saddam Hussein, vice-president of the faction that had toppled the Iraqi monarchy in 1972, and Colonel Muammar Qaddafi, who had taken control in Libya in June of 1973, had nationalized all oil interests within their borders. The Organization of Oil Producing Countries (OPEC) was at its apex. Saudi Arabia was content to remain on the sidelines as the Yom Kippur War erupted on October 6, 1973, and sat idly by through most of the struggle. King Faisal decided to finally step in when all appeared lost as Israeli troops, under the command of Ariel Sharon, crossed the Suez Canal on October 16. By October 20, troops were within 63 miles of Cairo. Faisal then cut off oil supplies to the US and ordered other OPEC members to do the same. They complied, and on October 21, stopped the flow of oil to the US sixth fleet in the Mediterranean. Suddenly, Israel's allies were selfishly urging her to sign a cease-fire.

Though the war ended with neither side conceding defeat, the only real winners were the Saudis, who had never fired a shot. They had shown other Arab nations that they possessed the power pan-Arab Nasserites and Syrians did not. This might have had enough of a ripple effect on its own, but the embargo would have an unexpected additional benefit: oil prices soared. Saudi oil revenues in 1972 had been $2.7 billion; but in 1973 rose to $4.3 billion. In 1974 numbers skyrocketed to $22.6 billion,[57] and suddenly Faisal had nearly unlimited resources with which to propagate Saudi and Wahhabist interests.

Saudi Arabia soon boasted the leading economy among Arab countries, and became a destination for Muslims who could not find decent-paying jobs in their own countries. Wahhabist *ulemas* would use this to their advantage. These immigrants would be indoctrinated with Wahhabism while in Saudi and eventually, when they had earned enough money, would return to their own countries with changed minds. Wahhabism would become the cry for Islam to ascend to a place of dominance in the world system. Saudi Arabia became the ideal of every other Muslim nation and Saudis preached Wahhabism as the belief system that Allah blessed so richly. The Muslim world looked to Saudi Arabia both for financial deliverance from poverty and for enlightenment. Wahhabism was proclaimed the seed of revival for true Islam.

Additionally, with Saudi control over the holy cities of Mecca and Medina, to which every Moslem had to travel at least once in their lifetime as part of the *Hajj* (a pilgrimage which is one of the five pillars of Islam). This afforded them another way of showing the rest of the world "true" Islam. Pilgrims were introduced to extreme-fundamentalist Wahhabi doctrine which was deemed the true Islam of Muhammad. As interest grew, Wahhabism spread throughout the Muslim world and became a standard curriculum in schools, mosques, and universities—Saudi grants and donations to Islamic charities made sure of this.

The West glossed this over, calling the movement "Islamism." The US State Department, intelligence community, and other concerned branches of the government paid it little attention. In a relativist culture of "separation of church (religion) and state," Islamism was viewed simply as a cultural movement to uplift the spirits of some of the poorest nations in the world. The thought that a religious teaching could actually be dangerous bordered too closely on intolerance (the greatest sin of political correctness) and went against the grain. The US wouldn't begin to take notice until after the attacks on September 11. Even then it would take more than two years before any governmental agency publicly announced that Wahhabism might be a threat.[58] Until that day, no one in the US government was willing to suggest that someone could hate this country enough to hijack a plane and commit suicide in the hope of killing thousands. The narcotic power of Wahhabism and the hatred it created had been totally underestimated.

The Yom Kippur War also brought other changes in the Islamic world and the Middle East. After Egypt and Syria's defeat in a conventional war, it became evident, especially when the US began to back Israel as a military ally and bolster her military with advanced US weaponry, that there was little chance of winning a direct conventional war against Israel. Despite the fact that it held only one-eighth of one percent of the land of the Arab states, this little country was much more than a David against their Goliath. Somehow Israel had become *the* Middle-Eastern superpower, especially since it was the only country in the region with the atomic bomb. This brought about concern that Israel might attack Iraq with nuclear weapons if provoked during the 1991 Gulf War, again causing America to rush weaponry to defend Israel—this time the Patriot missile— in exchange for Israel's promise to stay on the sideline. As a result, Israel absorbed thirty-nine missile strikes without retaliating even once, all the while keeping Baghdad in her nuclear crosshairs.

As a result, at a 1974 meeting in Rabat, Morocco, the Arab League appointed the terrorist organization, the PLO, as the sole, legitimate representative of the Palestinian people, and Egyptian-born Mohammed Abdel-Raouf Arafat al Qudwa al-Hussaeini, as its leader. He would become known as Yasser Arafat.

Another result was also the brightest ray of hope seen in the Arab-Israeli conflict in the last Century: the peace treaty and normal relations between Egypt and Israel and returning the Sinai Peninsula to Egypt on the guarantee that it remains demilitarized. Even with this agreement came signs of dissention. After Egyptian President Muhammad Anwar al-Sadat made his unprecedented trip to Israel in 1977 and became the first Arab Leader to address the Israeli parliament, the Knesset, I asked Prime Minister Menachem Begin what he thought of the Egyptian leader in an informal meeting we had some time later. He responded, "I didn't like his tie, and I didn't like his letter." Although I didn't know what he meant at the time, I felt it was inappropriate to pursue the matter. Later I discovered that as Sadat addressed the Knesset he wore a tie with a dazzling pastiche of large Nazi swastikas. Rumors spread in 1953 that Adolph Hitler may have escaped capture and was alive and well in Brazil. An Egyptian weekly, *Al-Musawwar,* asked Sadat what he would write to the fuehrer. Sadat (who played a role in Nasser's coup to oust King Faruk) replied:

> "I congratulate you with all my heart, because, though you appear to have been defeated, you were the real victor. You were able to sow dissention between Churchill, the old man, and his allies on one hand and their ally, the devil, on the other . . . That you should become immortal in Germany is reason enough for pride. And we should not be surprised to see you again in Germany, or a new Hitler in your place."[59]

Prior to this, and in the midst of World War II, Sadat had spent time in jail for his openly pro-Nazi stance and frank endorsement of Hitler in British-ruled Egypt. Sadat would thus sign a peace treaty with Israel while flagrantly sporting his anti-Semitic tie.

Despite this, Sadat was assassinated in 1981 for his efforts to bring peace to the Middle East. Normal relations broke down. Egypt withdrew its ambassador to Israel in 2001. Sadat's move did, however, set a precedent that would be followed by Jordan as it signed a peace treaty with Israel in 1994. To date, Egypt and Jordan are the only two Arab countries to agree to such treaties; other Arab nations have remained openly hostile towards Israel. However, anti-Semitism is again rising in Egypt.

If direct military confrontation were not the answer to defeating Israel, what was? Ayatollah Khomeini provided part of the answer in ousting the Shah of Iran, and the PLO provided the rest when invading Lebanon. The Arabs aimed to fight a war of attrition against Israel, defeating her little by little and destroying her will to fight back. This would be through spreading the virus of rabid anti-Semitism and asymmetrical terrorism. Khomeini showed how to unify secular, social, and religious groups in their hatred for the Shah and the US and used it as a political and military tool to overthrow the government. With the storming and capture of the US Embassy on November 4, 1979, he showed that the West was far from all-powerful. Suddenly Islam became the new Goliath determined to defeat the US and Israel.

The revolution was a surprise in Washington and Langley. A 1978 Mossad report to US officials that Shah Muhammad Reza Pahlavi was in eminent danger of being deposed was soundly rejected. When the Shah fell roughly a year later, it was not only shocking to President Jimmy Carter, but extremely embarrassing. Unfortunately this would not be the last event of this magnitude about which the CIA would fail to inform the president or that Carter would mishandle.

Despite the US's surprise, the Saudis welcomed the overthrow in more ways than one. Saudi Arabia benefited from the Iranian revolution as it cut off Iranian oil to the West. Saudi oil revenues again grew disproportionately as a result just as they had after the OPEC embargo of 1973: their royalties were $32.2 billion in 1978, $48.4 billion in 1979, and $102.1 billion in 1981.[60] As a result, between 1982 and 2002, 1,500 mosques, 210 Islamic centers, and 2,000 Muslim schools were built in non-Muslim countries alone in order to promote Wahhabism. The Saudis also donated academic chairs for Islamic studies to Harvard Law School and the University of California at Berkley, as well as grants supporting Islamic research at American University (in Washington, D.C.), Howard University, Duke, and Johns Hopkins.[61] In a two-year period in the 1980s, according to Muslim World League internal documents, the Saudis spent $10 million to build mosques in the United States.[62] Since 1973, Saudis have spent well over $87 billion to spread Wahhabism throughout the US and the Western Hemisphere.[63]

The Saudis also began to purchase arms from the United States about that time. It was in February of 1978 that Jimmy Carter informed Congress he planned to sell fifty F-15 fighters to Saudi Arabia. Despite objections from Israel, pro-Israel lobbyists and demonstrators marched in the streets with signs bearing such slogans as "Hell No to the PLO" and "Aid to Israel! Best Investment for America." The sale was eventually approved.[64] America was now selling advanced arms to both Israel and the Arabs.

The PLO and Hezbollah (Party of Allah) contributed to the rise of Islamism by creating something that eventually became known as asymmetrical terrorism, used to indicate that the strategy and tactics of one side differs significantly from the other. These were not battles with visible soldiers wearing identifying uniforms and shooting at each other over no-man's land. These were sudden, surprise *kamikaze*-type attacks aimed at killing as many as possible with no opportunity to retaliate because there was no one alive at which to return fire. Under careful manipulation by zealous minds, a new "H" bomb—the Human bomb—had been created. It was one that could be used to zero in on any target with greater precision than any of America's smart bombs and cost millions less to produce. Loss of human life has never been a consideration for terrorists.

Using H-bombs, the PLO and Hezbollah demonstrated how to use asymmetrical terrorist tactics to scare an enemy into retreat. I was in Beirut in October 1983 when two truck bombs were used against US and French troops stationed there. The explosions killed 241 US military personnel and fifty-eight French paratroopers. I remember the chaos and panic that rippled through the streets that day. The result was that the foreign troops withdrew and Lebanon was turned into a terrorist incubation center where Christians were killed and Muslim children in daycare centers and kindergartens were taught the glory of being martyred for Allah as suicide-bombers against Israel. America had lost its first significant battle in the war on terrorism and its citizens didn't even know they were at war.

(6)

THE HIGH COST
of APPEASEMENT

"For thou hast been a shelter for me, and a
strong *tower from the enemy,"*
(Psalm 61:3.)

While Wahhabism focused its hatred on the West, the Communist East was also in its crosshairs. When the Soviets invaded Afghanistan at the end of 1979 to protect its puppet government from the *Mujihadeen* (Persian for warriors) rebel uprising, Osama bin Laden, the twenty-three-year-old heir to the largest construction business in Saudi Arabia, left the Middle East to fight the Soviets for the freedom of his Islamic brothers in Afghanistan. He received support from Saudi, Pakistan, and the US to fight a guerilla war against sophisticated Soviet military might.

The Saudis spent $4 billion in aid to various Afghan rebel groups between 1980 and 1990, which excludes the amount given through various Islamic charities and private funds of the princes.[65] Bin Laden received special training from the CIA and created a network throughout the Muslim world to successfully recruit fighters and secure equipment for the *Mujihadeen* cause against Soviet infidels. After nearly a decade of fighting, the Soviets finally withdrew in February of 1989. It was apparent they were no longer able to move into a region and suppress an uprising as they had throughout Soviet Bloc countries in previous decades. As a result, Soviet republics began to secede from the USSR, one by one declaring their independence. Moscow had no resolve to fight a civil war to stop the succession. As a result, the Berlin wall fell on November 9, 1989 and the Union of Soviet Socialist Republics was finally dissolved in December of 1991.

Fighting in Afghanistan did not end with the Soviet withdrawal however, as rebel forces continued their drive to take over the government that had precipitated the Soviet intervention. The government held out against these forces for some time until, before its demise, the Soviet Union signed an agreement with the United States to stop giving aid to either side. Over the next few years various groups claimed control until a Wahhabish movement headquartered in Herat called the *Taliban* finally won out and set up a government. This movement was organized with the help of the former Saudi construction engineer who was suddenly a George Washington to the Arab world. Bin Laden had not only helped to topple the Soviet Union, but also made way for the first Wahhabist government outside of Saudi Arabia.

Intoxicated by his success in vanquishing the Soviets, bin Laden would turn his attention to the only remaining superpower that threatened the Wahhabist worldview: the United States. In 1988, the incredible network this Muslim folk hero had formed to defeat the Soviets became *al Qaeda* (The Base.) With its inception, more than a decade of violence against the US would not really be noticed until fifteen Saudis and four other Muslim members of *al Qaeda* high-jacked four US airliners, crashed two into the World Trade Center Towers, and one into the Pentagon on September 11, 2001. The hijackers on the fourth plane targeted Washington, D.C. but it crashed in a field near Shanksville, Pennsylvania, after passengers bravely tried to overcome the terrorists.

Meanwhile Saudi leaders sat back and watched, quietly funding terrorism and securing more advanced military hardware and protection from the United States to safeguard its oil interests. The threat to Saudi Arabia was real, however. In 1990 Saddam Hussein could easily have pushed through Kuwait to Riyadh had he so desired because of Saudi Arabia's poor defensive ability. While they possessed some of the most sophisticated US weapons available, Saudi troops weren't combat ready and could hardly have been expected to operate effectively. The Iraq war was no more than a bump in the US economy; gas prices temporarily soared in response to the possibility that the war might bring shortages, then quickly returned to normal. Martin Indyk, former US Ambassador to Israel said:

> We've struck a Faustian bargain, turning a blind eye
> to Saudi Arabia's domestic policies . . . and a blind eye to
> Saudi Arabian efforts to export Wahhabism.[66]

In roughly that same time period (1990-2001), the Saudis were the number one world customer for advanced US conventional weaponry with sales totaling over $45 billion. Saudis have also invested about $200 billion back into the US economy through the years. However, despite having the most sophisticated weaponry in the region, without mercenaries or US troops to operate and maintain it, they are little more than fancy, and extremely dangerous, toys. Like much else that has been done in Saudi Arabia, great sums of money have been spent to look good, but no infrastructure has been built for arms maintenance.

Saudi Arabia's wealth is based solely on its oil reserves, but all those billions have created no lasting industry in the country where few Saudis are trained to run anything. The entire country has been kept afloat by engineers and experts from the West and cheap labor from the rest of the Muslim world. Saudi Arabia seems to have benefited little from the reign of the House of Saud. Instead of creating more wealth and raising the standard of living in the country, riches have been wasted on the opulent lives of its government officials (almost all of whom are relatives of the 7,000-member strong royal family), and on exporting the hatred of Wahhabism.

Right after the Iraqi invasion of Kuwait in August of 1990, Osama bin Laden offered the aid of his well-trained *Mujihadeen* forces to protect his Saudi homeland from Saddam Hussein's continued march through Kuwait to Riyadh. This would keep Saudi Arabia free of a possible infidel influence by allowing Western troops into the country to defend it. The Saudi Government did not take Bin Laden seriously, and soon US troops landed in Saudi Arabia to form the Desert Storm invasion force. The presence of American troops in his homeland became another mark against the United States for bin Laden, and one against what he must have viewed as Western corruption. This was further evidenced by the fact that bin Laden became more and more critical in his comments about the Saudi regime to the point that in 1994, the Saudi government revoked his citizenship. There is also evidence that it was this sentiment that motivated *al Qaeda* members to carry out the four Riyadh bombings in May and November of 2003 claiming the lives of forty-two individuals, including eight Americans, and wounding hundreds in an attempt to remove all Westerners from Saudi soil.

In April of 1991 Arab rage began to become more consolidated and focused. Radical Islamic sympathizers with Iraq during Desert Storm convened in Khartoum at the invitation of Hassan al-Turabi. Islamic militants called the National Islamic Front (NIF) had toppled the Sudanese government in June of 1989 and Sudan moved into the Islamist world (after the Soviet withdrawal from Afghanistan, bin Laden made trips to Sudan to help organize the NIF.) Many of the groups attending received Saudi financial support. Fifty-five nations were represented including several from the Middle East as well as representatives from Hamas (an acronym for the "Islamic Resistance Movement") and Islamic Jihad, as well as Yasser Arafat and bin Laden. Bin Laden even set up residence in Khartoum from 1991 until he was expelled in 1996 (at which time he returned to

Afghanistan to set up new headquarters). In those few years he initiated various businesses there as money-collecting fronts for *al Qaeda*.

What these groups all had in common was their hatred for the United States and its Middle East proxy, Israel. From it came the Popular Arab and Islamic Congress (PAIC) that met every couple of years until Sudan closed its offices in Khartoum in February of 2000. In a parting shot, al-Turabi blamed the US among other nations for the closure of offices because the United States "is well known for its hostile attitudes towards Islam."[67] In that time span, PAIC became a terrorists' convention where they could make new relationships and alliances, share bomb-making secrets, coordinate efforts and logistics, and encourage one another in their hatred. *Al Qaeda* blossomed as a result of the connections bin Laden made there and at the next conference held in January of 1993. On his own, Bin Laden would coordinate efforts with Hezbollah in 1992 and Hezbollah would attend PAIC's 1995 conference. PAIC became a *"Who's Who?"* of international terrorists.

It was during the early days of William Clinton's presidency, that the United States received its second wake-up call from bin Laden's organization: the February 26, 1993 truck bombing of the World Trade Center. The first *al Qaeda* attack was in 1992 against the Goldmore and Aden Hotels in Yemen, a temporary barracks for US Marines in transit to Somalia. While this first WTC attack went relatively unnoticed, in it were seeds of the eventual September 11 attacks, and not only in the same location. The actual aim of the bombing was to topple the towers and kill as many as 250,000.[68] If they had succeeded in even one percent of this instead of killing seven, we would be remembering February 26, 1993, not September 11, 2001.

In *Losing bin Laden*, author Richard Miniter wrote of Clinton's ineptitude in dealing with bin Laden throughout his presidency:

> In 1993, bin Laden was a small-time funder of militant
> Muslim terrorists in Sudan, Yemen, and Afghanistan. By
> the end of 2000, Clinton's last year in office, bin Laden's

network was operating in more than fifty-five countries and already responsible for the deaths of thousands (including fifty-five Americans) . . .

Clinton was tested by historic, global conflict, the first phase of America's war on terror. He was president when bin Laden declared war on America. He had many chances to defeat bin Laden; he simply did not take them. If, in the wake of the 1998 embassy bombings, Clinton had rallied the public and the Congress to fight bin Laden and smash terrorism, he might have been the Winston Churchill of his generation. But, instead, he chose the role of Neville Chamberlain (whose appeasements of Hitler in Munich in 1938 are credited with paving the way to the Nazi invasion of Poland that began World War II the next year).[69]

The 1993 WTC bombing had been planned and organized by Sheikh Omar Abdel Rahman who said:

> The obligation of Allah is upon us to wage *jihād* for the sake of Allah. . . . We have to thoroughly demoralize the enemies of Allah by blowing up their towers that constitute the pillars of their civilization . . . the high buildings of which they are so proud.[70]

In an uncompromising fit of moral relativistic blindness, FBI agents dismissed the very reason for the attacks, failing to connect the bombing to the worldwide Wahhabist movement that had fueled it. Rahman's fanatical Islamists were viewed as a splinter group.

Rahman, who was involved in the assassination of Egyptian President Anwar Sadat, came to America in 1990, free to set up his terrorist shop in New Jersey. A PBS special aired in 1994 documented a patchwork of

Islamic groups and terrorist sponsors that had sprung up across America after the Iranian revolution. These groups include arms of Islamic Jihad, Hamas, and Hezbollah with cells in New York, Florida, Chicago, Kansas City, and Dallas. The groups hide behind a smoke screen of small businesses and religious and charitable groups. These team members operate in the US to raise funds, recruit volunteers, and lay plans for terrorist missions for the ultimate battle against "The Great Satan." Their primary mission is to succeed in obtaining widespread media coverage, maximizing psychological and economic damage through terror.

By 1993, Jew-hatred empowered by US oil royalties was rampant in Arab countries. Terrorists had been trained in toppling superpowers through organizations such as the PAIC. Terrorist-harboring states worldwide, as well as business and charities in the US were donating money to fund attacks against the US and Israel. Another piece of the puzzle leading to 9/11 was the December 1994 attempt by the Algerian Groupe Islamique Armé's hijacking of an Air France plane they planned to crash into the Eiffel Tower. Most in the group were Arabs who had fought in Afghanistan. The plan failed, because none of the hijackers could fly the plane, so it landed in Marseilles instead, where it was stormed by French police. No direct connection was made to *al Qaeda*, but the attempt likely influenced the September 11 hijackers. They made sure there were terrorists on board who could fly the airliners, even if they didn't need to know how to land them. The United States was now directly in the sights of Islamic rage.

(7)

LUNATICS,
LIBERALS, *and* LIARS

He who says to the wicked, "You are righteous,"
Him the people will curse; Nations will abhor him.
(Proverbs 24:24 NKJV)

As the nation that helped the Jews return to the land that had been theirs some two millennia before, and as the nation that had raised Arab countries from obscurity by the power of the petrodollar, the United States moved from the eye of the prophetic squall on September 11, 2001, into the fury of the hurricane. It was also the day the fragile economic house of cards for which the Clinton administration took credit began to topple. The nation went from a time of unprecedented hope and economic confidence to despair in a matter of minutes.

The presidential election of 2000 was filled with debates about what America should do about its incredible budget surplus—pay down the national debt? Save Social Security? Give tax cuts back to the taxpayers? The government enjoyed budget surpluses in 1997 and 1998—the first since 1957. Projected estimates in January 2001 suggested that by the year 2010 the US government could have as much as $5.6 trillion dollars in surplus income with which to work. By March 2002 that forecast dropped to $1.6 trillion. In 2000, the United States budget had a surplus of $237 billion, which fell by almost half to $127 billion in 2001 following the 9/11 attacks. It dropped $158 billion into the red in 2002, and hit at that time a record deficit of roughly $374.2 billion in 2003 in the wake of the Iraqi war. In mid- 2010, national forecasts for 2010 were cut from the $1.6 trillion surplus to a slightly less than $1.3 trillion deficit.[71] The 2013 budget shortfall is projected to be $977 billion.

When the Stock Market reopened on Monday, September 17, 2001 following the attack on the Twin Towers, it saw record losses in the first few hours of trading. Not only did the US economy take a dive, but also did those countries around the world that depend largely on US consumer trade. In the weeks following, the market rebounded, only to be hit again and again as consumer confidence deteriorated. Tech stocks corrected from being grossly overvalued. Corporate accounting scandals hit companies like Enron, WorldCom, and Tyco. Americans had been robbed by the inflated economic optimism preached in the 1990s and by corrupt corporate leaders. At the same time the airline industry took a devastating hit as a result of the attacks, and United Airlines was forced to file for Chapter Eleven Bankruptcy.

However, one industry did boom—the security industry—as Americans spent large sums trying to provide safety. The new Department of Homeland Security created by the Bush administration was allotted $37.70 billion for its 2003 budget—an increase from $19.5 billion in 2002. A department that didn't exist when Bill Clinton's second term ended was demanding an ever-growing infusion of US tax dollars.

Eclipsing that were the lives forever changed on that day: children who lost mothers or fathers, those who lost a spouse, a friend, or a son or daughter. Driving home a few days after the attacks, I listened to the account of a father calling his sister in the minutes before the second tower fell. He gave her a final message to pass along to his wife and children. I felt the real loss and madness of those attacks. Innocent lives were scarred in an instant because of a murderous doctrine of hatred. No moment has better defined the senselessness and horror of terrorism.

The moral clarity that could have prevented the attacks on September 11 also could have saved countless lives and a tremendous amount of money. Unfortunately, despite increased awareness of real needs brought about by September 11, deep ties to the Arab world still determine the federal government's response. It appears that warning signs continue to be ignored.

One example of this is that a group of Americans on a federal commission tried to sound a warning twice: In September 1999 and in January 2001, just 11 days after the Bush inauguration. The preliminary report by former Senators Gary Hart and Warren Rudman, co-chairs of the Commission on National Security, was given to then-President Clinton. It stated:

> A direct attack against American citizens on American
> soil is likely over the next quarter century. The risk is not
> only death and destruction but also a demoralization that
> could undermine US global leadership.[72]

This warning was virtually ignored by top officials and the news media. The commission continued its work, however, and on January 31, 2001, seven months before the attacks on the World Trade Center and the Pentagon, Hart and Rudman presented the commission's final report of 150 pages to newly elected President Bush. It was called "Road Map for National Security: Imperative for Change." In it the commissioners reissued their warning, along with a detailed plan of action to make America safer from terrorism. Again, the report was ignored.

On April 24, 2002, some seven and a half months later, an eight-plane delegation of Saudi officials landed at Ellington Field in Houston, Texas. The group onboard was on its way to meet with President George W. Bush at the Western White House in Crawford. What should have been an international incident instead turned into a State Department cover-up. Why? Among the passengers in Crown Prince Abdullah's entourage was one person on the FBI's most wanted list and two others on the terrorist watch list. The feds were ready to storm the plane and arrest the three men; however, the State Department had other priorities—after all, it had been that organization which had issued visas in the first place. The State Department's intervention resulted in the planes' leaving without incident. The FBI and Secret Service made certain the men got nowhere near Crawford.[73] Once again, economics and oil carried more weight than national security.

Worse, perhaps, was the Visa Express program that issued US visas to the Saudis through travel agents rather than with a trip to the embassy, as is required elsewhere in the world. At least three of the fifteen Saudi terrorists responsible for 9/11 entered the US via Visa Express, yet the program continued to run uninterrupted. It took another ten months and extreme media pressure to finally force closure.

In the wake of September 11, Saudis hired several public relations firms to repair their image in the eyes of the US public. According to Justice Department filings, approximately $17 million was spent on that project. The firms hired included one of Washington's most prominent, Patton Boggs, which reportedly received some $200,000 a month. Patton Boggs is especially known for its contacts among Democrats. It was founded by Thomas Hale Boggs, Jr., a well-connected Democratic lobbyist, and son of the late Hale Boggs, House majority leader. His sister is journalist Cokie Roberts.

The *New York Times* reported the Saudi government also hired Akin, Gump, Strauss, Hauer & Feld, a company founded by Robert W. Strauss, former head of the Democratic National Committee. The firm was paid $161,799 in the first half of 2002. Frederick Dutton, a former special assistant to President John F. Kennedy and long-time adviser to the Saudis, received $536,000 to help manage the aftermath of September 11.

The Saudis ran hundreds of television and radio commercials in virtually every major American media market and placed advertisements in publications such as *People* magazine and *Stars & Stripes*, presumably to influence US troops in Iraq. The latter was apparently an attempt to divert attention from Saudi reluctance to respond to President Bush's call for support during the Gulf War. The Saudi memory lapse regarding how the US prevented Saddam Hussein from targeting the kingdom during the 1991 Gulf War was obvious.

Three well-connected Washington lobbying and law firms were hired and paid handsomely from the Kingdom's coffers to polish their image. Ex-Washington officials have also been paid handsomely by the Saudis. The list included such former government figures as Spiro T. Agnew, Jimmy Carter, Clark Clifford, John B. Connally, and William E. Simon. A Saudi source was quoted as saying that his countrymen had contributed to every presidential library in recent decades.

Despite attempts by the Saudis to hone their image, the 2013 Amnesty International report stated:

> The authorities severely restricted freedoms of expression, association and assembly and clamped down on dissent. Government critics and political activists were detained without trial or sentenced after grossly unfair trials. Women were discriminated against in law and practice and inadequately protected against domestic and other violence. Migrant workers were exploited and abused. Sentences of flogging were imposed and carried out. Hundreds of people were on death row at the end of the year; at least 79 people were executed . . . .Torture and other ill-treatment of detainees and sentenced prisoners were reported to be common, widespread and generally committed with impunity. Reported methods included beating, suspension by the limbs and sleep deprivation.

Those tortured reportedly included detained protesters, who were held incommunicado for days or weeks without charge or trial.[74]

The US must emerge from its lethargy. All is not well, and it must no longer be deceived by appearances. It has obviously been no deterrent to discover that fifteen of the nineteen hijackers on September 11 were Saudis, and that Saudi Arabia is the largest supporter of *al Qaeda*. These details are conveniently overlooked in order to maintain the flow of oil that lubricates our nation's economy. The US has been lulled to sleep with whispers of "Everything will be all right. Islam is a peaceful religion. You have nothing to fear."

The rivulets of prophetic utterances are beginning to flow and quickly merge with the rapids ahead. The next key events of biblical prophecy are easily identifiable as the players slip into position:

1. Israel

Against all odds and unprecedented opposition, the Jews rose from obscurity and Israel was reborn. Israel had much for which to thank several American presidents. It stands on the world stage as a nuclear power, and has on more than one occasion brandished that power in the face of invasion and possible defeat (the Yom Kippur War of 1973 is one of the best examples). Israel seems ready today to take on the world if need be—and may soon be forced to do just that.

2. The European Union (EU)

Occupying the same lands as did the Roman Empire these nations have traditionally been seen as the "ten toes" of Nebuchadnezzar's dream revealed in Daniel 2:31-45. This mix of iron and clay cannot truly join together, i.e., oil and water. It will more likely be an alliance of two governments such as Middle Eastern monarchies and European democracies. Whatever this alliance is, it seems likely the EU will be central. During the presidency of George W. Bush, the US, UN, EU, and Russia tried to force Israel to accept yet another land-for-peace deal. That cooperative could easily be part of the end time government that will ratify a seven-year peace agreement between Israel and the Antichrist.

This second member of the Quartet has become a major proponent of Arab League anti-Semitism in past decades. While it has done much to worsen the Palestinian refugees' plight since 1948, its Secretary General has also spoken frequently against Israel. In the company of North Korea, China, Saudi Arabia and other *Shariah* law nations, Israel alone has been uniquely criticized and scrutinized for so-called human rights violations. This masquerade extends further when terrorist-supporting states such as Syria head the Security Council or Libya leads the Human Rights Commission. No wonder that arm of the UN proclaims that Palestinians can use "all available means, including armed struggle"[75] to regain their "occupied territories"—a clever endorsement of suicide bombings.

At an Anti-Racism Conference in Durban, South Africa in 2001, most conference attendees banded together to condemn one nation as patently racist—Israel. It is, incredibly, the only democracy in the Middle East committed to civil rights, the rule of law, and Arab participation in democratic government, but was unjustly accused of genocide, ethnic cleansing, and apartheid.[76] Representatives of Israel and the United States walked out on September 4, exactly one week before the attacks on the World Trade Center and the Pentagon—the only two nations willing to acknowledge the lunacy and prejudice of the entire proceeding. During the conference, streets were filled with protesters carrying banners reading, "The blood of the martyrs irrigates the tree of revolution in Palestine" and "George W. Bush: Palestinian blood is on your hands." It is all too easy to see that this organization has changed greatly from its original intent and has become a repository for the vengeful whims of Islamic fanatics in these latter days.

3. Russia

Since the fall of communism in Russia, most Americans no longer view this super power as a threat. The Cold War (which some called World War III) may have ended, but as the world edges towards another World War to be fought over control of the world's known oil supplies, this former superpower will be a key player. Why? It likely harbors oil reserves rivaling those of Saudi Arabia, Iraq, Iran, and Kuwait which at one time were considered to be as much as two-thirds of the world's remaining oil. As a third member of the Quartet, Russia, former leader of the Communist world, a nuclear power, and the probable reincarnation of Gog and Magog will prophetically sweep down from the North to attack Israel; its role in the final conflict also seems apparent.

4. China and the East

These nations can also be seen easily fitting into an anti-Israel coalition because of links with the former Soviet Union and an utter dependence on outside sources of oil. We also know from Revelation 16 that the "kings of the east" will join with those at the river Euphrates (Babylonia) in the final battle.

5. The Terrorists

Their most vocal cry has been for the destruction of Israel and the return of the third holiest site in Islam, Jerusalem (and in particular the Temple Mount), to Arab control. Most experts agree the terror war begun with the US on September 11 will never truly end. The US has been lumped together with Israel in this fight. The anti-Semitism that has infected Arab countries is again spreading in Europe and Russia. It is an ingredient that binds the anti-Israel faction in the Battle of Armageddon.

6. The United States

The country stands in the midst of the gathering clouds of this storm. As a member of the Quartet, the US was the only one that really had the voice to urge Israel's acceptance of the Road Map. The strategic alliance with Israel also makes the US her greatest defender. This position in the last days will be determined by a choice of allegiance: will the growing liberal tendencies of the US push her to join the EU, UN, and Russia in a globalization move that will, in the end, force a false peace on Israel and begin the Tribulation? Or will the US with its moral clarity, large Jewish populace, and Christian consciousness align itself so closely with Israel that the two countries are literally indistinguishable in the final chapter of Bible prophesy?

As you should be able to tell from this brief summary of the players, such a decision will be one made by the US alone, and not imposed by outside forces. Those nations will influence the United States either through negotiations or terrorist attacks. What will the US do? Will freedom be bartered for plentiful but expensive oil, globalization, and moral relativism, or will Americans stay the course and hold to biblical principles? Will the US nation be on God's side in the final conflict? Will we acquiesce to lunatics, liberals, and liars in weakness, or stand strong and seek a revival of moral clarity?

(8)

BATTLE LINES ARE DRAWN *through the* HEART *of* JERUSALEM

But I have chosen Jerusalem, that my name might be there;
and have chosen David to be over my people Israel,"
(2 Chronicles 6:6.)

Lines for the approaching Battle of Armageddon have been drawn
by UN resolutions, terrorist demands, and US acceptance of the Israeli
boundaries of 1967 that declared the Golan Heights, Gaza Strip, West
Bank, East Jerusalem and the Temple Mount "occupied territories." On
three different occasions between 1991 and 2001, the PLO was offered
that land minus control of East Jerusalem. Each time the offer was
refused and violence escalated. The conclusion is only too obvious: the
PLO now referred to as the Palestinian Authority or PA, will not sign a
final agreement with Israel until control of East Jerusalem is included.
The battle line has indeed been drawn through the heart of Jerusalem,
the Old City and the Temple Mount.

Israelis and Palestinians both claim Jerusalem as their capital, yet most countries including the United States have embassies in Tel Aviv. The reason is found in the hesitancy to be seen as backing one side against the other. To back Israel would send a strong message to the Arab nations that the US has as yet been very hesitant to make.

Several years ago, I met with former New York Mayor Rudolph Giuliani to discuss Jerusalem. I asked him what the most important things were that Jerusalem and New York had in common. He replied:

> We are both blessed with freedom and democracy. Much of the world doesn't have freedom and democracy. Because we share the same principles on which government and society are based, than all of the other friendships become even stronger.
>
> The relationship of blood also exists between New York and Jerusalem. There are so many who have family in both places.
>
> We have the relationship of religious significance for Jews, Christians, and Muslims—the historical significance and the reality that we are two of the world's great cities. Jerusalem is older than New York. A good deal of the world passes through both places. We share great bonds. [77]

New York and America indeed share a great bond with Jerusalem—the city that will be the center of global attention in the final days. Even after over four decades of visiting Israel and studying the conflicts and prophecies surrounding her, I still don't fully comprehend why this is so. The Temple Mount is the holiest place in Judaism, perhaps second only to Golgotha to Christians. It is considered the third holiest place in the world to Muslims (behind Mecca and Medina), though Jerusalem, the city Muslims call *al-Quds,* is not mentioned in the Quran. For Jews, it is the place of which God said, ""In this house and in Jerusalem, which I have chosen out of all the tribes of Israel, I will put My name forever," (II Chronicles 33:7, NKJV.)

Why has Jerusalem been a bone of contention to the world? Why is such a tiny city so often in the world news? It is because of that ancient prophecy whose fulfillment Jehovah himself guaranteed!

Every nation that has come against Jerusalem has been cursed. In 586 B.C., the Babylonian army besieged Jerusalem and ransacked the Temple. On Friday, April 11, 2003, the Iraqi National Museum in Baghdad was plundered by a lawless society. More than 170,000 ancient and priceless artifacts were stolen. These relics covered the entire 7,000 years of Babylonian history.

Saddam Hussein, who claimed to be Nebuchadnezzar incarnate, was cursed just as the first Nebuchadnezzar was cursed. Saddam should have read the Bible. Who would ever have believed that the man who caused nations to tremble would end up hiding in a hole in the ground, hair matted, beard dirty and unkempt, and dining on rotten food. Bums living under bridges look better than Hussein did when captured.

In Madrid, I was the first to challenge then-Secretary of State James Baker over Jerusalem. I asked, "Why can't America recognize Jerusalem as Israel's capital?" Baker was incensed by my question and said he refused to be entangled in a fruitless debate, and that the status of Jerusalem would be determined by negotiations.

Why have I been so concerned? There is no other city in the world on which Jehovah pronounces a blessing to those who bless it, and a curse on those who curse it. The nations that divide Jerusalem will be cursed beyond their ability to comprehend. If that happens, no amount of prayer or repentance will reverse the curse on that nation. Once prophecy is touched, Jehovah's anger will not be assuaged.

This revelation is amazing. Presidents have placed their hands on the prophecy of King Solomon found in II Chronicles 7:14 while being sworn into office. They trusted that Jehovah would bless America as well as their term in office. It is unlikely, however, that many have read the prophecy by Solomon found in 2 Chronicles 6:6: "But I have chosen *Yerushalayim*, that my name (*shem*) might be there," (paraphrased.) This amazing prophecy denotes that Jerusalem is the only city in the world on which Jehovah has chosen to place His name.

Is it important that Jerusalem not be touched? Unequivocally, yes! Heaven and earth met in Jerusalem after the birth of Jesus and will meet again upon His return. The prophecies declare that Jerusalem will be united—not divided—when the Messiah returns. He is not coming back to a Muslim city.

At the end of the age, Jerusalem will be the center of all prophecy:

> "I saw the Holy City, the new Jerusalem, coming down out of heaven from God, prepared as a bride beautifully dressed for her husband," (Revelation 21:2 NIV.)

The prophet Amos proclaimed:

> "The LORD also shall roar out of Zion, and utter his voice from Jerusalem," (Joel 3:16, NIV.)

The prophet Zechariah declared:

> "I will return to Zion and dwell in Jerusalem," (Zechariah 8:3 NIV.)

It is no coincidence that the first words of the New Testament are:

> "A record of the genealogy of Jesus Christ the son of David, the son of Abraham," (Matthew 1:1 NIV.)

David, the first king of Jerusalem, was forerunner of the true King, Jesus Christ.

The final Battle of the Ages will be over Jerusalem. If America's leaders choose to line up against the Scriptures, she will find herself fighting against Jehovah, a battle that will definitely be lost!

Satan's challenge to Jehovah can be found in Isaiah 14:12-15, NIV:

> How you have fallen from heaven, O morning star, son of the dawn! You have been cast down to the earth, you who once laid low the nations! You said in your heart, "I will ascend to heaven; I will raise my throne above the stars of God; I will sit enthroned on the mount of assembly, on the utmost heights of the sacred mountain. I will ascend above the tops of the clouds; I will make myself like the Most High." But you are brought down to the grave, to the depths of the pit.

Notice he says he will sit on the Temple Mount in Jerusalem, on the north side. Yet Jehovah says, "You will be cursed and brought down to the lowest pit of hell." Most wars have been fought over ownership disputes, over land and over property. Personal battles have raged over someone illegally using the name of another person to write a check or to buy goods. It is called "fraud." The person who commits fraud can be punished severely. America even has laws that grant a citizen the right to bear arms to protect his property. Jerusalem's title deed does not belong to anyone; it belongs exclusively to Jehovah. He placed His Name there!

The prophets declare :

> "Then shall the LORD go forth, and fight against those nations, as when he fought in the day of battle. And his feet shall stand in that day upon the mount of Olives, which is before Jerusalem on the east, and the mount

of Olives shall cleave in the midst thereof toward the east and toward the west, and there shall be a very great valley; and half of the mountain shall remove toward the north, and half of it toward the south," (Zechariah 14:3-4, NIV.)

It's amazing that the US, supposedly a Christian nation, would move to divide Jerusalem and give East Jerusalem over to the PLO, a terrorist regime, to become the capital of an Islamic state.

There is, indeed, in ancient prophecy, a curse that Jehovah will place on the nation that divides Jerusalem:

> Behold, I will make Jerusalem a cup of trembling unto all the people round about, when they shall be in the siege both against Judah and against Jerusalem. And in that day will I make Jerusalem a burdensome stone for all people: all that burden themselves with it shall be cut in pieces, though all the people of the earth be gathered together against it. In that day will I make the governors of Judah like an hearth of fire among the wood, and like a torch of fire in a sheaf; and they shall devour all the people round about, on the right hand and on the left: and Jerusalem shall be inhabited again in her own place, even in Jerusalem. In that day shall the LORD defend the inhabitants of Jerusalem; and he that is feeble among them at that day shall be as David; and the house of David shall be as God, as the angel of the LORD before them, (Zechariah 12:2, 3, 6, 8 NIV.)
>
> And this shall be the plague wherewith the LORD will smite all the people that have fought against Jerusalem; Their flesh shall consume away while they stand upon their feet, and their eyes shall consume away in their holes, and their tongue shall consume away in their

mouth. And Judah also shall fight at Jerusalem; and the wealth of all the heathen round about shall be gathered together, gold, and silver, and apparel, in great abundance, (Zechariah 14:12,14 NIV.)

The Mosque of Omar with the golden dome that dominates the skyline of Jerusalem is more commonly known as the "Dome of the Rock." It is built over the stone upon which Abraham reportedly laid Isaac as a sacrifice. In Muslim tradition—echoing the jealousy of Ishmael, the eldest but not favored son—it was he, not Isaac, who was offered here. It is also said to be the place from which Muhammad ascended into heaven for a special visit. Muslims do not refer to the area as the Temple Mount, but as the Noble Sanctuary.

Some believe this is also the location of the altar of the first two Hebrew Temples—though this may be due more to the Crusaders' confusion of it and the Temple of Solomon than any actual archeological evidence. The Muslim edifice was built sometime around AD 700. Caliph Omar I, successor to the prophet Muhammad, took Jerusalem in AD 637. Though it is the more famous of the two mosques of the Noble Sanctuary because of its brilliant dome, it is not considered the holiest.

That designation rests with the second mosque on the Mount, called the *al-Aqsa* Mosque (which means "the farthest place of worship of the One God" and refers to its distance from Mecca.) It sits just to the south of the Dome of the Rock, and is the largest mosque in Jerusalem. It was built soon after the Dome of the Rock and is dedicated to Muhammad's night visit to heaven and supposedly rests upon the place from which he took that journey.

It was also this location that became the focal point for the beginning of the second *Intifada*, which is also called the *al-Aqsa Intifada* because it began when then-Israeli Prime Minister Ariel Sharon visited that holy site. The violence began in smaller outbreaks days before this, but on September 28, 2000 it reached new heights after Sharon stood at the door of the *al-Aqsa* Mosque. Though Sharon entered none of the mosque buildings on the Temple Mount, his mere presence on the Noble Sanctuary (all of which Arabs actually consider a mosque) caused an eruption of shouting and rock throwing. The melee resulted in twenty-eight Israeli policemen being injured, three of whom had to be hospitalized. There were no reported Palestinian injuries that day. The following day, however, orchestrated violence erupted after the Muslims' Friday prayers which resulted in deaths and casualties on both sides. The worst period of Palestinian violence in Israeli history ensued. From September 29, 2000 to September 11, 2002, some 427 Israeli civilians and 185 members of the Israeli Defense Forces were killed, 3,202 civilians and 1,307 IDF members injured.

Though the violence had likely been set to start the moment Arafat walked out on the Camp David talks with Israel in July, it was Sharon's visit to the Noble Sanctuary that was purportedly the catalyst for violence to begin in earnest. It is a testimony to how control of the Temple Mount is at the heart of the conflict. It has also been the site of other outbreaks of tension such as the one on September 24, 1996 that led to four days of fighting with tanks and attack helicopters being employed. When the dust and smoke settled more than seventy had died with hundreds more wounded. The pretext of that battle was the opening of a new exit to the Hasmonean Tunnel, an archeological site running along the Western Wall and under part of the Old City of Jerusalem. At the time visitors had to enter and exit by the same opening.

It is traditionally believed that the Dome of the Rock will have to be removed before the third, and last, Temple can be built—a prophecy well known to the Arabs and a reason to further distrust Jewish oversight of the Mount. Some believe, however, that the original site of the Temple may have been on the northern part of the Temple Mount, which is open, not in the south where the Dome of the Rock sits today. If that is the case, it is possible the Temple could be rebuilt without harming the two mosques, which would be more peaceable considering the importance to both the Jews and the Muslims. One way or the other, it seems likely that the rebuilding of the Temple will be one of the bargaining chips used by the Antichrist to draw Israel into the seven-year pact mentioned in the Book of Revelation.

(9)

THE CITY *of the* GREAT KING

"For the LORD Most High is awesome;
He is a great King over all the earth,"
(Psalm 47:2.)

Bestselling author Leon Uris in his book, *Jerusalem: Song of Songs,* described the city as:

> . . . the center of the world, the eye of the world, and the navel of the world. She is regarded as the halfway house between heaven and earth. . . . Jerusalem is the greatest of the great, for she alone has achieved immortality on moral and ethical grounds.[78]

The Psalmist wrote:

> "It is high and magnificent; the whole earth rejoices to see it! Mount Zion, the holy mountain, is the city of the great King!" (Psalm 48:2, NLT.)

Ultimately, the fate of Jerusalem, the City of David, will become the paramount reason for false hope in this world as the pact is signed with the Antichrist. It will also be the site of the final loss of hope as the Antichrist enters the rebuilt temple and desecrates it, marking the beginning of the Tribulation. I believe it is the spirit of Antichrist which provokes the actions of the PLO and other terrorist groups. It adds a spiritual dimension to why Jerusalem is the key to the Palestinian Authority's acceptance of a treaty with Israel, and why it is such a sticking point for anyone proposing peace for the region. It is about much more than how many have died in suicide bombings or Israeli police actions; it is about who controls the center of the world and the rock upon which God made His covenant with humanity.

Not only has the line been firmly drawn, but each side knows what it is willing to sacrifice to get what it wants. The Palestinians wish to chase Israel from what they consider their land; the Jews want to protect their place in the Holy Land. Though America and the USSR desire to avoid an arms race in the Middle East, they can not while maintaining their loyalties. The Soviets, therefore, armed Nasser's Pan-Arabists and the United States eventually promised to keep Israel one step ahead of her neighbors after the Yom Kippur War. This proved more difficult as the US also agreed to supply weapons to Saudi Arabia, Egypt (after Sadat signed a treaty with Israel in 1978), The United Arab Emirates, Kuwait, Bahrain, Jordan, Oman, Lebanon, Qatar, and Yemen (based on previous sales from 1990 to 2001).[79]

One report stated:

> US weapons sales more than tripled in 2011, reaching a record high, according to a new congressional report.
>
> The country sold $66 [billion] worth of arms last year, up from $21.4 [billion] in 2010. The previous record had been $31[billion] in 2009; global arms sales declined slightly after that because of the economic crisis.

America's largest customer was Saudi Arabia, which purchased more than $33 [billion] worth of weapons from the US, including dozens of F-15 fighter jets, missiles, and other materiel.

The United Arab Emirates and Oman also both spent billions, purchases driven in part by fears over Iran's regional ambitions. The Obama administration has touted these deals as a major stimulus for the US economy, saying the Saudi arms sales alone would generate some 75,000 new jobs . . . .All told, the US sold 78 per cent of the world's arms in 2011. Russia was a distant second, with $4.8 [billion] in arms sales.[80]

Thanks to the US, those on opposite sides of the line running through Jerusalem are well prepared to wage conventional warfare in order to control it.

So far the edge has gone to the Israelis, not only because of promises to keep them one step ahead in this race to obtain US arms, but because of Israel's nuclear strike potential. Almost from Israel's rebirth in 1948, Prime Minister David Ben-Gurion saw that nuclear power would be useful in making the Negev desert bloom by supplying electricity and powering desalinization plants to provide drinking water. However, as author Seymour Hersh wrote:

> "Nuclear power was not Ben-Gurion's first priority; the desert would glow before it bloomed."[81]

Ben-Gurion had his eyes set on Israel becoming a nuclear power. Throughout his contacts with the United States, Ben-Gurion continued to push for a promise that Israel would find sanctuary under the umbrella of US nuclear weapons. He could never secure this promise. Israel began a game of cat-and-mouse with her ally. On the one hand, she tried to persuade the US to promise protection, and on the other, developed protection of her own.

By 1953 the Weizmann Institute in Israel had developed an improved ion exchange mechanism for producing heavy water and a more efficient method for mining uranium, which it bartered with the French for a formal agreement to cooperate in nuclear research. By 1958, Israel had begun construction of its own nuclear facility near the Negev Desert town of Dimona, which was based upon visits to the French nuclear research facility at Marcoule. The Israeli government would continue its research for a decade before the first nuclear bombs were manufactured at Dimona in 1968. The facility went into full-scale production at that point, turning out four or five bombs each year. During this time, the US tried through various means to figure out just what was going on at Dimona and Israel tried to conceal it. However, evidence seems to suggest that the US had a pretty good idea of Dimona's purpose, but simply looked the other way knowing that Israel didn't have much choice. Some members of congress even supported Israel's actions. A few days before meeting with President Kennedy to further discuss the Hawk missile purchases, Shimon Peres met with Senator Stuart Symington, a Kennedy supporter and ranking member of the Senate Armed Services Committee. As Peres told his biographer, Symington said, "Don't be a bunch of fools. Don't stop making atomic bombs. And don't listen to the administration. Do whatever you think best."[82]

However, this struggle didn't come without its political casualties. In the spring of 1962, President Kennedy was pushing Prime Minister Ben-Gurion for some solid answers about Dimona, or at least promises that its research was not for military purposes. Ben-Gurion held his ground. According to Yuval Neeman, a physicist and defense ministry intelligence officer who was involved in Israel's nuclear weapon's program, "It was not a friendly exchange. Kennedy was writing like a bully. It was brutal."[83]

As a result, Kennedy shut out Ben-Gurion in the midst of a growing threat. It was in April that Iraq joined Egypt and Syria in the short-lived

Arab Federation, making the threat of another Arab invasion similar to the War of Independence much more likely. Author Seymour Hersh described the situation:

> He [Ben-Gurion] instinctively turned to Washington, and proposed in a letter to the President that the United States and Soviet Union join forces to publicly declare the territorial integrity and security of every Middle Eastern state. "If you can spare an hour or two for a discussion with me on the situation and possible solutions," Ben-Gurion asked, "I am prepared to fly to Washington at your convenience and without any publicity." Kennedy rejected Ben-Gurion's offer of a state visit and expressed "real reservations," according to Ben-Gurion's biography, about any joint statement on the issue with the Soviets. Five days later, a disappointed Ben-Gurion sent a second note to Kennedy: "Mr. President, my people have the right to exist . . . and this existence is in danger." He requested that the United States sign a security treaty with Israel. Again the answer was no, and it was clear to the Mapai Party that Ben-Gurion's leadership and his intractability about Dimona were serious liabilities in Washington. Golda Meir acknowledged to Ben-Gurion's biographer, "We knew about these approaches. . . We said nothing, even though we wondered."
>
> A few weeks later, on June 16, 1963, Ben-Gurion abruptly resigned as prime minister and defense minister, ending his fifteen-year reign as Israel's most influential public official.[84]

By 1973 Israel was thought to have about twenty-five nuclear warheads with three or four missile launchers in place and operational at Hirbat Zachariah. Israel also had a number of mobile Jericho I missile launchers at her disposal. This provided the capability of launching nuclear weapons and hitting targets as far away as Tbilisis and Baku in southern Russia. Damascus and Cairo were within easy range.

When the Yom Kippur War erupted in 1973, the US was slow to respond. Several sources suggested that Nixon and Kissinger planned for Israel to suffer a severe setback before responding in order to teach her a lesson. It was at this point that Israel had developed what became known as the Samson Option. It was based on Israel's determination that there would never be another Holocaust at the hands of a foreign power. It was better to die by their own hand than be captured by an oppressive force, whether that be Romans, Germans, or Arabs. It was the biblical character Samson from whom they took their example. In his last hour, a blinded and weakened Samson was marched into the temple of Dagon as a show of Philistine pre-eminence over the Jews. As the mocking catcalls swirled about him, Samson prayed, "O Lord God, remember me, I pray thee, and strengthen me, I pray thee, only this once, O God, that I may be at once avenged of the Philistines for my two eyes," (Judges 16:28, NIV.) Then, placing his hands firmly on two pillars supporting the roof of the temple, he prayed again, "let me die with the Philistines," (Judges 16:30, NIV) and with all his might pushed the columns over, bringing the roof down upon himself and all the Philistines. The Bible tells us that in this final act he killed more Philistines than he had in all his previous battles.

The Samson Option thus illustrates Israel's willingness to bring the world into a nuclear war and suffer annihilation. Israel's leaders knew the consequences of a pre-emptive attack against Egypt and Syria—the Soviet Union would launch an all-out nuclear attack: Armageddon would ensue. Once the US was appraised of Israeli resolve, Nixon pulled out all stops to help Israel win a conventional war that prevented nuclear proliferation in the Middle East. He ordered that the US come to Israel's aid by launching military airlifts to rival those directed at Berlin after World War II.

Since Israel had nuclear weapons and her neighbors did not, this further bolstered her position as a nation that could not be defeated in open warfare. If the Arabs developed nuclear weapons however, this distinct advantage would be lost. So it was that on June 7, 1981, Israel used US F-15s and F-16s purchased for defensive purposes only, to take out the Osirak nuclear reactor twelve miles southwest of Baghdad before it became operational. Israel did not want another David vs. Goliath scenario.

While the world fumed, the US gave Israel only a mild reprimand for this pre-preemptive strike. According to Richard V. Allen, Reagan's national security advisor, when President Ronald Reagan was informed of the attack, the conversation went like this:

> "Mr. President, the Israelis just took out a nuclear reactor in Iraq with F-16s." . . .
>
> "Why do you suppose they did it?"
>
> The President let his rhetorical question hang for a moment, Allen recalled, and added:
>
> "Well. Boys will be boys."[85]

The White House announced that the next installment of a 1975 sale of seventy-five F-16s would be suspended because of the attack. However, two months later the suspension was lifted and a shipment of four new F-16s was delivered to Israel without incident.

It appears Israel had also found a way to get around restrictions required for use of America's extremely advanced and secret KH-11 spy satellite system. President Carter had agreed the Israelis could receive satellite pictures of areas within one hundred miles of their borders so they could detect troop movements in neighboring countries that might portend an invasion by Arab forces—again for defensive purposes only. However, somehow in addition they received enough images of Osirak— roughly 550 miles from Jerusalem—that they could also launch a surgical strike against Iraq without being detected until they had reached the target.

Soon Israel added nuclear submarines to its inventory and in June 2000 an Israeli submarine launched a cruise missile that hit a target 600 kilometers away. Israel became the third nation, after the US and Russia, to have that capacity. However, in the spring of 2002, Iran launched a missile that covered a similar distance. When asked about Iran's nuclear capabilities in May of that same year, Russian Deputy chief of the General Staff, General Yuri Baluyevshy said, "Iran does have nuclear weapons. Of course they are non-strategic nuclear weapons. I mean these are not ICBMs with a range of more than 5,500 kilometers..."[86]

They may not have the range to reach Moscow or Washington, but they could certainly reach Tel Aviv and Jerusalem. Goliath is quickly closing in on David's military edge. But, it doesn't matter how many times you can blow someone up, just that you *can*.

While in the USSR in 1999, I met with a former KGB head. I said to him, "It is wonderful how the world is now a much safer place to live." He responded, "Listen, the world is not a safer place to live. Our republics are cash-poor and crime-rich. We have thousands of nuclear bombs. Last month in the Ukraine, two missing bombs were reported. Only the casings were left. When I asked where they were, I was told, 'Russian entrepreneurs.' While your country was celebrating the end of the cold war, we were panicking over the beginning of a hot war."

I asked him about Israel. He responded, "We have been targeting their cities, and they have had their big bombs trained on us for years. So, what else is new?" I knew he was telling me the truth, for I had heard this from a key advisor to two of Israel's prime ministers years before.

The Washington Post reported:

> In the ethnic conflicts that surrounded the collapse of the Soviet Union, fighters in several countries seized upon an unlikely new weapon: a small, thin rocket known

as the Alazan. Originally built for weather experiments, the Alazan was transformed into a weapon of terror, packed with explosives and lobbed into cities.

Military records show at least 38 Alazan warheads were modified to carry radioactive material, in effect creating the world's first surface-to-surface dirty bomb. Experts and officials say the warheads have disappeared.[87]

During the 1991 Gulf War, Reuben Hecht, who had been a senior advisor to Israel's prime ministers, lived in Haifa, a target of Saddam Hussein's SCUD missiles. He said to me, "We have picked up intelligence that Saddam has given the order to load chemical and biological weapons in SCUDs. I can assure you that if they hit our cities, Baghdad will be a radioactive dustbowl. Israel has mobile missile launchers armed with nuclear weapons. They are facing Baghdad even as I speak, and are ready to launch on command. We are on full-scale nuclear alert."

Today in Israel names like Dimona, the Samson Option, Project 700, the Zechariah Project, the Temple Weapons, and Z-Division are all part of one of the most massive nuclear arsenals in the world. Now new names are being heard: Pumped X-ray Lasers, Hydrodynamics, and Radiation Transport—the new Armageddon-generation of weapons. It is thought that Israel has over 300 tactical and strategic weapons including more than 100 nuclear artillery shells, nuclear land mines, and neutron bombs that will with massive doses of radiation destroy human life. It also has lasers for its planes and tanks and electro-magnetic weapons that will shut down radar. As of November 14, 2003, Israel took her first order of US F-16I fighter jets, which signaled the largest arms deal in Israeli history. The new jet can reach nations as far away as Iran and Libya and can be armed with AMRAAM air-to-air missiles and equipped with Northrop Grumman APG-68 radar. That would give the Israeli Air Force the capability to shoot down other jets from over thirty miles away.

At *least* nine nations currently have the capability of attacking an enemy with a thermonuclear bomb: Russia, the United States, China, Israel, France, Great Britain, India, Pakistan, and, it appears, soon Iran. This gives them all the possibility to unleash a plague of nuclear or neutron bombs that would be very much like what is described in Zechariah 14:12, NKJV:

> And this shall be the plague with which the Lord will strike all the people who fought against Jerusalem: Their flesh shall dissolve while they stand on their feet, Their eyes shall dissolve in their sockets, And their tongues shall dissolve in their mouths.

Others such as North Korea claim to be closing in on it. In the last battle, Russia, the European countries (Great Britain and France), and the Eastern countries (Iran, Pakistan, India, China, and North Korea) will be on the other side of the line from Israel. But where will the United States be?

Thus far, the war on terrorism has taken us from the attacks of 9/11 to lengthy campaigns in Iraq and Afghanistan. But if we are ultimately to win this war and prevent another, perhaps nuclear attack on US cities, where must we go from here?

Americans have no idea what they could face if the nation continues to ignore the call of God for prayer and repentance. As George Santayana said, "Those who cannot remember the past are doomed to repeat it."[88]

(10)

WINNING THE WAR
on TERROR

"Blessed is the nation whose God is the Lord,
The people He has chosen as His own inheritance,"
(Psalm 33:12, NKJV.)

As the US entered a new millennium, America truly faced the greatest threat ever to its existence and way of life. While atheistic communism once posed the greatest potential of a new imperialistic culture, it significantly decreased with the disintegration of the Soviet Union and the end of the Cold War. This current struggle in the war on terrorism is no longer just a fight for the supremacy of a political ideology through military might; it is a battle for hearts and minds through a twisting of truth that turns our enemies into zealous sociopaths willing to give their lives to murder others.

This is not Christianity which can be lived with righteousness through love, but a tyrannical system that envelopes cultures and governments and dictates truth for its own interests. The repressive Taliban government is perhaps the best example of how Wahhabists really want the world to appear.

Islam is the force empowering impoverished nations against their economic superiors. It has become the greatest threat to our nation with a foreign policy that denies truth for the sake of a Clinton-style house-of-cards prosperity and a lack of resolve to win the war on terror.

Many seem to believe that the United States needs to return to the more isolationistic stance it had at the beginning of the twentieth century, letting the rest of the world take care of itself. This is no longer possible in a time when live television signals can be broadcast all over the planet and where journeys that once took months can now be completed in hours. We have come a long way from Jules Verne's fantastic idea of going *Around the World in Eighty Days* to a time when satellites circle the globe in ninety minutes. Since most consumer products are made abroad, we are irreversibly tied to the rest of the world as never before.

Because of this, I believe the areas of Foreign Policy and National Security will dominate election debates over the coming years, as will the question "How do we win the war against terrorism?" I see winning the war on terror as perhaps the greatest solution to securing peace for the nation. For the first time in history a war must be fought against a deadly religious ideal, Wahhabism, rather than a political idealist or a madman bent on universal rule. We can no longer tolerate every belief in the hope that this will lead to global brotherhood.

When Wahhabists call Christians "polytheists" and "crusaders," it is more than just demonizing our point of view or a misunderstanding of who we are. When pamphlets are circulated referring to American Christians as polytheists because of a belief in the Trinity, we merely shake our heads and mark those materials as "irrelevant religious stuff." However, when Wahhabists label us polytheists, we become targets for *jihad*, animals for the slaughter. Brutally murdering *mushrikun* (polytheists) is an act of worship and devotion for Wahhabists today just as it was for the original followers of Muhammad ibn Abd al-Wahhab in the mid-1700s.

The Crusades are often viewed as a mistake of the Church in the

Middle Ages. Wahhabists refer to Crusaders as the forces which wrested Jerusalem and the Noble Sanctuary from their control, amassed to wipe out Islam in the same way *jihadists* hope to extinguish Judaism and Christianity. It also lowered the Crusaders' status to something less than human, as was exemplified by Sallah al-Din's breaking of his peace treaty to recapture Jerusalem. Apparently, there was no need to keep one's word to "apes and pigs."[89]

This brings a spiritual dimension to the war on terrorism. There can be no ceasefire in a war against people hoping to be martyred. Such a war cannot be won without tremendous dedication to spiritual truth and Christian people praying to win this battle for hearts and minds.

The Bible tells us in I Timothy 6:10 KJV, that the "love of money is the root of all evil." This has never been more evident than it is today when much of what is good and holy in America is traded for economic gain. While money is good to have, we need to realize that nothing is more valuable than God's blessings of peace, freedom and security.

We cannot win the war on terrorism by vowing to defeat terrorists while at the same time trying to appease them. We must realize that the major front in the war on terrorism is the battle line Muslims wish to see drawn through the heart of Jerusalem.

Though liberals in the United States have painted the struggle of the Palestinians as a political revolution for freedom from oppression, no nation has ever aimed strictly at civilians in order to overthrow its enemies. The terrorists fight a war on the innocent—not caring who their victims are as long as it generates headlines—even if it means killing children or babies in strollers as has happened all too often. The truth must be recognized: terrorists are not freedom fighters; they are murderers. Israel's struggle against the PLO, Hamas, Islamic Jihad, and other such organizations is a war on terror. How can we ignore an ally's fight against terrorists—trying to force them to appease the terrorists—and expect to win our own? If we hope to win the battle against terrorism, all must be treated as criminals, not diplomats. If a man breaks into your house to steal or to harm your family, you don't negotiate with him about which rooms he can invade; you dispatch him, or at the very least have him arrested! The US can no longer afford to legitimize terrorism as a negotiating technique to win more concessions from sovereign governments. As we have seen, there is no appeasing these thugs; they want it all!

On October 12-14, 2003, I attended the first annual Jerusalem Summit—a forum to discuss establishing peace in the Middle East. I had the honor of being the keynote speaker on the first evening of the conference alongside world leaders and media celebrities such as Israeli Prime Minister Benjamin Netanyahu, former Prime Minister Ehud Olmert, Director of the Middle East Forum Daniel Pipes, Benny Elon of the Israeli Ministry of Tourism, the Honorable Richard Perle, syndicated columnist Cal Thomas, and former Ambassador Dr. Alan Keyes. Interestingly enough, the theme of this first summit was "Winning the War on Terrorism through Moral Clarity." The scripture from Zechariah 8:19 on the cover of the program read: " . . . so love truth and peace."

As he addressed the conference, former Prime Minister Netanyahu had this to say:

> Conscience is a moral compass. Conscience is absent in some societies and they endorse terrorism. Terrorism is deliberate and systematic action to kill innocent civilians. Israel is fighting terrorism. But the UN doesn't make the distinction between these two kinds of "violence", because that would say some of the UN members are perpetuators of war crimes, or terrorism. . . .
>
> The UN will not stop the terrorists; only an alliance of free states led by the US, geared to bring down regimes that fuel and propagate terrorism, can do that. We must implant values and morality in civilizations. Salvation will not come from the UN . . .
>
> The Israeli Defense Forces must continue to fight

terrorism, for Israel's survival as a nation, and to uphold justice and morality.[90]

The Minister of Strategic Cooperation between the US and Israel, Uzi Landau, added this:

No cause justifies terror . . . Israel is a small target; America is the big one. But we are on the front line. If terror is not defeated here, it will move to the US and to Europe. Our war is a war of free societies against terror.[91]

And as Ambassador Keyes said:

In the wake of September 11th we should have taken a stand clearly and unequivocally, that if you practice terrorism you lose your claim to legitimate participation in all and any international processes whatsoever . . .The hope and heritage of righteousness and faith . . . says, "Come what may, do evil what it will, God is God and I shall stand for Him." This, I believe, is the moral heritage that transcends any struggle for evil. . . . We shall fight the fight as it is necessary in the world but we shall win it first in our own souls and spirit. So that at the end of the day we shall stand—not as people who have defeated evil, but as people who have once again vindicated the truth that— come what may—you cannot crush out that faith which holds on forever to the righteous will of God.[92]

(11)

TENACITY *to* THWART
TERRORISM

Bow down thine ear to me; deliver me speedily:
be thou my strong rock, for an house of defense to save me,"
(Psalm 31:2, KJV.)

The war on terrorism cannot be won without a resolve for victory,
without a conviction to call terrorism evil (whoever may be instigating it),
and without the determination to win the battle first in the spirit realm
through prayer. Natural insight is not enough to win this fight; we need
God's guidance. When tenacity and conviction begin to weaken, a tolerance
for viewing children with no legs and allowing those who maimed them
to walk free develops. I'm not talking about being hateful or mean-
spirited, nor am I preaching a racist hatred of Arabs and Muslims—what
I'm talking about are values. We cannot violate rules of law and evidence
to go after such men, but we must not let terrorists and murderers walk
free for political reasons when we have evidence to convict them. What
I am talking about is real love—God's love—that includes justice, but not
vengeance. If we are to win the overall battle against terrorism, we must
win it first in Israel.

I believe that in order to do that, we must also take some clear and concise step towards that end. Many of the things America needs to do, in fact, are already in place. If we want to send a strong, clear message to the terrorists that their reign of terror is over, here is what we must do first:

1. Support Israel's construction of a security fence in order to save Palestinian and Israeli lives.

Israel has exhausted every means to provide security for Israeli citizens. The last resort was to build a security fence to deter terrorists from slipping across the border into Israel from the West Bank. This decision by the Israeli government was not an ill-conceived plan. There are similar barriers along the borders with Lebanon, Syria, Jordan, and the Gaza Strip.

In places where no security barrier exists, terrorists only have to walk across an invisible line to get from the West Bank into Israel. US forces captured Saddam Hussein because a security fence was built around Saddam's hometown of Tikrit, in order to control traffic in and out. This limiting of access eventually enabled the military to capture him. Israel must be allowed to do what the US would do in its place.

2. Recognize Jerusalem as Israel's capital and ratify the Jerusalem Embassy Act.

The Jerusalem Embassy Act of 1995 echoes other such legislation supporting Israel that the US Congress passed, but Presidents Clinton, Bush and Obama have resisted based on perceived National Security issues. The Act called for US recognition of Jerusalem as Israel's capital with the move of its embassy from Tel Aviv to Jerusalem by

1999. Listed below are a few basic tenets of the Jerusalem Embassy Relocation Act:

» The United States maintains its embassy in the functioning capital of every country excepting the case of our democratic friend and strategic ally, the State of Israel.

» The United States conducts official meetings and other business in the city of Jerusalem in *de facto* recognition of its status as the capital of Israel.

» Jerusalem should remain an undivided city in which the rights of every ethnic and religious group are protected;

» Jerusalem should be recognized as the capital of the State of Israel; and

» The United States Embassy in Israel should be established in Jerusalem no later than May 31, 1999.[93]

The first positive step the US must take is to show solidarity with Israel and send a message to terrorists that continued violence will only diminish their negotiating power.

3. Ratify the 1987 Anti-Terrorism Act.

The 1987 Anti-Terrorism Act is also being held up on a National Security Waver, perhaps mainly because of one thing: it names the Palestinian Liberation Organization as a terrorist group and accepting this would end our ability to negotiate with them.

If the US stepped forward to declare the PLO a terrorist organization and remove it once and for all from being a valid representative to negotiate for the Palestinians, it would first of all send a clear message that terrorism no longer pays. Secondly it would clear the way for municipal and rural council elections as Israel and Jordan had first planned in the late 1980s. Such a move would be tremendously positive towards peace in the region. The Palestinian people can never have peace, nor can Israel, so long as a terrorist organization presides over their destinies.

Once the PA is back on the list as a terrorist organization, it should be targeted in the same way we are have tried to eliminate al Qaeda. The Obama administration should freeze its billions of dollars in assets and imprison, or at least allow Israel to imprison, its leaders. Such actions would be an easy next step to take in winning the war on terrorism and trying them for their crimes.

4. Require the Arabs to end the Palestinian Refugee problem by taking the refugees into their nations just as Israel, Germany, the United States, Jordan, and other countries have done with refugee groups.

The Palestinian refugee camps are the longest standing camps of their kind in the world; the *only* ones where the children and grandchildren of those in the camps have been born as refugees. Jordan has been the only nation willing to give citizenship to those within its borders. Neither Lebanon, nor Syria, or any other Arab nation has offered to do the same, nor allowed those in the camps to resettle elsewhere. They keep these people boxed in, prisoners held by their own Arab brothers and yet lay the blame squarely on Israel. After three generations these refugees continue to be pawns in the game of the Arab States to de-legitimize the state of Israel in any way they can.[94]

Journalist Joseph Puder in an article for *FrontPage Magazine* wrote:

The humanitarianism of the American people is wasted on people who care more about destroying the Jewish state than attending to the needs of their Palestinian people. Israel absorbed a greater number of refugees from Europe and the Arab states in the 1950's, and gave them back their dignity . . . Palestinian political gangsters thrive on the misery of their Palestinian people.[95]

Perhaps in light of the violence they breed, refugee camps *are* Israel's problem, but they cannot truly be considered her responsibility. The refugees have grown from 700,000 to over four million under the UN and Arab League's watchful eyes—a vast disgraced and disgruntled horde with no hope of a home or a homeland. No wonder many have become suicide bombers!

Many other nations have dealt with refugees, but the Arab States have refused to take in those they call "brothers." After agreeing to a ceasefire with Israel in 1949, the Arab states forcibly expelled 900,000 Jews from their lands, all of which Israel absorbed, in addition to the continual flow to the Holy Land of displaced persons from Europe.

As one writer noted:

Israel has allowed more than 50,000 refugees to return to Israel under a family reunification program. Arabs who lost property in Israel are eligible to file for compensation from Israel's Custodian of Absentee Property. As of the end of 1993, a total of 14,692 claims had been filed. Claims were settled for more than 200,000 dunams of land (each equal to about ¼ acre), more than 10,000,000 NIS (New Israeli Shekels) had been paid in compensation, and more than 54,000 dunams of replacement land had been given in compensation. No compensation has ever been paid to any of the more than 600,000 Jewish refugees from Arab countries who were forced to leave and abandon their property.[96]

Yet as Jamal Abd al-Nasser said, "The return of the refugees will mean the end of Israel."[97] The Arabs need to discard this trump card in favor of doing the humanitarian thing of helping their fellow Arabs. They must dismantle these terrorist incubation centers and give the Palestinian people homes.

5. Land for peace is not an option until a true representative of the Palestinian people can be raised.

The current Palestinian populace is a tainted and brainwashed people. These are the people who danced in the streets when told about the attacks of September 11. These are the people who raise their children to be suicide bombers, dress their sons as guerilla fighters with automatic weapons, some toys, some real, and have their daughters dip their hands in liquid symbolizing Israeli blood.[98] These are the people who celebrate Israeli deaths with suicide attacks as Jewish doctors treat Arab casualties in the same hospitals. This cycle of rabid anti-Semitism in the Palestinian territories must be reversed.

Until a legitimate Palestinian leadership emerges, there is no one with whom Israel can negotiate. Intervention is needed to develop such a group and reverse the propagation of hatred in Palestinian-controlled areas. This is a very unlikely role for either Israel or the US. Instead it should be handled in cooperation with an Arab partner such as Jordan—essentially the same plan Israel and Jordan were working on in the late 1980s.

6. We need to fight the racism of anti-Semitism as fervently as we fight racism in our nation.

Anti-Zionism and anti-Semitism need to be squelched. This hatred fuels, feeds and spreads terrorism and suicide bombers. The United States cannot financially aid nor should it supply weapons to nations that regularly air anti-Semitic television programming or endorse anti-Semitic literature.

The war on terrorism is a battle for hearts and minds; only God can touch a person's heart and change it. While taking these steps would be a decisive move politically towards a return to truth as a governing principle in the US, they will never be taken without an almost miraculous return to God. Presently, though, the US is still contaminated with the idea that money, education, and charm will suffice.

In the Great Commission Jesus told the disciples "you shall be witnesses to Me in Jerusalem, and in all Judea and Samaria, and to the end of the earth, (Acts 1:8, NKJV.) Regrettably, the Great Commission has become the Great Omission. Christ's love is no longer taught in Judea and Samaria (the area of the West Bank) as God had ordained. If we are to reverse the hatred fueling Palestinian terrorism, we must revert to God's first instructions to the Church.

Is America headed for a great awakening and a revival? Or are we headed for a rude awakening; the discovery that our confidence has been misplaced? Prophecy indicates that we are ultimately heading towards an event that will dwarf the impact of September 11 a thousand times over—will that event lead to the end of our nation, or its salvation? In order to answer that question, we must first come to grips with what was the greatest moral issue of the twentieth century, one that promises to be even more significant in the twenty-first.

(12)

THE NEW
ANTI-SEMITISM

"The voice of thy brother's blood crieth unto me from the ground,"
(Genesis 4:10, KJV)

As the ink was drying on the newly penned Constitution of the United States, many of those taking part in crafting it saw that the silver lining of promise for America's future was overshadowed by a dark cloud. One issue threatened to halt the proceedings before the young country could be birthed. The delegates struck a compromise with the "three-fifths clause." The question was based on how slaves would be counted in the census. The *Rutgers Law Journal* addressed this question:

> Delegates opposed to slavery generally wished to count only the free inhabitants of each state, but delegates supportive of slavery, on the other hand, generally wanted to count slaves in their actual numbers. Since slaves could not vote, slaveholders would thus have the benefit of increased representation in the House and

the Electoral College. The final compromise of counting *"all other persons"* as only three-fifths of their actual numbers reduced the power of the slave states relative to the original southern proposals, but increased it over the northern position.[99]

Rather than revert to colonies that the British could easily conquer, the delegates negotiated the outcome. The black cloud seen by our forefathers was the issue of slavery, and the hatred and racism that accompanied it. It was an issue they felt could have eternal ramifications. Thomas Jefferson, himself a slave owner, described it in this way:

> The whole commerce between master and slave is a perpetual exercise of the most boisterous passions, the most unremitting despotism on the one part, and degrading submission on the other. Our children see this and learn to imitate it; for man is an imitative animal. This quality is the germ of all education in him. From his cradle to his grave he is learning to do what he sees others do. . . . The parent storms, the child looks on, catches the lineaments of his wrath, puts on the same airs in the circle of smaller slaves, gives a loose rein to the worst of passions and thus nursed, educated and daily exercised in tyranny. . . .
>
> Can the liberties of a nation be thought secure, when we have removed their only firm basis, a conviction in the minds of the people that these liberties are of the gift of God? That they are not to be violated but with his wrath? Indeed, I tremble for my country when I reflect that God is just: that his justice cannot sleep forever: that considering numbers, nature and natural means only, a revolution of the wheel of fortune, an exchange

of situation is among possible events: that it may become probable by supernatural interference!

The Almighty has no attributes, which can take side with us in such a contest. [100]

Jefferson obviously felt that America's racism, despite whatever Christian principles our nation was founded upon, could well bring its destruction at the hands of a just and moral God. In the midst of the Civil War, Abraham Lincoln included this thought in his second inauguration address of 1865:

> If we shall suppose that American Slavery is one of those offences which, in the providence of God, must needs come, but which, having continued through His appointed time, He now wills to remove, and that He gives to both North and South, this terrible war, as the woe due to those by whom the offence came, shall we discern therein any departure from those divine attributes which the believers in a Living God always ascribe to Him? Fondly do we hope—fervently do we pray—that this mighty scourge of war may speedily pass away. Yet, if God wills that it continue, until all the wealth piled by the bondmen's two hundred and fifty years of unrequited toil shall be sunk, and until every drop of blood drawn with the lash, shall be paid by another drawn with the sword, as was said three thousand years ago, so still it must be said, "The judgments of the Lord are true and righteous altogether."
>
> With malice toward none, with charity for all, with firmness in the right as God gives us to see the right, let us strive on to finish the work we are in, to bind up the nation's wounds, to care for him who shall have borne the battle and for his widow and his orphan, to do all which

may achieve and cherish a just and lasting peace among ourselves and with all nations.[101]

Racism did not end with the Civil War, but lingers even today. If God's hedge of protection was removed from the Christian nation in the 1860s to the point that Civil War erupted, what can be expected to happen to us if we tolerate the racism of anti-Semitism arising today just as it did in Germany in the 1920s and 30s?

The Jew-hatred that surfaced in Germany between the World Wars has found a new home, and not only in the Arab nations today. As we saw earlier from Theodor Herzl's experiences in France, Germany was not the only European nation that disliked the Jews. Anti-Semitism was concealed beneath the guilt of the Holocaust, but not extinguished. Nearly seven decades after the Holocaust, it is reemerging. Today's detestation of the Jews has returned in the form of hatred for the nation of Israel. It now hides behind the politics of opposing Israel.

This anti-Zionism is spread democratically by fanatics across the ideological spectrum, from the extreme Liberal Left to the extreme Right.

Comments by Malaysian Prime Minister Mahathir Mohamad at the Organization of the Islamic Conference summit in October of 2003 are typical:

> I will not enumerate the instances of our humiliation and oppression, nor will I once again condemn our detractors and oppressors. It would be an exercise in futility because they are not going to change their attitudes just because we condemn them. If we are to recover our dignity and that of Islam, our religion, it is we who must decide, it is we who must act. . . .
>
> We [Muslims] are actually very strong. 1.3 billion people cannot be simply wiped out. The Europeans killed 6 million Jews out of 12 million. But today the Jews rule

this world by proxy. They get others to fight and die for them.[102]

While former National Security Advisor and later Secretary of State Condoleezza Rice said she did not believe Mohamad's ideology represented that of the Muslim world, it seemed unlikely that the delegates of over fifty-seven nations to whom he spoke agreed with her. At the conclusion of his speech, all stood and applauded loudly as they shouted their approval.

Newspapers around the world are noting the rise and new openness of anti-Semitism; how different are such remarks from those of Hitler's propaganda secretary Paul Joseph Goebbels on, of all dates, September 11—but in 1937, not 2001:

> Who are those responsible for this catastrophe? Without fear, we want to point the finger at the Jew as the inspirer, the author, and the beneficiary of this terrible catastrophe: look, this is the enemy of the world, the destroyer of cultures, the parasite among the nations, the son of chaos, the incarnation of evil, the ferment of decomposition, the visible demon of the decay of humanity.[103]

Early in 1937, Goebbels documented a meeting on church affairs, where Hitler freely expressed his vision. In his diary, Goebbels wrote:

> The Fuhrer explains Christianity and Christ. He [Christ] wanted to act against Jewish world domination. Jewry had him crucified.[104]

Similar language of this common doctrine of accusing the Jews of responsibility for virtually all the world's ills has resurfaced today in the halls of European government, academia, and the media, and through worldwide distribution over the Internet. Of course, if all these ills are because of the Jews, the next logical step is to begin shutting them out of positions of power, taking away what they own, and boycotting their businesses—the same steps Hitler took in 1933. He expressed his gospel of redemptive anti-Semitism in 1922, which sounds eerily similar to diatribes being shouted by Muslim leaders today:

> My first and foremost task will be the annihilation of
> the Jews . . . until all Germany has been cleansed.[105]

In July 2013, the European Union declared war on Israel—economic warfare. This is far from surprising since biblical prophecy indicates that the Antichrist will come from within EU confines. In Daniel 8:24-25, KJV, the prophet describes events surrounding his rise:

> And his power shall be mighty, but not by his own power;
> and he shall destroy wonderfully, and shall prosper, and
> practice, and shall destroy the mighty and the holy people.
> And through his policy also he shall cause craft to prosper
> in his hand; and he shall magnify himself in his heart, and
> by peace shall destroy many: he shall also stand up against
> the Prince of princes; but he shall be broken without hand.

In a recent move designed to cause Israel great financial hardship, the EU voted to forbid all twenty-eight members from having any interaction with Israeli territories outside the original 1949 lines. This would include, according to news sources, "cooperating, transferring funds, giving scholarships or research grants to organizations or individuals based in Judea and Samaria, eastern Jerusalem, and even the Golan Heights."[106] The instructions target the years 2014–2020. The decision dictates that Israel must disavow settlements that are not part of the 1949 mandate.

Subtle, and many times not so subtle, anti-Semitism is spreading across Europe once again. In 2012, a German court ruled that Jewish children could not be circumcised until old enough to consent. Citing animal cruelty, Poland has banned the practices surrounding kosher meat production. The dominant view regarding Jews in the EU now coincides with that of Muslim countries, and it is no surprise that those feelings are now being asserted in the political arena.

This action by nations comprising the European Union is a move that could easily backfire. As previously noted, Genesis 12:3 records, "I will bless those who bless you and I will curse him who curses you." It is no small thing to curse the nation on which rests the hand of God.

Just as traditional anti-Semitism sought to deny Jews rights as individuals in society, today it attacks the Jewish people as a nation. Just as they were exploited as scapegoats for their host countries' problems, Israel is being singled out as the root of all the world's evil. It explains what happened at the UN's international Conference on Racism in Durban, South Africa in August of 2001. As far as delegates were concerned, racism would be a thing of the past if just the one nation, Israel, were eliminated. Consider Israel's November 2003 General Assembly draft resolution calling for the protection of Israeli children from Palestinian terrorist attacks—the first resolution introduced by Israel to the UN since 1976. It was soundly rejected by the assembly's Social, Humanitarian, and Cultural Committee, even though a similar resolution to protect Palestinian children had passed just weeks before.

Opposition to Israel's policies and Jew-hatred has become utterly indistinguishable. Foes of globalization and US intervention in Iraq blame Israel by attributing these policies to Jewish control over Washington, as part of the historically anti-Semitic canard that the Jews aim to take over the world.

Of what are the Jews usually accused? How is it that they have gained control of the world by proxy? What are perceived as their greatest sins? Don't be surprised if you can answer this yourself; you have probably been more exposed to such anti-Semitic propaganda than you realize. The big three always seems to be: 1) the Jews control the media, 2) the Jews control the money, and 3) the Jews killed Jesus.

Is this actually true? Among the wealthiest people in the world, only six percent are Jewish. Who does control the money? According to a recent BBC report, seven of the ten wealthiest heads of state in the world are Arabs; none are Jewish. Nor are Jews CEOs of any of the world's ten largest companies.

Do they control the media? Of the ten largest media companies in the world, only one has been run in recent years by a Jew, Michael Eisner, former chief executive officer of the Walt Disney Company, hardly a pro-Israel propaganda machine.

Did the Jews kill Jesus? Read your Bible. The Sanhedrin had to go to the Romans to have Jesus killed. It was Roman soldiers who nailed Him to the cross and a Roman spear that pierced His side. What of the angry mob that called for his death? I have stood in the courtyard where that happened and it would hold no more than a hundred people. The Sanhedrin would have probably rallied at least half that number or more. That is a pretty small sample for which to blame an entire race.[107] Today, no one holds today's young Germans accountable for the Holocaust that happened less than a century ago; how can we still hold Jews responsible for an act that occurred two thousand years ago? You might as well hold Italians liable for the destruction of Jerusalem; Titus was a Roman. Besides, it was the sin of all humankind that nailed Jesus to the cross.

While anti-Semitism is on the rise again in Europe, nowhere is it more vehemently expressed than in the Arab World, and especially in Egypt, Israel's first Arab peace partner. A recent mini-series on Egyptian state television based on the infamous forgery *The Protocols of the Elders of Zion* is only one example. Egyptian schoolbooks fill the minds of impressionable youngsters with hate propaganda against Jews. State-controlled newspapers publish Nazi caricatures of Jews; and a vast array of anti-Semitic literature in Arabic or translated from the original language are readily available in bookstores. Both the fraudulent *Protocols* and Hitler's *Mein Kampf* are bestsellers in Arab states today. They are illustrated, as are the daily newspapers, with depictions of grotesque hook-nosed, bearded, thick-lipped Jews, Israelis indistinguishable from that published during the Holocaust by Nazi propaganda chief Josef Goebbels in *Der Sturmer*.

Just before the visit of Shimon Peres to Cairo on April 29, 2001, the front page of the newspaper *Al-Arabi* boasted a swastika and a photomontage of Peres in a Nazi uniform. On April 18, journalist Ahmad Regev wrote in the official Egyptian newspaper *Al-Akhbar*:

> Our thanks go to the late Hitler who wrought, in advance, the vengeance of the Palestinians upon the most despicable villains on the face of the earth. However, we rebuke Hitler for the fact that the vengeance was insufficient.[108]

Syrian Defense Minister Mustafa Tlas's 1983 book, *The Matzah of Zion*—an Arab variation on the medieval claims of blood libel that sparked the Damascus incident of 1840—accuses Jews of baking Passover matzo with the blood of Muslim children. It was recently reprinted. A television program, "Sucking the blood of Arabs" has been aired repeatedly in the Arab media. The Egyptian weekly *October* has informed its readers about "the loathsome qualities of the Jewish race throughout its long history." Meanwhile, the official Syrian daily *Tishrin* frequently accuses Israel of fabricating the Holocaust, as have numerous Iranian politicians in recent years.

Holocaust denial is a frequent theme in the Arab media, with *The Palestine Times* writing of "God's lying people" who are "the Holocaust worshippers,"[109] and the Palestinian Authority's TV channel: "No Chelmno, no Dachau, no Auschwitz, only disinfecting sites . . . the lie of extermination." The PA mufti of Jerusalem, Sheikh Sabri Ikrama, excuses the Holocaust, stating:

It is not my fault that Hitler hated the Jews. Anyway,
they hate them just about everywhere.[110]

Other Muslim clerics call upon worshipers in the mosques to "have
no mercy on the Jews, no matter where they are, in any country . . .
wherever you meet them, kill them."[111]

(1 3)

CONSEQUENCES *of* ANTI-SEMITISM

"Show me a sign of your favor, that those who hate me
may see and be put to shame because you,
LORD, have helped me and comforted me,"
(Psalm 86:17, ESV.)

Palestinian terrorists practice a form of anti-Semitism: a combination of savoring the murder of Jews along with their dehumanization by the Nazis, all for the sake of annihilating the Jewish people. While most European countries have faced the past ensuring that anti-Semitism will never again become official policy, the Arab world has done nothing to douse the flames of Jew-hatred within its borders.

The Palestinian Authority television station broadcasts movies in which children kill Israeli soldiers. Reports aired from PA summer camps show children training with weapons and singing songs filled with hatred for Jews and songs of praise for the *shahids* (suicide bombers.) The studio map of Greater Palestine covers the area of the entire State of Israel—but Israel is not mentioned and all Israeli cities are identified as the cities of Palestine.

SITAmnesty writer Amos Nevo penned:

Esti Vebman, an expert on anti-Semitism from the Institute for the Study of Anti-Semitism and Racism at Tel Aviv University, has been following the topic in the Palestinian Authority and Arab world for more than eight years. "Back in the Middle Ages," says Vebman, "the Christians used this motif of poisoning wells. The Arabs are now adopting the Christian anti-Semitism of the Middle Ages and Nazi anti-Semitism; they are adding Islamic motifs and integrating it into their anti-Israel propaganda."[112]

Amos Nevo continued in his article:

"It was a good day for the Jews, when the Nazi Hitler began his campaign of persecution against them," writes Sif Ali Algeruan of *Al-Hayat al-Jedida.*

They began to disseminate, in a terrifying manner, pictures of mass shootings directed at them, and to invent the shocking story about the gas ovens in which, according to them, Hitler used to burn them. The newspapers are filled with pictures of Jews who were mowed down by Hitler's machine guns, and of Jews being led to the gas ovens. In these pictures they concentrated on women, babies, and old people, and they took advantage of it, in order to elicit sympathy towards them, when they demand financial reparations, contributions and grants from all over the world. The truth is that the persecution of the Jews is a myth, that the Jews dubbed "the tragedy of the Holocaust" and took advantage of, in order to elicit sympathy towards them.[113]

Since the beginning of the second *intifada* in September 2000, Israel has been subjected to a worldwide campaign of de-legitimization in the media as well as international forums by political leaders and intellectuals. Extremists of the Left and Right have joined together in their hatred of the Jewish State, resulting in a dramatic increase in anti-Semitic incidents including physical attacks on Jews. These attacks on Israel's legitimacy have been accompanied by attacks on Jewish targets worldwide, but particularly in Europe. Anti-Semitic incidents have included bombings of synagogues and Jewish schools, vandalism and desecration of Jewish cemeteries, death threats and unprovoked violence against Jews, including murder. These hate crimes are often disguised as "anti-Zionist" actions.

One of the consequences of Palestinian anti-Semitism has been an increase in attacks on Jewish targets in the Arab world, such as the April 2002 terrorist attack on the ancient synagogue in Djerba, Tunisia, where 12 European tourists, four local Arabs, and a Jew were murdered. In Istanbul in November 2003, twenty-three persons were murdered, six of them Jews, and hundreds were wounded in suicide bombing attacks on two synagogues.

The following are excerpts from a report on anti-Semitism in Europe in 2002 by the European Union's European Monitoring Center on Racism and Xenophobia:

> Physical attacks on Jews and the desecration and destruction of synagogues were acts often committed by young Muslim perpetrators . . . Many of these attacks occurred either during or after pro-Palestinian demonstrations, which were also used by radical Islamists for hurling verbal abuse. In addition, radical Islamist circles were responsible for placing anti-Semitic propaganda on the Internet and in Arab-language media . . . . In the heated public debate on Israeli politics and the

boundary between criticism of Israel and anti-Semitism, individuals who are not politically active and do not belong to one of the ideological camps mentioned above become motivated to voice their latent anti-Semitic attitudes (mostly in the form of telephone calls and insulting letters). Opinion polls prove that in some European countries a large percentage of the population harbors anti-Semitic attitudes and views, but that these usually remain latent.... Observers point to an "increasingly blatant anti-Semitic Arab and Muslim media," including audiotapes and sermons, in which the call is not only made to join the struggle against Israel but also against Jews across the world. Although leading Muslim organizations express their opposition to this propaganda, observers assume that calling for the use of violence may influence readers and listeners. . . . We recommend that the EUMC request state authorities to acknowledge at the highest level the extraordinary dangers posed by anti-Semitic violence in the European context.[114]

France, with its large Muslim minority, stands out as the country in which the greatest number and most serious anti-Semitic incidents have occurred in comparison with other countries globally. These include: physical attacks and harassment of Jews all over the country, torching of synagogues, desecration of cemeteries, and threats and dissemination of radical anti-Semitic and anti-Israel propaganda. The perpetrators come mainly from among young North African Muslim immigrants.

It should be noted that a number of attacks have been the result of organized action, rather than spontaneous mob activity or vandalism, which target Jews in reaction to events in Israel and are part of efforts to delegitimize Israel. These attacks are not limited to Israel, but are blatant manifestations of anti-Semitism involving Jews everywhere, generally beginning in mosques and other large concentrations of Muslims.

In other European countries, especially those with large Arab populations, Jews have been physically assaulted, and often suffer verbal harassment, graffiti, and cemetery desecrations. They have been physically attacked in Belgium, in addition to attacks on Jewish community facilities. Universities throughout Europe have become active centers of anti-Semitic and anti-Israel propaganda and threats. Even in Britain, Jews have been attacked and synagogues and other community facilities have been desecrated.

Numerous anti-Semitic incidents have occurred in Scandinavian countries, especially Denmark and Sweden, whose governments have been extremely critical of Israel. In Germany in recent years there have been a large number of anti-Semitic incidents by neo-Nazi and Islamic elements.

In Eastern Europe and Russia anti-Semitic activities have mostly taken the form of propaganda and demonstrations. In Russia a number of Jews were injured and synagogues and other Jewish facilities have been damaged. One Russian innovation is placing booby-trapped signs with anti-Semitic slurs along highways, which explode when someone tries to remove them.

As an analysis that appeared in the London *Spectator* regarding the attitude of the British clergy acknowledged: "Animosity towards Israel has its roots in a deep hatred of the Jews."[115] This was echoed by the late Italian journalist, Oriana Falacci, who strongly denounced the double standard often practiced in Europe:

> One standard for the Jews and another for Christians and Muslims, one *vis-à-vis* Jewish blood that has been spilled and another *vis-à-vis* other blood. And there is the lack of proportion between attacks on Israel, which

are not political criticism but saturated with anti-Semitic terms, and what Israel actually does.[116]

There is an ironic Jewish joke that defines anti-Semitism as a disease suffered by gentiles that is often fatal to Jews. As such, there is not much that is new about the so-called "new anti-Semitism" at the beginning of the twenty-first century.

Israeli historian Robert Wistrich noted that it is radical Muslims and not necessarily white Europeans who are leading the present wave of anti-Semitism. The Islamic world imported anti-Semitism from Europe, converted it to Islam as part of the Israeli-Palestinian conflict, and exported it back to Europe and the West in general by means of the Muslim migration and anti-West and anti-globalization elements.

Regarding the blood libels of the new century, Wistrich concluded:

> Arab governments are doing nothing against these fabrications, and in essence legitimize them in order to protect themselves from the wrath of their own embittered citizens, deprived of democracy, freedom of speech and basic human rights.
>
> Against this background it is clear how millions of Muslims are prepared to believe every falsehood, including the blowing up of the World Trade Center by the Mossad.
>
> This "Semitic" antisemitism is especially threatening when it is on a mission from Allah, and the 1979 revolution in Iran against the "Great Devil" (America and the "Crusader" West) and the "Jewish-Zionist Devil" bears witness to this. This is total war, because it is mainly a religious war. Antisemitism of this kind has diverted the Jihad from its original objective and turned into a death cult.[117]

This growing trend has gradually become not an echo but an amplification of what transpired in pre-World War II Germany. While cries against the Jews grew louder, the rest of the world simply shrugged it off with comments such as "Oh, I don't think that is emblematic of *all* the Germans." Their silence made those nations accomplices in the Holocaust. Are we any less guilty if we stand quietly by and let the cry to kill Jews grow among Arabs and Europeans? How far must such blatant hatred go before we do something about it? I feel that it has already gone too far.

There is perhaps no better sign that the spirit of Antichrist is again on the rise with this reemergence of rabid anti-Semitism. Satan hates Jews because they were the first with whom God made a covenant. The US can be no less guilty as a nation for being silent about racism towards Jews because of its acquiescence to racism towards African-Americans as its constitution was being written. As Thomas Jefferson said:

> Indeed, I tremble for my country when I reflect that God is just; that His justice cannot sleep forever.[118]

It was the director of Israeli Mossad Isser Harel who told me:

> Hitler first killed Jews, and then he killed Christians.
> Our culture and our democracies are the root of the rage.
> If we're right, then they are wrong.

September 11, 2001 was a tragic day in American history. The attack was a physical manifestation of a battle lost weeks, months, and possibly years before because of a lack of prayer. Osama bin Laden had been verbally attacking America for years, but the Church was asleep. The demonic powers that were influencing him should have been violently confronted by holy angels on assignment through the power of prayer—as it was in the Prophet Daniel's time.

Praying for the peace of Jerusalem is not praying for stones or dirt; it is praying for God's protection over the lives of the people there. It is praying for revival, for God's grace to be poured out on the Bible land and all over the Middle East—prayer that demonic powers will be defeated by holy angels in a battle not seen with the natural eye. Mother Teresa was one of the first people who told me she prayed daily for the peace of Jerusalem according to Psalms 122:6. She said to me, "Love is not something you say, it's something you do." I believe that with all my heart.

Is it possible that America might have been spared the Great Depression if she had not ignored the plight of the Jews? Is it possible that tens of thousands of Americans would not have died in World War II if America had not closed her doors to the house of Israel? If so, God-fearing Americans must stand up now before it is too late. Where will end time prophecy place the United States of America: on God's side in support of the Jewish people, or on the side of the Enemy?

In the last quarter century many have cursed again and again that which God calls them to bless. Are they inviting God's blessings or curses? President Obama and others before him want East Jerusalem as the capital of an Islamic Palestine (a Jew-free state.) If this happens, prayer will not prevent the wrath of Almighty God from falling upon America for touching prophecy and dividing Jerusalem.

Consider this for a moment: Deuteronomy 28 is perhaps the most widely quoted chapter of the Bible concerning the blessings and curses of God. I have numerous times heard ministers read verses 1-14 of that chapter listing the blessings of God available to Believers; how often have we heard the curses read? Let me end with one of the last curses in this chapter: Read it very prayerfully:

> The LORD will bring a nation against you from far away, from the ends of the earth, like an eagle swooping down, a nation whose language you will not understand, a fierce-looking nation without respect for the old or pity for the

young. They will devour the young of your livestock and the crops of your land until you are destroyed. They will leave you no grain, new wine or oil, nor any calves of your herds or lambs of your flocks until you are ruined. They will lay siege to all the cities throughout your land until the high-fortified walls in which you trust fall down. They will besiege all the cities throughout the land the LORD your God is giving you . . . , (Deuteronomy 28: 49-52 NIV.)

It is time to decide: Will the US live under God's blessings or incur His wrath? It is time to answer the trumpet call, and correct the nation's course. Americans often look to the White House to make course corrections, so it is only fitting to look back at its leaders to see how each has dealt with Israel.

PART II

PRESIDENTS

(14)

PRESIDENTS *and* PROPHECY

While people are saying, "Peace and safety,"
destruction will come on them suddenly, as labor pains
on a pregnant woman, and they will not escape,
(I Thessalonians 5:3, NIV)

Virtually every United States President has in some way been impacted by prophecy. Beginning with George Washington through every other presidential decision concerning the direction of the United States and its relationship to Israel and the Arab states, leaders have navigated the murky waters of foreign policy and the US role in world affairs. Domestic conscience has elected men to office and directed how the US will account for its stewardship of the power entrusted to them. Though we were prophetically called upon to be used of God in the world, the nation will also assuredly have much to answer for because of apathy in taking its appointed place of leadership.

In the early 1900s Palestine was a desert wasteland in the hands of the unfriendly Turks—America held much greater promise for the displaced Jews of the world. Many came to view the US as their Promised

Land; they were comfortable in the US and felt no need to seek peace elsewhere. This sentiment was not without repercussions, however. As many of the indigent Jews of Europe flooded to the US, it not so much answered what some deemed to be "the Jewish problem" but brought it to America. US leaders determined the influx was too great and another answer would have to be sought.

In 1921, Congress passed a quota mostly targeting Europe's unskilled workers. Another law passed that same year limited immigrants from each country to the equivalent of only three percent of its nationals already residing in the US in the year 1910. This law limited total annual immigration to 357,000 people. Three years later the Johnson-Reed Immigration Restriction of 1924 lowered this quota to only two percent, also resetting the base year to 1890—when just 150,000 people were allowed into the country. The government's restrictive immigration policy thus drastically cut immigration from 800,000 in 1921 to 23,000 in 1933. Ellis Island's role quickly changed from an immigration depot to that of a detention center. In 1915, Ellis Island processed 178,000 immigrants; by 1919 that number fell to just 26,000. What some saw as the Jewish problem would have to be further resolved in a manner other than allowing them into the US.

However, before this issue came to the fore, God had prepared someone to step forward with a solution—William Eugene Blackstone. Blackstone was born into a Methodist home in upstate New York in 1841, but followed his fortunes west to Oak Park, Illinois after the Civil War. Though he was not an ordained minister, but rather the founder of a construction and investment company, Blackstone had been an ardent student of the Bible from his boyhood. In 1878, he published a book called *Jesus Is Coming* that sold over a million copies (no small feat in a nation of only about fifty million—roughly a sixth of America's population today). While the book was offensive to many who had grown comfortable with their own brand of Christianity, it was welcomed by such men as Dwight L. Moody and Cyrus I. Scofield. Those two men and others of similar stripe appreciated Blackstone's literal interpretation of the scriptures. They favored a more active and evangelical, missions-minded Christianity. It so touched the US conscience that it "in a large measure set the tone for this period of history."[119]

Blackstone's book was so well documented it was actually more scripture than commentary, listing hundreds of Bible passages for the reader to review at his own pace. It was a book difficult for any true Believer to ignore. Suddenly, America was becoming a beacon to the world pointing to Bible prophecy. The book was eventually translated into forty-eight languages, including Hebrew, and is still in print today. Blackstone wrote:

> You may say, "I don't believe the Israelites are to be restored to Canaan, and Jerusalem to be rebuilt."
> Have you read the declarations in God's Word about it?
> Surely nothing is more plainly stated in the Scriptures.[120]

Blackstone then listed eighty-nine Scripture passages that support his assertion. Later in the chapter he further states:

> It would seem that such overwhelming testimony would convince every fair-minded reader that there is a glorious future restoration in store for Israel. . . .
> I could fill a book with comments about how Israel will be restored, but all I have desired to do was to show that it is an incontrovertible fact of prophecy, and that it is intimately connected with our Lord's appearing.[121]

Perhaps Blackstone's remarks seem somewhat overstated to us some six-and-a-half decades after the birth of Israel as a state, but in his time, the confidence of his assertions was no less than prophetic. Many in US churches gave little credence to the possibility that the Jews would ever have their own land and state again, let alone in their ancient homeland with Jerusalem as its capital. Many Jews themselves actually had little interest in the idea. By the outbreak of World War I, only about 20,000 of the 2.5 million Jews in the US belonged to a Zionist organization.[122] American Jews were quite happy where they were.

Blackstone, however, looked upon Israel as "God's sun-dial." He even went so far as to say, "If anyone desires to know our place in God's chronology, our position in the march of events, look at Israel."[123] For Blackstone, it was the next milestone along the river of prophecy.

In what light did churches in the US interpret the scriptures quoted by Blackstone? How could the certainty of these prophecies concerning the rebirth of Israel been missed? It was interpreted as referring to "spiritual Israel"—the modern-day Church. Wisely, Blackstone had a few things to say about this as well. His book would touch on some of the darkest episodes for the descendants of Jacob. He saw quite plainly that Israel and the Church were separate entities, each with a future that signified two different covenants. God had not forsaken one for the other, he argued, but rather had a unique plan for each.

However, by replacing literal Israel, it appeared the Church no longer had to feel any responsibility to the Jews as God's Chosen People. This "Replacement Theology" would quiet the Church in Germany during World War II as the death camps were rushed into full operation. There was no feeling of obligation to the Jews. They were instead "suffering for their sins of rejection of the Messiah." It was as if Jesus' death cut the Church free from God's chosen people rather than grafting the Gentiles into the olive tree. However they saw it, this insidious virus—an invisible anti-Semitism—allowed the mainstream German Church to look the other way as the most horrific and ungodly acts were perpetrated on the Jewish people.

Blackstone's words did not fall on deaf ears in the United States, however. As his popularity rose, so did his activity. In 1888, he and his daughter Flora visited Palestine, and concluded their trip in London during their year-long sabbatical.

When he returned, Blackstone was more zealous for the cause of reestablishing the state of Israel than ever before. Soon thereafter, the burden of his heart was to initiate a conference between Jews and Christians to discuss this very topic. The "Conference on the Past, Present, and Future of Israel" took place November 24-25, 1890 at the First Methodist Episcopal Church in Chicago. It was attended by some of the best-known Christian and Jewish Leaders of the day.

The assembly passed resolutions of sympathy for oppressed Jews living in Russia, and copies were forwarded to the Czar and other world leaders. However, Blackstone knew it was not enough to beg mercy from these leaders—the Jews needed a land to call their own within borders that afforded peace and security. He wanted these world leaders to grant the Jews permission to return to Palestine and establish just such a state. Out of these meetings came the inspiration for the document that would eventually be known as "The Blackstone Memorial."

On March 5, 1891, Secretary of State James G. Blaine introduced William Blackstone to President Benjamin Harrison. Blackstone personally handed the President his memorial, originally titled "Palestine for the Jews." President Harrison seemed like a man who would favor Israel as well, since he chose Psalm 121:1-6, KJV as the Scripture on which he would place his hand as he took the Oath of Office as the twenty-sixth President of the United States:

> I will lift up mine eyes unto the hills, from whence cometh my help. My help cometh from the Lord, which made heaven and earth. He will not suffer thy foot to be moved: he that keepeth thee will not slumber. Behold, he that keepeth Israel shall neither slumber nor sleep. The Lord is thy keeper: the Lord is thy shade upon thy right hand. The sun shall not smite thee by day, nor the moon by night.

The first paragraph of Blackstone's memorial began simply, "What shall be done for the Russian Jews?" and the second, "Why not give Palestine back to them again?"[124] It was signed by 413 prominent Americans including John D. Rockefeller, J. P. Morgan, Cyrus McCormick, the Chief Justice of the Supreme Court, heads of several major newspapers, the Speaker of the House, other members of congress, the mayors of Chicago and Philadelphia, and several other businessmen, ministers, and clergy. It called for a conference to discuss the possibilities of a Jewish homeland—the first step on the road to a Jewish state—and copies were also sent to the head of every European nation. The letter that accompanied his memorial ended with these words:

> That there seem to be many evidences to show that we have reached the period in the great roll of the centuries, when the ever-living God of Abraham, Isaac, and Jacob, is lifting up His hand to the Gentiles, (Isaiah 49:22) to bring His sons and His daughters from far, that he may plant them again in their own land, (Ezekiel 34, &c). Not for twenty-four centuries, since the days of Cyrus, King of Persia, has there been offered to any mortal such a privileged opportunity to further the purposes of God concerning His ancient people.
>
> May it be the high privilege of your Excellency, and the Honorable Secretary, to take a personal interest in this great matter, and secure through the Conference, a home for these wandering millions of Israel, and thereby receive to yourselves the promise of Him, who said to Abraham, "I will bless them that bless thee," Genesis 12:3.[125]

While many in the US have probably never heard of William E. Blackstone, the same could not have been said of presidents from Harrison through Truman. Blackstone, believing the Church could well be raptured (being caught up to heaven) at any moment, became increasingly preoccupied with the Jewish people and their promised return to Palestine. He kept the issue before every US president until his death in 1935. Blackstone not only personally handed the memorial to Harrison, but would also see it presented to Presidents William McKinley, Grover Cleveland, Theodore Roosevelt, and Woodrow Wilson—William McKinley signed it before being elected president.[126] Blackstone's words so saturated those presidents, that in 1949, some fourteen years after Blackstone's death, Harry Truman, who by his action made the US the first nation to recognize the newborn state of Israel, virtually quoted Blackstone's letter. When he was introduced to some Jewish scholars that year as "the man who helped create the State of Israel," Truman responded with, "What do you mean 'helped create'? I am Cyrus, I am Cyrus!"[127] He referred to the biblical king who allowed the Jews to return to Jerusalem from their captivity in Babylon.

Blackstone's memorial was written five years before the father of modern-day Zionism, Theodor Herzl, published his book, *The Jewish State* and founded the Zionist Movement. When Blackstone discovered that Herzl's book was practical and political, not prophetic, he marked all the prophecies in the Old Testament concerning Israel's rebirth in a Bible, and sent it to Herzl. Blackstone informed Herzl that his proposal to have the Jewish state in Argentina, Uganda, or any other country was unacceptable—it had to be in the promised land of Palestine with Jerusalem as its capital. Blackstone so greatly influenced Herzl that the Bible containing those marked prophecies was, for a time, displayed in Herzl's tomb in Israel.

Because of his zeal, Blackstone is among those recognized and honored in Israel today. While righteous gentiles such as Corrie ten Boom and Oskar Schindler have a tree dedicated to them for saving lives during the Holocaust, Blackstone has a forest named after him and is mentioned in some textbooks on the history of Israel.

Despite his presence before presidents and his popularity, Blackstone would be to them what Moses was to Pharaoh—a voice calling from God,

"Let My people go!" And, like Moses, his voice would—for the most part—go unheeded. Just as Pharaoh vacillated in his decision to release the Jews to go to Canaan (ancient Palestine), so would US presidents waver in making decisions regarding God's Chosen People. As God hardened the heart of Pharaoh, so He would harden the hearts of those in the US State Department during various administrations.

While State Department employees had incited US protests against the murder of Jews in Damascus in 1840, it would silence any response to Blackstone's plea. Actually it welcomed US apathy towards the murder of Jews during the Holocaust. The death knell that sounded over the Blackstone Memorial came in a penciled note from Alvey A. Adee, Assistant Secretary of State. He held the office from 1886 to 1924, an incredible thirty-eight years. Adee left his fingerprints everywhere in US foreign policy throughout his tenure and beyond. If Adee felt one way, then it was a good indication of the way any up-and-coming young State Department officer should feel if advancement was desired. His note read:

> For thirty years and I know not how much longer, Turkey has writhed under the dread of a restoration of the Judean monarchy. Every few months we are asked to negotiate for the cessation of Palestine to the Jewish "nation." The whole project is chimerical [fanciful].[128]

While the project was not an impossible and foolish fancy as Adee suggested, his note was enough to infect the State Department. The idea arose that any action towards helping Israel become a nation again was not only a waste of time, but also not in the interests of peaceful relations with the powers that controlled the region at the time—namely the crumbling Ottoman Empire. The tone was also set in those intellectual halls that the simplistic, black-and-white values and ideals of evangelical Christians such as Blackstone were naïve and quixotic. Well-informed diplomats, it was thought, knew more about the values and cultures of the regions involved, so they were in a better place to make policy regarding issues concerning them.

Slowly the US State Department began to make its decisions based more on what other nations thought than using the values upon which the country was founded. This trend away from the moral clarity of our forefathers and towards the relativism of humanistic secularism is what turned the State Department into what it is today: a friend of the United Nations and globalization—more than the friend of its own nation.

Further prophetic insight was realized when William Blackstone's friend, Cyrus Scofield, published his famous study Bible in 1909. It was greatly inspired by Blackstone's interest in biblical prophecy and the simple, straightforward interpretation of Scripture. In his notes, Scofield interpreted Ezekiel 38 and 39 to mean that Russia would invade Israel during the end time. That interpretation was challenged and even mocked. Many asked, "How can you possibly say that? Russia is a Christian Orthodox nation; there is no Israel. . . nor any possibility it will ever exist." Scofield reportedly answered, "I don't understand it, and I can't explain it, but the Bible says it, and I believe it." Today no one doubts that Russia might attack Israel—especially since it has been known to regularly pinpoint Israeli cities as targets for possible nuclear strikes—and Scofield's interpretation is now usually taken for granted.

William Blackstone was God's voice to a generation. He called Believers to Zionism before the movement was even founded. Through Blackstone, God was prevailing upon the US conscience that had called on Him to save it from the tyranny of the British, and from its own divisive internal strife over slavery. God answered willingly and faithfully, keeping the country whole through these, and other, conflicts. Now God was calling on the United States to act on behalf of His chosen people, the Jews—and for more than fifty years, His call went ignored. Had any of the presidents who received Blackstone's memorial acted instead of disregarding it—lives of six million Jews who died in the Holocaust as well as the lives of those persecuted in Russia and elsewhere in the world might have been saved. It was Dietrich Bonhoeffer who said:

> Silence in the face of evil is itself evil: God will not hold us guiltless. Not to speak is to speak. Not to act is to act.[129]

About a century before Israel's rebirth, the groundwork had been laid within the American conscience for its support of and relationship with the descendants of Isaac. The call had begun for America to become an international ambassador to help the Jews reestablish a land and state. Over the next century, almost every American president would be faced with the issue of being part of or ignoring prophecy stating that the people of Isaac would again have their own homeland. Amazingly, the battle continues today with Arab hatred for the Jews, and the numerous conspiracy myths that the Jews blew up the World Trade Center towers. Such fabrications are propagated by the radical Islamic fanatics of the world.

GEORGE WASHINGTON
and HAYM SALOMON

"Judah, you are he whom your brothers shall praise;
Your hand shall be on the neck of your enemies;
Your father's children shall bow down before you,"
(Genesis 49:8, NKJV)

PRESIDENT GEORGE WASHINGTON, 1789 INAUGURAL
(BIBLE OPENED TO GENESIS 49)

The United States of America was built on Judeo-Christian principles, with the Ten Commandments and the tenets of the Bible as the basis for its laws. The newly-born nation eschewed tyranny, creating a constitution of checks and balances to control governmental power. It also refused to embrace Old World struggles—such as that of Christian against Jew—as part of its culture. The fledgling government took literally the verse of Scripture, "Old things are passed away; behold, all things are become new," (2 Corinthians 5:17 NKJV.) From this admonition sprang the idea of "separation between church and state"—that all faiths would have the right to the freedom of religious gathering, worship, and expression.

Moreover, the state would not dictate what church to attend, nor would it silence anyone from expressing their faith in public office or in the halls of government.

The founding fathers saw no conflict between these freedoms and openly expressing their religious beliefs, whether going about their daily business as citizens or civic leaders. The American government was not formulated to sanction oppression of any kind. With regard to religion, the government was not to be amoral or secular as some seem to think today; rather, governance was to be based upon the Judeo-Christian virtues of love and prayer: to love and pray for others instead of trying to force them to change.

As early settlers continued to make their way to the colonies from Great Britain so too did people from other countries. Among them were the first Jews to reach North America. They set foot on Manhattan Island in September 1654. The four men, six women, and thirteen children had sailed from Brazil aboard a leaking and filthy French ship rampant with disease. It was a miracle any survived the difficult journey. When the Jews arrived in the new colonies, they proved to be a conundrum for their neighbors. They were a people without a homeland, wanderers—often unwelcome—in whatever land they chose to settle. The Jewish immigrants were by nature a close-knit group, and their commonality was often viewed as being conspiratorial.

In 1790, the first census was taken of the thirteen colonies of the United States. The total population was nearly four million, and approximately two thousand were Jews. George Washington wrote a letter to the Sephardic congregation of Newport, Rhode Island, in August of 1790, and thanked them for the contributions of the Jewish people in the fight for independence:

> May the children of the stock of Abraham who dwell in
> the land continue to merit and enjoy the goodwill of the
> other inhabitants. While everyone shall sit safely under

his own vine and fig-tree and there shall be none to make him afraid.[130]

The second president of the United States, John Adams, had an equal admiration for the People of the Book. Near the end of his life, Adams expressed, "For I really wish the Jews again in Judea an independent nation."[131] This became a slogan among early Jewish nationalists.

Then later, it is quite possible that an incident of 1840 opened the American ear—that of both Jew and Christian—to the need for Hebrew people worldwide to have a homeland within whose borders they could finally find security from persecution. What had brought the affair to the attention of President Martin Van Buren and his Secretary of State John Forsyth was a dispatch from the American consul in Beirut describing the massacre of Jewish men, women, and children in Damascus. Jews there had been accused of ritual murder in order to obtain the blood of Christians for use in their Passover services—the old and ever-present charge of "blood libel." (This false accusation has been revived in Islamic nations today.)

The accusations were used as a justification to destroy Jewish property and murder Jews in the streets. In the end, it was found that the rumor had been started by French agents to incite Muslims and enhance France's position as the protector of Christians in the area.

While the issue was undeniably a gross violation of basic human rights, the end result was that it placed the United States unequivocally and officially on the side of the Jews, forcing the nation to, through formal diplomatic channels, support the Jews for the first time in its history. This action came so fast, in fact, that by the time the American public raised the issue to the government in order to persuade President Martin Van Buren to officially object, complaints had already been raised. The US consul in Egypt was called upon to file a formal protest. The incident was such an epitome of Old World prejudices the United States had been trying to escape, that it was the first and only time the government, especially the State Department, acted on behalf of the Jews without first being prodded by the American people.

Thus, a little more than a century before Israel's rebirth, the groundwork was being laid in the American conscience for its support of and relationship with the nation of Israel. The call had begun for America to become an international ambassador in helping the Jews reestablish a land and a state for themselves. Over the next century, almost every American president would be faced with the issue of being part of or ignoring the prophecies stating that the people of Israel would return to the Land and form their own government. Unfortunately, however, these same presidents, on the advice of the State Department and because of the pressures of their own times, would take no action to answer this cry until after World War II.

Virtually every American president has in some way been impacted by the Jewish people. From George Washington to Barack Obama, leaders have navigated the murky waters of foreign policy and what America's role should be in world affairs—and in recent years how foreign policy relates to Israel. This will not change with future presidents. Domestic conscience has directed and will continue to direct how America will account for its stewardship of the power entrusted to it, particularly with regard to Israel. There have been times that sluggishness in responding to that call and taking the appointed place of leadership has caused the loss of lives, much pain, and not a little consternation.

Today, Israel is the closest ally the United States has in the Middle East, though that claim may be argued in light of recent governmental action—or inaction. While the reborn Jewish state seeks succor from its big brother for military support and political assistance, as well as financial aid, the United States has benefited equally. Israel has offered staunch support against the enemies of democracy in the region, shared outstanding industrial advances, and succeeded in areas of research and development that have benefited the United States as well.

Is this a recent phenomenon, this cooperation between the Jewish people and the United States? Hardly! In a letter to Reverend F. A. van der Kemp, John Adams wrote of the influence of the Jews on western nations:

> I will insist that the Hebrew have done more to civilize men than any other nation. If I were an atheist, and believed in blind eternal fate, I should still believe that fate had ordained the Jews to be the most essential instrument for civilizing the nations. If I were an atheist of the other sect, who believe, or pretend to believe that all is ordered by chance, I should believe that chance had ordered the Jews to preserve and propagate to all mankind the doctrine of a supreme, intelligent, wise, almighty sovereign of the universe, which I believe to be the great essential principle of all morality, and consequently of all civilization.[132]

President Woodrow Wilson felt strongly that the ancient Hebrews set the standard for the unfolding United States of America:

> Recalling the previous experiences of the colonists in applying the Mosaic Code to the order of their internal lives, it is not to be wondered that the various passages in the Bible . . . [were] held up before the pioneer Americans the Hebrew Commonwealth as a model government. . . . In the spirit and essence of our constitution, the influence of the Hebrew Commonwealth was paramount in that it was not only the highest authority for the principle, 'that rebellion to Tyrants is obedience to God,' but also because it was in itself a divine precedent for a pure democracy.[133]

President Calvin Coolidge praised the contributions of the Jews to the American Revolution:

> The Jewish faith is predominantly the faith of liberty. [He listed] some among the merchants who unhesitatingly signed the nonimportation resolution of 1765: Isaac Moses, Benjamin Levy, Samson Levy, David Franks, Joseph Jacobs, Hayman Levy Jr., Matthias Bush, Michael Gratz, Bernard Gratz, Isaac Franks, Moses Mordecai, Benjamin Jacobs, Samuel Lyon, and Manuel Mordecai Noah.[134]

Coolidge also recounted the story of Haym Salomon, Polish Jew financier of the Revolution:

> Born in Poland, he was made prisoner by the British forces in New York, and when he escaped set up in business in Philadelphia. He negotiated for Robert Morris [the superintendent for finance in the Thirteen Colonies] all the loans raised in France and Holland, pledged his personal faith and fortune for enormous amounts, and personally advanced large sums to such men as James Madison, Thomas Jefferson, Baron Steuben, General St. Clair and many other patriot leaders, who testified that without his aid they could not have carried on in the cause.[135]

Near the beginning of the Revolution, when the colonial soldiers were poorly armed, starving to death, and on the verge of defeat, Salomon went to the Jews in America and Europe and gathered a gift of one million dollars (an incredible amount at that time). He sent the funds to General George Washington, who used them to buy clothing and arms to outfit American troops, an act that ultimately helped the Colonies win the war. Salomon pledged his personal fortune. It is said that altogether, Salomon gifted the Continental Army with $25 million dollars and later died a pauper. Neither he nor his heirs has ever collected a dime of what was due from the Government. He never even received a medal for his services . . . a glaring example of history often forgetting its heroes.[136]

In addition to his gifts, Salomon loaned the US government at least another $800,000. It has been calculated that were his loan to be repaid today at 7 percent interest, the amount owed the Salomon family would equal at least $2.5 trillion. The aid given to Israel today is but a drop in the bucket compared to the debt of gratitude due Haym Salomon.

To show his appreciation, Washington instructed the engravers of the US one-dollar bill to include a memorial to the Jewish people over the head of the American eagle. It is still there today. If you look closely at the reverse side of a one-dollar bill, you will see thirteen stars over the eagle's head that form the six-pointed Star of David. Surrounding that is a cloudburst representing the Glory in the tabernacle in Jerusalem. President Washington specified that this was to be a lasting memorial to the Jewish people for their help in winning the war for independence.

Washington was not alone in his faith or feelings of brotherhood for the Jews. At the Continental Congress of 1776, Benjamin Franklin suggested that the Great Seal of the United States bear the likeness of a triumphant Moses raising his staff to divide the Red Sea with the waters crashing in on the armies of Pharaoh in the background. Thomas Jefferson, on the other hand preferred an image that showed more perseverance: that of the children of Israel marching through the desert following rays from the pillar of fire.[137] The final design of the Great Seal included a pyramid (Egypt), and eagle (protection), rays of fire and a cloud (Divine leadership.) All were symbolic of the Red Sea experience of the Children of Israel.

Because Salomon was very sympathetic to the cause of the men fighting the Revolution against England, he soon joined the Sons of Liberty. He was captured by the British, charged as a spy, and incarcerated on a British warship for eighteen months. He was pardoned because he was fluent in several languages. His interpretive skills enabled him to persuade the German Hessian regiments hired by the British as mercenaries to abandon the cause. Salomon was also responsible for the escape of a number of Patriot prisoners.

Salomon married Rachel Franks in 1777. She was the daughter of a leading Jew, Moses Franks. When the elder Salomon's loyalist activities were exposed in 1778, he was again arrested and sentenced to death by the British. He once more managed to escape and slip into Philadelphia.[138] There, he used his skills as a broker to become the French consul's agent and paymaster for French forces aiding the Americans in their fight for independence. As a sympathizer to the Patriots, he offered them below-market interest rates and never sought repayment.[139]

Author Dr. David Allen Lewis wrote:

> Salomon had a dream for the Jewish people, that America would be the place where they could find rest, and that one day this nation would be the instrument for reestablishing the national homeland for the Jewish people in Eretz Israel.[140]

In 1941, a memorial to George Washington, Robert Morris, and Haym Salomon was erected on Wacker Drive in Chicago. In 1975, Salomon was honored with a commemorative ten-cent stamp to mark his true patriotism as a "financial hero."

(16)

JOHN ADAMS, THOMAS JEFFERSON, *and* THEODORE ROOSEVELT

"Thus saith the LORD of hosts; In those days [it shall come to pass], that ten men shall . . . take hold of the skirt of him that is a Jew, saying, We will go with you: for we have heard [that] God [is] with you," (Zechariah 8:23, KJV)

Each president who succeeded George Washington had some contact with the Jewish population in the United States. Some had personal and intimate relationships, while some hid behind a cloak of bare civility. John Adams knew about the Jews as a people through his religious upbringing. Adams had been raised a Congregationalist but later became a Unitarian. Whatever involvement he had with the Jewish constituents who helped elect him began only after the inaugural on March 4, 1797. Adams once commented:

> My religion is founded on the love of God and my neighbor; on the hope of pardon for my offenses; upon

contrition; upon the duty as well as the necessity of [enduring] with patience the inevitable evils of life; in the duty of doing no wrong, but all the good I can, to the creation of which I am but an infinitesimal part.[141]

Adams had a deep appreciation for God's Chosen People and for their contributions to make the world a better place for all.

Under his administration, thousands of Jews living under oppression in Russia, Prussia, and Austria petitioned for admission to the United States. The Naturalization Act, a part of the 1798 Alien and Sedition Acts was passed to limit French immigration, making it impossible for Jews from Russia and regions of Europe to move to America. A clause in the legislation included the words *other foreigners*, which many American Jews considered a pointed reference to their race.

This legislation was the result of what came to be known as the XYZ Affair. When French privateers began to pursue and raid American trading ships, President Adams dispatched a delegation to France to try to settle the issue. The refusal of French Foreign Minister Charles Maurice de Talleyrand to entertain the envoys and the insistence on a bribe in the amount of $250,000 in order to end the conflict offended Adams. Refusing to accept the severity of the problem, Thomas Jefferson and his associates demanded to see the diplomatic communiques in Adams' possession.

Attempts to negotiate a settlement with France were rebuffed, leading to the undeclared Quasi-War of 1798. The president eventually made the documents available, but with names omitted. He had instead replaced those with the letters *X, Y,* and *Z*. The anti-French sentiment resulted in the aforementioned Alien and Sedition Acts. Adams lost the Jewish vote and the election in 1800 to Thomas Jefferson, an anti-Federalist Republican.

He also once expressed to a Jewish petitioner his wish that:

Your nation be admitted to all the privileges of citizens in every country of the world. This country has done much. I wish it may do more, and annul every narrow idea in religion, government, and commerce.[142]

In 1818, long before the Zionist movement was formed, Adams wrote to Mordecai Manuel Noah, a journalist and politician:

I really wish the Jews again in Judea, an independent nation; as I believe the most enlightened men of it have participated in the amelioration of the philosophy of the ages. . . . I wish your nation [of Jews] may be admitted to all privileges of citizens in every country of the world. This country has done much. I wish it may do more, and annul every narrow idea in religion, government, and commerce.[143]

Adams was gracious in his loss to Thomas Jefferson and retired to his farm. He was not so congenial, however, as to attend Jefferson's inauguration in 1801. John Adams died on July 4, 1826, two years after he saw his son, John Quincy, elected to the White House.

From the charters drafted by Pilgrims who first colonized what would one day become the United States of America, its forefathers purposed in their hearts to be a force for good on the earth as defined by the Bible and its prophecies. As stated in the Declaration of Independence, they believed these truths to be "self-evident, that all Men are created equal, that they are endowed by their Creator with certain unalienable Rights, that among these are Life, Liberty and the Pursuit of Happiness." Thomas

Jefferson, one of the writers of that Declaration, and who would become the third president of the newly-formed nation, further said: "Can the liberties of a nation be secure when we have removed a conviction that these liberties are the gift of God? That they are not to be violated but with His wrath?"[144] From this first declaration and by invoking the blessings of God in its foundation, the founders placed this new nation into the hands of God for its existence and its future. Little did Thomas Jefferson and his companions realize how closely this "one nation under God" would be tied to an as yet unborn Jewish nation that would be settled on a scrap of land along the Mediterranean Sea.

While Thomas Jefferson was arguably the most erudite president to ever occupy the White House, he was sadly lacking in knowledge of the Jews. Jefferson was a deist: He believed in a Creator, but not in a God who was daily involved in the lives of His creation. However, as president of the United States, he felt compelled to attend church. Once, when challenged on his outwardly hypocritical attendance, he replied:

> Sir, no nation has ever yet existed or been governed without religion. Nor can be. The Christian religion is the best religion that has been given to Man, and I as chief magistrate of this nation am bound to give it the sanction of my example.[145]

Jefferson took office in 1801 and appointed Reuben Etting, a Jew, as United States Marshal for Maryland. Uriah Phillips Levy, although not a Jefferson appointee, so greatly admired the third president that he purchased Monticello after Jefferson's death and refurbished the sadly neglected, dilapidated home. His mother was buried on its grounds, and his nephew, Congressman Jefferson M. Levy, used the property as a summer home.

Jefferson was also acquainted with Mordecai Manuel Noah and received the same communique from him as did Adams following the dedication of the Mill Street Synagogue in New York City. Jefferson responded to Noah's missive with:

> Sir, I thank you for the discourse on the consecration of the Synagogue in your city, with which you have been pleased to favor me. I have read it with pleasure and instruction, having learnt from it some valuable facts in Jewish history which I did not know before. Your sect by its sufferings has furnished a remarkable proof of the universal spirit of religious intolerance in every sect, disclaimed by all while feeble, and practiced by all when in power. Our laws have applied the only antidote to this vice, protecting our religious, as they do our civil rights, by putting all on an equal footing. But more remains to be done, for although we are free by the law, we are not so in practice; public opinion erects itself into an Inquisition, and exercises its office with as much fanaticism as fans the flames of an *auto-da-fé* [public penance prescribed for condemned heretics].[146] A staunch believer in the value of education, Jefferson helped found the University of Virginia in 1819. He once wrote to a friend: "If a nation expects to be ignorant and free, it expects what never was and never will be."[147]

Even in death Jefferson chose to highlight his love for independence, liberty, and education. When he retired from public life, he went home to his beloved Monticello. His days there were spent reading and corresponding with friends and acquaintances. As Jefferson neared the end of his life, he set his affairs in order, and then turned his thoughts to designing his headstone.

His role in national politics had been an important one in the establishment of a new nation. He had served as president, vice president, secretary of state, Minister to France, and governor of Virginia. Any or all of those designations could have been written as his epitaph. Instead of outlining his accomplishments, he chose rather to have the artisan's chisel carve:

> Here was buried Thomas Jefferson, Author of the Declaration of American Independence, of the Statute of Virginia for Religious Freedom, and Father of the University of Virginia.[148]

Thomas Jefferson died on July 4, 1826, the fifth anniversary of the independence of the nation he had governed as its third president. He predeceased former President John Adams by just a few hours exactly fifty years from their signing the Declaration of Independence. He and Adams were the only two signators to attain the highest office in the new land.

Years later, in a White House speech to a group of Nobel laureates, President John F. Kennedy, hinting of Jefferson's gifts and talents, alleged:

> I think this is the most extraordinary collection of talent, of human knowledge, that has ever been gathered together at the White House, with the possible exception of when Thomas Jefferson dined alone.[149]

Although elected president in 1904, Theodore Roosevelt was born a sickly child in New York City in 1858. He was determined to leave behind weakness and set about to improve his health through weightlifting, boxing, and hiking. He was an ardent hunter, which is attributed to the creation of the "Teddy Bear."

The story is told of a hunting expedition during which Roosevelt failed to bring down a single bear. One of his fellow huntsmen found a hapless bear cub and tied it to a tree. Roosevelt's refusal to shoot the orphaned bear earned him accolades as "gentle" and "cuddly," despite his widely-known daring. Two Jewish immigrants created a cuddly stuffed bear and sought the future president's permission to give it the nickname "Teddy." Permission was granted, and Rose Michtom and her husband Morris began to market the toy as a "Teddy Bear." It was a resounding success and remains so today, over one hundred years later.

Meanwhile, Roosevelt began his rise in the world of politics, first as police commissioner in New York City and then as secretary of the navy. In 1898, Teddy was elected governor of the state of New York. It was during that same year that he organized the "Rough Riders" and led the charge up San Juan Hill near Santiago de Cuba during the war with Spain. Following his success, Teddy was chosen by President William McKinley to run as his vice president. Six months after McKinley's inauguration, the president was felled by an assassin's bullet while visiting the Pan-American Exposition in Buffalo, New York. A young anarchist, Leon Czolgosz was arrested and charged with the crime.

While each succeeding president had interaction with the Jewish residents of the United States, the first significant government appointment came through Theodore Roosevelt after the heavy mantle of the presidency settled on his shoulders. He turned for advice and encouragement to Oscar Straus, brother of Nathan Straus, who had purchased Macy's department store in 1895 and continued to develop it into what became one of the world's largest retailers (and for whom the city of Netanya in Israel is named). In 1906, Roosevelt appointed Straus secretary of commerce and labor making him the first Jew ever to serve in a US cabinet post. Straus and Roosevelt remained close friends after Teddy left office in 1909.

Roosevelt penned a letter to Jacob H. Schiff, a prominent Jewish philanthropist, businessman and community leader, during a celebration in Carnegie Hall to commemorate the 250th anniversary of the first Jewish settlement in the United States. He wrote:

> I am glad to be able to say, in addressing you on this occasion, that while the Jews of the United States, who now number more than one million, have remained loyal to their faith and their race traditions, they have become indissolubly incorporated in the great army of American citizenship, prepared to make all sacrifice for the country, either in war or peace, and striving for the perpetuation of good government and for the maintenance of the principles embodied in our constitution. They are honestly distinguished by their industry, their obedience to law, and their devotion to the national welfare.[150]

(17)

PRESIDENT WILLIAM TAFT
vs. HENRY FORD

"So give your servant a discerning heart to govern your people
and to distinguish between right and wrong.
For who is able to govern this great people of yours?"
(I Kings 3:9)

PRESIDENT WILLIAM TAFT,
1909 INAUGURAL SCRIPTURE

Theodore Roosevelt's successor, William Howard Taft, held the distinction of being the first sitting president to attend a Passover Seder at the invitation of his Jewish friends. Taft's father had been a close friend of Rabbi Isaac Mayer Wise, who led B'nai Yeshurun, Cincinnati, Ohio's largest synagogue. Taft and his father would often visit the temple to listen to Wise's sermons. A rabid opponent of Abraham Lincoln, Wise was extremely interesting. He led the battle of equality for women. He crusaded for the ordination of female rabbis, for women's suffrage, and even for the banishment of "obey" from the marriage ceremony. He was not a proponent of the return of the Jews to Palestine, however. He errantly decried the thought of the Jews as a nationality:

> If facts are eloquent witnesses and prove anything, they prove, in this case at least, that the Jews do not wish to and will not go back to Palestine; furthermore, that most of them, being citizens of this and other countries of advanced civilization approaching the ideals of Moses, want no Jewish state; would join none, if the establishment of such a state were possible. They will not separate themselves from the powerful organizations of the great nations of the world to set up a miniature statelet, a feeble dwarf of a government of their own in Palestine or in any other country.[151]

The president also enjoyed a close friendship with Judge Mayer Sulzberger, a stalwart of the Republican Party. After his election as president, Taft offered the judge the post of ambassador to Turkey, but due to his age, the judge declined the post and elected to remain on the bench.

Another of Taft's closest Jewish friends was Julius Rosenwald, president of Sears, Roebuck and Co. The prominent Jewish businessman was a loyal Republican and a strong Taft supporter. Taft was vocal in his abhorrence of anti-Semitism, and after leaving office continued to write articles and lecture across the country in his role as president of the American Bar Association.

Taft's term as president ended in an overwhelming defeat in the election of 1912. In 1921, President Warren G. Harding, a close friend of Taft, appointed him to fill the vacancy on the Supreme Court created by the death of Chief Justice Edward D. White. Taft served nine years on the Court, thus becoming the only man to hold both the offices of chief executive and Supreme Court justice. Health issues forced his resignation in 1930, and William Howard Taft died on March 8, 1930, at the age of seventy-two.

Earlier in 1920, during a speech to the Anti-Defamation League of B'nai

B'rith in Chicago, Taft had launched a full-scale attack against Henry Ford for having published *The Protocols of the Learned Elders of Zion*. The former president clearly and forcefully condemned the wave of anti-Semitism that followed Ford's allegations of a Jewish capitalist conspiracy. One can but wonder how this diabolical lie was ever perceived as truth.

The basic story contained in *The Protocols*, which Taft found so abhorrent, was composed by Goedsche, a German novelist and anti-Semite who used the pseudonym of Sir John Retcliffe. Goedsche plagiarized the main story from another writer, Maurice Joly, whose *The Dialogue in Hell between Machiavelli and Montesquieu* (1864) involved a hellish plot aimed at opposing Napoleon III.

According to Robert T. Carroll and *The Skeptic's Dictionary*:

> *The Protocols of the Learned Elders of Zion* is a forgery made in Russia for the *Okhrana* (secret police), which blames the Jews for the country's ills. It was first privately printed in 1897 and was made public in 1905. It is copied from a nineteenth century novel by Hermann Goedsche (*Biarritz*, 1868) and claims that a secret Jewish cabal is plotting to take over the world.
>
> *The Protocols* were exposed as a forgery by Lucien Wolf in *The Jewish Bogey and the Forged Protocols of the Learned Elders of Zion* (London: Press Committee of the Jewish Board of Deputies, 1920). In 1921, Philip Graves, a correspondent for the *London Times*, publicized the forgery. Herman Bernstein in *The Truth About "The Protocols of Zion": A Complete Exposure* (1935) also tried and failed to convince the world of the forgery ... Even after [it was] exposed as a forgery, Ford's paper continued to cite the document. Adolf Hitler later used *The Protocols* to help justify his attempt to exterminate Jews during World War II.[152]

The Protocols was first published in the United States in 1920 in the *Dearborn Independent*, a Michigan newspaper purchased by Henry Ford mainly to attack Jews and Communists. Ford had become a pacifist at the beginning of World War I and required an outlet for his ever-growing anti-Semitic leanings. He engaged a journalist, E. G. Pipp, as managing editor of the newspaper. William Liebold, Ford's personal secretary and watchdog, was named business manager; and a Detroit journalist, William Cameron, was employed as staff writer. Cameron was responsible for articles penned under Ford's name on what was touted as his "Own Page." It afforded the owner a way to espouse his ideas and theories regarding what he called the "working man."

Ford began to build the framework to place the blame for World War I at the feet of Jewish international bankers. These shadowy, nameless men could, according to Ford, "manipulate certain instincts and passions with a skill which could only emanate from Satan himself."[153] In a meeting with peace activist Rosika Schwimmer, whose plan was to appeal to Henry Ford, the pacifist, she and the other guests in attendance were stunned when Ford blurted out, "I know who caused the war—the German-Jewish bankers! I have the evidence here. Facts! I can't give out the facts now because I haven't got them all yet, but I'll have them soon."[154]

Shortly thereafter, Ford's first issue of the *Independent* hit the stands with articles blaming the Jews for having caused the war and the world economic upheaval. It was followed later in the year by his book *The International Jew*, which had been translated into German. It is said Hitler had a dog-eared copy on his desk. That would not have been unusual, since Ford and Hitler held common beliefs regarding the Jews. So close was their relationship that Henry Ford was the only American named in *Mein Kampf.* In it Hitler wrote:

> It is Jews who govern the stock exchange forces of the American Union. Every year makes them more and more

the controlling masters of the producers in a nation of one hundred and twenty millions; only a single great man, Ford, to their fury, still maintains full independence.[155]

On July 30, 1938, Ford was awarded the *Verdienstkreuz Deutscher Adler* (the Grand Service Cross of the Supreme Order of the German Eagle) by the Third Reich. He accepted, no doubt aware of the extent of Hitler's vicious nature and the cruel and inhumane attacks against the Jews in Europe.

Why are Henry Ford, his association with Adolf Hitler, and *The Protocols of the Learned Elders of Zion* important in a study of Presidents and Prophecy? In his deprecatory writings about the Jews, Ford ultimately incited sympathy for them. As Fred Jerome wrote in his book *Einstein on Israel and Zionism: His Provocative Ideas About the Middle East*, "Nothing brings out nationalistic feelings and the sense of ethnic pride or racial identity as much as being attacked for being a member of a 'minority' group."[156]

In some churches, members were warned against Ford's acceptance of *The Protocols* as truth. And yet through the decades since its first printing, the lie still persists; born of fantasy, fueled with hatred, and supported by bigots. Dressed in the Emperor's new clothes it is palatable, but nonetheless, it remains a naked prevarication. It continues to feed Holocaust denial and Jew-hatred around the world.

One thing is certain: Much of the rise in fervency among the Jews to establish their own homeland in Palestine was fueled by the strident anti-Semitic attack of Henry Ford and the subsequent Jewish defense of President Taft.

(18)

WOODROW WILSON APPOINTS *the* FIRST JEWISH SUPREME COURT JUSTICE

*"Deal with thy servant according unto
thy mercy, and teach me thy statutes,"*
(Psalm 119:124)

WOODROW WILSON,
1913 INAUGURAL SCRIPTURE

William Howard Taft's successor was Woodrow Wilson, a man who had great regard and appreciation for the descendants of Abraham, Isaac, and Jacob. In an address to the Committee on Foreign Affairs of the House of Representatives on December 11, 1911, New Jersey Governor Wilson opined:

> Here is a great body, our Jewish fellow citizens, from whom have sprung men of genius in every walk of our varied life; men . . . who have conceived of its ideals with singular clearness and led its enterprise with spirit and sagacity. . . . They are not Jews in America, they are American citizens.[157]

The 28th president of the United States was well versed in biblical principles and theology. Both his father, Joseph Ruggles Wilson, and his maternal grandfather were Presbyterian ministers. Early in his life, the elder Wilson had made a commitment to pray morning and evening. His family prayed before meals—another habit Woodrow continued—and regularly attended midweek church services. As a young child, he felt that it was his destiny to become president of the United States and thereby achieve the goal of helping to restore the Jewish people to their homeland in Palestine. In his later life, Wilson was humbled: "To think that I, the son of the manse, should be able to help restore the Holy Land to its people."[158]

At the age of seventeen, Wilson left for Davidson College but had to return home due to poor health. When he was healthy enough to resume his academic studies, he chose Princeton University in New Jersey. Following his graduation, he entered the University of Virginia Law School, but Wilson's career as a lawyer was short-lived. He resumed his schooling, graduating in 1896 with a doctorate in history and politics.

Having opted for a teaching career, Wilson's efforts took him to several small colleges before he was invited back to Princeton as a professor of jurisprudence. (He is the only US president to have earned a doctorate.) From that position, he was elevated to president of the college in 1902. He then followed his political star and was elected governor of New Jersey. Fellow Democrats, sensing a winner, nominated him for the 1912 presidential race, and he emerged victorious due to a vote split three ways—between Wilson, Teddy Roosevelt, and William Howard Taft.

Wilson would be influenced by many during his White House years, but perhaps the most prominent was Louis D. Brandeis, a Jewish lawyer. Brandeis had attended Harvard Law School and opened his practice in Boston. In 1914, he wrote *Other People's Money*, a book that greatly impacted Wilson, its message coinciding with Wilson's New Freedom platform on which he had run in 1912.

Needing a qualified candidate for the Supreme Court in 1916, Wilson chose Brandeis. His selection threw both Wall Street and Washington into a dither—Brandeis was liberal, radical, and pro-union. But that wasn't what many considered to be the biggest strike against the nominee: Louis Dembitz Brandeis was a Jew, and although named after his uncle, who had been instrumental in securing the presidential nomination of Abe Lincoln, was deemed by some to be unfit to ascend to the hallowed halls of the nation's highest court. The fact that he had been raised in the Kentucky heartland and had little to commend him as a Jew held no sway with his detractors. He considered himself to be first and foremost a citizen of the United States. Besides, he averred that there was "no inconsistency between loyalty to America and loyalty to Jewry."[159]

Brandeis had been elated to learn that his beloved uncle had joined an experimental farm—or a *moshav*—in Haifa and had with one accord been selected as its chairman. The young lawyer was soon to find that he too was drawn to Zionism. When the World Zionist center of operations was moved from an increasingly bellicose Berlin to New York City, he played a decisive role, not only in the welfare of Jews in Palestine but in their very survival.

President Wilson, in his nomination speech, listed his grounds for wanting the appointment of Brandeis to the Supreme Court to be approved:

> I cannot speak too highly of his impartial, impersonal, orderly, and constructive mind, his rare analytical powers, his deep human sympathy, his profound acquaintance with the historical roots of our institutions and insight into their spirit, or of the many evidences he has given of being imbued to the very heart with our American ideals of justice and equality of opportunity; of his knowledge of modern economic conditions and of the way they bear upon the masses of the people, or of his genius in getting persons to unite in common and harmonious action . . .

This friend of justice and of men will ornament the high
court of which we are all so justly proud.[160]

Brandeis drew the ire of many special interest groups, for which
President Wilson was unprepared. When challenged, he said of his long-
time friend, "He is a friend of all just men and a lover of the right; and
he knows more about how to talk about the right—he knows how to set
it forward in the face of its enemies."[161] It took the president four long
months to finally secure the votes to have Brandeis confirmed by a margin
of forty-seven to twenty-two, thus becoming the first Jew to serve in that
august body.

Brandeis traveled to the Holy Land only once, in 1919. When he
returned to the United States, he penned his unfortunately erroneous
opinion in his journal:

So far as the Arabs and Palestine are concerned, they
do not present a serious obstacle. The conditions under
which immigration must proceed are such that the Arab
question, if properly handled by us, will in my opinion
settle itself.[162]

Although Brandeis eschewed a role in political circles in his later
life, he was induced to lead the Palestine Development Council, a private
organization of Jewish banks. A young labor leader, David Ben-Gurion,
applied to the organization for a home loan. Ben-Gurion would later say,
"[Brandeis was] the first Jew to be great both as an American, quite apart
from what he did for the Jews, and great as a Jew, quite apart from what
he did for America."[163]

In 1937, a kibbutz in the fledgling country was named *Ein Hashofet*,
"The Judge's Book," in honor of Louis Brandeis. It is reported that between
1912 and 1939, the year he resigned from the Supreme Court, Brandeis

donated over $600,000—much more in today's dollars—"to Jewish organizations, with most of the money donated toward Zionism."[164]

Louis Brandeis died on October 5, 1941, of a heart attack. Wayne McIntosh, an associate professor in the Department of Government and Politics at the University of Maryland, wrote of Brandeis:

> In our national juristic temple, some figures have been accorded near-Olympian reverence . . . a part of that legal pantheon is Louis D. Brandeis—all the more so, perhaps because Brandeis was far more than a great justice. He was also a social reformer, legal innovator, labor champion, and Zionist leader . . . And it was as a judge that his concepts of privacy and free speech ultimately, if posthumously, resulted in virtual legal sea changes that continue to resonate even today.[165]

Another of President Wilson's inner circle, along with Brandeis and Wise, was multimillionaire Bernard Baruch, a long-time admirer of President Wilson and a campaign contributor. As an advisor, he was decidedly anti-Zionist and openly against a Jewish homeland. He considered himself an American first and a Jew second. However, by the time the issue landed on the floor of the United Nations for debate in 1947, he had had a change of heart.

Baruch was joined in his admiration for the president by Henry Morgenthau, whose German-Jewish family had immigrated to the United States just as the Civil War ended. Henry was educated in New York City, graduating from Columbia Law School in 1877. He began to invest in real estate and became quite wealthy. He served the Democratic Party as chair of the finance committee and in 1913 was dispatched to Turkey as US ambassador. In 1920, he was appointed to the commission charged with the establishment of the International Red Cross.[166]

While World War I and the German war machine devastated most countries of Europe, President Wilson was able to keep American troops at home. However, in February 1917, German naval forces breached an agreement not to attack merchant ships in the Atlantic and began to sink American vessels, including the British-owned *Lusitania*, with 128 Americans onboard. Wilson abruptly ended diplomatic relations with Kaiser Wilhelm, and on April 2, petitioned Congress for a declaration of war. Four days later Congress granted the request, and the United States entered the battle—the one Wilson fervently hoped would be the "war to end all wars."

The following year, the Kaiser and the Central Powers (Austria-Hungary, Italy, Bulgaria, and the Ottoman Empire) petitioned for peace. On November 11, 1918, at 11:00 AM, a ceasefire was signed and implemented. Kaiser Wilhelm and Crown Prince Frederick Hohenzollern fled to Holland, where they were given asylum. Dutch officials refused to extradite the two to face war-related charges. On November 28, 1918, Wilhelm II submitted his proclamation of abdication:

> I herewith renounce for all time claims to the throne of Prussia and to the German Imperial throne connected therewith. At the same time I release all officials of the German Empire and of Prussia, as well as all officers, non-commissioned officers and men of the navy and of the Prussian army, as well as the troops of the federated states of Germany, from the oath of fidelity which they tendered to me as their Emperor, King and Commander-in-Chief. I expect of them that until the re-establishment of order in the German Empire they shall render assistance to those in actual power in Germany, in protecting the German people from the threatening dangers of anarchy, famine, and foreign rule.[167]

In preparation for the Paris Peace Conference, which followed in

January 1919, President Wilson prepared a fourteen-point program he believed would provide a fair and just settlement of war claims and conditions.[168] As part of his presentation, Wilson put forth an appeal for a League of Nations, which he hoped would "guarantee political independence and territorial integrity to all countries and nationalities, large and small."[169] This interpretation of the fourteen points was derided by the Arabs and mocked by the French premier, Georges Clemenceau, who chided, "God has ten commandments. Wilson needs fourteen points."[170]

Wilson's attempt to introduce the concept of a League of Nations was successful, and the organization was founded in 1919, with a total of 63 nations joining in what would become the United Nations that we know today. Unfortunately for Wilson, a charge against the organization was mounted by Senator Henry Cabot Lodge of Massachusetts, and the United States declined to join the body. Wilson was devastated by Lodge's success and launched a whistle-stop tour of the country to try to win grassroots support for his vision. While en route from Kansas to Colorado, the stress of his campaign caused the president to suffer a debilitating stroke from which he never completely recovered.

At the end of his term in office, Wilson and his wife Edith Galt Wilson retired to their home in Washington, D.C., which Bernard Baruch had arranged for them. Wilson died just short of three years later, on February 3, 1924. He left behind the legacy of a man friendly to the Jewish people, uncompromising in his stand against anti-Semitism, and a man of conviction and honor. Wilson's steadfast devotion to the ideal of a return to the homeland of the Jewish people in Palestine would later be even more deeply appreciated.

(19)

WARREN G. HARDING,
CALVIN COOLIDGE, *and*
HERBERT HOOVER

Where [there is] no vision, the people perish:
but he that keepeth the law, happy [is] he,"
(Proverbs 29:18)

PRESIDENT HERBERT HOOVER,
1929 INAUGURAL SCRIPTURE

In an era when every move by political candidates is closely
scrutinized by the media, it is highly unlikely that Warren G. Harding
could have been elected president. He had two strikes against him that
would have felled other, stronger men: 1) At the age of twenty-two,
Harding suffered his first nervous breakdown, followed by four additional
episodes over a span of twelve years; and 2) Harding allegedly fathered
an illegitimate daughter with Nan Britton. (Modern DNA testing would
resolve the issue, but Britton's daughter, Elizabeth Ann Britton Harding
Blaesing, refused to submit to paternity tests during her lifetime. She died
in Oregon in November 2005.)

Harding was the first of eight children born to Dr. George Tryon Harding Sr. and Phoebe Elizabeth (Dickerson) Harding. Warren's mother had been a midwife, and later earned a license to practice medicine. It was rumored, supposedly by a recalcitrant thief, that Harding's great-great-grandfather may have been African-American, a claim which was discounted by his family. His career was launched at the age of ten, when his father acquired the *Marion Daily Star*, a declining Ohio newspaper. The elder Harding rebuilt the publication into a top broadsheet, at which Warren was taught the basics of operation.

Harding was raised by a deeply religious mother, which is what could account for his signing the Lodge-Fish joint resolution of approval to establish a Jewish homeland in Palestine when he was president. It was perhaps one of the only positive notes regarding the Jews to emerge from his lackluster stay in the White House. Harding stated:

> A long-time interest, both sentimental and practical, in the Zionist movement causes me to wish I might meet the members of the organization and express the esteem which I feel in behalf of that great movement.[171]

As a candidate for the White House, Harding had cozied up to such rabid anti-Semites as Thomas A. Edison and Henry Ford. Bubbling beneath the surface, Jew-hatred began to roil and force its way above ground. It was under Harding's watch that, in 1920, Henry Ford began his pointedly anti-Semitic rant against the Jews by the dissemination of the *The Protocols of the Learned Elders of Zion*.

As president, Harding was clearly out of his depth. Historians credit him with being more interested in his weekly poker games, visits to vaudeville theaters, regular golf games, and boxing contests than affairs of state. To his credit, he was instrumental in establishing the Tomb of the Unknown Soldier, and among his accomplishments were "income tax and federal spending reductions, economic policies that reduced what became known as stagflation, a reduction of unemployment by 10 percent, and a bold foreign policy that created peace with Germany, Japan, and Central America."[172]

Harding's term in office, however, was plagued by scandal, perhaps the most infamous of which was the Teapot Dome. Harding learned of the duplicity of Secretary of the Interior Albert B. Fall while on an Alaskan tour. He was devastated to discover that his intimate friend had betrayed his trust by accepting a bribe estimated at $400,000 in exchange for lease rights to federal oil reserves. Others of Harding's close associates were also involved in the scandal. Harding packed his bags and headed home. He stopped in San Francisco, where he became ill and developed pneumonia. Warren Harding succumbed to the sickness on August 2, 1923. The remaining two years of his term were served by Calvin Coolidge.

★ ★ ★

During the watches of Woodrow Wilson, Warren G. Harding, and Calvin Coolidge, inhabitants of southern Russia and the Ukraine were actively engaged in pogroms against the Jewish population. As a result, some eighty thousand-plus Jews emigrated to Palestine. Many of the victims of the pogroms would have made their way to the United States, but were barred from entry by the austere allocations regulated by Congress. Between March 1920 and May 1921, marauding Arabs struck Jewish quarters and farms, maiming and killing. The British were appalled by the violence, but they disingenuously called in the fox to guard the henhouse.

Hajj Muhammad Amin al-Husayni, well-known for his virulent anti-Semitism, was elevated to an office created especially for him—that of Grand Mufti. It was, according to the Jewish settlers, a conciliatory move by Britain. Thus began a repeating pattern of conflict: Anti-Semitism in

Europe and the USSR would drive displaced Jews out of those nations and into Palestine, creating a no-win situation for the Jews and producing even more Jew-hatred in the region.

This same precedent was reproduced in 1924, when yet another wave of Jewish refugees from Poland fled to Palestine. Rumors that the new arrivals had plans to overrun the Temple Mount spurred an all-out attack against Jewish settlements near Jerusalem and in outlying areas. When the smoke settled, 133 Jews and 116 Arabs had been killed.

Government officials in the United States had no wish to become entangled in the ongoing struggle, so they not surprisingly chose the path of neutrality toward both parties. The entire conflict, as it was explained, fell under the authority of the League of Nations—the organization to which the United States did not belong. Despite tiptoeing through the minefield of Palestinian politics and Jew and Arab hostility, Washington would eventually be drawn into the chaos that gripped the region, then and now.

Although Coolidge was not noted for his interaction with the Jews in America, he did voice his "sympathy with the deep and intense longing which finds such fine expression in the Jewish National Homeland in Palestine."[173] He later became friends with Adolph Ochs, a Tennessee newspaperman, and Louis Marshall. Ochs had purchased the near-defunct *New York Times* and turned it into a successful publication. Coolidge repaid their friendship by signing the Johnson–Reed Act limiting immigration. It was also during Coolidge's presidency that Henry Ford decided it was in his best business interests to "apologize" for publishing *The Protocols* in the *Dearborn Independent*. Ford products had been boycotted by both Jews and Gentiles to the point that it was causing serious concern for Ford's bottom line. Author David L. Louis wrote of Ford's dilemma:

> Mass meetings in various cities denounced Ford,
> and a resolution of protest was introduced in Congress.

Representatives of almost all national Jewish organizations and religious bodies issued a common declaration deploring the campaign. One hundred nineteen widely known Christians, including Woodrow Wilson, William Howard Taft, and William Cardinal O'Connell called upon Ford to halt his "vicious propaganda."[174]

After having been sued by Aaron Shapiro for his role in printing the fraudulent document, Ford issued a weak apology:

> I deem it to be my duty as an honorable man to make amends for the wrong done to the Jews as fellow-men and brothers, by asking their forgiveness for the harm that I have unintentionally committed.[175]

Before his death, Ford apparently repented of his repentance and declared his signature on the apology had been forged by Harry Bennett, his private investigator.

★ ★ ★

Herbert Clark Hoover was waiting in the wings to assume the role as the first Quaker president of the United States. Orphaned at an early age, Herbert was reared in Oregon by an aunt and uncle. He was educated by the Quakers in a secondary school which afforded him one of the most comprehensive educations of any of the presidents who had preceded him. Hoover enrolled in the first class to pass through the doors of Stanford University, destined to become one of the premier universities in the country. After graduation, he accepted a job with a British mining enterprise, Bewick Moreing and Company, in Australia. Hoover excelled in developing mines that produced zinc and silver, and soon made his fortune. He established his own mining company, which developed natural resources in countries such as Russia, adding to his international stature.

Hoover's humanitarian endeavors earned him accolades worldwide, especially during World War I in Belgium. He organized the distribution of food to almost ten million starving French and Belgian refugees stranded between the German armed forces and the British navy. His actions are thought to have been one of the greatest humane and noble initiatives in history and gained him international acclaim. It was through his effort that American and Allied troops received the necessary food to survive during the German submarine blockade.

When the war ended, he once again stepped into the fray and provided incalculable assistance to a war-decimated Europe through President Wilson's newly established American Relief Administration (ARA). As head of the Allied Food Council, Hoover also directed the distribution of goods to European civilians nearing the end of the conflict. In 1919 and the early months of 1920, Hoover and his workforce supervised delivery of over thirty million tons of food to twenty-three European countries. Without those efforts, many would not have survived.

Hoover's expertise won him the job as secretary of commerce to both Warren Harding and Calvin Coolidge. When Coolidge decided not to pursue another term in office, Hoover easily won the Republican Party's nomination. He faced opponent Al Smith, the first Catholic candidate to run for the White House, and Hoover won with a margin of 444 to 87 electoral votes, the most since Ulysses S. Grant's presidential victory.

Hoover had a number of active Jewish supporters in his corner: Lewis L. Strauss, an investment banker; Herbert Strauss; Julius Rosenwald, president of Sears, Roebuck and Co.; Harry Guggenheim; Felix Warburg, a New York German Jew; and Louis Marshall, a lawyer and president of the American Jewish Committee. From these select men, Hoover would choose several for his administration.

Lewis Strauss had served as Hoover's secretary during his term as director of the ARA and became one of the president's closest friends and confidants. According to Strauss' personal papers:

> In February of 1917 [Strauss] chanced to read about Herbert Hoover's efforts to save the Belgians from starvation and Hoover's recent appointment as USFood Administrator. Acting on his mother's advice, Strauss decided to volunteer his services without pay for a few months as Hoover's administrative assistant. Hoover soon came to appreciate the initiative and executive abilities of his young assistant, giving him ever larger and more challenging assignments.[176]

According to his papers, in which can be found tidbits and pieces of the puzzle that was Lewis Strauss:

> According to legend, Hoover provided Strauss with an uncharacteristically fulsome recommendation in which Hoover promised to refund all of the salary paid to Strauss over the next ten years if his employers did not feel that they had gotten their money's worth. Several months before the expiration of the trial period, the senior partners announced Strauss' elevation to full partnership.[177]

Strauss was an ardent supporter of Hoover and campaigned untiringly for his reelection. He raised more than twenty thousand dollars to boost Hoover's coffers, but it wasn't enough to propel Hoover to a second term.

Julius Rosenwald was one of the most prestigious Jewish humanitarians in the United States. He invested millions of dollars in various charities, universities, and institutes across the country. One of his major concerns was the trouble facing Jews in Europe. Because of this disquiet, he founded the American Jewish Relief Committee for War Sufferers and donated over one million dollars to the relief effort. It was through this organization that Rosenwald befriended Herbert Hoover and worked closely with the humanitarian to provide food for Russian sharecroppers in 1917. The two men were partially responsible for saving the lives of thousands of Russian Jews who would otherwise have starved to death.

Rosenwald was born in Springfield, Illinois in 1862 and was apprenticed to his uncles in the clothing business in New York City. By 1890, he had married Augusta Nusbaum, the daughter of a rival clothier. When Sears, Roebuck and Co. encountered financial difficulty, the co-owners, Richard Sears and Alvah C. Roebuck, offered to sell half of the business to Rosenwald's brother-in-law, Aaron Nusbaum. He, in turn, invited Julius to invest. In 1895, Nusbaum and Rosenwald owned half of the company for an investment of $75,000. In 1908, when Sears faced declining health, Rosenwald became president of the multimillion-dollar company.

Having worked with Hoover during the war years, Rosenwald evolved into an articulate and vocal supporter who believed his friend would go down in history as one of America's greatest presidents. He was a hearty contributor to Hoover's campaigns and worked diligently to enlist support for the Republican presidential nominee.

Hoover was so appreciative of his Jewish friends Rosenwald and Strauss, and so confident in their abilities, that he attempted to appoint each to public office. Rosenwald declined an appointment as secretary of commerce due to his age and ill health. (He died in Highland Park, Illinois, on January 6, 1932.) Strauss declined Hoover's several offers to serve in his administration. That did not deter the president from appointing a number of Jewish acquaintances as ambassadors and heads of special commissions. Rabbi Abba Hillel Silver, a noted American Zionist, was appointed to a national advisory committee on jobless relief; and Harry

Frank Guggenheim was assigned to the National Advisory Committee on Aeronautics, and then served as ambassador to Cuba.

One of Hoover's most celebrated choices was that of Benjamin N. Cardozo as a Supreme Court justice to replace Oliver Wendell Holmes Jr. Cardozo's nomination by Hoover made him only the second Jewish man in the history of the Court to be nominated. Considered one of the country's most brilliant judges, Cardozo was a descendant of Rabbi Gershom Mendes Seixas, who spoke at George Washington's inauguration. His father, Albert Cardozo, a Spanish-Portuguese Jew, was a noted member of the New York State Supreme Court.

The young Cardozo owed his superb education to the likes of Horatio Alger, who tutored the young man before his entry into Columbia College and then Columbia Law School. After successfully working his way up from law school to the New York Court of Appeals, in 1927 he was elevated to the position of chief judge. President Calvin Coolidge offered Cardozo an appointment to the International Court of Justice at The Hague, but Cardozo declined the honor.

Hoover bucked the trend of most presidents when he entered the name of Cardozo as a nominee to the Supreme Court. He was first of all a Jew during a time of increasing anti-Semitism, and he was a Democrat who had supported Al Smith during the 1928 election. Yet Hoover was able to transcend partisan politics and appoint the man he felt best suited for the position. So popular was Cardozo that he was confirmed without debate or roll call. The *New York Times* said of Cardozo's appointment: "Seldom, if ever, in the history of the Court has an appointment been so universally commended."[178] History would record that it was one of the president's paramount and most long-lasting accomplishments.

Justice Benjamin Cardoza died in 1938, leaving only a six-year legacy on the bench. He, along with Louis Brandeis and Oliver Wendell Holmes Jr., was named among the ten most distinguished justices in history to sit on the Supreme Court. Hoover was lauded for his foresight in selecting this renowned jurist.

After a mere eight months in office, tragedy struck. As the Great Depression began to settle over the country, Hoover's popularity began to fade. Although he ran for reelection in 1932, Hoover was defeated by Democrat Franklin Delano Roosevelt in a rout equal to or exceeding his own election margins four years prior. Despite Hoover's pro-Jewish leanings and his staunch support of the Zionist movement, the majority of American Jews backed Roosevelt.

When the public began to be aware of the heinous treatment of Jews in Germany well after the outbreak of World War II, Hoover took a strong pro-Jewish stance. On October 29, 1932, the fifteenth anniversary of the Balfour Declaration, Hoover wrote to Lewis Strauss:

> I have watched with genuine admiration the steady and unmistakable progress made in the rehabilitation of Palestine which, desolate for centuries, is now renewing its youth and vitality through the enthusiasm, hard work and self-sacrifice of the Jewish pioneers who toil there in a spirit of peace and social justice. It is very gratifying to note that many patriotic American Jews, Zionists as well as non-Zionists, have rendered such splendid service to this cause which merits the sympathy and moral encouragement of everyone.[179]

Herbert Hoover lived to the age of ninety and died in New York City on October 20, 1964.

(20)

FRANKLIN D. ROOSEVELT
AVOIDS *the* JEWISH ISSUE

"Though I speak with the tongues of men and of angels, and have not charity, I am become as sounding brass, or a tinkling cymbal,"
(1 Corinthians 13:1-3, KJV)

PRESIDENT FRANKLIN D. ROOSEVELT,
1933 INAUGURAL SCRIPTURE [180]

Although history has dealt Franklin Delano Roosevelt some harsh criticism for his handling of the Holocaust years, especially with regard to attempts by Jews to immigrate to the United States to escape death, he had a number of close Jewish friends. Roosevelt, who was the scion of a wealthy upper-class family of Dutch-English heritage that resided in Hyde Park, New York, was born on January 30, 1882. He was educated in the best schools and claimed then-New York governor Theodore Roosevelt as a cousin.

Franklin completed the illustrious Groton School, where he was greatly influenced by Headmaster Endicott Peabody. Peabody taught his students that it was a Christian's duty to help those less fortunate and urged his charges to enter a life of public service in order to achieve that goal. In midlife, Franklin would say of the headmaster, "It was a blessing in my life to have the privilege of [his] guiding hand."[181] Roosevelt's son, James, called his father a "frustrated clergyman at heart." As senior warden at St. James Episcopal Church in Albany, New York, one of his greatest desires was to be asked to stand in for the rector.

It was no surprise to James, then, that in 1934, Roosevelt surprised everyone by inviting the crews of three escorting vessels (two American cruisers and one British) to anchor near where Columbus had landed in San Salvador. "He [Roosevelt] handed out printed programs he had secretly prepared" for Divine Easter Service. He then led the prayers. "On the *Nourmahal* that day, [Roosevelt] delivered a simple sermon, stressing the religious significance of the spot where we were anchored. He said that Columbus had arrived there and discovered America only through his belief in divine guidance . . . a Supreme Being gave Columbus courage to sail on when threatened by disaster and mutiny." Roosevelt told the party with some elation that this was the first time he ever conducted a service or preached a sermon "all by myself." He seemed delighted. [Roosevelt told Churchill that the Beatitudes and the thirteenth chapter of St. Paul's letter to the Corinthians were two of the most influential passages in his life. He chose I Corinthians 13 the four times that he was sworn into office.][182]

After graduating from Groton, he went to Harvard and studied political history and government, and then his next stop was Columbia Law School.

In 1905, Roosevelt married a fifth cousin (twice removed), Anna Eleanor Roosevelt. She was the niece of Theodore Roosevelt, who gave the bride away at the wedding. In 1921, polio robbed Franklin of his ability to walk and forced him into a wheelchair for the rest of his life. He could stand or walk no more than a few steps without the aid of crutches. This early tragedy cemented the relationship between Franklin and Eleanor, but alas, it was not to be a lifetime commitment. They had six children: Anna, James, Franklin (who lived less than one year), Elliot, Franklin (the second child to be so named), and John.

Roosevelt's religious beliefs would eventually be summarized by Frances Perkins, whom he would later appoint as secretary of labor, the first female to serve in a presidential cabinet:

> His sense of religion was so complete that he was able to associate himself without any conflict with all expressions of religious worship. Catholic, Protestant, and Jew alike were comprehensible to him, and their religious aspirations seemed natural and much the same as his own. He had little, if any, intellectual or theological understanding of the doctrinal basis of the major religions. But he had a deep conception of the effect of religious experience upon a man's life, attitudes, moral sense, and aspirations.[183]

Roosevelt's liaisons outside marriage with two women, Lucy Mercer and Marguerite "Missy" LeHand, have been widely documented. His choices caused a cataclysmic rift in his marriage to Eleanor, who moved out of the home, but the two chose to remain married, becoming an indomitable political and social duo. So deep was the chasm between them, Eleanor firmly refused to move back into Franklin's home in Warm Springs, Georgia, when his health began to fail and in the months before his death.

Eleanor had been instrumental in much of what Franklin achieved politically. Even though he was confined to a wheelchair, it was she who persuaded him to enter the political arena. He acquiesced and, despite his handicap, was elected governor of New York. Just four short years later, he entered the presidential race as the Democratic candidate with the bouncy campaign song, "Happy Days are Here Again," and defeated incumbent Hoover in the election.

As Roosevelt took the oath of office on March 4, 1933, he was faced with a country still under the thumb of severe economic depression. It struggled with events such as "Black Tuesday," the collapse of the stock market. He faced the task of amassing a group of advisors who could help him overcome the devastating blow to the American marketplace. He found those men among current or former college professors, many of whom were Jewish.

The Jewish population was ecstatic over Roosevelt's victory, which was accomplished with a vote of over 82 percent of its people. That number increased to 85 percent in 1936 and 1940, and 90 percent in 1944. Jonah Goldstein, a Jewish Republican Congressman in the 1930s, quipped, "The Jews have three *velten* [worlds]: *die velt* [this world], *yene velt* [the next world], and Roosevelt."[184] Some close Jewish advisors to Roosevelt included Justice Louis Brandeis, Judge Joseph Proskauer, attorney Benjamin Cohen, and the brothers Herbert and Irving Lehman.

Among Roosevelt's most trusted advisors was Rabbi Stephen S. Wise. A free-thinking spirit, Wise was a passionate proponent of organized labor and aided in the establishment of the National Association for the Advancement of Colored People (NAACP). Wise's efforts to elevate the underdog caught the attention of Roosevelt, and the two men became fast friends. The friendship was strained when Wise and another close associate, Rev. John Haynes Holmes, sought help from then-governor Roosevelt to oust New York City Mayor Jimmy Walker from office. Roosevelt was concerned that Walker's base, which included the powerful Democrats at Tammany Hall, would impede his run for the presidency. When the two clerics persisted in their efforts against Walker after Roosevelt won the presidency, Wise became unwelcome in the Roosevelt White House. The president extended an olive branch to Wise in 1935, just a year away from his second run for the presidency. Apparently he was successful, given the percentages by which the Jewish population voted for him.

Arthur M. Schlesinger Jr. later noted:

> For a long time [Roosevelt] was a hero. No president had appointed so many Jews to public office. No president had surrounded himself with so many Jewish advisers. No president had condemned anti-Semitism with such eloquence and persistence. Jews were mostly liberals in those faraway days, and a vast majority voted four times for FDR.[185]

One of the most outstanding members of Roosevelt's advisory team was Felix Frankfurter. According to Louis Brandeis:

> [Frankfurter was] the nation's most useful lawyer. Oliver Wendell Holmes remarked that he displayed "an unimaginable gift of wiggling in wherever he wants to." General Hugh Johnson denounced him as the most influential single individual in the United States. . . . William O. Douglas remembered him as "brilliant and able, friendly yet divisive . . . People either loved or hated Felix."[186]

Felix was born into a practicing Jewish family in Vienna, Austria, and moved to New York City at the age of twelve. He attended school on the Lower East Side, and at graduation moved on to City College then to Harvard Law School, where he was editor of the Harvard Law Review and an honors graduate. He boasted the best scholastic achievements since the graduation of Louis Brandeis.[187] At the age of thirty-two Frankfurter was invited to join the faculty at Harvard as a law professor, where he was known as a radical liberal.

Roosevelt met Frankfurter when the aspiring president served as assistant secretary of the navy. He acknowledged and appreciated Felix's legal brilliance. It was no surprise that when Roosevelt was elected to the presidency, he chose Frankfurter to replace Supreme Court Justice Benjamin Cardozo upon his death.

Robert Burt wrote of the affection the judge held for the president:

> Two days before his death, Frankfurter told his chosen biographer, "Tell the whole story. Let people see how much I loved Roosevelt, how much I loved my country, and let them see how great a man Roosevelt really was."[188]

Frankfurter retired in 1962 and was recipient of the Presidential Medal of Freedom in 1963. President Lyndon B. Johnson said of the honoree, "Jurist, scholar, counselor, conversationalist, he has brought to all his roles a zest and wisdom which has made him teacher to his time."[189]

Justice Felix Frankfurter died from congestive heart failure in 1965 at the age of eighty-two.

While Roosevelt was busily occupied with the development of his New Deal programs and the exodus from the Depression that had held the country in its grip, the National Socialist German Workers' Party (Nazi) in Germany was equally busy laying the foundation for another attempt at world domination.

In 1921, Hitler claimed the chairmanship of the National Socialist German Workers' Party and began to dazzle crowds with his formidable gift of oratory. Soon thereafter, the party had a new logo —the swastika— which Hitler believed symbolized the triumph of the Aryan man. It also adopted a new greeting, *"Heil!"* and eventually *"Heil, Hitler!"* (This can be translated as "Hail Hitler," or more ambiguously as "Salvation through Hitler.")

The mustachioed little man mesmerized his listeners with his gravelly, impassioned voice—never mind that his speeches contained little of actual value. Near the end of 1921, he had come to be known as the Führer (leader.) He formed gangs to maintain control at his assemblies and to apply goon-squad tactics to disrupt those of his adversaries. These were the beginnings of the infamous storm troopers, the SS, Hitler's black-shirted and dreaded bodyguards.

Hitler declared the Jewish people to be Germany's No. 1 enemy, the race accountable for the nation's internal problems. He strongly stressed what he saw as "the anti-Semitism of reason" that must lead "to the systematic combating and elimination of Jewish privileges. Its ultimate goal must implacably be the total removal of the Jews."[190]

German lawmakers made a disastrous error in judgment in 1925. They removed the prohibition against the Nazi Party and granted permission for Hitler to address the public. Moreover, when he needed it most in order to expand the reach of the party, a worldwide economic crisis reached Germany. Ironically, the resulting magnitude of unemployment, panic, and anger afforded Hitler the opportunity to step forward and claim the role of redeemer and savior of the nation. On January 30, 1933, Weimar Republic of Germany President Paul von Hindenburg was persuaded to nominate the Führer as Reich Chancellor. Germany had lost its last chance to avoid a Second World War and the Holocaust.

Hitler's determination to outfox his opponents and remove the conservatives from any role in the government took little time or effort. He abolished free trade unions, removed communists, Social Democrats, and Jews from any participation in politics, and consigned his rivals to concentration camps. He solidified his hold on Germany in March 1933 with the use of persuasive argument, indoctrination, fear, and coercion. The façade was firmly in place, and the people of Germany were intimidated into subjugation.

By August of 1934, the Third Reich had a determined dictator who held the reins both of Führer and chancellor, as well as all powers of the state accorded to a leader. He abandoned the Treaty of Versailles, conscripted a massive army, supplied it with war materiel, and in 1938 forced the British and French into signing the Munich Agreement. Soon to follow were concentration camps, laws against Jews, the destruction of the state of Czechoslovakia, the invasion of Poland, and a non-aggression pact with the USSR. The only obstacles standing between Hitler and the rest of the world were Franklin D. Roosevelt, Winston Churchill, Joseph Stalin, and the armies of the Western civilization.

Just one week after President Roosevelt was sworn in for his first term as chief executive, German laborers had completed Dachau, the original concentration camp. Within its confines some 40,000 individuals would be murdered, most of them Jews. Hitler would follow the opening of the camp by nationalizing the Gestapo and bringing it under his full control. Just three months later, he had successfully combined all commands under the aegis of the Nazi Party.

The events of *Kristallnacht* in 1938, in which the Reich looked the other way while the citizenry attacked Jews and their businesses throughout the country, did little to move Roosevelt toward a more proactive stance on rescuing European Jews caught in Hitler's reprehensible assault. Roosevelt had entered the office of the presidency with no firm policy regarding the Jews and a Palestinian homeland. It was not until Rabbi Wise and a group of his close friends talked with the president in the early months of 1939 that Roosevelt expressed an interest in the manifest destiny of the Jewish people.

Roosevelt and Wise would also become close friends with Nahum Goldmann, founder and president of the World Jewish Congress. At a weekend meeting with the president's aide, Samuel R. Rosenman, Roosevelt glimpsed the men on the verandah. He called out, "Imagine what Goebbels would pay for a photo of this scene—the president of the United States taking his instructions from the three Elders of Zion!" It was also Rosenman who, upon hearing FDR comment about erecting a barbed-wire fence around Palestine, said it would not only keep Arabs out of a Jewish homeland, it would keep the Jews inside.[191]

As events of the 1930s led ominously toward a Second World War, the Nazis under Hitler had already been searching for a "final solution" for what they considered the Jewish problem. Initially, steps had been implemented to allow German Jews to immigrate to whatever countries would accept them, but the move proved to be too slow for the Führer and the Reich. It was decided that Jews were to be purged, beginning in Germany, Bohemia, and Moravia. After that, they were to be expunged in Europe from east to west.

Since the summer of 1941, more than a half million Jews had been murdered behind army lines. The question was how to attain the goal of mass extermination in areas outside the battle zone. A more efficient way needed to be found to eliminate larger numbers. No, the meeting was not called to determine how to begin the process but rather to spell out how the "final solution" would be achieved. By January, death camps equipped with gas chambers were under construction.

Franklin Roosevelt's lack of support for the European Jews caught in Hitler's slaughterhouses and his lack of action caused another rift with Rabbi Wise who had launched a campaign to persuade the president to sign a boycott against German imports. Roosevelt's response was to issue a concerned communique, but he instituted no corresponding action.

(21)

FDR'S TRAGIC DECISIONS

And though I bestow all my goods to feed the poor,
and though I give my body to be burned,
but have not love, it profits me nothing,"
(I Corinthians 13:3)

PRESIDENT FRANKLIN D. ROOSEVELT,
1937 INAUGURAL SCRIPTURE

On May 23, 1939, a shipload of 925 Jews, including families with small children, some of them toddlers, left the port of Hamburg for Cuba. They were grateful to be escaping Nazi discrimination. Though every one of them carried a visa for Cuba, none were admitted. The ship, the *St. Louis*, then turned its prow toward America, hoping to find a safe harbor there. Instead, they found that door closed as well. Michael Barak, one of the small children aboard the ship, described the US "welcome" at a 2002 reunion of those passengers in Jerusalem:

> When approaching Miami of the "free" country,
> Roosevelt sent the US navy to prevent any entry. On top
> of that he warned any country in the region from letting

any of the "damned" Jews to land safely on their soil. In Canada, the head of immigration said, after being asked how many Jews of that ship could be accepted, "None is too many."[192]

The ship sailed along the coast of Florida for five days while its captain did what he could to find an open door somewhere in the world. In all, three weeks were spent trying to find refuge. Urgent cables were sent to every level of the US government, including two personal appeals to President Roosevelt. No reply was forthcoming. Instead, Coast Guard boats patrolled to prevent anyone from swimming to shore. On June 7, the *St. Louis* was forced to set sail back across the Atlantic, where it was allowed to disembark its precious cargo between England, Holland, France, and finally Belgium. Of the passengers aboard the *St. Louis*, most of the families were separated when the Nazis took control of Holland, Belgium, and France the following year (1940). About 260 were deported immediately to killing centers,[193] and nearly half of them died in the Holocaust.

The president's inaction regarding the *St. Louis* caused a change of heart among some of his supporters, who felt that Roosevelt bore some responsibility for the devastating tragedy. It would be a visit from a Polish diplomat, Jan Karski, that would provide even more evidence of the chief executive's lack of sympathy for the plight of European Jews. Karski was dispatched to London and Washington to deliver a firsthand account of the atrocities being visited on the Jewish people. He met first with Justice Felix Frankfurter who, though not convinced, took Karski to the White House to meet with Roosevelt. Karski reported to the president:

> There is no exaggeration in the accounts of the plight of the Jews. Our underground authorities are absolutely sure that the Germans are out to exterminate the entire

Jewish population of Europe. Reliable reports from our own informers give us the figure of 1,800,000 Jews already murdered in Poland up to the day when I left the country.[194]

Karski later gave a firsthand report of the president's response to his plea:

You will tell your leaders that we shall win this war. You will tell them that the guilty ones will be punished for their crimes. You will tell them that Poland has a friend in this house.[195]

Roosevelt then changed the subject and moved on to the next topic for discussion. Eleanor said this about the way her husband dealt with unpleasant things: "If something was unpleasant and he didn't want to know about it, he just ignored it. He always thought that if you ignored a thing long enough, it would settle itself." [196]

According to Michael Soltys of the *Buenos Aires Herald*, in London, Karski's pleas again fell on deaf ears:

[Karski] was told that if the Germans were so foolish as to lose sight of military strategy with such "secondary" objectives as the extermination of the Jews, the Allies had no intention of repeating the error.

"If Hitler wants to waste his trains transporting Jews to concentration camps, let him!" and "What do you expect us to do? Bomb the camps so that they die quicker?" were among the responses he received. The writer H. G. Wells, a lifelong socialist, told Karski: "You've got to look at the reasons why anti-Semitism has emerged in all the countries where Jews live."

It was no better in the United States where President Franklin D. Roosevelt . . . pumped Karski for four hours for information on Europe behind the lines but showed zero interest in the plight of the Jews. Frankfurter, a Jew himself, simply refused to believe his story, as did other US Jewish leaders.[197]

At the end of the war, Jan (Kozielewski) Karski was honored by the State of Israel as a righteous Gentile. In 1994, Israel bestowed on him an honorary citizenship. The following year, he received Poland's highest honor, Knight of the White Eagle, from President Lech Walesa. Jan Karski died in the Georgetown area of Washington, D.C., in 2000 at the age of eighty-six. In 2012, Karski was posthumously awarded the Presidential Medal of Freedom.[198]

It was during Woodrow Wilson's presidency that a politician named Breckinridge Long unfortunately entered the political arena. He had been awarded a minor post because of his contributions to the president's campaign. By the time Roosevelt became president, he had parlayed that appointment into the oversight of Jewish refugees trying to flee Hitler's Germany. How this rabidly anti-Semitic buffoon rose to that position is an unanswerable question, especially perusing some of his comments regarding the Jews. Herbert Druks wrote of Breckinridge:

> Long was the fellow who had been so impressed with [Benito] Mussolini [the Italian dictator] because the *Duce* made the Italian trains run on time, and on April 7, 1936, had written to William E. Dodd, US Ambassador to Germany: "From a purely objective point of view, I think the suggestions made by Hitler if they are sincere, afford the biggest, broadest base for discussion made by any European statesman since the World War." . . . It was Long who . . . wished to convince Roosevelt to impose

even stricter visa regulations to protect America from "undesirables." [Long was convinced] Jews were "lawless, scheming, defiant" and "the same kind of criminal Jews who crowd our police dockets in New York."[199]

Eleanor Roosevelt wrote that Long had been "rhapsodizing about the achievements of Mussolini's new "corporate state," saying: "Italy today is the most interesting experiment in government to come above the horizon since the formulation of the Constitution 150 years ago. [Mussolini] is one of the most remarkable persons . . . And they are doing a unique work in an original manner, so I am enjoying it all."[200]

Long's simple philosophy toward Jewish refugees was not his alone. Others felt as he did: that all were rabble-rousers and should be refused admittance to the United States. The story is told of a well-known journalist who was approached by a State Department official in an American embassy in Europe. The politico challenged, "I hope you're not helping Jews to get into the United States."[201] Such was the antipathy toward those targeted by Hitler.

In an article for Yahoo! Voices, Brandon Moran summarized *Paper Walls*, a book by author David Wyman. Moran wrote:

> The "Paper Wall" around Central Europe in the summer and fall of 1940 slowed the migration of Germans into the US dramatically. This wall consisted of stringent legislation and policy passed during this period, tightening the strangle hold on immigration into the US Avra Warren played a large role in doing so. Warren worked to raise legislation for stricter immigration controls. His goal was to protect the country from subversive aliens. The new legislation suspended temporary immigration because temporary immigrants could have subversive connections or intentions. Warren and Assistant Secretary of State, Breckinridge Long,

devised a plan that effectively walled out any applicants the State Department wished to exclude. [202]

Citing Long, Wyman provides an issued memorandum spelling out his intent:

> We can delay and effectively stop for a temporary period of indefinite length the number of immigrants into the United States. We could do this by simply advising our consuls to put every obstacle in the way and to require additional evidence and to resort to various administrative advices which would postpone and postpone and postpone the granting of the visas. However, this could only be temporary. [203]

Consular officers were instructed to decline visas to applicants who had "parents, children, husband, wife, brothers, or sisters in residence in territory under the control of Germany, Italy, or Russia. Many bills and laws were introduced at this time, adding cement to the Paper Wall. The flow of immigrants into the US had slowed to a trickle. By July 10, the US government ordered all German consulates closed. . . . By late 1941, the doors into the US had been all but closed.[204]

When Rabbi Wise and a group of concerned individuals approached President Roosevelt about the exclusion policies barring immigration of Jews, they were referred to the person most responsible: Breckinridge Long. He reacted to their pleas as though he were the one being persecuted. He justified his anti-Semitism with the paranoia of the infiltration of German agents embedded within immigrating Jews. With politicians like Long in high places, Hitler's "final solution" was guaranteed success.

In August 1942, the rabbi received a devastating cable from Gerhart

Riegner, the World Jewish Congress representative in Switzerland, which read:

IN FUHRER'S HEADQUARTERS PLAN
DISCUSSED AND UNDER CONSIDERATION
[THAT] ALL JEWS IN COUNTRIES OCCUPIED
OR CONTROLLED [BY] GERMANY... SHOULD
AFTER DEPORTATION AND CONCENTRATION
IN EAST AT ONE BLOW BE EXTERMINATED.[205]

As Wise had no way of knowing that the US State Department had received an identical message, he sent a copy to Undersecretary of State Sumner Welles. Welles petitioned Wise not to circulate the information until it could be corroborated. Two months later, in a press conference, Wise revealed that Jews in all German-controlled areas were being transported to Poland, where they were being murdered. What should have been front-page, above-the-fold news in US newspapers was relegated to the inside pages.

By December, the president had been convinced to meet with Wise and a group of rabbis in order to examine Hitler's sickening plot. The leaders presented a memorandum to President Roosevelt that read, in part:

> We ask you now once to raise your voice—on behalf of the Jews of Europe. We ask you again to warn the Nazis that they will be held to strict accountability for their crimes. We ask you to employ every available means to bring solemn protest and warning to the peoples of the Axis countries so that they may be deterred from acting as the instruments of the monstrous designs of their mad leaders.[206]

Breckinridge Long was infuriated that he had not received a copy of the Riegner Report before it was shown to Rabbi Wise. As a result of his anger, a telegram was dispatched to the American Legation in Bern, Switzerland, on February 10, 1943, which read (paraphrased):

> In the future we would suggest that you do not accept reports submitted to you to be transmitted to private persons in the United States unless such action is advisable because of extraordinary circumstances.[207]

(2 2)

FDR FINALLY ACTS

[Charity] does not behave rudely, does not seek its own,
is not provoked, thinks no evil;"
(I Corinthians 13:5, NKJV)

In 1943, Treasury Secretary Henry Morgenthau, Jr. launched an investigation into the role of the US State Department regarding the destiny of the Jews in Hitler's Europe. He was not allowed to see the telegram sent to Switzerland and was told politely, of course, that it was of no concern to the Treasury Department.

On the surface, Morgenthau did not seem the man to take up any banner for any cause and plant it on top of the mountain of Washington bureaucracy. He was what some might call a fragile man. He had suffered from migraines and spasms of nausea all of his life and spent hours and days stretched out in dark rooms trying to recover from them. When Rabbi Wise enlightened him of what was happening in the death camps and through other Nazi pogroms, it could not have helped these bouts. As Wise told him of the millions murdered, that the Nazis were making soap from the remains and lampshades from the skin of the Jews, Morgenthau's confidential aide Henrietta Klotz recalled that he "grew paler and paler, and I thought he was going to keel over." Morgenthau even cried out for Rabbi Wise to stop, "I can't take any more!"[208]

In Morgenthau, however, Wise had found his David to take on the Goliath prejudice of the State Department and the Washington career-path bureaucrats. When Morgenthau learned of Breckinridge Long's hostility to refugees, especially to Jews, and that Long was deliberately hindering the funds, information, and passports that could save Jews from Hitler's "final solution," he decided to confront him. In December of 1943 Morgenthau told Long:

> Breck, we might be a little frank. The impression is all around that you particularly are anti-Semitic. [When Long denied this, Morgenthau continued,] Breck, the United States of America was created as a refuge for people who were persecuted the world over, starting with Plymouth. And as Secretary of the Treasury for 135 million people, I am carrying this out as Secretary of the Treasury, and not as a Jew.[209]

Morgenthau then took the matter to Long's superior, Secretary of State Cordell Hull, whose wife happened to be half Jewish, though Hull had done everything he could to keep that fact quiet. Morgenthau, however, would now pull no punches. He told Hull that if he "were a member of the Cabinet in Germany today, you would be, most likely, in a prison camp, and your wife would be God knows where."[210]

Morgenthau got no more than bewilderment from either of these men. He then determined he had to take the matter to President Roosevelt. Knowing the president's previous attitudes on these issues, Morgenthau knew the matter could well cost him his position in the cabinet, as well as his friendship with Roosevelt. It no longer mattered to him though; his conscience would not let him escape. He had to see it through to the end—one way or the other.

Meanwhile, in downtown Manhattan, a crowd of about 75,000 waited outside Madison Square Garden while another 21,000 pressed inside for a rally on March 1, 1943. As one voice the people shouted, "Stop Hitler Now!" Dr. Chaim Weizmann, the articulate and persuasive leader of the Jewish Agency, moved the gathering with his plea:

> The world can no longer believe that the ghastly facts are unknown and unconfirmed. At this moment expressions of sympathy without accompanying attempts to launch acts of rescue become a hollow mockery in the ears of the dying. The democracies have a clear duty before them. Let them negotiate with Germany through the neutral countries concerning the possible release of the Jews in the occupied countries.[211]

Rabbi Wise had hoped to secure more congressional support as well as assistance from President Roosevelt, but he had little success. Weizmann moved those listening to his speech with the concluding words, "When the historian of the future assembles the black record of our days, he will find two things inconceivable: first, the crime itself; second, the reaction of the world to that crime."[212] Still, he failed to move the administration in Washington, D.C.

Rabbi Stephen Wise was roundly condemned for his belief that FDR would rally in support of Europe's Jewish population. However, when he died on April 19, 1949, at the age of seventy-five, he was remembered by Israeli Ambassador Eliahu Elath, who said:

> The people of Israel will join with Jews and non-Jews all over the world in mourning the death of one of the great humanitarians of this century. We of Israel owe him much for he was, half a century ago, among the pioneers in Zionism who lifted their voice in the cause of Israel's redemption. A fearless and tireless advocate of the causes he held dear, he fought our battle tenaciously decade after decade until it was won.[213]

Perhaps one of the most damning charges brought against Roosevelt and his administration was the failure to acquiesce to bombing the railroad lines leading to Auschwitz and the gas chambers inside its compound. It was possible that by the spring of 1944, such action would have been practicable, yet it was rejected with the explanation that it would have taken necessary men and airplanes away from definitive operations in other areas. That was seen as a smokescreen, especially since the Allies had already marked for destruction industrial complexes near the death camp. Historians believe that had American bombers been sent to target the railroads, thousands of Jews from Hungary and Slovakia might have lived.

November 1943 found Franklin Roosevelt, British Prime Minister Winston Churchill, and Joseph Stalin (premier of the Soviet Union) headed to Tehran for a military strategy conference. En route, the president had instructed his pilot to fly low over Palestine. As he viewed the country from his window, Roosevelt excitedly pointed out sites from his childhood Bible lessons, "from Beersheba to Dan." Once in Iran, Stalin was eager to create a second war front in Europe, a move with which neither Churchill nor Roosevelt agreed. Both felt the resulting casualties would be too great. Stalin's fear was that the two leaders would agree to a peace plan with Germany which would open the door for the defeat of Russia. After much discussion and wrangling, Churchill and Roosevelt agreed to launch a major offensive in the spring of 1944.

Before the offensive could begin, however, two of Morgenthau's researchers in the Treasury Department, Randolph E. Paul and John Pehle, produced a document titled, "Report to the Secretary on the Acquiescence of this Government in the Murder of the Jews." In the account the two men concluded:

> The tragic history of the Government's handling of this
> matter reveals that certain State Department officials are
> guilty of the following:

1. They have not only failed to use the Governmental machinery at their disposal to rescue Jews from Hitler, but have even gone so far as to use this Government machinery to prevent the rescue of these Jews.

2. They have not only failed to cooperate with private organizations in the efforts of these organizations to work out individual programs of their own, but have taken steps designed to prevent these programs from being put into effect.

3. They not only have failed to facilitate the obtaining of information concerning Hitler's plans to exterminate the Jews of Europe but in their official capacity have gone so far as to surreptitiously attempt to stop the obtaining of information concerning the murder of the Jewish population of Europe.

4. They have tried to cover up their guilt by:

   a) concealment and misrepresentation;
   b) the giving of false and misleading explanations for their failures to act and their attempts to prevent action; and
   c) the issuance of false and misleading statements concerning the "action" which they have taken to date.[214]

Morgenthau forwarded the statement to Roosevelt. It produced immediate action from the chief executive, who formed the War Refugee Board and placed John Pehle at its helm. It effectively removed all Jewish liberation and relocation issues from the hands of State Department employees. Deplorably, by the time this action had been taken, some four million Jews had been slaughtered.

As March 1944 began to flow into April, President Roosevelt submitted to a routine physical at Bethesda Naval Hospital. Although his diagnosis was not made public, Franklin's doctors ordered him to take a brief sabbatical to rest and recuperate. He accepted an offer from his good friend Bernard Baruch to travel to his estate in Hobcaw, South Carolina. After a month of sleeping long hours and relaxing during the day, Roosevelt returned to the White House, refreshed and ready to resume daily activities.

While the president convalesced, a major battle was shaping up in Western Europe. The opening salvo of "Operation Overlord" would be fired on D-Day, June 6, 1944, on the beaches of Normandy. When the smoke cleared, the invasion was deemed successful; the casualty count, however, was devastating to the Allied forces:

> The cost of the Normandy campaign had been high for both sides. From D-Day to 21 August, the Allies had landed 2,052,299 men in northern France. There were around 209,672 Allied casualties from 6 June to the end of August, around 10 percent of the forces landed in France. The casualties break down to 36,976 killed, 153,475 wounded, and 19,221 missing. Split between the Army-Groups; the Anglo-Canadian Army-Group suffered 16,138 killed, 58,594 wounded and 9,093 missing for a total of 83,825 casualties. The American Army-Group suffered 20,838 killed, 94,881 wounded and 10,128 missing for a total of 125,847 casualties. To these casualties it should be added that 4,101 aircraft were lost and 16,714 airmen were killed or missing in direct connection to Operation Overlord. Thus total Allied casualties rose to 226,386 men.[215]

(23)

FDR'S IDEA *for a* JEWISH HOMELAND

"And now abideth faith, hope, charity, these three;
but the greatest of these [is] charity,"
(I Corinthians 13:13, KJV)

PRESIDENT FRANKLIN D. ROOSEVELT,
1945 INAUGURAL SCRIPTURE

As a leader, Roosevelt often seemed either unable or unwilling to act, to use his considerable influence to counter the indifference and ignorance that seemed to have gripped Europe during the Holocaust. While the president appeared to have the will to help, it was quite obvious that he could not find the way. Pulitzer Prize-winning author Doris Kerns Goodwin wrote of Frances Perkins' intuitive description of Roosevelt's mindset, especially where the topic of authenticity was concerned:

> He would have one of these flashes [of almost clairvoyant knowledge and understanding] now and then
> .... He couldn't always hold on to it or verbalize it, but

when it came, he suddenly understood how all kinds of disparate things fit together[216]

Perhaps this helps to explain Roosevelt's reaction in late 1939 and 1940, when he brooded over a plan to resettle Jews as a means of escape from Hitler's assault. As a student of geography, he became engrossed in maps and excitedly shared the news when he felt he had found yet another spot where the Jews of Europe might thrive. He eventually platted 666 possible landing spots around the world that could accommodate those threatened by extinction. Some of the places he touted were Angola, Cuba, Northern Rhodesia, Brazil, Mexico, Tanganyika, Bolivia, Cameroon, and Santo Domingo. At one point, the president's excitement led him to telephone Henry Morganthau and enlist his help in getting together one thousand of the richest Jews in the country so that Roosevelt could inform each how much they were to contribute to his resettlement plan. Morganthau managed to tactfully table that suggestion.

It was also about this same time that Roosevelt directed his secretary, Grace Tully, to initiate a file on Palestine. Meant to be only a temporary file for his personal use, it ultimately grew to gigantic proportions during the president's three terms in office.

It had been just two years prior that an article in *Harper's Magazine* commented regarding the Near East Division of the State Department: "[It] is not often marked with excitement . . . our relations with these peoples [in the Middle East] are not important."[217] The world would soon know just how important that region would become.

The Near East Division of the State Department was ruled by the dictatorial and short-tempered Wallace Murray, who sported a British accent. He was inflexible in his oversight, taking on the character of a feudal lord rather than that of an employee compensated by taxpayer dollars. The anti-Semitic Murray had little interest in happenings in Europe and in the destiny of the Jews there. He supported the entire Arab world—Turkey, Iran, and Afghanistan and he and his cohorts believed Jews who had already immigrated to Palestine were unwelcome intruders and had no right to be there. Murray fueled the department's already well-developed hostility against the Balfour Declaration, vowing that Palestine was a British problem, and American diplomats were not to be involved.

Murray's superior, Secretary of State Cordell Hull, thought the Palestine issue a provincial one. It mattered little that his wife was Jewish; he was overtaken by more weighty matters. Hull tended to pass Palestinian matters along to Sumner Welles, his undersecretary. Welles, a graduate of Harvard and a close friend of President Roosevelt, was one of the few friends the Zionists had in the State Department. In his position, he was able to forestall some of Murray's more anti-Semitic policies and acted to provide information to the heads of many Jewish organizations. For all of his access to information, Welles, like so many others, failed to comprehend the reality and scope of Hitler's "final solution." He did, however, intercept a proposal made by Alexander C. Kirk, US Ambassador to Egypt, which outlined a plot to "bring Zionist leaders into the United States to revise their views on the Palestine problem in the light of the demonstrated impracticability of the present policy."[218] Murray fully supported Kirk's request, but Welles intervened. President Roosevelt never saw the proposal.

The aforementioned "Palestine" file, thought to be only temporary, had burgeoned with information from Zionists such as Wise, Frankfurter, and Benjamin Cohen, but not from the State Department. Indeed, Cohen presented what he called a radical proposal to the Department in 1942. His memo consisted of four pages and suggested that Palestine be made "an unquestioned sphere of Jewish influence by reason of the numbers of Jews who will be settled there."[219] Murray lost no time in adding two additional pages to the memo, outlining his objections to the plan. It was ultimately decided that Cohen's suggestions were of no interest to the United States, as Murray felt a US military presence would be required to facilitate Jewish statehood.

July 1942 found Roosevelt again in the company of Chaim Weizmann, thanks to a plea from Winston Churchill. As stated before, rather than discuss the plight of the Jews, the president launched a barrage of questions regarding the chemist's knowledge of synthetic rubber. Weizmann, at the White House to discuss a Jewish homeland in Palestine, was completely foiled in his every attempt. He left the residence frustrated. Just days later, Roosevelt was asked by Frankfurter to entertain David Ben-Gurion; the president emphatically denied the request.

Roosevelt had not totally abandoned his plan to move the Arabs out of Palestine, however. In a rambling conversation with Secretary Morganthau, he outlined his idea:

> What I think I will do is this. First, I would call Palestine a religious country. Then I would leave Jerusalem the way it is and have it run by the Orthodox Greek Catholic Church, the Protestants, and the Jews have a joint committee to run it. They are doing it all right now and we might as well leave it that way. I actually would put a barbed wire around Palestine, and I would begin to move the Arabs out of Palestine. . . . I would provide land for the Arabs in some other part of the Middle East, and I know there are plenty of places. Each time we move out an Arab we would bring in another Jewish family.[220]

Winston Churchill, an unabashed Zionist, had openly presented his position about a Jewish state in Palestine during a visit to Cairo in 1943. He was also quick to cite Roosevelt as a stalwart: "I am committed to the establishment of a Jewish state in Palestine, and the president will accept nothing less."[221]

In a conversation with Undersecretary of State Edward Stettinius, Roosevelt was voluble in his vision for Palestine. Stettinius recorded in his diary: "[Roosevelt] thinks Palestine should be for the Jews and no

Arabs in it, and he has definite ideas on the subject . . . . It should be exclusive Jewish territory."[222]

State Department minions tried desperately to muzzle the president to avoid pro-Zionist comments, but they had little success. They were unaware that in private, Roosevelt was openly profuse in his statements about a Jewish homeland in Palestine. Welles, his most trusted friend and disciple, was often his sounding board, and it was he who suggested that Roosevelt engage Lt. Col. Harold B. Hoskins, an Arabic-speaking intelligence officer, as a special emissary to provide unimpeachable information for his "Palestine" file, apart from the State Department. Hoskins, unfortunately, leaned more toward the anti-Semitism displayed by Murray. As a confidant to Roosevelt, the duplicitous Hoskins was able to provide an even better picture to Murray and his cohorts of Roosevelt's true thoughts and feelings about Palestine.

Again, Zionist leaders were not privy to information from the State Department but had to use other means to secure information about Roosevelt's plans regarding Palestine and Jewish immigration. In October 1943, those organization heads appealed to Eugene Meyer, publisher of the *Washington Post*, for assistance. It was suggested that Meyer wrangle an invitation from Roosevelt rather than petitioning the president for an audience. Meyer was successful, but during an almost hour-long chat, he succeeded in gaining nothing of real import in concessions regarding the issue, except for a plea from the president to assure the leaders that he would not fail them. Left with no other option, Zionist leaders continued to put their eggs in Roosevelt's basket.

In backroom meetings with leaders of these various organizations, suggestions of coexistence were being voiced. Contrary to Roosevelt's views, it was thought that the Arabs and Jews could share governance of the region. The president was aware that his vision of a Jew-only state was at that time unattainable. On December 3, 1944, FDR penned a personal letter to New York Democratic Senator Robert Wagner, in which he wrote about Palestine:

There are about half a million Jews there. Perhaps
another million want to go. They are of all shades—good,
bad, and indifferent. On the other side of the picture there
are approximately seventy million Mohammedans who
want to cut their throats the day they land. The one thing
I want to avoid is a massacre or a situation which cannot
be resolved by talking things over.[223]

FDR's economist, James Landis, reinforced King Ibn Saud's hatred
for what he considered to be the Jews' trespassing on Arab lands in a
memorandum dated January 17, 1945. Political scientist Dr. Winberg Chai
wrote:

Landis began by noting that the king felt very strongly
about the matter, had refused, to date, all suggestions
from the United States that there might be some middle
ground, and recently in the presence of a member of
Landis's staff had threatened to see to the execution of
any Jew who might seek to enter his country. The director
added that Ibn Saud politically represented the Wahhabis
sect, which was the spearhead of the pan Islam movement
and was unwilling to have any dealings with infidels, let
alone Jews.[224]

Even as his health failed, Roosevelt was consumed with the desire
that had possessed so many succeeding presidents: to settle the Palestine
issue during his final term in office. To do so, he felt, he would need to
personally talk with Saudi Arabian King Ibn Saud. In January, before
Roosevelt's inauguration for a fourth term was to take place, he revealed
his strategy to the newly elevated Secretary of State Stettinius. The
president's plan was to produce a map to convince the king of the small
amount of land that is Palestine. He would patiently explain why letting

go of a portion of that region for a Jewish homeland would harm no one, especially not the Arabs. He would then point out to Ibn Saud that the Jews would confine themselves to the land assigned. FDR had already assured the monarch in May of 1943 and again in February 1945 that "No decision would be taken with respect to the basic situation in that country without full consultation with both Arabs and Jews."[225]

Before he was to meet with Ibn Saud, FDR had scheduled a February conference with Churchill and Stalin in Yalta, an ancient city on the Black Sea in the Crimean region. That meeting produced the "Yalta Agreement" the document that would become a "Declaration on Liberated Europe." The document would outline the destiny of Europe after Germany was defeated, the division of Berlin, the formation of the United Nations, and the future of Japan. It is interesting to note that the pronouncements made at Yalta would define much of the modern political, military, and economic world as we know it. It would also signal the beginning of the Cold War and the cultivation of Middle Eastern potentates, whose countries held two-thirds of the world's known petroleum reserves.

FDR casually mentioned to both Churchill and Stalin that he would visit with Ibn Saud on his return trip to Washington, D.C. He asked Stalin his opinion of Zionism and his thoughts on a Jewish homeland. On February 10, Stalin inquired how the king might benefit from such a meeting. With a twinkle in his eye, Roosevelt joked that "he might offer the king the six million Jews in the United States."[226]

In reality, the meeting with the monarch proved to be less than satisfying for FDR, who still harbored a desire to see a homeland for the Jews in Palestine. When he broached the subject with Ibn Saud, the king's response was unequivocal: "The Arabs and the Jews could never cooperate, neither in Palestine, nor in any other country. . . . The Arabs would choose to die rather than yield their lands to the Jews."[227]

Upon his return, the president addressed a joint session of Congress to deliver an overview of his trip. He stunned some of his advisors by ad-libbing:

I learned more about that whole problem—the Moslem problem, the Jewish problem—by talking with Ibn Saud for five minutes than I could have learned in the exchange of two or three dozen letters.[228]

The president had learned with resounding finality that the Arabs were adamantly opposed to having the Jews share Palestine. It was a truth that was difficult for him to accept. He placed a call to Rabbi Wise and asked him to help set the minds of the various Zionist leaders at rest. Frightened that Jews already in Palestine would face war or yet another massacre by their Arab neighbors, Roosevelt even called in a member of the anti-Zionist faction, Judge Joseph Proskauer. He petitioned the judge to add his voice of reason to calm the fears and diminishing hopes for a much-awaited Jewish state.

On March 3, the president invited Colonel Hoskins for what would be the last White House meeting between the two. They were joined in the family dining room by Mrs. Roosevelt and their daughter, Anna Roosevelt Boettiger. As the two men discussed the Palestine problem, the First Lady enjoined that the Zionists were "much stronger, and perhaps willing to risk a fight with the Arabs."[229] FDR replied that there were fifteen to twenty million Arabs in the region. He thought that when all was said and done, they would prevail over the massively outnumbered Jews.

A year later, in March 1945, Roosevelt returned to his estate in Warm Springs, Georgia. Approximately two weeks after his arrival, on April 12, 1945, he was awakened for his morning routine of a nourishing breakfast in bed. He was presented with a number of drafts of letters to various Middle East leaders. Citing them as "typical" correspondence, he signed them and handed them back to his aide. Three hours later and just prior to lunch, he complained of a severe headache, then sank back in his chair and drew his last breath.

The president died before his great-grandson, Joshua Boettiger, was born. He never knew that his granddaughter would marry and produce a son, John, who would wed a Jewish woman. Joshua Adler Boettiger was born and reared by his mother as a Reformed Jew. Today, the thirty-second president of the United States could boast a great-grandson who at this writing is a rabbi at Congregation Beth El in Bennington, Vermont, the only rabbi who can trace his roots to the White House.

When studying the presidency of FDR, it is difficult to ascertain exactly where his actual thoughts and feelings about a Jewish homeland in Palestine lay. To Morgenthau, he expressed his concerns about Arab acceptance of a Jewish state when his own government refused entry to refugees. When Roosevelt surveyed the Holy Land during his flight to the Tehran Conference, he expressed reservations about the sustainability of life in the rocky terrain. The president's erratic policies toward the Jewish people, both in Europe and in Palestine, left little if any precedent for his successor. His statements were often hard to interpret, and his actions even more difficult to decipher. At his death, he left behind more questions than answers in this regard, even though his White House was rife with Jewish advisers.

History, of course, has yet to write the closing pages on Franklin Delano Roosevelt and the Holocaust, which claimed the lives of six million Jews. Does the fact that Jews in the United States overwhelmingly supported the Roosevelt presidency term after term somehow balance the scales regarding his refusal to do anything constructive to save the lives of European Jews? Or will history record that he shuffled responsibility first to one and then another in his cabinet in an attempt to pass the buck?

It would be his vice president and successor, Harry S Truman, who would make famous the statement, "The buck stops here." It was a simple way to say that responsible action would not be delegated to anyone else— it would be the duty of the president to act. The nagging questions remain: Had Roosevelt not succumbed to ill health, and had Harry Truman not become president of the United States, would the events of May 14, 1948, have taken place with the blessing of the United States? Would FDR, with his desperate longing to be liked by everyone and his concern that Jews in Palestine would be massacred by the Arabs, have capitulated to the pressure from Ibn Saud and his ilk and denied Israel recognition?

Roosevelt dreamed of a Jewish state and the Arab countries in the region working side by side to promote development, to build cities and infrastructure, and to irrigate the desert so that it could produce a variety of foods to nourish and prosper the people. Today, the US State Department is still trying to realize that dream by promoting a two-state solution: That Israel would occupy a small area of the region; the Palestinian Arabs would occupy an adjacent area; and the small State of Israel would be surrounded by hostile Arabs bent on its destruction. Like Roosevelt, many in government today still choose to live in denial of the Arab world's intentions and believe the impossible to be possible.

(24)

HARRY TRUMAN
DECISIVELY MOVES
FORWARD

"Blessed [are] they that mourn: for they shall be comforted,"
(Matthew 5:4, KJV)

PRESIDENT HARRY TRUMAN,
1945 INAUGURAL SCRIPTURE

When Franklin D. Roosevelt succumbed to what was reported as an unexpected and massive stroke, Vice President Harry S Truman assumed the mantle of chief executive. He and House Speaker Sam Rayburn were reportedly ensconced in Mr. Rayburn's office, sipping whiskey and discussing the political climate in Washington, when their reverie was disturbed by the ringing of the telephone and a summons to the White House. Truman, knowing the delicate state of the president's health, imagined the worst.

Upon arriving at the official residence, he was immediately taken to Roosevelt's second-floor study, where Eleanor waited. "Harry, the president is dead," she declared as he entered the room.

Stunned, Truman responded, "Is there anything we can do for you?"

She replied, "Is there anything we can do for *you*, you're the one in trouble now."

That evening, around 7 o'clock, Truman was sworn in as president. He later remarked to reporters, "Boys, if you ever pray, pray for me now. I don't know if you fellows ever had a load of hay fall on you, but when they told me yesterday what had happened, I felt like the moon, the stars, and all the planets had fallen on me."[230]

Harry S Truman was born to John Anderson Truman and Martha Ellen Young Truman on May 8, 1884, in Lamar, Missouri. Harry's middle name is "S" in honor of both his grandfathers whose names were Anderson Shipp Truman and Solomon Young. Rather than be accused of favoritism, his parents opted for the single initial, which is common among those of Scots-Irish ancestry. The family moved frequently during Harry's early years, but finally settled in Independence, Missouri, when he was six years old, so that he could attend the Presbyterian Church Sunday school. He began his formal education at the age of eight.[231]

Harry badly wanted to attend West Point but was rejected because of poor eyesight. He invested several semesters at various colleges, but would ultimately be the only president after 1897 to serve without a college degree. Instead, he joined the Missouri Army National Guard where he served six years. With the onset of World War I, he rejoined the Guard and was eventually dispatched to France as a battery commander. At the end of the war, he married his long-time sweetheart, Bess Wallace. One daughter, Mary Margaret, was born to the couple.

Lieutenant Truman and an army buddy, Sgt. Edward Jacobson, served together in the 129th Field Artillery and after the war ended opened a haberdashery in Kansas City. The joint venture store would be a victim of the 1921 recession. During his later life, Truman would credit Jacobson as the person whose advice had a major impact on his decision to recognize Israel as an independent state.

Truman entered the political arena and eventually served as

Missouri's Jackson County judge. His chief political desire was to serve as governor of Missouri or in the US House of Representatives, but his advisor and Democratic Party boss, Tom Pendergast, urged him to set his sights higher and run for the US Senate.

When he arrived in Washington, D.C., as a senator, Truman realized that Zionist organizations were pushing for a Jewish homeland in Palestine, but he was clearly in unfamiliar territory. The early whispers of Hitler's anti-Semitism and finger-pointing at the Jews proved unsettling to Truman, as was the 1939 White Paper issued from the halls of British Parliament that severely restricted Jewish immigration to the Holy Land. Truman wrote that the document made trash out of the Balfour Declaration and served only to swell the already lengthy list of British capitulations to the Führer's Nazi regime. He had been so disturbed that in 1941 he became a member of the American Christian Palestine Committee, a pro-Zionist organization. When seventy-seven US senators supported a Jewish state, Truman cautiously explained his reservations in a form letter sent to all those urging him to add his name. He wrote:

> My sympathy of course is with the Jewish people, but I am of the opinion that a resolution such as this should be very circumspectly handled until we know just exactly where we are going and why. . . .
>
> . . . with Great Britain and Russia absolutely necessary to us in financing the war I don't want to throw any bricks to upset the applecart, although when the right time comes I am willing to help make the fight for a Jewish homeland in Palestine.[232]

Little did the junior senator from Missouri know he was about to become an historic figure and that the "right time" was just around the corner. His brief stint in that office was quite uneventful. He drew some criticism during those early days for attending the funeral of his friend and mentor Tom Pendergast. Truman replied, "He was always my friend, and I have always been his."[233]

After making his mark in the Senate, and to the astonishment of all and the chagrin of some, Truman was tapped by Franklin Roosevelt to serve as his fourth vice president. He was selected to replace Henry Wallace. Although Truman reluctantly acquiesced to the demands of the president and the Democratic National Party, the label of the "Second Missouri Compromise" was firmly affixed by some to the selection of Truman as the vice presidential candidate.

Truman was an odd choice for Roosevelt as a running mate, as they had been on opposite ends of several issues while Truman was a senator. However, the choice made good political sense to the party because Roosevelt's prior vice president, Henry A. Wallace, was seen as being too liberal. Due to Truman's record for honesty and efficiency in facing tough issues (he was credited with saving the country roughly $15 billion in defense contracts through the toughest years of the Second World War), his name rose to the top of the list.

Harry S Truman was sworn in as vice president of the United States on January 20, 1945. Roosevelt and Truman rarely conferred, and when Roosevelt died just eighty-two days into Truman's vice presidency, the new president knew very little of his predecessor's plans for the end of the war and its aftermath. However, Truman's Midwestern values and ability to meet difficult issues head-on seemed to guide him. His love for the Bible (he had read it through twice by age twelve) gave him a natural inclination to favor "God's Chosen People" in their quest for a safe homeland. Just as FDR had been a student of the land of Palestine, Truman was a student of its people.

As a young man, one of his most cherished belongings had been a set of essays edited by Charles Francis Horne. The eight volumes contained essays about "Great Men and Famous Women." It was in the pages of these books that he read and reread the stories of David, Solomon, and others. He had pored over the story of Nebuchadnezzar's capture of the children of Israel and his ensuing madness. Young Harry studied the life of Cyrus the Great, who willingly allowed the captives to return to Palestine. He would later compare himself with that ruler.

In April 1943, almost two years before he would take office, Truman accompanied Rabbi Wise to a meeting in Chicago Stadium. There the future president delivered a scalding volley directed at those ambivalent listeners who had not raised a hand to help the Jews:

> This is the time for action. Today—not tomorrow—we must do all that is humanly possible to provide a haven and place of safety for all those who can be grasped from the hands of the Nazi butchers. Free lands must be opened to them. To do all of this, we must draw deeply upon our tradition of aid to the oppressed, and on our great national generosity. This is not a Jewish problem, it is an American problem—and we must and we will face it squarely and honorably.[234]

Just two days after he was sworn into office as chief executive, Truman delivered another passionate speech:

> Merely talking about the Four Freedoms is not enough. This is the time for action. No one can any longer doubt the horrible intentions of the Nazi beasts. We know that they plan the systematic slaughter throughout all of Europe, not only of the Jews but of vast numbers of other innocent peoples. . . . Their present oppressors must know that they will be held directly accountable for their bloody deeds. To do all this, we must draw deeply on our traditions of aid to the oppressed, and on our great national generosity.[235]

The State Department, headed by Secretary Edward R. Stettinius

Jr., held a decidedly pro-Arab stance. On Wednesday, April 18, 1945, Secretary Stettinius wrote to the newly inaugurated president:

> It is very likely that efforts will be made by some of the Zionist leaders to obtain from you at an early date some commitments in favor of the Zionist program which is pressing for unlimited Jewish immigration into Palestine and the establishment of a Jewish state.... The question of Palestine is, however, a highly complex one and involves questions which go far beyond the plight of the Jews in Europe. If this question shall come up, therefore, before you in the form of a request to make a public statement on the matter, I believe you would probably want to call for full and detailed information on the subject before taking any particular position in the premises. I should be very glad, therefore, to hold myself in readiness to furnish you with background information on the subject at any time you may desire.[236]

Perhaps it was Secretary of Defense James Vincent Forrestal, who best summed up these views when he said, "You don't understand. There are four hundred thousand Jews and forty million Arabs. Forty million Arabs are going to push four hundred thousand Jews into the sea. And that's all there is to it. Oil—that is the side we ought to be on."[237] (Secretaries of state have seemed not to waiver from that stance to this day: Oil trumps reliable allies.)

Years later, Truman would write of this memo from "the striped pants boys," saying that they were "in effect telling me to watch my step, that I didn't really understand what was going on over there and that I ought to leave it to the experts." However, the new president was not to be intimidated. He felt that "as long as I was president, I would see to it that I made policy."[238]

While it may seem unlikely that the memos pushed Truman to support Zionism, what it did ensure was that whatever his decision on the subject, it would be made quite independent of anti-Semitic State Department pressure. Two days later, the new president entertained a Zionist group in his office.

(25)

TRUMAN *and the* JEWISH DELEGATION

Thou shalt not take the name of the LORD thy God in vain;
for the LORD will not hold him guiltless that taketh his name in vain,"
(Exodus 20:7, KJV)

PRESIDENT HARRY TRUMAN,
1949 INAUGURAL SCRIPTURE

Even as President Harry Truman was finding his way through the minefield that was Palestine, Rabbi Abba Hillel Silver, a contemporary of Herbert Hoover, pushed the Zionist agenda in individual states and among politicians. Under his urging, thirty-three state legislatures, which characterized 85 percent of the US population, approved proclamations supporting creation of a Jewish state in Palestine. Thirty-seven governors were joined by fifty-four senators and 250 representatives in signing an appeal to the president. While the political movement made little impact congressionally, it did pave the way for open discussion.

In September 1945, Rabbi Silver and Rabbi Wise visited with Truman. The outcome was less than satisfactory, as the president grumbled about all the various factions that were applying pressure for their personal projects. He advised the two Jewish leaders that the best course of action would be patience on their part.

The stress must have reached a fever pitch when the president's own mother petitioned on behalf of a Jewish friend who wanted an item added to the agenda at the upcoming London Conference. Truman replied to his mother peevishly in a letter:

> There isn't a possibility of my intervening in the matter. These people are the usual European conspirators and they try to approach the President from every angle. The London Conference is for a specific and agreed purpose... Don't ever let anybody talk to you about foreign affairs. It is a most touchy subject and especially in that part of the world.[239]

The enigmatic and mysterious Middle East fascinated Truman, who kept a worn, plastic-covered copy of a map of the area in his desk drawer:

> Unfolding the map on his desk, Truman then proceeded to give a 15-minute dissertation on the historical importance and present-day significance of the area, which at least one person present described as "masterful." As he concluded, Truman turned good-humoredly toward General Eisenhower and asked if he was now satisfied that the situation was understood. Eisenhower joined in the general laughter of all those present and admitted that he was indeed satisfied.[240]

Another factor that would influence Truman's support of Zionism was the plight of the remainder of the Jews in Europe. With the Germans finally defeated and the death camps liberated, the world was not only stunned by what had been done to these people, but over the months to follow shock abounded at what was done with them in their "liberation." Death camps were replaced by displaced persons (DP) camps, but there seemed little difference between their accommodations except that one had been set up to kill them and the other was attempting to save them.

The DP camps were horribly sparse; there were few resources at the end of the war to dedicate to them. Additionally, those who for so long had nothing to cling to but the hope to survive had little idea what to do, now that they were "free." There was nothing for them to return to in Europe. They were caught in a no-man's land—no place to go and no place to stay. Solving this problem would become a key issue for Truman throughout his deliberations about the destiny of Palestine. One of his first acts was to request that Britain open the doors again for the immigration of 100,000 displaced Jews into Palestine. James Grover McDonald, who would become Truman's first ambassador to Israel, wrote that the president was "hell bent on the 100,000."[241] Truman's decision to push the envelope on immigration numbers would effectively countermand the British White Paper, which guaranteed the Arabs a majority in the region.

McDonald had become interested in the plight of Jewish refugees in 1933, when he was a history and politics professor. His concern led to an appointment as the League of Nations Officer of High Commissioner for Refugees from Germany, which included a department of Jewish affairs. He was hampered in his efforts to render aid because of the United States' refusal to join the newly formed League, while the British and French were members but not overly concerned about the refugee situation. Add to that a lack of sufficient funding, and it was obvious to McDonald that his efforts—at least at that time—would be futile.

In 1935, he resigned his appointment as High Commissioner and charged the government of the Third Reich with plotting to exterminate an entire race—the Jews. He condemned the membership of the League of Nations for its apparent lack of concern over the issue. Shortly thereafter, FDR established the President's Advisory Committee on Political Refugees and enlisted McDonald as chair. Deeply disturbed over restrictions on Jewish immigration into Palestine, McDonald resigned the president's commission. He was recruited to serve on the Anglo-American Committee of Inquiry on Palestine and supported the call for allowing 100,000 Jewish refugees into Palestine.

Following liberation of the camps at Bergen-Belsen, Buchenwald, and Dachau, Treasury Secretary Henry Morgenthau began to push President Truman to seek the advice of his cabinet regarding the fate of survivors—where they would go, how aid would be delivered, and other equally vital issues. Not taken with Morgenthau or his plans, Truman was nevertheless hoodwinked by the secretary's proposal to send an envoy to visit the camps and file a report with the State Department. Truman selected Earl G. Harrison, dean of the University Of Pennsylvania School of Law. Harrison had also served as Commissioner of Immigration and Naturalization during the war. His fact-finding trip in the summer of 1945 would define Palestinian policy for years.

On his first night in Munich, Harrison hosted Abraham J. Klausner, a young rabbi from the United States. Never having been much of a Zionist, Klausner's life was changed dramatically after being assigned to help the survivors of Dachau, and he was transformed into a militant Zionist. Through their discussion, which lasted through the night, Harrison's views were altered as the rabbi described the horrors of the concentration camps. The envoy's report to Truman was one of introspection and soul-searching. His report made the front page of many newspapers in the United States when he questioned the treatment of the survivors:

> As matters now stand, we appear to be treating the Jews as the Nazis treated them, except that we do not exterminate them. They are in concentration camps in large numbers under our military guard instead of S.S. troops. One is led to wonder whether the German people, seeing this, are not supposing that we are following or at least condoning Nazi policy.[242]

Harrison's retrospective contained a decisive summation of what should be the fate of the displaced Jews, and he also supported 100,000 immigrants to the Middle East:

> Palestine is definitely and pre-eminently the first choice. Many now have relatives there, while others, having experienced the intolerance and persecution in their homelands for years, feel that only in Palestine will they be welcomed and find peace and quiet and be given an opportunity to live and work. . . . there are many who wish to go to Palestine because they realize that their opportunity to be admitted into the United States or into some other countries in the Western Hemisphere is limited if not impossible.[243]

Truman responded to Harrison's report by writing immediately to General Dwight Eisenhower with an order to provide immediate assistance:

> We must intensify our efforts to get these people out of camps and into decent houses until they can be repatriated or evacuated. These houses should be requisitioned from the German civilian population. That is one way to implement the Potsdam policy that the German people "cannot escape responsibility for what they have brought upon themselves." . . . I know you will agree with me that we have a particular responsibility toward these victims of persecution and tyranny who are in our zone. We must make clear to the German people that we thoroughly abhor the Nazi policies of hatred and persecution. We have no better opportunity to demonstrate this than by the manner in which we ourselves actually treat the survivors remaining in Germany.[244]

Truman diligently read his Bible and fervently believed in a homeland for the Jewish people. He also believed that the Balfour Declaration was the basis for "a solemn promise that fulfilled the age-old hope and dream of the Jewish people."[245] With that in mind, he too kept a private folder in his desk drawer throughout his presidency; it was labeled "Palestine." After having read Harrison's indictment, he was forced to look at the possibility that the *She'erith Hapletah*, or saved remnant who had survived the Holocaust, were inextricably interwoven with the future of Palestine.

The president forwarded a copy of Harrison's study to British Prime Minister Clement Attlee, asking for quick action to evacuate as many of the refugees to the Holy Land as could possibly be achieved. State Department officials were completely in the dark regarding Truman's actions. He was unaware that while he was coming forward with a proposal to repatriate the Jews, the very determined "striped pants boys" were working on a memo in opposition—obviously still more concerned with reaction of the Arabs in the region than with the devastation left in Hitler's wake. At the same time, Britain was thrown into a state of panic by Truman's proposal, a state from which it never recovered during its remaining rule over Palestine.

Some Christian writers of the day went so far as to confront the refugees and demand they decide once and for all if they were willing to be reintegrated into the nations from which they were disgorged into the death camps, or if they would rather attach themselves to the hopes of a Jewish homeland. Commentaries and journals outlined God's Divine plan for the end times as it concerned the children of Israel and the Land, which God had given to Abraham. There were even calls for repentance by Evangelicals for the horrors that had been done to God's Chosen People.

On December 4, 1945, Truman met Chaim Weizmann—whom he repeatedly referred to as "Cham," although he had been warned innumerable times that the *C* was silent.[246] The men were poles apart regarding their wishes for a Palestinian refuge for the victims of Hitler's Holocaust. Truman was pushing Britain for a total of 100,000 immigrants to Palestine; Weizmann saw the need for 1.5 million Jews to be allowed into the protectorate. The Zionists believed that the Jewish immigrants could reclaim the "waste places":

For the Lord will comfort Zion, He will comfort all her waste places; He will make her wilderness like Eden, And her desert like the garden of the Lord; Joy and gladness will be found in it, Thanksgiving and the voice of melody, (Isaiah 51:3 NKJV.)

You shall shoot forth your branches and yield your fruit to My people Israel, for they are about to come, (Ezekiel 36:8 NKJV.)

Israel shall blossom and bud And fill the face of the world with fruit, (Isaiah 27:6 NKJV.)

I will put in the desert the cedar and the acacia, the myrtle and the olive, (Isaiah 41:19 NIV.)

Following his introduction to Truman, Weizmann was determined to try the smooth rhetoric that had earlier convinced the likes of Lord Balfour and other British diplomats of the need for a homeland. He typed a seven-page, single-spaced missive in which he presented his arguments for Palestine as a "secular state on the pattern of those in the United States and Western Europe"[247]—not a religious state or a theocracy.

As Weizmann was ushered into Truman's office, two men were being ushered out another door: Lessing J. Rosenwald, president of the American Council for Judaism—an anti-Zionist organization; and David J. Stern, publisher of the *Philadelphia Record* and a dissident Zionist.

These two mavericks were arguing for a universal Palestine that would be homeland neither to Jews nor Arabs; it would be a utopia for all world religions and all faiths equally, in which all would be responsible for its governance. As he exited the White House, Rosenwald leaked the information that President Truman was opposed to establishing a totally Jewish homeland in Palestine and would not commit to such a move.

Just days later, Weizmann attempted again to persuade Truman with the same tactics that had worked on the British. He wrote the president that a new Jewish state would not be a theocratic one; rather, it would be a secular state. The Jewish leader was edging ever more closely to an argument that would hit home with Truman, the Bible scholar, when he later proclaimed that the Jews must be rescued from homelessness. Weizmann pleaded with Truman for a homeland for his dispossessed people.

Many believe the president's ultimate change of policy was a direct result of his encounters with powerful White House bureaucrat David Niles, as well as Max Lowenthal, Clark Clifford, and long-time friend Eddie Jacobson. It was Niles who confessed his reservations about FDR's commitment to the Jewish cause. Niles admitted to having "serious doubts in my mind that Israel would have come into being if Roosevelt had lived."[248] He recommended Major General John H. Hilldring, a determined cavalry officer, to be Truman's Assistant Secretary of State for Occupied Areas.

Hilldring had an affinity for the refugees' vision of a homeland. Again, Niles urged Truman to appoint the general as his watchdog on the General Assembly delegation to assure that the president's position was expressly and accurately conveyed. By so doing, Truman forestalled any planned sabotage against his Middle East policies. Hilldring, a tough military man, performed his job with the full authority of the president of the United States. Had it not been for his efforts, there might never have been a declaration of statehood on May 14, 1948.

Truman would meet with Eddie Jacobson several more times—

specifically in November 1947 and March 1948—and each succeeding encounter would yield distinct results. His daughter, Margaret Truman Daniels, refuted in her book, *Harry S Truman*, that the two met repeatedly; however, Truman expert and foremost journalist on the subject, Frank Adler, says the exact opposite is true. He contends that Mrs. Daniels' version is categorically incorrect. Adler indicates in his writings that the two men met over twenty times in the Oval Office and several times in New York, Key West, and Kansas City. He contends that the president's old friend and former partner even traveled with Truman onboard the train that carried the president on his whistle-stop tour across the United States.[249] Regardless of Margaret Daniels' perception of the relationship between her father and Jacobson, the president indicated that he trusted his friend totally. In a letter from Vera Weizmann, Chaim's wife, to Jacobson, she wrote in reference to efforts to swing the pendulum in favor of the Jewish people, "One day the world will know the part you played in helping my husband achieve his goal."[250] Ambassador McDonald said of Jacobson, "Just because Eddie Jacobson is so thoroughly American—and so Jewish—he has played quiet but effectively his large constructive role."[251] In the end, however, it would be Weizmann, with Jacobson's help, who would secure Truman's backing and loyalty.

(26)

TRUMAN VERSUS *the* STATE DEPARTMENT

"Thou shalt have no other gods before me,"
(Exodus 20:3, KJV)

PRESIDENT HARRY TRUMAN,
1949 INAUGURAL SCRIPTURE

It was in response to the Balfour Declaration that Truman first made his feelings known on the issue of Zionism. He alleged the British had hedged on the Declaration until it was little more than a worthless bit of paper. He described the measures as a "Munich mentality" and a shameful denial of Britain's obligations to the Jewish people. Although Truman was charged with ambivalence in his own actions toward European Jews and their bid for a homeland in Palestine, American Zionists were encouraged when he wrote to his friend A. M. Levin, "fight for the Jewish homeland in Palestine."[252] He would discover that there were some hard choices to be made regarding the issue before his first term ended.

As Roosevelt's successor, Truman made new discoveries daily. He was soon informed that FDR had made a pact with King Ibn Saud of Saudi Arabia, stating that "no action would be taken with respect to the basic situation in that country [Palestine] without full consultation with both Arabs and Jews," and that he would "take no action, in my capacity as Chief of the Executive Branch of this Government which might prove hostile to the Arab people."[253]

Given the state of FDR's health when the letter was penned, some speculate that the assurances given to Saud were not penned by the president. When challenged about this so-called promise, Truman retaliated by saying there was no proof that FDR had ever signed such a document or made such a commitment. Not one of his years in the public eye had prepared Truman for the minefield of following in the footsteps of Roosevelt. He soon learned it took infinite skill to traverse the deadly territory that was Middle East politics. Every presidential successor to date has encountered many of the same problems caused by an all-consuming Jew-hatred in the Arab world.

Despite the uncomfortable territory in which the president found himself, his biblical beliefs were so deeply ingrained that he supported the Jewish people in their quest to immigrate to Palestine. But therein lies the rub: His feelings about an actual Jewish state were a bit ambivalent. Truman made it abundantly clear that every possible opportunity must be seized to give a chance for a renewed life to as many Holocaust survivors as humanly possible—a kind of "refugee Zionism." Thus, the basis for his Middle East policy was compassionate and charitable in nature. It has been said that he viewed the Jewish refugees' struggle in Palestine as very similar to the battles for independence fought by his country's Founding Fathers. He saw the neighboring Arabs as the modern-day parallel to Britain's King George III.

Nahum Goldmann, founder and president of the World Jewish Congress, wrote a letter to a friend in Israel regarding Truman's ambivalence. He felt that the president had not yet accepted the real need for a state, and that Truman did not fully understand the reasoning behind that need. The president, it seemed, was in a constant maelstrom of dissent from both his own anti-Zionist advisors and the Zionist organizations. The Zionists were pushing Truman for more immigration relief, even as they sought his support for a homeland for the unwelcome and unwanted survivors of Hitler's wrath. Zionist activists would soon find that one of their greatest champions occupied the Oval Office at 1600 Pennsylvania Avenue.

Truman, however, was so frustrated with the constant upheaval that he wrote to Eleanor Roosevelt:

> The action of some of our US Zionists will eventually prejudice everyone against what they are trying to get done.[254]

After a year of campaigning for massive Jewish immigration to Palestine, many of Truman's Arab friends had become estranged and America's standing in the Middle East was in tatters. The president had been cautioned by King Saud that only Allah knew what the consequences of Truman's actions would bring.[255] Truman later wrote to an associate that the situation in Palestine seemed to be unsolvable, even as he wrestled with the issues of a Jewish homeland there. On October 4, 1946—Yom Kippur—he announced that he was going on record in support of a "viable Jewish state."[256] The Arabs were incensed by the statement. King Saud accused Truman of waffling on his earlier avowal to consult with all parties involved before making any policy statement regarding Palestine.

Upon hearing of the king's displeasure, Truman wrote to King Saud:

> The Government and people of the United States have given support to the concept of a Jewish National Home in Palestine ever since the termination of the first World War, which resulted in the freeing of a large area of the Near East, including Palestine, and the establishment of a number of independent states which are now members of

the United Nations. The United States, which contributed its blood and resources to the winning of that war, could not divest itself of a certain responsibility for the manner in which the freed territories were disposed of, or for the fate of the peoples liberated at that time. It took the position, to which it still adheres, that these peoples should be prepared for self-government and also that a national home for the Jewish people should be established in Palestine . . . . The Jewish National Home, however, has not as yet been fully developed. . . . It was my belief, to which I still adhere, and which is widely shared by the people of this country, that nothing would contribute more effectively to the alleviation of the plight of these Jewish survivors than the authorization of the immediate entry of at least 100,000 of them to Palestine. No decision with respect to this proposal has been reached.[257]

He closed his missive to the king by saying: "I take this opportunity to express my earnest hope that Your Majesty . . . will use the great influence which you possess to assist in the finding in the immediate future of a just and lasting solution."[258]

Truman's pronouncement of support did little to sway the British from their intractable position of disallowing massive immigration of Jews to Palestine. Its leaders, in fact, began to talk of evacuating Palestine and leaving Jews already there to their fate. British Secretary of State for Foreign Affairs Ernest Bevin reacted to the establishment of a UN Special Committee on Palestine established in the early months by saying, "After two thousand years of conflict, another twelve months will not be considered a long delay."[259]

Truman said of Bevin's statement, "It was an ignominious thing to say. [Bevin] went on to say that if I had not meddled with the thing, they would have had the thing settled. That didn't help my Missouri good nature one little bit."[260] Truman thought Bevin's pronouncement showed contempt for the wretchedness in which the refugees found themselves—especially in light of the delays and miserable conditions in which they awaited permission to travel to Palestine.

The Soviets, on the other hand, were highly critical of a Jewish state and made it known that any attempts to carve one out in Palestine would be met with opposition. A memo dated May 10, 1947, from the chargé d'affaires in Moscow, Elbridge Durbrow, regarding the Soviets' long-term policy in the region read in part: "Opposition to formation in all or part of Palestine a Jewish state, which USSR would regard as Zionist tool of west, inevitably hostile to Soviet Union."[261]

Within four days of the release of Durbrow's memo, Soviet representative to the UN Andrei Gromyko would stride to the stage at the UN General Assembly and startle all its members. He vowed that the USSR fully understood the Jews' desire for a homeland, calling it a "legitimate right," and would propose identical Arab and Jewish states as the ideal way to proceed. Neither the Jews, the United States, nor the British were prepared for the Soviet announcement.

US leaders in the State Department spent nearly two weeks evaluating and debating the Soviet stance. They finally determined that Gromyko's magnanimous gesture was a ploy to gain the trust of liberal Jewish leaders in the West. It would allow the Soviets to retain the freedom to act as they pleased. The move, however, led almost immediately to prompt leaders of various Jewish organizations to line up outside the Russian mission in Manhattan for protracted meetings, including toasts of "L'Chayim" (to life), which would ring through the meeting rooms.

It was Kermit Roosevelt, son of Teddy Roosevelt and long-time Middle East intelligence operative, who would ultimately define the Russians' purpose. He thought the division of Palestine would open the door in the Middle East for a Soviet toehold based on the assumption that maintaining any attempt at partition would result in the need for force, which would require the assistance of the USSR. Kermit felt a separation would almost certainly guarantee turmoil in the region. He was not the only one concerned about the resulting upheaval. Loy Henderson, a Foreign Service officer attached to the State Department's Near East Division, wrote to Secretary of State Marshall:

> I consider, therefore, that it is my duty briefly to point out some of the considerations which cause the overwhelming majority of non-Jewish Americans who are intimately acquainted with the situation in the Near East to believe that it would not be in the national interests of the United States for it to advocate any kind of plan at this time for the partitioning of Palestine or for the setting up of a Jewish State in Palestine.[262]

While the General Assembly was in session in November 1947 at an old ice rink that had been built for the 1939 World's Fair, various groups met in different venues, some in Flushing Meadow, Queens, others in a Long Island community named "Lake Success." Even the most ardent Zionists in the US delegation—among them Hilldring and Eleanor Roosevelt—were unsettled after hearing of reservations regarding the division of the Holy Land. Others of the delegates suggested passivity would be the best course: accept the idea of partition while refraining from persuading members to join in support of the move. As the meeting in Lake Success moved forward, it was revealed that US delegates were pursuing two decidedly different sets of instructions. One came from the State Department, the other from the White House.

The various factions involved busily argued about the partition map suggested by the United Nations Special Committee on Palestine (UNSCOP). The State Department supported that division; Truman and Jewish leader Chaim Weizmann did not. On that map, the Negev was assigned to Arab Palestine, a stance that US Ambassador to the UN Herschel Johnson was expected to confirm. In the president's mind, it was clearly Jewish land. As the meeting progressed on November 19, Truman called Johnson, who was in the process of delivering a statement supporting the State Department's position. Johnson was forced to leave the podium for a twenty-minute conversation, and upon his return revised his intention to report that the Negev was to go to the Jews.

When the roll call was finally taken, UN membership, which consisted of fifty-seven voting nations, was apportioned along these lines: thirty-three votes for partition including the United States and the USSR—two more than the two-thirds required; thirteen votes against, including Saudi Arabia, Syria, Iraq, Lebanon, Egypt, Iran, Pakistan, Afghanistan, Greece, Turkey, Cuba, Yemen, and India; ten abstentions, among them Great Britain; the delegate from Siam was absent. France typically waivered throughout the process due to worries about Arab oil on the one hand and US financial support on the other. Finally, Bernard Baruch, who had made the transition from anti- to pro-Zionist, challenged the French delegation. He strongly suggested that if they voted against partition, American aid—all American aid—would be cut off. It was the tipping point, and France voted for partition. There is an interesting side note: The Arabs in Palestine were offered a separate state and rejected the offer.

Listening from the sidelines in Jerusalem was Haganah leader, Yitzhak Sadeh, who prophesied: "If the vote is positive, the Arabs will make war on us. And if the vote is negative, then it is we who will make war on the Arabs."[263]

Menachem Begin, the head of *Irgun* (a Zionist paramilitary group operating in Palestine), found little in the UN vote for which to rejoice. He said: "The Partition of Palestine is illegal. It will never be recognized.... Jerusalem was and will forever be our capital. *Eretz Israel* [the land of Israel] will be restored to the people of Israel. All of it. And forever."[264]

In his memoirs Truman wrote:

> The question of Palestine as a Jewish homeland goes
> back to the solemn promise that had been made to them

[the Jews] by the British in the Balfour Declaration of 1917 a promise which had stirred the hopes and the dreams of these oppressed people. This promise, I felt, should be kept, just as all promises made by responsible, civilized governments should be kept.[265]

In early 1948, Eddie Jacobson sent a telegram to Truman in a last-ditch effort to secure a meeting with him and Weizmann. Truman refused. With little to lose, Jacobson flew to Washington and marched into the White House unannounced. He implored the president to meet with Weizmann:

> Harry, all your life you have had a hero. You are probably the best-read man in America on the life of Andrew Jackson. . . . Well, Harry, I too have a hero, a man I never met but who is, I think, the greatest Jew who ever lived. I too have studied his past and I agree with you, as you have often told me, that he is a gentleman and a great statesman as well. I am talking about Chaim Weizmann; he is a very sick man, almost broken in health, but he traveled thousands and thousands of miles just to see you and plead the cause of my People. Now you have refused to see him because you were insulted by some of our American Jewish leaders, even though you know that Weizmann had absolutely nothing to do with these insults and would be the last man to be a party to them. It doesn't sound like you, Harry, because I thought that you could take this stuff they have been handing out to you. I wouldn't be here if I didn't know that if you will see him you will be properly and accurately informed on the situation as it exists in Palestine, and yet you refuse to see him.[266]

Jacobson's success in moving the president was evidenced by a terse reply that Truman would receive Chaim Weizmann as soon as possible after the president's return from New York on March 17, 1948.[267] The two men finally met on the following day and spent almost an hour together. Among the issues discussed by the two statesmen were the hope to see a homeland established without bloodshed, ideas for development of the area, and the desperate need for land to support the immigrants. When the dust settled, Truman had given his word—which to the man from Independence was as good as a signed document—that the United States would immediately recognize the State of Israel once it had been declared and would back the plan for partition. Unfortunately, Truman had failed to notify "the striped pants boys" of his promise.

The following day and without Truman's knowledge, Senator Warren Austin, his emissary to the UN, addressed the Security Council. He informed the Council that partition in Palestine was no longer a viable option. *The New York Times* reported that a "pin-drop silence and bewilderment" settled over the hall.[268] Members of Truman's cabinet adamantly avowed that Austin was a maverick, acting alone; others declared that the senator had spoken with the full authority of the president behind him. White House Counsel Clark Clifford and advisor Oscar Ewing categorically denied the president had given his approval to Austin. Clifford insisted he had warned that State Department heads desired to reverse Truman's position on partition, yet the president replied, "You are unduly concerned. I know how Marshall feels, and he knows how I feel. They are not going to change our policy."[269]

The passage of time has not dispelled the "What did Truman know and when did he know it?" aspects of the senator's speech, nor has it lessened Truman's response. A note on his personal calendar explains his ire:

> The State Department pulled the rug from under me today. I didn't expect that would happen. In Key West, or

en route there from St. Croix, I approved the speech and statement policy by Senator Austin to the UN meeting. This morning I find that the State Department has reversed my Palestine policy. The first I know about it is what I see in the papers! Isn't that hell? I'm now in the position of a liar and a double-crosser. I've never felt so low in my life. There are people on the 3rd and 4th levels of the State Department who have always wanted to cut my throat. They are succeeding in doing it. Marshall's in California and [Undersecretary Robert] Lovett's in Florida.[270]

After about ten years as a private citizen, the former president was interviewed by Edward R. Murrow. The broadcast journalist asked Mr. Truman if he had any second thoughts about recognizing Israel as a state. Truman answered:

Not the slightest for this reason. I'm going to brag a little if you'll allow me. I know the history of that section of the world fairly well. When it came time to make the decision and there was a chance to create the State of Israel, as had been promised, I just carried out the agreements that had already been made on the subject, and I've never been sorry for it because I think it's necessary that there be a State of Israel.[271]

Truman became the punching bag for some of his own friends, definitely for the Zionists in America, and for the media. *The New York Times* screamed:

A land of milk and honey now flows with oil, and the homestead of three great religions is having its fate decided by expediency without a sign of the spiritual and ethical considerations which should be determined at least in that part of the world. Ancient Palestine was once described as "not the land of philosophers, but the home of prophets." It would take a prophet sitting on a rapidly spinning turntable to have foreseen the course which our government has pursued during the last few months."[272]

While the president endured some of the darkest days of his term in office, Truman tapped Clifford to determine how the debacle had happened. While the dust was swirling about him, Clifford dispatched White House Special Council Samuel I. Rosenman to Chaim Weizmann's hotel in an effort to reassure the Jewish leader that the president would stay the course and honor his word. The Zionist declared to his cohorts that he was assured of Truman's support, and as Eddie Jacobson reported, "[Weizmann] was the only human being outside of myself who expressed the utmost faith in the word of President Truman."[273]

The partition vote was accomplished and the Jews, who had been homeless for two thousand years, would be homeless no longer. Rabbi Isaac Herzog proclaimed, "After a darkness of two thousand years the dawn of redemption has broken."[274]

(27)

TRUMAN RECOGNIZES
THE STATE *of* ISRAEL

Blessed [are] the peacemakers:
for they shall be called the children of God,"
(Matthew 5:9, KJV)

PRESIDENT HARRY TRUMAN,
1949 INAUGURAL SCRIPTURE

President Harry Truman is said to have viewed Army General George C. Marshall, who had been tapped as secretary of state in January 1947, as perhaps the greatest American alive in his day. Despite the high regard, however, the two men were destined to butt heads regarding the Palestine issue and the as-yet unnamed Jewish state. Marshall was joined in his antipathy toward US recognition by Undersecretary of State Robert Lovett; his predecessor, Dean Acheson; Secretary of Defense James V. Forrestal; Charles Bohlen, third in command in the State Department; and Director of the Office of United Nations Affairs Dean Rusk. Forrestal was violently against the move and expressed his opposition vociferously:

> You fellows over at the White House are just not facing
> up to the realities in the Middle East. There are thirty

million Arabs on one side and about six hundred thousand Jews on the other. It is clear that in any contest, the Arabs are going to overwhelm the Jews. Why don't you face up to the realities? Just look at the numbers! . . . [If Truman supports a Jewish state] then he's absolutely dead wrong.[275]

As I have mentioned previously, the State Department was and still is peopled with a majority of pro-Arab experts, greatly enamored of the abundance of Middle East oil. They apparently felt it their calling to either avert or delay any move by Truman to recognize a Jewish homeland in the region. Those individuals were more closely aligned with the British position on the question rather than with those of the president.

At midnight on May 14, 1948, the British Mandate would expire. Sixty seconds following the end of that era, the world was assured that David Ben-Gurion would step to the microphone and boldly declare the rebirth of a Jewish homeland. The name of the new nation had not been decided—would it be Israel? Would it be Judaea? One thing was almost certain—full-scale war would erupt immediately, as had been threatened by the Arab nations surrounding the tiny state. Of course, there were those who were convinced that the only way out was to turn the entire area over to the United Nations as its caretaker. Clark Clifford was much opposed to that move, which he felt would see the demise of a Jewish homeland before it had come to life.

Clifford had prepared a possible announcement for Truman to deliver shortly after the stroke of midnight. At their usual meeting days before the event was to take place, Truman outlined what he wanted the White House counsel to do in order to convince Marshall to endorse the idea of a Jewish state:

> You know how I feel. I want you to present it just as though you were making an argument before the Supreme Court of the United States. Consider it carefully, Clark,

organize it logically. I want you to be as persuasive as you possibly can be.[276]

When all the players on Truman's team—Marshall, Lovett, Niles, Clifford, and various aides—came together late in the afternoon on May 12, dominant in the room was the famous sign on the president's desk: THE BUCK STOPS HERE. As the men filed into the Oval Office, a mere two days separated them from the rebirth of the still-unnamed state. The surface calm in the room belied the underlying tension.

The meeting began with an overview of the situation and the Jews' confidence that things would go smoothly in the transition. Marshall assured everyone present that he had given the Zionists notice not to expect assistance from the United States, even in light of the possibility of increased hostility. The secretary of state was angry because it was said that he had dispatched someone with a message to David Ben-Gurion—a statement he implacably denied. Marshall unwaveringly avowed no knowledge of a message, and also stated he had no idea who Ben-Gurion was. (He was, of course, the head of the Jewish Agency, and the projected first prime minister of the new state.)

Next in the rotation of speakers was Clifford, who presented his points succinctly. It was his last point that would fuel the fire of Marshall's intransigence. Clifford said:

> Mr. President, I strongly urge you to give prompt recognition to the Jewish state immediately after the termination of the British Mandate on May 14. This would have the distinct value of restoring the president's firm position in support of the partition of Palestine. Such a move should be taken quickly, before the Soviet Union or any other nation recognizes the Jewish state. [He concluded:] I fully understand and agree that vital national interests are involved. In an area as unstable as the Middle East,

where there is not now and never has been any tradition of democratic government, it is important for the long-range security of our country, and indeed the world, that a nation committed to the democratic system be established there, one on which we can rely. The new Jewish state can be such a place. We should strengthen it in its infancy by prompt recognition.[277]

When Marshall indignantly objected, not only to the content of his statement but to Clifford's presence at the meeting, Truman laconically replied, "Well, General, he's here because I asked him to be here."[278]

The debate raged on as first Marshall and then Lovett joined the attack against recognition. Marshall was so incensed that he actually threatened Truman during the discourse. He wanted the president to be assured that should he side with Clifford (which he had already), the vote of the secretary of state would go to his opponent in the next election.[279]

Truman ended the meeting with the issue still unresolved between him, Marshall, and Lovett. Not only did Marshall record the entire discussion in the official record of the meeting, it has been said that from that time forward, he refused to even speak the name of Clark Clifford.

May 14, 1948, in the US capital dawned unusually warm and humid. The anticipation in government halls was palpable: Would the president recognize a Jewish state or would he acquiesce to his secretary of state and postpone any acknowledgement? Unlike today's "instant news instantly" mindset, the transmission of information took a bit longer. What was going on in Jerusalem? How high was the anticipation there? How great was the threat of annihilation?

In the White House, Clifford was still trying to sway Marshall and Lovett to the side of recognition. He approached Lovett with the question that if the secretary of state refused to support Truman on the matter, would he at least not openly defy him? After much vacillation, the general finally agreed to do nothing, neither positive nor negative. He would simply make no comment.

Clifford also contacted Eliahu Epstein, head of the Jewish Agency, and requested his assistance:

> Mr. Epstein, we would like you to send an official letter
> to President Truman before twelve o'clock today formally
> requesting the United States to recognize the new Jewish
> state. I would also request that you send a copy of the letter
> directly to Secretary Marshall.[280]

Working with several advisors, Epstein drafted a succinct missive that reached the White House by noon on the fourteenth. His request as an agent of the Provisional Government of Israel read as follows:

> I have the honor to notify you that the State of Israel
> has been proclaimed as an independent republic within
> frontiers approved by the General Assembly of the United
> Nations in its Resolution of November 29, 1947, and that a
> provisional government has been charged to assume the
> rights and duties of government for preserving law and
> order within the boundaries. . . . The Act of Independence
> will become effective at one minute after six o'clock on the
> evening of 14 May 1948, Washington time. . . . I have been
> authorized by the provisional government of the new state
> to tender this message and to express the hope that your
> government will recognize and will welcome Israel into
> the community of nations.[281]

In the original document, Epstein had referred to the new state simply as "Jewish state." As the letter was being delivered to Clifford by aide Harry Zinder, Epstein was advised by shortwave radio that the official name of the newly-established state would be "Israel." He immediately dispatched a second aide to overtake Zinder, strike the phrase "Jewish state," and insert "Israel" into the document.

At 6:11 that evening, White House Press Secretary Charlie Ross read the following statement dated May 14, 1948, approved and signed by President Harry Truman:

> This government has been informed that a Jewish state
> has been proclaimed in Palestine, and recognition has
> been requested by the [provisional] government thereof.
> The United States recognized the provisional government
> as the de facto authority of the new [State of Israel].[282]

Just as Epstein's document had the added word "Israel," so had Truman's document. The United States of America, in the year of its 172nd anniversary, was the first foreign nation to recognize the sovereign State of Israel; the USSR followed three days later. The president's pro-Zionist advisors bore the brunt of criticism for Truman's actions; however, it was the feisty, fedora-wearing Missourian who made the final decision.

One of the president's most coveted messages landed on his desk at about 10 pm on the night of May 14. It was in the form of a thank you from his long-time friend and ally, Eddie Jacobson.

What would the outcome have been if the president had yielded to the Marshall crowd? We will never know the answer; however, support from the United States' chief executive gave Israel an advantage that was essential for its survival. Without the deterrent offered by US backing, Israel's enemies on all sides may well have been much more pro-active in waging war, and the outcome could have been completely disastrous for the new Jewish state.

The account of a meeting with David Ben-Gurion in New York City after Truman left office had the president leaving the hotel in tears.

The Israeli prime minister was asked what he thought had caused the president's emotional response. Ben-Gurion answered:

> These were the tears of a man who had been subjected to calumny and vilification; who had persisted against powerful forces within his own administration determined to defeat him. These were the tears of a man who had fought ably and honorably for a humanitarian goal to which he was deeply committed. These were tears of thanksgiving that his God had seen fit to bless his labors with success.[283]

Chaim Weizmann was entertaining guests at teatime when his political advisor, Ivor Linton, interrupted the gathering. The Jewish leader was overjoyed to learn of Truman's actions. Meanwhile, traffic on Sixty-sixth Street, in front of the offices of the Jewish Agency, screeched to a halt as a blue and white flag—with the Star of David—was unfurled for the first time. It waved over the newly designated Israeli Embassy.

The president expressed the outcome of the day when he said:

> One of the proudest days of my life occurred at [6:11] P.M. on Friday, May 14, when I was able to announce recognition of the new State of Israel by the government of the United States. In view of the long friendship of the American people for the Zionist ideal, it was particularly appropriate that our government should be the first to recognize the new state.[284]

In September 1948, Truman wrote to Chaim Weizmann. In the letter he made no mention of the fighting and bloodshed that had gripped the region since the rebirth of Israel, but did express concerns for the battered Jewish people: "I hope that peace will come to Palestine ... and that we will eventually be able to work out proper location for all those Jews who suffered so much during the war."[285]

The tale of President Harry S Truman's choice to back the formation of a Jewish state and immediately recognize it is in actuality the account of how God grooms an individual to make a momentous decision that becomes the fulfillment of biblical prophecy. Truman was a student of the Scriptures and of Jewish history. His path to the presidency led him through the military during World War I, where he met Eddie Jacobson, a young Jewish man who would become Truman's best friend. Harry was profoundly touched by the horrors of the Holocaust. Two of his presidential advisors were devoted advocates of Israel and strongly supported him in his decision to recognize the State of Israel. Perhaps time and again, Truman had read in his Bible and believed:

> 'See, I have set the land before you; go in and possess the land which the Lord swore to your fathers—to Abraham, Isaac, and Jacob—to give to them and their descendants after them,'(Deuteronomy 1:8 NKJV.)

Approximately a year after Truman acknowledged the newly formed State of Israel, Isaac Halevi Herzog, the chief rabbi of Israel, visited the White House. As tears flowed down Truman's face, the Israeli dignitary blessed the president with the words: "God put you in your mother's womb so you would be the instrument to bring about Israel's rebirth after two thousand years."[286]

Truman said about the rebirth of the State of Israel:

> I had faith in Israel before it was established, I have in it now. I believe it has a glorious future before it - not just another sovereign nation, but as an embodiment of the great ideals of our civilization.[287]

Truman chose not to run for a third term in the White House. He felt it was time to revert to the traditional two-term policy. He retired in 1953, on the day General Dwight D. Eisenhower was inaugurated. The two men were less than cordial when they met for the swearing-in ceremony. However, Eisenhower immediately noticed that his son John, who was supposed to be on active duty in Korea, was in attendance for the ceremony. He questioned Truman about it, and the president replied to the query:

> The president of the United States ordered your son to attend your inaugural. The president thought it right and proper for your son to witness the swearing-in of his father to the presidency. If you think somebody was trying to embarrass you by this order, then the president assumes full responsibility.[288]

Following his retirement from public service, Truman lectured and taught while working on his memoirs. He worked with architects on the development of the Truman Library in Independence, Missouri. Eleanor Roosevelt was the keynote speaker when it opened on July 6, 1952. His health began to fail at the age of eighty-eight. He was hospitalized for a lung condition in December 1972, and on the day after Christmas, Harry S Truman died. He, his wife, Bess, and their daughter, Margaret, are buried on the grounds of the library named for him.

In the aftermath of his valiant defense of a Jewish homeland, Truman could have rejoiced in the knowledge that the Jews became faithful and committed defenders of the Christian holy sites in the Holy Land. Moreover, he would have been pleased that no American troops have ever occupied the Holy Land. Instead, Israel has become a powerful military presence in the region, and the nation and its people have never been overrun by communist ideology. The truth is: The two nations—Israel and the United States of America have long been bound by strong cords of Judeo-Christian beliefs.

(28)

EISENHOWER'S IMMEASURABLE CONTRIBUTION *to* HISTORY

"If my people, which are called by my name, shall humble themselves,
and pray, and seek my face, and turn from their wicked ways; then will
I hear from heaven, and will forgive their sin, and will heal their land,"
(II Chronicles 7:14, KJV)

PRESIDENT DWIGHT D. EISENHOWER,
1953 INAUGURAL SCRIPTURE

Eisenhower (also spelled Eisenhauer) is a name which in Hebrew means "iron worker." When the family came to the United States from Switzerland, the family name was misspelled by immigration authorities. It was because of their surname that the family of the 34th president of the United States was sometimes thought to be Hebrew. Born and raised in Denison, Texas, and the third of seven boys in the Eisenhower family, the future leader was not reared in the company of Jewish people, but nonetheless Dwight grew up being infused with an appreciation for God's Chosen People at his mother's knee.

At birth, he was named David Dwight Eisenhower and called

Dwight. He would later be nicknamed Ike— or "ugly-Ike" by some. He was educated in the school system in Denison and graduated from high school in 1909. Having devoured his mother's treasury of books, he determined that a military career was his destiny. He applied to the Naval Academy but was denied entrance because he was too old, having just passed his twentieth birthday. In 1911, he was accepted into the Military Academy at West Point. When he enrolled, Dwight inexplicably reversed the order of his name and became Dwight David Eisenhower. He was commissioned as a second lieutenant in 1915, and while posted at Fort Sam Houston in San Antonio, Texas in 1916, met and married Mamie Doud.

Eisenhower served under Generals John J. Pershing, Douglas McArthur, and Walter Krueger. He was summoned to Washington, D.C., by General George Marshall and in 1942 was made commander of the landing of Allied Forces in North Africa. Ike's career with the armed forces was stellar, and he ultimately attained the highest rank of five-star general during his service in World War II.

In December 1943, Eisenhower was appointed Supreme Allied Commander of the Expeditionary Forces. As such, he was informed of the Nazi concentration camps, but nothing could have prepared him for the reality he would find at Ohrdruf, a camp outside the town of Gotha in south central Germany. When the 89th Infantry Division, accompanied by the 4th Armored Division, marched into the camp, the troops had no way of knowing that it was an arm of the monstrous Buchenwald extermination facility. Ohrdruf had a capacity of 11,000 detainees, but when the Allies arrived, it held only about a thousand bodies—victims of starvation, abuse, disease, or a German bullet. Captives still able to walk had been assembled and marched to Buchenwald.

An eyewitness reported that mounds of bodies, little more than skin and bones, smoldered throughout the camp—an attempt by the departing German SS members to destroy the evidence. In a letter to General Marshall, Ike wrote:

I have never felt able to describe my emotional reaction when I first came face to face with indisputable evidence of Nazi brutality and ruthless disregard of every shred of decency ... I visited every nook and cranny of the camp because I felt it my duty to be in a position from then on to testify firsthand about these things in case there ever grew up at home the belief or assumption that the stories of Nazi brutality were just propaganda.[289]

The Eisenhower Memorial Commission later released the following account:

When General Eisenhower learned about the camp, he immediately arranged to meet Generals Bradley and Patton at Ohrdruf on the morning of April 12th. By that time, Buchenwald had been captured. Consequently, Ike decided to extend the group's visit to include a tour of the Buchenwald extermination camp the next day. Eisenhower also ordered every American soldier in the area who was not on the front lines to visit Ohrdruf and Buchenwald. He wanted them to see for themselves what they were fighting against. . . . He ordered that every citizen of the town of Gotha personally tour the camp and, after having done so, the mayor and his wife went home and hanged themselves. He cabled General Marshall to suggest that he come to Germany and . . . He encouraged Marshall to bring Congressmen and journalists with him. It would be many months before the world would know the full scope of the Holocaust—many months before they knew that the Nazi murder apparatus that was being discovered at Buchenwald and dozens of other death camps had slaughtered millions of innocent people.

General Eisenhower understood that many people would be unable to comprehend the full scope of this horror. He also understood that any human deeds that were so utterly evil might eventually be challenged or even denied as being literally unbelievable. For these reasons he ordered that all the civilian news media and military combat camera units be required to visit the camps and record their observations in print, pictures, and film.[290]

Lt. Col. Lewis H. Weinstein, chief liaison of Eisenhower's staff, wrote of the general's reaction to the scene at Ohrdruf on April 12, 1945:

> I saw Eisenhower go to the opposite end of the road and vomit. From a distance I saw Patton bend over, holding his head with one hand and his abdomen with the other. And I soon became ill. I suggested to General Eisenhower that cables be sent immediately to President Roosevelt, Churchill, DeGaulle, urging people to come and see for themselves. The general nodded.[291]

The future president seemed to have a firm grasp on human nature. Today the world is beset by Holocaust deniers who disparage the truth of the extermination of six million Jews. They have learned from Hitler that "a lie is believed because of the insolent inflexibility with which it is propagated."[292] Those who deceive themselves refute official documents, multitudes of photographs, filmed testimonies of those who endured and survived the camps, and thousands of feet of filmed footage that support the horrific results of Hitler's heinous crime spree.

Three days later, on April 15, the two camps that were referred to as Bergen-Belsen were liberated. Though these Nazi death camps were devoid of gas chambers, the overlords were held responsible for the deaths of 35,000 captives by starvation, relentless work conditions, sickness, cruelty, and brutal and inhumane medical experiments. When the British Royal Artillery 63rd Anti-Tank Regiment marched into the camp, it still held more than 60,000 prisoners in the two facilities, which were little more than a mile and a half apart. After those incarcerated were freed, the death toll continued to rise due to malnourishment and typhus. Another nearly 14,000 died as a result of their previous treatment at the hands of their Nazi captors. So great was the death toll, that many had to be buried in mass graves to prevent the spread of disease.

Dachau was liberated on August 29, and accompanying the soldiers into that camp was noted CBS correspondent Edward R. Murrow. As he had from Buchenwald, Murrow reported entry into the camp with a horror-filled voice fully cognizant of the terror that had gripped the men and women inside. His account brought the reality of Hitler's "Final Solution" home to the United States—a reality unmatched to this day. It fully surpassed Roosevelt's description of the attack on Pearl Harbor as "a day of infamy." As the troops moved from one concentration camp to another and uncovered the abominations, the time could well have been described in words such as shame, disgrace, ignominy, revulsion, shock, and repulsion. The Third Reich had earned every one of those words and much more.

Following the end of World War II, Eisenhower was offered and accepted the position of president of Columbia University. In 1951, he took a leave of absence after being given the role of supreme commander over NATO forces. A group from the Republican Party sought Ike out in Paris and prevailed upon him to seek the presidential nomination in 1952. Armed with the catchy slogan, "I like Ike," Dwight David Eisenhower was elected in a landslide and inaugurated on January 20, 1953. He would serve two terms in the White House.

The eight years of Eisenhower's presidency that followed Truman's were perhaps the iciest of US-Israeli relations. Eisenhower refused to meet with Jewish leaders, kept Israel at arm's length for the most part, and courted the Arabs hoping to turn them away from the Soviets.

As president, Eisenhower inherited one of the most problematical decisions he would have to make as chief executive. During the Truman administration, Ethel and Julius Rosenberg, her brother David Greenglass, Harry Gold, and Morton Sobell were charged with espionage. The Rosenbergs, who were Jewish, were found guilty and sentenced to death. The other three defendants received prison sentences. After Eisenhower took office, he was approached by Rabbi Abraham Cronbach and others, who asked for clemency for the husband and wife. The president rejected the appeal on June 19, 1953:

> Only most extraordinary circumstances would warrant executive intervention in this case. I am not unmindful of the fact that this case has aroused grave concern both here and abroad. In this connection, I can only say that by immeasurably increasing the chances of atomic war the Rosenberg's may have condemned to death tens of millions of innocent people all over the world. The execution of two human beings is a grave matter, but even graver is the thought of the millions of dead whose death may be directly attributable to what these spies have done.
>
> When democracy's enemies have been judged guilty of a crime as horrible as that of which the Rosenberg's were convicted; when the legal processes of democracy have been marshaled to their maximum strength to protect the lives of convicted spies; when in their most solemn judgment the tribunals of the United States have adjudged them guilty and the sentence just, I will not intervene in this matter.[293]

That same evening at Sing Sing Prison in New York State, the Rosenbergs were executed—Julius at 8:05 and Ethel at 8:15. For years afterward the guilt of this couple was questioned again and again, primarily because the testimony and evidence at trial seemed insufficient. Finally, the reason behind this insufficiency was made known when Democratic Senator Daniel Patrick Moynihan had the Venona Project declassified in 1995. Venona clearly showed that Julius was guilty, but it cast doubt upon Ethel; she was guilty by complicity, if anything. Unfortunately, the evidence of Venona could not be presented at their trial because the project was still ongoing and classified. It must be noted that the Rosenbergs were not executed because of anti-Semitism, but because a crime was committed and the guilty had to be punished.

The conviction of the Rosenbergs cast a shadow on the entire American Jewish community, and both those with anti-Semitic beliefs and passions and those who merely favored the Arab cause in the Middle East rose to take advantage of it. Once in office, Eisenhower's Secretary of State John Foster Dulles attempted to sway the new chief executive in favor of the Arabs, and principally Egypt's President Gamal Abdel Nasser. Unfortunately for Egypt, on July 26, 1956, the Eisenhower administration withdrew funds designated for erection of the Aswan Dam in Egypt, and Nasser became incensed. He proceeded to nationalize the Suez Canal—which connects the Mediterranean and Red Seas.

Nasser's actions took the entire world by surprise, and especially British and French stockholders of the Suez Canal Company. Leaders in Britain and France immediately began to make plans to wrest the canal from Nasser. The seizure of the area surrounding the Suez Canal was of great concern to Israel as well, because it would be impossible to ship goods through the Arab-controlled locale. Joining with Britain and France in what became known as the "tripartite collusion," Israel attacked the Egyptians across the Suez on October 26, which allowed the other two countries to join the battle on Israel's side.

When the Russians become involved in support of Egypt and issued threats to Britain, France, and Israel, President Eisenhower responded with, "If those fellows start something, we may have to hit 'em—and, if necessary, with everything in the bucket."[294]

It was Canadian External Affairs Minister Lester Pearson who brought a bit of sanity to bear on the parties involved. He suggested the formation of a United Nations Emergency Peace-keeping Force to be sent to Egypt to form a buffer zone between the Egyptians and the tripartite group. During one of the meetings, and angered by the unfairness of the UN's placing all blame on Israel, Australian Prime Minister Robert Gordon Menzies took the group to task:

> The United Nations made Israel a victim of a double standard of belligerent rights. Egypt sought to justify her denial of passage throughout the [Suez] Canal of Israeli ships on the grounds that she was at war and had belligerent rights, and thus she had been in contempt of the United Nations for six years. Israel, having accepted the proposition that she was at war with Egypt, attacked, but was ordered out of the Gaza strip and the Sinai peninsula; and Egypt still refuses to allow her ships safe passage; I cannot believe this kind of thing is a triumph of international justice.[295]

The presence of the peacekeeping forces slowly dispelled the threat. (The Nobel Committee presented Lester Pearson with its Peace Prize in 1957 because of his efforts to avoid an all-out war in the Suez region.) The UN units were withdrawn in December 1956, and the canal returned to Egypt's oversight. Israel, however, remained at Sharm-el-Sheik and in Gaza.

Eisenhower had been spared the move for military intervention, but having taken Dulles' advice, the president proceeded to alienate the pro-Israel lobby in Washington with his attempts to placate the Arabs, who had been soundly defeated by the Israelis during the Sinai Campaign. The president took to the airwaves in February 1957 to demand Israel's immediate and unconditional withdrawal from Sharm el-Sheikh and

Gaza. He threatened sanctions if his demands were not met. His actions did not endear him to the Jewish community and particularly not to I. L. Kenen, the head of the American Israel Public Affairs Committee (AIPAC). The group had achieved its goal in securing Congressional backing for the fledgling State of Israel. Senators and representatives had been convinced that a tough and robust Jewish state would be a safeguard against Arab expansion in the Middle East.

The members of the organization rallied to counter Dulles' influence on Eisenhower. Both the president and the secretary of state were infuriated when Ike received a letter from Congressional members outlining their disagreement with his plan to implement sanctions. So upset were the two, that a plan was developed to disallow private contributions to Israel through Jewish organizations and the purchase of Israeli bonds. AIPAC leaders went straight to Congress with this ploy and were rewarded when Eisenhower was forced to drop the proposal.

Democratic Senate Majority Leader from Texas Lyndon Baines Johnson warned Dulles that coercion would not be allowed, as it would damage the genial association between Israel and the United States. Republican Minority Leader William Knowland of California joined forces with Johnson in opposing sanctions.

Eisenhower was then placed in the position of having to soothe the rightfully ruffled feathers of Israeli Prime Minister David Ben-Gurion. The president asked the prime minister to consider withdrawal and assured him he would be amply rewarded for his statesmanship. Israeli Foreign Minister Golda Meir traveled to New York to deliver a speech before the UN General Assembly. So it was that:

> Israel agreed to a withdrawal from the Sinai in 1957, on the basis that a United Nations Expeditionary Force would shield Israel's southern border from attack, and that international guarantees would ensure freedom of navigation through the Strait of Tiran. Significantly, it

was the failure of these guarantees and the withdrawal of UNEF that resulted in the war of 1967.[296]

While seeking the office of president, Eisenhower had been unable to capture the Jewish vote. His challenger Adlai Stevenson carried that vote both in 1952 and 1956. The lack of support for the man responsible for directing the liberation of Europe could have been due to Eisenhower's apparent reluctance to support a Jewish state in 1948. The president did, however, have several highly visible Jewish men in his administration: Maxwell Rabb, who helped push the 1953 Refugee Relief Act through Congress; Arthur Burns, an economics professor at Columbia University, who advised the president on economic affairs and graduated to the role of Richard Nixon's economic advisor; and Norman Cousins, editor of the *Saturday Review.*

After serving two terms, President Dwight David Eisenhower and his wife Mamie left Washington, D.C. They would have died with few worldly goods had Congress not reinstated his rank of five-star general, complete with its accompanying pension and medical benefits. It was sufficient to allow them to purchase a small farm in Gettysburg, Pennsylvania.

It was in 1965 that the general chairman of the United Jewish Appeal, Max M. Fisher, sought an audience with the retired Eisenhower to seek his permission to award Ike a medal for his role in liberating the Jews from German concentration camps. As Fisher rose to leave the president's farm in Gettysburg, Ike said contemplatively, "You know, Max, looking back at Suez, I regret what I did. I should never have pressured Israel to vacate the Sinai."[297] According to an interview with Peter Golden for his biography, Fisher recalled the president adding, "Max, if I'd had a Jewish adviser working for me, I doubt I would have handled the situation the same way."[298]

(29)

JOHN F. KENNEDY– LYNDON B. JOHNSON ERA

"Yet you do not know *what your life will be like tomorrow.
You are just a vapor that appears
for a little while and then vanishes away,"
(James 4:14, NASB)

The young senator from Massachusetts, John F. Kennedy, addressed the Zionist Organization of America convention in June 1947. He articulated his undeniable support for a Jewish homeland:

> It is my conviction that a just solution requires the establishment of a free and democratic Jewish commonwealth in Palestine, the opening of the doors of Palestine to Jewish immigration, and the removal of land restrictions, so that those members of the people of Israel who desire to do so may work out their destiny under their chosen leaders in the land of Israel. If the United States is to be true to its own democratic traditions, it will actively and dynamically support this policy.[299]

John Fitzgerald Kennedy was the first president to be born a child of the twentieth century, and the first president to have been a Boy Scout. Born to Joseph and Rose Fitzgerald Kennedy, he was named after his maternal grandfather, who had been both a congressman and mayor of Boston, Massachusetts. The future president's father was a wealthy entrepreneur, who had served Franklin D. Roosevelt as chair of the Securities and Exchange Commission and as ambassador to Great Britain. He proved to be a provocative figure because of his opposition to US entry into World War II.

Young "Jack," as his friends called him, completed high school at The Choate School in Wallingford, Connecticut, before matriculating at Harvard. After graduation in 1940 with a degree in international affairs, Kennedy assisted with the writing of his father's memoirs before trying to enlist in the army. He was rejected because of chronic back problems, but was accepted by the navy. After completing training, he was assigned first to Panama and later to the Pacific Theater. Kennedy was given command of the patrol torpedo boat *PT-109*. While on patrol in the Solomon Islands, his boat was struck by a Japanese destroyer, the *Amagiri*. The impact ripped away the starboard aft side of the boat, and two of its crewmembers were never recovered.

Kennedy gathered his surviving crew together in the water around the wreckage and asked them to vote on whether to "fight or surrender." Kennedy stated, "There's nothing in the book about a situation like this. A lot of you men have families and some of you have children. What do you want to do? I have nothing to lose." [300] Shunning surrender, the men swam toward a small island. Kennedy, despite re-injury to his back in the collision, towed a badly burned crewman through the water with a life jacket strap clenched between his teeth.[301] He towed the wounded man to the island and later to a second island, from where his crew was subsequently rescued.[302] Kennedy was awarded the Navy and Marine Corps Medal for his heroic actions. Once asked by a reporter how he became a hero during the war, Kennedy quipped: "It was involuntary. They sank my boat."[303]

Joseph Kennedy had groomed his oldest son, Joseph P. Kennedy Jr. (Joe), to fulfill the family's political aspirations. The elder Kennedy was crushed when Joe, a pilot, was killed in a freak air accident over England during World War II. The political mantle then fell on Jack, who was thrust into the political arena in 1945, shortly after his discharge from military service. With the seemingly unlimited funds of the Kennedy patriarch, Jack was easily elected, besting nine rivals for a Congressional House seat. In 1952, he sought the Senate seat that had been held by Henry Cabot Lodge Jr. and won with a margin of 74 percent.

As senator, Kennedy stood in strong opposition to an arms embargo of Israel. The embargo had stayed firmly in place during the Eisenhower years despite a small "one-time only" sale of a hundred unsophisticated anti-tank guns in the last days of Ike's term. The decade-old nation of Israel had to wonder if its old friend had turned cold toward her. Congressional voting records for Kennedy's terms in office reflect that except for one vote in opposition to monetary aid for Israel and the Arab countries, he backed the pro-Israel bloc.

In 1960, Kennedy leveraged his senate seat for a Democratic presidential nomination and ultimately a victory over Eisenhower's vice president, Richard M. Nixon. In doing so, he overcame opposition to his candidacy because of his Roman Catholic beliefs. The Jews in the United States were particularly wary of his bid for the White House, because charges of anti-Semitism had been lodged against Jack's father while ambassador to the Court of St. James in the 1930s. Herbert Druks wrote:

> In 1934 Ambassador Kennedy asked his son Joe P. Kennedy Jr. to visit Germany, Austria, and Hungary and to report on conditions in those countries. Joe Jr. traveled there and wrote to his father that the Jews had too much power in those countries and that many were lawyers,

businessmen, and judges. Nationalists and Nazis planned to change all that. Joe observed that it was unfortunate that innocent Jews would be hurt because of the guilty.[304]

Based on the exchange of letters between father and son, Druks also revealed:

> Joe Senior believed that Hitler's anti-Semitism was a means by which he aimed to win control over Germany. Anti-Semitism seemed all right to Joe Senior and Joe Junior, but they could not understand why the Nazis picked on the Catholics.[305]

Arthur Hertzberg wrote of a rabbi who sought an audience with Ambassador Kennedy in London. The man had family members, who were US citizens, stranded in Europe. He wanted to petition the ambassador for help in rescuing them. Kennedy was less than amiable as Hertzberg recounted:

> Kennedy received [the petitioner] coldly and told him to stop being a pest. The rabbi was so disheartened and so outraged that he uttered a curse: May God have as much compassion for your children as you have for mine.[306]

At first glance, it would seem that Jack was the more amenable to working with the Jewish population and had more compassion for them than his brother Joe—Daddy's first choice for the White House—would have had. As a presidential candidate, Jack tried to allay any fears from Jewish citizens by staging a meeting with a powerful group of Jewish leaders in New York City in August 1960. He was able to convince these high-ranking men that, should he be elected, he would instruct that the door to the Oval Office would always be open to them. It was enough to elicit $500,000 in campaign donations and to draw further support from the Jewish community.

It would be the warm personality of John F. Kennedy that would take US-Israeli relations out of Eisenhower's deep freeze and into a new place of prominence in the eyes of America. "Let every nation know," Kennedy announced in his inaugural address, "whether it wishes us well or ill, that we shall pay any price, bear any burden, meet any hardship, support any friend, oppose any foe, to assure the survival and success of liberty."[307] It was Kennedy's aim to find out just who did wish us well or ill in the Middle East, who would support democratic liberty there, and solidify our friendships with those nations to promote further promote freedom and peace in the world.

While it was Nasser's Egypt that Kennedy aggressively pursued initially, for a number of reasons that friendship never developed, not the least of which was Nasser's aggression into Yemen in an attempt to join the Arabs by force since his coercion had failed. Nasser would slide from the world stage as that struggle turned into a winless Vietnam for him. Thus when Kennedy was ready to look elsewhere in the Middle East for friends, Ben-Gurion was already knocking at the door.

Israel knew it needed the support of a major power to survive, and with the largest population of Jews being in the United States, it seemed the best friend to make, especially after the debacle of the Suez Crisis left things with England and France on a questionable footing and with the Soviet Union supplying weapons to Israel's enemies. As one Israeli diplomat once put it, "The Almighty placed massive oil deposits under Arab soil. It is our good fortune that God placed five million Jews in America."[308] Thus Ben-Gurion knocked, because it was time for Israel to take its relationship with the US beyond simple economic support.

Ben-Gurion told Kennedy that there was a missile gap in Egypt's favor and that Egypt's new Soviet MiG-19's were superior to Israel's fleet of French-manufactured Super-Mystères. Thus if Egypt attacked, Israel would be at a deficit. The Hawk missile—whose name was an acronym for "Homing All the Way Killer"—was a ground-to-air defensive weapon that would home in on attacking jets and knock them out of the sky. Such a weapon could balance arms technology between the two countries and discourage a possible Egyptian offensive. Since it was also strictly a defensive weapon, it could not be used for another Suez-type Israeli invasion. As Shimon Peres would one day word it, they just wanted to ask President Kennedy for a few Hawks on behalf of Israel's doves.[309] Kennedy seemed to think that this sort of help to Israel might just be a possibility. He knew the full ramifications of the sale, so he knew it was a major step to a new relationship with Israel.

A Hawk sale would also set a precedent, however. The Hawk had a technologically advanced system that the US had not even made available to many of its allies. While the tactical necessity of Israel acquiring this weapon was the main discussion of the day, the symbolism of the sale was evident. This was much different than Eisenhower's "one time only" sale of anti-tank rifles. If Kennedy agreed to sell Israel the Hawks, he was letting Israel into the US's closest military confidence, throwing open the door for Israel to request anything else it wanted in the US arsenal. The arms embargo would be a thing of the past. Opinion ranges widely on why Kennedy seriously considered, and finally agreed to, this request.

During Kennedy's 1,036 days in office, he made several decisions in favor of the Jewish people. In 1961, he met in New York City with David Ben-Gurion. In their meeting, the prime minister shared with the president, "We are the remnant of a people struggling for its last hold of its existence. Israel is our last stop."[310] Throwing tradition to the wind, Kennedy decided to sell surface-to-air Hawk missiles to the Israelis to help defend against Arab attacks. He was the first president to do so, and in acquiescing to Ben-Gurion's request, defied the powerful and mostly anti-Semitic State Department and Pentagon. Then he tripled Israel's financial assistance from the United States.

The president seemed to understand what so many in the State Department refused to acknowledge: Tension between Israel and her

Arab neighbors was, and is, much more than a proliferation of arms. In his book *John F. Kennedy and Israel*, Herbert Druks wrote:

> The Arab leaders used Israel as their scapegoat and a means to gather popular support from their people. They claimed that all their troubles came from the fact that Israel existed. Instead of improving the life of their people in such countries as Egypt, Syria, Jordan, Lebanon, Arabia, Iraq, the Sudan and Libya they bought weapons with which to dominate and control other countries and to control their own people.
>
> For Israel it was a basic question of survival and not a desire to dominate or rule the world. It was not a question of an arms race. Israel needed weapons in order to protect itself from such countries as Egypt, Syria and Iraq that sought its annihilation.[311]

As president, Kennedy was the first to select two Jews for his cabinet—Secretary of Labor Arthur Goldberg and Secretary of Health, Education, and Welfare Abraham Ribicoff. A well-liked former governor of Connecticut, Ribicoff had served as a representative, and following his stint as a cabinet member would run for a Senate office. He served in that capacity until his retirement in 1981.

Goldberg was an important labor lawyer, who had graduated to the role of counsel for the AFL-CIO by the time JFK took office. He had played a supporting role in Jack's bid for the White House and would be rewarded with a Cabinet appointment. When Justice Felix Frankfurter chose to retire in 1962, Goldberg was tapped to fill the vacancy on the Supreme Court.

As a senator, one of Kennedy's first undertakings had been to support a resolution condemning the harsh treatment of Jews in the Soviet Union. In September 1963, just months after his inauguration, President

Kennedy flew to New York to address the UN General Assembly on that topic. He admonished those present that:

> Man does not live by bread alone and the members of this organization are committed by the Charter to promote and respect human rights. Those rights are not respected when a Buddhist priest is driven from his pagoda, when a synagogue is shut down, when a Protestant church cannot open a mission, when a Cardinal is forced into hiding, or when a crowded church service is bombed.[312]

Just before that fateful trip to Dallas, Lewis H. Weinstein, a major political contributor and friend from Boston, visited Kennedy in the Oval Office. He was there to talk about doing more to secure freedoms for Soviet Jewry. Weinstein reminded the president that no chief executive since Theodore Roosevelt had done anything to intervene with the Soviet leaders on the behalf of Russian Jews. When the two men parted, it was with Kennedy's promise that when he returned from his trip to Texas, he would set up a conference in the capital to discuss the Soviet Jews who were being deprived permission to exercise their religious beliefs. The president would not live to fulfill the vow to his old friend. He had, however, proved to be the friend of the Jews that his father was not.

While riding through Dallas in a motorcade that was to take the President and First Lady Jacqueline to the Dallas Trade Mart to address those assembled on the topic of national security, Kennedy was assassinated in Dealey Plaza. Texas Governor John Connally was also wounded. The Warren Commission established by Lyndon Johnson would conclude that the president was shot by Lee Harvey Oswald, a disgruntled American citizen with ties to Russia. Oswald would be gunned down while in police custody by a local Dallas bar owner, Jack Ruby.

The casket of John Fitzgerald Kennedy, the thirty-fifth president of the United States would lie in repose in the East Room of the White House. His casket then was borne to the Capitol Rotunda, where he lay in state until moved to St. Matthew's Cathedral for the funeral service, then his body was transported by caisson to Arlington National Cemetery, where today a simple eternal flame marks the site of his burial.

The Saturday before the funeral, Rabbi Levi Olan of Temple Emanu-El in Dallas eulogized the fallen president as his congregation sat in all-consuming grief and shock. It was unbelievable that this tragedy had happened, and in their city.

In Jerusalem, a memorial stands with the name of John F. Kennedy emblazoned over the door. It resembles a large tree hewn down before its time. Fifty-one columns rise from the base of the monument, each symbolizing the fifty states of the union and one indicating the District of Columbia. Inside the memorial is a bust of the fallen president with an eternal flame rising from its center. The memorial was funded by contributions from Jewish organizations in the United States. Adjacent to the memorial is the Kennedy Peace Forest, filled with beautiful trees. Israel remembers those who have made contributions in support of the Jewish people and the home of her rebirth.

While in Dallas with President Kennedy and riding only two cars behind on that fateful day, Vice President Lyndon Baines Johnson (LBJ) would within hours become the chief executive of the United States. As the crowds gathered around Parkland Memorial Hospital awaiting word of President Kennedy's condition, Johnson was rushed back to Love Field to board Air Force One. Two hours and eight minutes after the assassination of John F. Kennedy, Johnson was sworn in—flanked by Lady Bird Johnson on his right and Jacqueline Kennedy on his left.[313] Federal Judge Sarah T. Hughes, a friend of the Johnsons, would make history on that date: She became the first—and so far the only—woman to swear in a US president. LBJ was also the only president to be sworn in to office on Texas soil—albeit stained with the blood of his predecessor. A Catholic missal was substituted for the Bible, as none could be found on the martyred president's plane.[314]

Born in Stonewall, Texas, in 1908, to a mother from a long line of Baptist preachers, Lyndon gained his early education from his mother and was greatly influenced by the biblical beliefs of his forebears. His father, Sam Johnson Jr., was a Christadelphian. Like many earlier presidents, Lyndon had been taught of the Jews' place in antiquity and of their heritage in Palestine. It was, perhaps, because of his early childhood instruction that he was so amenable to surrounding himself with the best of American Jewish leaders.

In 1918, at the age of ten, Lyndon eagerly told his father that one day he would be president of the United States. He could not have known how true that statement would be or under what tragic circumstances he would attain the office. From a childhood wish to a stunning reality, from a farm in central Texas to a career in politics, LBJ rose from shoeshine boy to representative to senator to vice president, and from there was catapulted into the limelight as the 36th president of the United States.

As Johnson shouldered the responsibilities of office, he also had to walk the tightrope of emotions that besieged the country. The prince was dead; Camelot was without its leader. While LBJ was known as a wheeler-dealer, neither he nor Lady Bird possessed the charisma and *savoir faire* of the Kennedys. However, having navigated the tricky halls of Congress for years, Johnson began to push through some of the late president's programs—particularly those surrounding civil rights and antipoverty. During those battles, LBJ was accompanied by numerous Jewish supporters and advisers.

One of Johnson's staunchest Jewish supporters was Abraham (Abe) Fortas, a powerful Yale lawyer and protégée of William O. Douglas. Fortas had served as undersecretary of the interior under FDR and was later appointed by Truman to sit on various delegations during organizational meetings of the United Nations in San Francisco. He also represented the United States at the 1946 General Assembly meeting in London.[315]

Fortas has been credited with assisting Johnson in his political achievements more than any other individual. Impressed by LBJ's management of his appointment as chairman of the Naval Affairs Subcommittee (established to investigate misuse in the conduct of naval operations), Fortas and then-congressman Johnson became fast friends. It was during the run for the Senate that Johnson called on Fortas for assistance. Having beaten challenger Coke Stevenson for the seat by only eighty-seven votes, this caused the election to be contested. Johnson asked his old friend Fortas to represent him. Fortas was successful, and Johnson was labeled with the moniker "Landslide Lyndon." Johnson called again upon Fortas in 1965 to fill Arthur Goldberg's vacant seat on the Supreme Court.

In 1964, President Johnson was approached by Israeli Ambassador Abraham Harman, who had been advised by Prime Minister Levi Eshkol to seek a military alliance with the United States. The president replied that such a treaty was unnecessary, as America was committed to Israel's security, a pledge recognized by other world powers and Arab countries. When Egypt closed the Straight of Tiran to ships bound for Haifa and to Israeli ships seeking passage, Prime Minister Eshkol sought Johnson's assistance. After conferring with former President Eisenhower, LBJ reiterated that the Israelis were guaranteed the "right of access to the Gulf of Aqaba" and that this "was definitely part of the 'commitment' we had made to them . . . the Gulf of Aqaba is an international waterway and the blockade of Israeli shipping is, therefore, illegal."[316]

Even as Johnson contemplated Nasser's move, the grandson of Winston Churchill, another Winston, was interviewing David Ben-Gurion at the King David Hotel in Jerusalem. A Kol Israel radio newsman announced the closure of the Strait. The Egyptian leader had effectively severed Israel's lifeline for oil imports. According to Winston:

Ben-Gurion, with a gesture of the hand, ordered his assistant to switch off the radio and, shaking his great mane of white hair gravely, declared with sorrow: "This means war. I am very frightened. Not for Israel, for she will survive—we cannot afford otherwise—but for the younger generation. It is always the best of their generation who never return."[317]

Israel was ultimately forced to take action against Nasser and the countries that backed him. In six days during June of 1967, the Israelis blitzed the Arab armies. Not only were they victorious in the conflict, but Jerusalem was once again reunited and in Jewish hands. Israeli commander Motta Gur expressed the feelings of a grateful nation:

> For some two thousand years the Temple Mount was forbidden to the Jews. . . . The Western Wall, for which every heart beats, is ours once again. Many Jews have taken their lives into their hands throughout our long history, in order to reach Jerusalem and live here. Endless words of longing have expressed the deep yearning for Jerusalem that beats within the Jewish heart. You have been given the great privilege of completing the circle, of returning to the nation its capital and its holy center ... Jerusalem is yours forever.[318]

Johnson was aided during his White House years by a number of highly placed Jewish Americans. Those included some of the nation's best legal minds: Arthur J. Goldberg, whom Johnson persuaded to resign his Supreme Court position and assume the role of ambassador to the UN; Sheldon Stanley Cohen, to whom LBJ turned to put his affairs in order following the assassination of Kennedy; Eric Frederick Goldman, who became a special consultant to the president; and Professor David

Riesman, whom he appointed as undersecretary of the Department of Health, Education, and Welfare, and who assisted with the Medicare and Medicaid programs. Johnson depended heavily on these gifted American Jews to assist him in carrying out his various programs.

One of LBJ's great disappointments was a scandal that broke when he nominated Abe Fortas to succeed Chief Justice Earl Warren. It was revealed that Fortas had accepted an annual stipend of twenty thousand dollars to serve on the board of a charity foundation headed by Louis E. Wolfson. A hue and cry arose because Wolfson had been incarcerated for stock manipulation. Not only was the tainted Fortas rejected for the seat of chief justice, he was forced to resign from the highest court in the land.

Johnson eschewed a second full term as president due to opposition surrounding his handling of the Vietnam War. When Robert Kennedy decided to seek the Democratic presidential nomination, Johnson announced that he would bow out of the contest. He stunned the nation with his announcement, "I shall not seek, and I will not accept, the nomination of my party for another term as your president."

He chose instead to retire to his ranch on the Pedernales River in the heart of the Texas Hill Country. Almost four years to the day following the inauguration of Richard M. Nixon, Lyndon Baines Johnson died of a heart attack while en route from his ranch to San Antonio. He is buried in the Johnson Family Cemetery on the ranch grounds.

(30)

RICHARD M. NIXON *and* GERALD FORD ACT *on* ISRAEL'S BEHALF

Yet you do not know what your life will be like tomorrow.
You are just a vapor that appears for
a little while and then vanishes away,"
(Isaiah 2:4, NKJV)

PRESIDENT RICHARD M. NIXON,
1969, 1973 INAUGURAL SCRIPTURE

Richard Milhous Nixon succeeded Lyndon Johnson as 37th president of the United States. He was born in Yorba Linda, California, to Quaker parents. His family moved to Whittier when Richard was nine, and his education culminated in a law degree from Duke University. In 1940, he married Thelma (Pat) Ryan and joined the navy during World War II. Upon resigning his commission in 1945, he and Pat returned to Whittier.

The Republican Party in California tapped Nixon to run against US Representative Jerry Voorhis. Nixon won the election and in 1947 began his political career in Washington, D.C. In 1950, he took a seat in the Senate, and because of his age (39), his strong stance against the advancement of Communism, and the size of his California political base, he was selected to run as Dwight D. Eisenhower's vice presidential candidate. The ticket won the election.

After the inauguration, Eisenhower broke with tradition—that of a vice president being mostly an honorary position—and assigned specific duties to Nixon. Irwin Gellman, who recorded the Nixon years in Congress, wrote also of his stint as vice president:

> Eisenhower radically altered the role of his running mate by presenting him with critical assignments in both foreign and domestic affairs once he assumed his office. The vice president welcomed the president's initiatives and worked energetically to accomplish White House objectives. Because of the collaboration between these two leaders, Nixon deserves the title, "the first modern vice president."[319]

Though groomed to succeed Eisenhower, Nixon lost the 1960 presidential election to the handsome and charismatic John F. Kennedy. Then, after Lyndon Johnson's refusal to run for a second full term as president, Nixon ran against and defeated Hubert H. Humphrey in 1968.

Having been painted as anti-Semitic in his early years, and with some corroborating evidence, Nixon somehow managed to disguise his wariness of Jewish people. Despite this bent, he scoured the country for the brightest and best Jewish minds and welcomed them into his administration. These included Leonard Garment, a liberal Democrat who assisted the newly elected president with cabinet selections; Arthur Burns, an economic advisor who served as White House Council and was later appointed to the post of chairman of the Federal Reserve; William Safire, a speechwriter and later a Pulitzer Prize–winning journalist; and Heinz Albert (Henry) Kissinger, a foreign policy advisor and later secretary of state.

In the annals of support for Israel, Nixon is perhaps best noted among American presidents for having literally saved that nation during the 1973 Yom Kippur War. Accounts of the activities which took place in the White House and Pentagon on that defining day in 1973 are as varied as the two men who were the main rivals: Secretary of State Kissinger and Secretary of Defense James Schlesinger. What is known from the differing accounts is that President Nixon was the catalyst.

On October 6, Yom Kippur, the Day of Atonement and holiest day of the Jewish year, the Arab Coalition, comprised of Egypt, Syria, and Jordan, struck Israel with a sneak attack in the hope of finally driving the Jews into the Mediterranean. Israel was tragically caught off-guard, as most of its citizenry were in synagogues, and its national radio was off the air. Because people were enjoying a restful day of reflection and prayer, Israel had no immediate response to the coordinated attacks. Israeli intelligence had not seen the assault coming, and the military was ill-prepared for war.

At the outset of hostilities, Egypt attacked across the Suez Canal. The battle raged for three days with Egyptian forces advancing nearly unopposed into the Sinai Peninsula. By the third day, Israel had mobilized its forces and halted the Egyptian army, resulting in a stalemate. On the northern border, Syria launched an offensive on the Golan Heights. The initial assault was successful but quickly lost momentum. By the third day of fighting, several thousand Israeli soldiers were killed. More Israeli soldiers fell on that first day than in the entire Six-Day War of 1967. Forty-nine planes, one-third (more than five hundred) of her tank force, and a good chunk of the buffer lands gained in the Six-Day War were also lost. The Israelis seemed to be on the brink of another holocaust.

On the fourth day of the war, Prime Minister Golda Meir reportedly opened up several silos and pointed the nuclear-tipped missiles toward Egyptian and Syrian military headquarters near Cairo and Damascus.[320] Army Chief of Staff Moshe Dayan was reported to have said, "This is the end of the Third Temple," in one of the crucial meetings. Later he told the press, "The situation is desperate. Everything is lost. We must withdraw."[321]

In Washington, Nixon intervened in inter-cabinet squabbles between Kissinger and Schlesinger and lit a fire under those who were inundated by legislative lethargy. As preoccupied as he was with Watergate about which more is written later, Nixon came straight to the point, announcing that Israel must not lose the war. He ordered that the deliveries of supplies, including aircraft, be sped up and that Israel be told that it could freely expend all of its consumables (ammunition, spare parts, fuel, and so forth) in the certain knowledge that these would be completely replenished by the United States without delay. Earlier in his presidency, "Nixon made it clear he believed warfare was inevitable in the Middle East, a war that could spread and precipitate World War III, with the United States and the Soviet Union squaring off against each other."[322] He was now staring down the barrel of that war.

Nixon's insistence that armaments be airlifted to Israel to ensure her victory was because the president assigned a great sense of exigency to the task. He said, "You get the stuff to Israel. Now. Now!"[323] White House aide Alexander Haig said of Nixon's focus on Israel:

> As soon as the scope and pattern of Israeli battle losses emerged, Nixon ordered that all destroyed equipment be made up out of US stockpiles, using the very best weapons America possessed . . . . Whatever it takes, he told Kissinger . . . save Israel. The president asked Kissinger for a precise accounting of Israel's military needs, and Kissinger proceeded to read aloud from an itemized list. "Double it," Nixon ordered. "Now get the hell out of here and get the job done."[324]

In a *Jerusalem Post* editorial, Nixon insider Leonard Garment was quoted as saying: "It was Nixon who did it. I was there. As [bureaucratic bickering between the State and Defense departments] was going back and forth, Nixon said, 'This is insane . . . .' He just ordered Kissinger, 'Get your [behind] out of here and tell those people to move.'"[325]

Secretary of Defense Schlesinger suggested that the United States dispatch three transports loaded with war materiel in what became known as "Operation Nickel Grass." When he presented the proposal to the president, Nixon angrily sent the secretary to do his bidding. When Kissinger returned later to explain yet another delay in the president's orders being carried out, Nixon snapped that the delayed planes were to get off the runway immediately.

Every available American plane transported conventional arms to Israel. The resulting supply to defend Israel was larger than the Berlin airlift that had followed World War II, and it literally turned the tide of the war. Nixon's quick action saved Israel from almost certain extermination and the world from possible nuclear war. He had carried Kennedy's agreement to militarily support Israel to the next logical level—a full military alliance.

The Israel Defense Forces (IDF) launched a counteroffensive within the week and drove the Syrians to within twenty-five miles of Damascus. Trying to aid the Syrians, the Egyptian army went on the offensive, all to no avail. Israeli troops crossed the Suez Canal and encompassed the Egyptian Third Army. When the Soviets realized what was happening, they scrambled to further assist Egypt and Syria. The Soviet threat was so real Nixon feared direct conflict with the USSR and elevated all military personnel worldwide to DefCon III, meaning increased readiness that war was likely. However, a ceasefire was finally worked out between the United States and the USSR, adopted by all parties involved, and the Yom Kippur War—called the Ramadan War by Muslims—was ended.

There are those who ascertain that Nixon acted only because of the threatened use of nuclear weapons by the original "Iron Lady," Golda Meir. That is rebutted by Mordechai Gazit, who thought Israel's relationship with the United States was not solidified sufficiently for

Nixon to have been so manipulated by Meir. It was J. J. Goldberg in his book *Jewish Power*, who wrote:

> [John F.] Kennedy initiated the first US arms sales to Israel . . . Johnson continued and intensified Kennedy's policy of warmth toward Israel. . . . In 1966 Johnson approved the first sale of American warplanes to Israel.
>
> Nonetheless, it remained for Richard Nixon, a Republican elected with little Jewish support, to create a now-familiar US-Israel alliance of more recent decades. It was Nixon who made Israel the largest recipient of US foreign aid; Nixon who initiated the policy of virtually limitless US weapons sales to Israel. The notion of Israel as a strategic asset to the United States, not just a moral commitment, was Nixon's innovation.[326]

Israeli President Chaim Herzog, when asked about Nixon's anti-Semitism, responded with: "He supplied arms and unflinching support when our very existence would have been in danger without them. Let his comments be set against his actions. And I'll choose actions over words any day of the week."[327]

Wily as he was, Richard Nixon had no misconceptions regarding how his role in the Israel airlift would be regarded by historians. By the time he was called upon to provide a means of assistance to the State of Israel, his administration was embroiled in the Watergate Scandal, the resignation of Vice President Spiro Agnew, and Nixon's impending impeachment.

In the summer of 1973, Agnew came under investigation by the US Attorney's office in Maryland; the charges: tax fraud, conspiracy, bribery, and extortion. He was eventually charged with having accepted bribes of over $100,000 during his tenures as a Baltimore County Executive, Governor of Maryland, and Vice President of the United States. In

October of that year, he was allowed to enter a plea of no contest to only one charge: failure to report $29,500 in income. He was instructed to resign from the office of vice president. Nixon named as his replacement: House Majority Leader Gerald Ford.

Nixon, too, left office under a swirling cloud of darkness following the eruption of the scandal which exploded due to the June 1972 break-in and burglary of the Watergate Complex in Washington, DC. The attempted cover-up by the president elicited threats of a Senate trial. On August 8, 1974, Nixon, accompanied by his family, made a television appearance to announce that he would resign his office and relinquish duties to Vice President Gerald Ford. A month later the Nixon family returned to San Clemente, California, and President Gerald Ford issued a "full, free, and absolute pardon."[328] When the dust from the debacle had settled, forty-three people had been tried, convicted and imprisoned—many of them Nixon's top aides.

Despite his exile from politics, Nixon was ultimately viewed as an elder statesman, his advice enthusiastically sought. On April 18, 1994, Richard Milhous Nixon suffered a severe stroke and died four days later. He was buried on the grounds of the Nixon Library in Yorba Linda. History has been kind to the former president, although the final chapter remains unwritten, but perhaps his greatest accolade came from Prime Minister Golda Meir:

> However history judges Richard Nixon—and it is probable that the verdict will be very harsh—it must also be put on the record forever that he did not break a single one of the promises he made to us.[329]

★ ★ ★

Upon Richard Nixon's resignation, Vice President Gerald R. Ford was sworn in as 38th president of the United States. Shortly after assuming his duties in the White House, Ford reassured the Israelis:

> America must and will pursue friendship with all nations. But, this will never be done at the expense of America's commitment to Israel. A strong Israel is essential to a stable peace in the Middle East. Our commitment to Israel will meet the test of American stead, fairness, and resolve. My administration will not be found wanting. The United States will continue to help Israel provide for her security. My dedication to Israel's future goes beyond its military needs to a far higher priority the need for peace. My commitment to the security and future of Israel is based upon basic morality as well as enlightened self-interest. Our role in supporting Israel honors our own heritage.[330]

President Ford was deeply concerned about those issues supported by Jews in America, among them the treatment of Jews in Soviet Russia. In an attempt to alleviate their suffering, Ford signed the Jackson–Vanik Amendment, which bestowed Most Favored Nation status on those countries that agreed to honor basic human rights. It provided an additional tool to seek the freedom of Jews under the thumb of the Soviets.

President Ford was unashamed of his overt support for the State of Israel. During a news conference on October 20, 1976, he reiterated:

> The United States is dedicated to the security and survival of Israel. The three million Israelis—they're a democratic state in an area where democracy doesn't flourish. . . . since I have been president . . . the Ford administration has either granted or sold about $2.5

billion worth of military equipment to the State of Israel. And the net result is, today Israel is stronger militarily than it was prior to the Yom Kippur War because of the support of the Ford administration.[331]

In addition to military support, Ford achieved some success in opposing an Arab boycott against companies trading with Israel. Writer Amy Goldstein aptly summed up the Ford presidency and his ties with Israel:

> While no person or President is perfect, President Ford's actions on behalf of the Jewish people (including the Helsinki Accords) during his presidency, and then his grace to stay out of the public debate afterwards, continues to be a stark contrast to the actions of his successor—both during and after his tenure.[332]

Ford would complete Nixon's term of office, but then lose his quest for a second full term to Washington outsider James Earl (Jimmy) Carter Jr. in 1976. After attending the inaugural of Jimmy Carter, Ford retired to his home in Rancho Mirage, California, with his wife, Betty. He pursued his hobbies of golf and tennis, and in 1981 attended the state funeral of Anwar Sadat in Cairo. He was once again thrust into the public limelight in 1994, when he was called upon to speak at the funeral of Richard M. Nixon.

When Gerald Ford died on December 26, 2006, he had reached a milestone unachieved by any other president: At the age of ninety-three years, he was the longest-lived among all his predecessors by 165 days. Because Ford had been selected to replace disgraced Vice President Spiro Agnew, he bore the label of being the first and only US leader never to have been elected as president or vice president. He is buried on the grounds of his presidential museum in Grand Rapids, Michigan.

(31)

JAMES EARL (JIMMY)
CARTER: PALESTINIAN
CHAMPION

"He has shown you, O man, what good;
And what does the LORD require of you But to do justly,
To love mercy, And to walk humbly with your God?"
(Micah 6:8, NKJV)

PRESIDENT JAMES EARL (JIMMY) CARTER,
1977 INAUGURAL SCRIPTURE

Jimmy Carter, successor to Gerald Ford, rocketed to the top of the charts as the number one advocate denying a most elementary right, that of self-determination for the Jewish people—despite his flowery platitudes to the opposite. In 1980, President Carter avowed:

> I am opposed to an independent Palestinian state, because in my own judgment and in the judgment of many leaders in the Middle East, including Arab leaders, this would be a destabilizing factor in the Middle East and would certainly not serve the United States interests. [333]

Since relinquishing the Oval Office to his successor, Carter had been able to achieve what others before him—and especially his good friend the late Yasser Arafat—had failed to do: define Israel's governing guidelines as "apartheid." Introducing this blatant racism into Israel's struggle for survival had been a work in progress for the former chief executive and a tribute to his determination to view the world only through his own narrow-mindedness. How did Jimmy Carter, a devout Southern Baptist deacon and Sunday school teacher, a man well versed in Scripture, reach this apex of error? How did he develop such a determined "blame Israel for everything" position? Perhaps a brief look at his life and the evolution of his beliefs will answer those questions.[334]

Jimmy's father, James Earl Carter Sr., landed in Plains, Georgia, when his father, Alton, decided to move the family to the small town in southwest Georgia. "Mr. Earl," as Jimmy's father was known around town, was an astute businessman. His ventures in peanut farming, forestry, and a small grocery made him successful, if not rich. He was a well-known local figure, and like other farmers in Georgia and elsewhere, worked hard for his living. It is likely the elder Carter could well sympathize with author and poet Andrew Nelson Lytle, who wrote: "A farm is not a place to grow wealthy; it is a place to grow corn."[335]

In his book *The Real Jimmy Carter*, Steven Hayward describes the area in which the future president grew into manhood:

> "Jimmy Carter . . . was the first American president to be born in a hospital . . . about the only modern appurtenance of Plains . . . There were few paved roads. Plains, with a population of about six hundred when Jimmy Carter was born, wouldn't get electricity for another ten years."[336]

Perhaps it was Carter's mother, the acerbic and outspoken Miss Lillian, who had the greater impact on the future president. Miss Lillian Gordy married James Earl Carter Sr. in 1923, the same year she completed her nurse's training in Atlanta. Jimmy, the eldest, was born in 1924. His three siblings, Gloria (1926), Ruth (1929), and Billy (1937), would all achieve some fame (or notoriety), but none would reach the pinnacle of the elder sibling. One of Miss Lillian's most famous quotes may have been the result of her exasperation with some of her children's antics. Said the witty lady: "Sometimes when I look at all my children, I say to myself, 'Lillian, you should have stayed a virgin.'"[337]

Jimmy rose through the ranks of local and state politics to become the 39th president of the United States. Along the way, he would realize a number of "firsts." He was the first president to graduate from the United States Naval Academy, and, so far, the first native-born Georgian to become president, the first president from the Deep South, the first president to walk with wife, Rosalynn, from the East Portico of the Capitol Building down Pennsylvania Avenue to the White House on the day of his inauguration, the first (and only) president to be interviewed by *Playboy* magazine, the first president to report an attack by a "killer" rabbit,[338] and one of only two presidents[339] to report a UFO sighting.

What is even more astounding about former president Carter is that he feels his short and arguably failed attempt at governing the United States somehow endows him with great influence in the world arena. This is the same man that, in his early days of campaigning for the White House, elicited the response, "Jimmy who?" Perhaps the better question would have been: "Jimmy? Why?" Even then Carter's duplicitous approach was evident. The ever-grinning Carter was an enigma. Journalist Bill Moyers observed: "In a ruthless business, Mr. Carter is a ruthless operator, even if he wears his broad smile and displays his Southern charm."[340]

After graduating high school in Plains, Carter attended Georgia Tech and Jackson State University. He received an appointment to the United States Naval Academy, from which he graduated with a BS degree in physics. In the summer of 1946, James Earl Carter Jr. married his sweetheart, Rosalynn Smith, following a one-year courtship. After graduation, he was assigned to a series of ships and diesel submarines in the Atlantic and Pacific fleets.

While Carter has claimed he was interested in politics at the young age of eight, he showed no real proclivity for political leadership during his high school years. His only stab at politics in college was an aborted run for class president during his freshman year. When asked about Carter's early political aspirations, an unnamed Naval Academy classmate replied:

> He didn't show any signs of greatness, and I don't recall that he held any strong political or religious views. . . . I think we were all amazed when he became governor of Georgia, and positively astounded when he ran effectively for president.[341]

At first blush it is incomprehensible to think of Jimmy Carter, the lay-preacher from Plains, Georgia, as being anti-Semitic. After all, he had read the same Scriptures that confirmed Christian Zionists have read; when and where did he make the leap from Bible-believer to enemy of the Jewish people? Was it during the Camp David talks, when he was ensconced with Menachem Begin and Anwar Sadat? Was it the Israeli prime minister's intractability when it came to giving away Israel in order for Mr. Carter to achieve his goal of a peace treaty? After all, one would have thought Mr. Carter and Mr. Begin would have been able to meet on common ground: the Bible. When I interviewed Mr. Begin in 1980, I asked him about his Bible study, and he eagerly explained:

> When we face our various problems, we should always strive to live by the Bible. That is true for all of humanity. This is the book which has kept the Jewish people alive—that is my belief. And I am proud to quote the Bible in substantiation of our rights. If anyone brings

it up, I tell them I plead guilty of quoting the Bible on matters of public policy, but I don't apologize. [David] Ben-Gurion had a wonderful saying . . . "Some people say that the mandate is our Bible, but it is not. The Bible is our mandate." And you know something? Every time you read the Bible, you find something new. Every Saturday night a group of sages gather in my home and we study the Bible together. And every time we find something new. The Book which has been studied for thousands of years by great rabbis, professors and sages still yields something new each time you study it. It's wonderful.[342]

Was it at Camp David that the president, despite their common leanings, developed his almost megalomaniacal determination to force a peace agreement—no matter the cost to Israel? We may never know; but what we do know is that no assessment of Carter would be complete without exposing a detractor who seems determined that the long-coveted and long-awaited Jewish homeland will become nothing but a memory in the Middle East.

Perhaps the answer lies in Mr. Carter's personal feelings and events that were set in motion prior to the Camp David meetings over the settlement issue. The president claimed that Prime Minister Begin had agreed to halt settlement construction prior to the meeting with Sadat, that he was open to giving up part of Jerusalem. The truth lies elsewhere.

On the subject of dividing Jerusalem, Mr. Carter wrote in his book *Palestine: Peace Not Apartheid* that Menachem Begin viewed the possibility favorably. Nothing could have been more inaccurate. Mr. Begin gave me a copy of a letter he had written to President Carter on September 17, 1978. In the letter, Begin penned, "On the basis of this law, the government of Israel decreed in July 1967 that Jerusalem is one city indivisible, the capital of the State of Israel."[343] That doesn't sound like Mr. Begin wished to divide Jerusalem to placate Mr. Carter. I refuted

Mr. Carter's assertions regarding Prime Minister Begin both in a review posted on Amazon.com and in my book *Jimmy Carter: The Liberal Left and World Chaos.*

The former president also wrote that Begin had agreed to a freeze on building Jewish settlements. Again, apparently not true. Begin told me he had only agreed to a three-month moratorium on building, from September 17 to December 17, 1978. Emory University professor and historian Kenneth Stein clarifies the issue:

> During his tenure as prime minister, Begin forbade the negotiation agenda to include the West Bank and those portions of Jerusalem that the Israeli government annexed after the 1967 Six-Day War. This refusal to negotiate became Carter's core disagreement with Begin .... With Begin not offering a fallback position, Carter could not initiate a conclusive Israel-Palestinian negotiating process. He never forgave Begin.[344]

The letter written by Prime Minister Begin to President Jimmy Carter on September 17, 1978, plainly stated Israel's stance toward relinquishing any territory, especially that in Jerusalem. In the letter, Begin penned:

> I have the honor to inform you, Mr. President, that on 28 June 1967 Israel's parliament (The Knesset) promulgated and adopted a law to the effect: "the Government is empowered by a decree to apply the law, the jurisdiction and administration of the State to any part of Eretz Israel (Land of Israel Palestine), as stated in that decree."
>
> On the basis of this law, the government of Israel decreed *in July 1967* that Jerusalem is one city indivisible, the capital of the State of Israel.[345] (Emphasis mine.)

Mr. Begin did not wish to divide Jerusalem or relinquish any land simply to placate Mr. Carter. Perhaps it must also have been a bit hard to swallow when both Begin and Sadat were awarded the Nobel Peace Prize for their efforts at Camp David, while Jimmy was overlooked.

At this writing, Carter is the oldest living former president and the Democratic Party's elder statesman, and he never overlooks an occasion to openly malign the State of Israel. He advocates the most extreme form of a Palestinian state—one that would succeed in wiping Israel from the map leaving Hamas, Fatah, and the Palestinian Authority in charge.

In his post-White House days, Jimmy Carter became quite adept at legitimizing terror and championing Yasser Arafat, the long-time PLO leader. The two first met in Paris in 1990 at the Hotel de Crillon for a ninety-minute session. According to a euphoric Carter, "He [Arafat] has done everything possible these last months to promote the [Middle East] peace process. He's explored all the possibilities to make progress toward a total peace settlement."[346] Arafat welcomed Carter with open arms. Why not? After all, Arafat was engaged in dialogue with the man Anwar Sadat considered a brother, the man who was the highest-level American to have met with him. It mattered not that Carter was a *former* president; it mattered only that he was sympathetic to the Palestinian leader's cause.

Israelis were appalled at Carter's fawning over Arafat, the man who just days before had been acting the sycophant to Saddam Hussein in Baghdad. During his visit to Iraq, Arafat had spewed his hate-filled rhetoric, designed to enrage the Arab world against Israel. Furthermore, he had threatened Israel with attacks using Baghdad's al-Abed missiles. In 2007, Carter was interviewed on Al-Jazeera Arab television. During the interview, the former president admitted: "Well, I don't really consider, I wasn't equating the Palestinian missiles with terrorism."[347] Perhaps that is why Arafat's threats from Baghdad were of so little concern to Mr. Carter.

Despite Arafat's record of murderous terrorist activities, Carter chose to embrace him. In fact, he went so far as to assist Arafat with writing a generic speech to be delivered to Western audiences. Carter's advice to

Arafat was to try to drum up as much sympathy as possible from world leaders and to show Israel in as bad a light as possible, as often as possible. He gave the PLO leader specific examples, sympathetic illustrations that could be changed or embellished to suit the audience in question.[348] This aid from Carter came regardless of the fact that, in 1980, Arafat bawled, "Peace for us means the destruction of Israel. We are preparing for an all-out war, a war which will last for generations."[349]

During his more recent visits to the Middle East, Carter has worked to build a bridge with the leaders of Hamas, who support the myths found in *The Protocols* and refuse to acknowledge a Jewish state. The former president has met with Khaled Mashaal, Hamas' exiled leader numerous times in Damascus. His last meeting with Mashaal took place during the final days of the George W. Bush administration. Mr. Carter openly defied the US State Department in order to visit with the terrorist leader, and he believes Hamas must be included in any peace negotiations. What a travesty of justice and what a slap in the face to the Israelis, who have long been targeted by Hamas rockets and terror attacks!

Apparently, Mr. Carter's playing footsie with Palestinian terrorists has paid off. He added another "honor" to his miniscule list of achievements when he was awarded the Palestine International Award for Excellence and Creativity. The dubious tribute was certainly well deserved. Carter has been very creative in his support for the terrorists that surround Israel. In his acceptance speech, he promised to support the campaign for an independent Palestinian state to the death. He also implored the Palestinians to halt internal strife. Was the implied intent that of uniting the warring factions into one cohesive unit in order to better attack their Jewish neighbors?

Said the former president in his speech, "I have been in love with the Palestinian people for many years," and he indicated that his family shared his devotion: "I have two great-grandsons that are rapidly learning about the people here and the anguish and suffering and deprivation of human rights that you have experienced ever since 1948."[350] Mr. Carter doesn't seem to share the same sympathy for the Jewish people, whose history has been riddled with pogroms, hate crimes, the Holocaust, and a continual struggle to survive as a nation surrounded by enemies. In his closing comments after receiving the award, Carter pledged his "assistance, as long as I live, to win your freedom, your independence, your sovereignty and a good life."[351]

Carter's push to be on the cusp of the birth of a Palestinian state reached a new pinnacle in September 2011, when he openly backed an attempt by Palestinian President Mahmoud Abbas to secure statehood recognition in the United Nations. Had such a move been successful, it would have negated all attempts to reach a peaceful agreement negotiated by the Israelis and Palestinians. Carter applauded the move and said recognition would be a step forward. Apparently, a world without Israel is preferable—by hook or by crook.

Carter has carried his Liberal Left political invective far beyond his presidency. He seems to have forgotten that as a citizen he still represents the United States, even though he doesn't rise every morning and trek downstairs to the Oval Office. Jimmy Carter's popularity seems to be at its height among those despots whose hatred of America is legendary. He is a man who considers himself to have been an ideal president and whose term was simply "unfinished." Carter has inserted his opinions in countries around the world, and in so doing has managed to regularly and repeatedly speak ill of those elected by the majority of Americans to conduct business on their behalf. Only time will determine if Jimmy Carter was this nation's worst ex-president, but the current consensus of opinion is that, at the moment, he holds exclusive rights to that appellation.

Has former president James Earl Carter, Jr. become a unifying force for peace, as he hoped he might, or has he become the divisive, sanctimonious, pacifist many see? In his book *Palestine: Peace Not Apartheid*, the former president summed up his proposal for peace in the Middle East:

It is imperative that the general Arab community and all significant Palestinian groups make it clear that they will end the suicide bombings and other acts of terrorism when international laws and the ultimate goals of the Roadmap for Peace[352] are accepted by Israel.[353]

Discord and wrangling still follow him nearly thirty years down the road from the White House. It is the sound of meaningless noise like a "noisy gong or a clanging cymbal," (1 Corinthians 13:1, NLT.) It grates on the nerves of any true believer in Jesus Christ, those who understand the biblical importance of Israel and who love the Jewish people.

Carter's Liberal Left policies during his administration and his outspokenness against things American since departing 1600 Pennsylvania Avenue should leave no skepticism regarding his past performance. It should, in fact, be a red flag to every American: Don't take the Carter road ever again. It is infinitely sad that Mr. Carter has allowed his bias and resentment against Israel to skew the facts and produce an erroneous interpretation of Israeli actions.

(32)

RONALD REAGAN: *a* FAITHFUL FRIEND

" . . . if my people, who are called by my name,
will humble themselves and pray and seek my face and
turn from their wicked ways, then I will hear from heaven,
and I will forgive their sin and will heal their land,"
(II Chronicles 7:14, NIV)

PRESIDENT RONALD WILSON REAGAN, 1981, 1985
INAUGURAL SCRIPTURE

The past several decades, especially those surrounding the rebirth of Israel, have produced US presidents most of whom were pro-Israel. None equaled or surpassed the 40th president of the United States, Ronald Wilson Reagan. He was, perhaps, the best friend of Israel ever to sit behind the desk in the Oval Office.

When the dust had settled following Reagan's 1980 election, it was obvious that the Iranian hostage situation[354] had aided his cause. As he placed his hand on his mother's Bible, open to 2 Chronicles 7:14,[355] the 52 American hostages that had been held in Iran for 444 days were released. As I watched the events unfold, I reminisced about a meeting I had had with Reuven Hecht and Isser Harel (head of Mossad from

1951 to 1963). I had asked Harel whom he thought would be the next US president. He responded:

> The word on the streets is that terrorists might have a say about that. They are going to attempt to influence your elections by releasing the hostages precisely when Reagan is sworn into office. They want Carter out because of his challenges to Islam.

The former intelligence officer was referring to the Camp David accords, and to Carter's advice that Sadat give a speech in Egypt stating that religion and politics must be separate. This speech was heard by a blind cleric named al-Rahman who issued the Fatwa to assassinate Sadat. It was carried out on October 6, 1981.[356]

Another factor in Reagan's victory was the support of approximately twenty million pro-Israel Christians. Those fundamentalist stalwarts had been appalled in March 1977, when Carter delivered a major policy address in which he said, "Palestinians deserve a right to their homeland."[357] Those seven words sent Evangelical Christians into a tailspin. The reaction was immediate: Lobbyists and Evangelicals launched a publicity campaign, buying advertisements in a number of major US newspapers, which carried the message:

> The time has come for evangelical Christians to affirm their belief in biblical prophecy and Israel's divine right to the land. . . . We affirm as US evangelicals our belief in the Promised Land to the Jewish people . . . We would view with grave concern any effort to carve out of the Jewish homeland another nation or political entity.[358]

The tide had turned—landing Ronald Reagan safely ashore and carrying a disgruntled Jimmy Carter out to sea.

Ronald Wilson Reagan was born in an apartment above the H. C. Pitney Variety Store in Tampico, Illinois, on February 6, 1911, to Jack and Nelle Wilson Reagan. As president, he was said to have joked that he was once again "living above the store."[359] At the tutelage of his mother, a devout member of the Disciples of Christ, Reagan learned compassion and faith, particularly a firm conviction that people were basically good.

Ronald was an unusual young man, in that he opposed racial discrimination at a time when it was widely accepted. In the book *God and Ronald Reagan: A Spiritual Life,* political science professor Paul Kengor told of a time when Reagan brought home two young black basketball players who could not find a place to stay in the town of Dixon, Illinois. He invited them to spend the night and have breakfast before their departure the next morning. When Ronald strode through the front door, the two young men remained outside, fearing they would be turned away because of their skin color. Nelle Reagan did not miss a beat; she smiled warmly and said, "Come on in!"[360]

Reagan's path to the White House led him through a career as a radio sports announcer, as an actor, then as president of the Screen Actors Guild. In 1940, he married actress Jane Wyman. They had two biological children, Maureen and Christine (who survived only one day), and then adopted Michael. Jane divorced Ronald because of disagreements over his political aspirations. He met actress Nancy Davis shortly afterward, and the two were married in 1952. Their union produced Patti and Ron. The Reagans' marriage has been described as "close, authentic, and intimate."[361]

Reagan began to move from the more liberal Democrat tag to the more conservative Republican label. In 1966, he tossed his hat in the ring for the nomination of governor of California and beat two-term incumbent Pat Brown. Reagan won reelection in 1970 and set his sights on attaining the White House in 1980. He bested President Jimmy Carter by an electoral vote tally of 489 to 49.

Even before he began his quest for the presidency, Reagan was known for his support of Israel. He spoke at pro-Israel rallies during the 1967 Six-Day War. As governor he persuaded the California State Legislature to permit banks to invest in Israeli bonds. He was greatly influenced by a strong, conservative, Jewish think tank, and appointed members of the group to posts in his administration—including Elliot Abrams, Richard Pipes, Richard Perle, and Eugene Rostow. While stumping for the presidency, he readily condemned the PLO and considered Israel to be a tactical resource in the region. In a reception for a Jewish group in New York, he averred that Israel was "the only stable democracy we can rely on as a spot where Armageddon could come."[362]

In a White House meeting with Jewish leaders in 1983, Reagan said:

> Since the foundation of the State of Israel, the United States has stood by her and helped her to pursue security, peace, and economic growth. Our friendship is based on historic moral and strategic ties, as well as our shared dedication to democracy.[363]
>
> The president further encouraged the ironclad bond between the two countries when he said, "The people of Israel and America are historic partners in the global quest for human dignity and freedom. We will always remain at each other's side."[364]

Once ensconced in the West Wing, Reagan became widely known as a resolute champion of Israel. He opened new lines of communication with his peer, Menachem Begin, the man alienated by Jimmy Carter. When he greeted the prime minister at the White House in 1981, Reagan assured Mr. Begin: "I welcome this chance to further strengthen the unbreakable ties between the United States and Israel and to assure you of our commitment to Israel's security and well-being."[365]

Reagan then set about to reestablish defensive and financial ties with which to cement friendly and interdependent relations between the two countries. Perhaps more importantly, the president enjoyed a spiritual intimacy that was later compared to that of George Bush (43) and the Israeli people. The two presidents understood that Israel is important not only because of her tactical location but because of her biblical history.

According to Americans For a Safe Israel Executive Director Helen Freedman:

> It seems that presidents like Reagan and Bush who have a foundation in the Bible have a better understanding of what Israel's role is in the world. Israel is not meant to be a nation like all the other nations. It's not meant to be absorbed into the Middle East or the Commonwealth of Nations. It is a nation that represents the biblical promise—the Promised Land, the chosen people, and its obligation to be a light unto the nations .... [Reagan] we had heard woke up every morning and asked to do God's will—not his will, but God's will.[366]

Despite the distractions of the Iran-Contra Affair,[367] Reagan worked tirelessly to secure the release of Soviet Jews from Russia and to persuade its leaders to tear down the physical wall of separation between East and West Germany. In 1985, I launched a national campaign to ask President Ronald Reagan to appeal to Soviet President Mikhail Gorbachev to release Natan Sharansky and a handful of other Russian dissidents who wanted to go to Israel. I wrote *Let My People Go*, a book on the plight of Jews in the Soviet Union, and I produced a television special spotlighting Sharansky's fight for freedom. The appeal was successful, and President Reagan's efforts eventually led to a flood of immigrants into Israel. The pro-Israel Reagan administration opened the door for me to attend a series of White House Seminars, which included meetings between the president and other Christian Zionists, such as Jerry Falwell, Hal Lindsey, and Dr. Tim LaHay.

Josh Block, a spokesperson for the American Israel Public Affairs Committee (AIPAC), said, "There are a number of things President Reagan did that are monumental in their importance to US-Israel relationship."[368] Among those achievements were the formation of the Joint Security Assistance Planning Group, a strategic security think tank that has promoted cooperation in the war on terror, and a free-trade accord that opened the door for more balanced business dealings with industries in Europe.

When he inked the document, Reagan stressed its importance:

> I believe this new economic relationship with our friends in Israel will further our historic friendship, strengthen both of our economies, and provide for new opportunities between our peoples for communication and commerce.[369]

Ronald Reagan was also instrumental in bolstering the Israeli economy when he appropriated $1.5 billion in aid, half paid in 1985, the remaining half in 1986. However, then a decision by Reagan to sell the Airborne Warning and Control System aircraft (AWACS) and other military equipment to Saudi Arabia caused a chasm in US–Israel relations that took almost a year to be bridged. The Saudis reiterated that the planes were to be utilized to monitor Iran's air maneuvers, but it was widely accepted that the same planes could be used against Israel. Despite an uproar from the conservative, pro-Israel bloc, Congress approved the sale to the Saudis in October 1981. Thankfully, even the strain caused by that transaction was not enough to seriously maim relations between Israel and the United States.

Israel's Prime Minister Shamir said of the Reagan White House:

This is the most friendly administration we have ever worked with. They are determined that the strong friendship and cooperation will continue and even be strengthened despite the differences that crop up from time to time.[370]

Reagan's empathy with leaders in Israel and with American Jews was based on his belief in the biblical concept of a Jewish homeland for the People of the Book. He also understood the necessity for a strong, democratic Israel in the Middle East. He admired the courage of the people whose state had been forged from the fires of adversity, who for centuries had vowed, "Next year, Jerusalem." He proclaimed:

In Israel, free men and women are every day demonstrating the power of courage and faith. Back in 1948 when Israel was founded, pundits claimed the new country could never survive. Today, no one questions that Israel is a land of stability and democracy in a region of tyranny and unrest.[371]

Reagan seemed to be at ease in his dealings with Israel, partly because experts believed he knew and recognized the importance of a strong Jewish state in the region. He was well aware that Jerusalem should not be divided and that a Palestinian state co-opted by terrorists would mean the end of Israel.

Although Reagan was the first president in several decades not to have had a Jewish cabinet member, he often called for advice from men such as Milton Friedman, who served on the President's Council of Economic Advisers. Friedman was a Nobel Prize winner in economics and taught at the University of Chicago. Ronald Lauder, son of cosmetics queen Estée Lauder, was tapped by Reagan to serve as deputy secretary of defense for European and NATO policy and later as ambassador to

Austria. Lenore Annenberg, wife of philanthropist Walter Annenberg, held the post of chief of protocol and directed the visits by the Reagans with heads of state. Marshall Breger became the first Orthodox Jew to serve a US president. He held the post of adviser on Jewish and Israeli affairs. Those were but a few of the distinguished Jewish men and women to advise Reagan.

When his second term neared its end, President Reagan supported Vice President George H. W. Bush in his run for the post of chief executive. After the newly elected Bush was sworn in to office on January 20, 1989, Ronald and Nancy Reagan left the cold Washington winters for his beloved ranch in Southern California. He went to work on his memoirs and raising funds for the Reagan Presidential Library, which stands today in Simi Valley, California. On a devastatingly sad day in 1994, the former president made the difficult announcement that he was suffering from Alzheimer's disease and would thereafter make no further public appearances. In his letter to the American people, he wrote:

> When the Lord calls me home, whenever that day may be, I will leave with the greatest love for this country of ours and eternal optimism for its future. I now begin the journey that will lead me into the sunset of my life. I know that for America there will always be a bright dawn ahead.[372]

President Ronald Wilson Reagan died of pneumonia on June 5, 2004, after a ten-year battle with Alzheimer's. His body was flown to Washington, D.C., to lie in state. A funeral service was held at the Washington National Cathedral, after which the casket was returned to the Reagan Presidential Library. After a memorial service there, his remains were interred on the library grounds.

His final resting place bears the words Reagan himself spoke at the dedication of the library:

> I know in my heart that man is good, that what is right will always eventually triumph and that there is purpose and worth to each and every life.[373]

(3 3)

GEORGE H.W. BUSH (41)

"Let your light so shine before men, that they may see
your good works and glorify your Father in heaven,"
(Matthew 5:16)

PRESIDENT GEORGE H. W. BUSH,
1989 INAUGURAL SCRIPTURE

Not all American presidents have been Zionists —neither George H. W. Bush, William Jefferson (Bill) Clinton, nor Barack Hussein Obama could be described as such. If challenged, each would vow their allegiance to Israel as a US ally, but also each have had issues with America's number one ally in the Middle East.

George Herbert Walker Bush was elected president following Ronald Reagan's second term. George was born on June 12, 1924, in Milton, Massachusetts. His father, Prescott Bush, was a US senator from Connecticut. His mother, Dorothy Walker, was a deeply devout woman who raised her children in a staunchly religious environment.

George joined the navy after the attack on Pearl Harbor in 1941 and was subsequently assigned as a pilot to the *USS San Jacinto* and Air Group 51. His aircraft was a Grumman TBM Avenger, used to attack

Japanese ships in the Bonin Islands. During one such attack, Bush's plane encountered severe anti-aircraft fire, and flak from one of the Japanese guns struck the Avenger. Although his engine caught fire, Bush completed his bombing run before heading back toward the home carrier. Bush's crew, Radioman Second Class John Delaney and Lieutenant Junior Grade William White, were both killed during the attack. Bush parachuted from his damaged plane and was later rescued by the submarine *USS Finback*. For serving his country, he was awarded a Distinguished Flying Cross, three Air Medals, and the Presidential Unit Citation was awarded the *USS San Jacinto.*[374]

Shortly after returning from assignment in the Pacific, George married Barbara Pierce, whose father, Marvin, was the publisher of *McCall's* and *Redbook* magazines. He enrolled at Yale, and after receiving his degree, he and Barbara headed for the wide, open spaces of Texas. George had oil on his mind. It paid off in a big way, because by the time he was forty, he was a millionaire. He campaigned for the House of Representatives and was elected in 1966. He tried twice for a senate seat but was defeated both times.

Richard Nixon appointed Bush ambassador to the United Nations. Gerald Ford followed that with an appointment as the chair of the Liaison Office in Beijing, China, and then as director of the CIA. George entered the 1980 presidential race, but lost the nomination to Ronald Reagan, who then chose him as his running mate. The team stayed together through two races, and then George entered the contest in 1988 as Reagan's successor. Despite the Jewish community supporting his opponent Michael Dukakis by a 2-to-1 margin, Bush became the 41st president of the United States by a margin of 54 percent.

George H.W. Bush's first major international challenge as president was the Persian Gulf War. The conflict was prompted by Iraqi dictator Saddam Hussein's invasion of Kuwait in August 1990. Hussein's invasion was presumed to be provoked by greed—a desire to procure Kuwait's oil-rich land and to expand Iraq's hold over the region. Fearing that Saddam entertained a more expansive vision for the countries in the region, the US acted under the auspices of the United Nations, eventually forming a comprehensive alliance of nations—including several Arab countries. Troops soon began to amass in northern Saudi Arabia.

The UN Security Council demanded that Iraq withdraw from Kuwait, and when Hussein missed the deadline the federation launched a massive air offensive against the Iraqi leader. He responded by lobbing ballistic missiles into coalition states and Israel. The Bush administration prevailed upon Israeli leaders not to respond to the Iraq SCUD missiles targeting the Jewish state. On February 24-28, 1991, coalition forces launched a ground war; victory quickly followed. Deaths in the Iraqi ranks were estimated at as many as 100,000; alliance forces lost approximately 300 troops.

In October, following the Gulf War, President Bush and Secretary of State James Baker developed the plan and objectives for a peace conference in Madrid, Spain. Partnered with the Soviet Union, an invitation was extended to Israel, Syria, Jordan, Lebanon, and the Palestinian Liberation Organization.

Prior to issuing the invitations, the Bush administration had stalled with $10 billion in loan guarantees to Israel in an attempt to appease Arab nations destined for the Peace Conference. The president told reporters:

> It is in the best interest of the peace process and of peace itself that consideration of this absorption aid question for Israel be deferred for simply 120 days.[375]

When Israeli emissaries visited Washington in early 1991 they discovered, much to their dismay, that President Bush was tying the $10 billion in loan guarantees to an Israeli assurance that no additional "settlements" would be erected in what Washington called the "occupied territories." Yitzhak Shamir was quoted in a Tel Aviv newspaper as saying, "What President Bush was telling us was very simple: If you won't behave yourselves in the peace process, and if you won't accept the principle of 'land for peace' you won't receive the loan guarantees."[376]

In August 1992, Bush finally agreed to allow the loan guarantees to be fulfilled. He insisted that the loans be offset by any funds spent on housing or improvements in what some referred to as "the territories," but the president's credibility among pro-Israel supporters had been badly, if not critically, damaged. His credibility may have been wounded prior to the loan guarantee issue. In 1990, he voiced his opposition to "new settlements in the West Bank or in East Jerusalem," inferring that parts of the Holy City were not a sovereign part of Israel. While some believe the major achievement of the Bush (41) administration was the Madrid Peace Conference that reopened the door for the Middle East peace process and the Oslo Accords, others feel that the accords were unsuccessful due to the increase in attacks against Israel.

George Bush (41) lost the 1992 election. His support from the Jewish bloc had fallen from 35 percent in 1988 to approximately 12 percent in 1992.[377] We will see later that his son, George W. Bush, would, without apology, ardently support the Jewish people. "Bush 43" would be the rightful heir to Ronald Reagan's Israel policies and arguably the most Christian Zionist president to follow Reagan in the White House.

(34)

WILLIAM JEFFERSON CLINTON

*"For he who sows to his flesh will of the flesh reap corruption,
but he who sows to the Spirit will of the Spirit reap everlasting life"
(Galatians 6:8, NKJV)*

PRESIDENT WILLIAM J. (BILL) CLINTON,
1993 INAUGURAL SCRIPTURE

The man we know today as Bill Clinton was born William Jefferson
Blythe III in Hope, Arkansas, on August 19, 1946. His father was a traveling
salesman who had been killed in an automobile accident three months
before Bill's birth. In 1950, his mother, Virginia Dell Cassidy, married a
local car dealer, Roger Clinton; and at the age of fifteen, Bill assumed his
stepfather's last name.

Bill was an excellent student, ultimately graduating from Georgetown
University and, as a Rhoades Scholar, attended Oxford University. He was
awarded a law degree from Yale in 1973. Having met President Kennedy
in 1963, Clinton developed a taste for politics and was determined to
enter the fray. He first ran an unsuccessful campaign for Congress before
marrying Hillary Rodham Clinton in 1975. He made a victorious run

for Arkansas attorney general in 1976 and two years later was elected governor for a single term. Four years after his defeat for a second term, he won reelection and served as governor until he ran for and won the office of the presidency in 1992.

Rev. W. O. Vaught, pastor of Immanuel Baptist Church in Little Rock, Arkansas, told his parishioner, Governor Bill Clinton:

> You might be president one day. You will make mistakes, and God will forgive you. But God will never forgive you if you abandon the state of Israel.[378]

Almost exactly a year before the September 11 attacks, on September 8, 2000, President Bill Clinton welcomed an incredible assembly of world leaders made up of dignitaries, ambassadors, and heads of state who were attending the United Nations Millennium Summit to a reception held in one of the most remarkable places in New York city: The Temple of Dendur, a Nubian shrine honoring the Egyptian goddess Isis. The temple was rebuilt stone by stone in the Sackler Wing of the Metropolitan Museum of Art, which is a glass room large enough to accommodate a house and overlooks Central Park. It was disassembled in the 1960's to preserve the ancient site as the Aswan Dam project would have covered it in water. It had been given to the United States in 1965 as a gift of friendship from Egyptian President Jamal Abd al-Nasser, and awarded to the Met the same year that Nasser provoked the Six-Day War.

The symbolism of the event and the location speak volumes about the Clinton presidency; not only the symbolism of meeting with U.N. members in a room housing a gift from a man who hated Israel, but also the symbolism of the temple itself. The temple was erected roughly fifteen years before Christ's birth as a Roman tribute to Egyptian heritage and even depicts the Roman Emperor Caesar Augustus (the emperor responsible for Mary and Joseph going to Bethlehem for Jesus' birth)[379] sacrificing to the Egyptian gods alongside other pharaohs, symbolizing the supremacy of such gods to people of that day. Isis, to whom the temple was dedicated, has been one of the most enduring goddesses of all time, being the great mother-goddess, maternal spirit, enchantress, goddess of magic, and protector of the dead; an archetype identified with mother earth; the earth goddess, Gaia; and similar worldly traditions—in their words, she symbolized of *Spiritus Mundi*, the "spirit of the world." If ever there was a gathering that epitomized the moral relativity of Bill Clinton's eight years in office this was it—perhaps even going one step further than the day he lied before a federal grand jury concerning his sexual harassment of Paula Jones.

Many liberals gloss over the issues surrounding Bill Clinton's impeachment as a right-wing Republican witch hunt to oust a progressive, educated, highly intelligent, and charismatic world leader—the man who, until now at least—has come the closest in history to bringing peace to the Middle East and the president who presided over the time of the greatest prosperity in American, if not world, history. Some say, "So the man had a few sexual scandals, so did President Kennedy, and look at what a great man he was!" Yet, as often happens, they have their facts confused. William Clinton wasn't impeached for having an affair with Monica Lewinsky or even for using his position as governor to sexually harass Paula Jones. He was impeached for placing his hand on the Bible, promising to "tell the truth, the whole truth, and nothing but the truth," and *lying* to cover up his own indiscretions. If the man would lie to do that, what else would he be willing to lie about? If he were willing to twist the reasoning of moral judgment to justify perjury, what else would he do to achieve the goals he set for himself? And would this president's lack of moral judgment make him a danger to the citizens of the United States?

As the facts emerge about him and his actions during his presidency, it appears that Clinton was indeed willing to lie about and justify a great deal more to carve a place in history for himself. Yet history will not remember President William Jefferson Clinton nearly as fondly as he would have liked, and, unfortunately, his sexual misbehavior is far outweighed by the gravity of what he did to America. If America falls into obscurity in the events of the final chapter of the Bible, it will have been Bill Clinton, his policies, moral relativity, and favoring of globalization and the U.N. over strengthening and protecting America that weakened its stability enough to begin that landslide. "Treason" may not be a strong enough word for what he did to America during his presidency.

Clinton's strengths were his uncanny charisma and his ability to make people hear what they wanted to hear in what he was saying without ever having said it. He also had the incredible aptitude of always understanding the pulse of American opinion and acting to stay in the good graces of the whims of popular sentiment. A large part of this was because of his unprecedented use of focus groups and his skillful exploitation of their findings. Focus group research is done by taking random collections of people into a room for a two or three-hour session, giving them a small hand-held device on which to indicate their responses, and showing them videotaped speeches and addresses. They rate what they see and hear to indicate what they like most and the least. Then the gestures, phrases, and expressions that receive the highest approval ratings can be incorporated into the next speech or debate to illicit the greatest positive response from the audience.

Clinton's solutions for the problems he faced in his initial election concerning his dodging of the draft, his affair with Gennifer Flowers, and other concerns that voters had about his moral character were all resolved through intense focus group research. He mastered the art of "spinning" issues to put them in their best possible light, thus making his corruption and immorality palatable to most of the American public.

This was also something he used widely during his presidency—in his first year he worked with more different focus groups than George H. W. Bush did in his entire four-year term as president. Through it, Clinton became a master at manipulating image and public opinion, and keeping a high approval level through most of his presidency while selling the United States and its allies down the river.

I remember sitting next to Jim Wright, a former Texas congressman and Speaker of the House, as Arafat spoke to an audience on the lawn of the Rose Garden at the September 1993 meeting when Arafat and Rabin shook hands. In his speech, as one reporter put it, Arafat said:

> "I assure you that we share your values of freedom, justice, and human rights for which my people have been striving," . . . his reading glasses and soft tone belying his ogre status. "Our two peoples want to give peace a chance," he said to applause from a crowd of 3,000, a Who's Who of the American establishment . . .
>
> "We are relying on you, Mr. President, and all the countries who know that without peace in the Middle East, peace in the world is incomplete."[380]

Afterwards, former Congressman Wright turned to me and said, "Wasn't Arafat's speech brilliant? He is a charming fellow, and I used to not like him."

Such comments left me astounded at how well glitz can succeed over substance. Yasser Arafat had left a trail of blood beginning with his involvement with *Fatah* in the 1960s, then with his later actions being a renewed call for a million martyrs—suicide bombers—to march on Jerusalem and kill innocent men, women, and children. However, all of this magically disappeared as Arafat and his entourage marched into the White House on thirteen different occasions during the Clinton era as welcome guests to negotiate the release of "Palestine's occupied territories."

Clinton's aim was to hold the hands of both Jew and Arab as he walked each of them through the "peace" process—and he did so by validating one and applying pressure upon the other. One of the things that he did to legitimize Arafat, perhaps with further aid from his focus groups, was to change the language of the discussion. The PLO would no longer be referred to as "terrorists," but as "freedom-fighters" or "militants." Somehow, the building of Israeli settlements on the West became morally equivalent to suicide-bombers murdering innocent people in major Israeli cities as each was pitched as the reason negotiations were continually failing. A clear example of the Clinton administration's moral makeover happened in 1997, when Sara Ehrman, a co-founder of *Americans for Peace Now* who became a senior advisor to Clinton, organized a conference call in New York between Secretary of State Madeleine Albright and some American Jewish leaders. Among the participants was Ken Bialkin, who noticed this tendency on the part of the Clinton administration. He asked Albright, "How can you compare building in the settlements [in the West Bank] to Arafat's terror? You are creating moral equivalence."

The conference call ended and everyone hung up. But one participant remained on the line and recorded the rest of what was said. Sarah Ehrman angrily asked her friend Steven Cohen, who had been Shimon Peres's contact man with the PLO during the 1980s, "How is it that there are people here asking such embarrassing questions? Don't they realize that Arafat has no choice but to use terror?"[381]

He had no choice? The PLO and similar organizations have no choice but to send some of their most dedicated youth to murder innocent people by committing suicide? Then of what value are all the peace talks? Do Arafat's successor, Mahmoud Abbas, and other Arab leaders really want peace with Israel any more than did Yasser Arafat? If so, why have they rejected it time and again? Why did they reject it in Madrid in 1981 when they were offered ninety-five percent of the lands won in the Six-Day War?

Why did they renew their *intifada* after they were given the Gaza Strip, Jericho, and Bethlehem if what they really want is peace? Do they really have no option but to renew violence time and again after Israel makes concessions? On the other hand, the Palestinian Authority—whose strings are pulled by the PLO—has yet to honor its word in any of these negotiations and blames the continued violence on the Islamist "splinter groups" of Islamic Jihad and Hamas—many of whose attacks were, however, coordinated with Arafat and the PLO before being carried out. Wouldn't a better choice be to follow through on what they have promised as Israel has done, rather than breaking agreement after agreement by reinitiating violence time and again? As Democratic Congressman Elliot Engel from New York put it:

> It's not poverty; it's fanaticism that causes terrorism. They are the product of a system that hates the Jews. Islamic Fundamentalism is against anything Western. Israel has the right to go after the terrorists everywhere. The fight against terrorism is a fight for world survival. We must speak with moral clarity—there is no equation between suicide bombers and Israeli actions.[382]

It is this type of moral relativism that has given birth to this mess, not "the love of truth" that provides transparency. It is the United States that has raised Muslim hopes that the US will help them achieve their demands. The Arabs refuse to settle for anything less than 100 percent of what Israel won in 1967. Once that is accomplished, they will continue to work to gain what was mandated to Israel in 1948.

As author and law professor, Dr. Alan Dershowitz said in the first pages of his book, *Why Terrorism Works*:

> Terrorism is often rationalized as a valid response to its "root causes"—mainly repression and desperation. But the vast majority of repressed and desperate people do not resort to the willful targeting of vulnerable civilians. The real root cause of terrorism is that it is successful— terrorists have consistently benefited from their terrorist

acts. Terrorism will persist as long as it continues to work for those who use it, as long as the international community rewards it, as it has been doing for the past thirty-five years.[383]

Why does terrorism work? In a word: Appeasement! The perpetrators of terrorism believe they are valid representatives of the cause even if the people they claim to represent do not. Their acts of violence gain more concessions or prompt intensification of negotiations. Whenever the violence increases, the US goes out of its way to ensure more concessions will be forthcoming. So why should the jihadists stop?

It was in doing just this—validating the PLO's acts of violence by pandering all the more earnestly to them—that Bill Clinton and his obsession with achieving historical notoriety as the author of a lasting peace in the Middle East caused unremitting erosion in Israel's negotiating positions with the Arab world in the 1990s. Then when Israel was forced to fight against terror—striking back at military targets to disable terrorists, Clinton did not give it his full backing.

As Israel was at the center, it was also the focus of Clinton's pressure to force agreements. According to the Oslo Accords, Israel would negotiate separate peace accords with Jordan, Syria, and the Palestinians, yet only one of these was ever signed: with Jordan on October 26, 1974. For Syria, Israel's deportation of 415 Hamas members in December 1992 precipitated a crisis in continuing the talks, so that they demanded the PLO be a part of their negotiations and that the PLO also be given the power of veto.

The fate of the Golan Heights was also a major issue as these mountains provide a natural protective barrier from which to launch attacks against Israel as Syria did in the Six-Day War. Prime Minister Yitzhak Rabin had stated during his election campaign in 1992 that "He who considers withdrawing from the Golan Heights forsakes the security of Israel."[384] So, at least for the meantime, Rabin saw no mutual basis upon which Jerusalem could negotiate with Damascus.

In the wake of the signing of the Oslo agreements, however, Clinton formulated a comprehensive peace plan for the Middle East, and Syria was the main objective. So in 1994-1995, he pressured contacts between Israel and Syria to shift into high gear. As a result, a peace agreement appeared to be emerging. The proposed peace settlement, which included Israel's withdrawal from the Golan Heights, awakened tremendous opposition within the Israeli populace. In the context of the contacts with the Syrians, Rabin gave President Clinton what became known as the "deposit," a paper stating that if all of Israel's security needs were addressed and its demands regarding normalization and a timetable were met, it would be willing to carry out a full withdrawal from the Golan Heights. The paper was not a diplomatic commitment, but rather intended only to serve to inform the president as to Israel's final position to ultimately attain a peace agreement. According to a different version, Rabin was willing later on to explicitly mention the June 4, 1967 borders.

To this day, it is not clear how this "deposit" was born. It is quite possible the US president's constant pressure for progress with the Syrians placed the Israeli prime minister in an untenable position. Given Clinton's later actions, it appears his role in the "deposit" may well have been greater than Rabin's. However, the result was that the Clinton administration was willing to exploit Rabin in order to attain Israel's withdrawal from the Golan Heights and a subsequent peace agreement.

Clinton betrayed Rabin and showed the Syrians the "deposit" that had been intended for his eyes, only. It was Rabin, however, who was seen as a traitor and assassinated by an Israeli extremist on November 5, 1995. Standing at Rabin's state funeral, I watched as a tiny bead of sweat rolled down Bill Clinton's face. He looked sullen and tired, but unfortunately not remorseful. The damage done to negotiations was irreversible and talks with the Syrians deteriorated until they finally ended in late 1998.

When Benjamin Netanyahu ran for the office of Prime Minister in

1996, Clinton did not find him as malleable as Rabin had been. In fact, Netanyahu posed such a barrier to Clinton fulfilling his dreams for history, that he did something unprecedented: Clinton sent his own democratic campaign advisors to help Netanyahu's incumbent opponent, Shimon Peres, win the election. (Peres had been foreign minister and an integral part of the peace negotiations under Rabin. After Rabin's assassination, he became leader of the Labor party and prime minister).

Why did Clinton see Netanyahu as such a threat to his plans? Benjamin Netanyahu was a man who realized that the problems in the Arab-Israeli conflict could not be resolved without moral clarity, and also saw through Clinton's double-talk. He would not sell Israel's security down the river for agreements from Arafat and the Palestinian Authority. After the violence was renewed in a series of murderous bus bombings in February and March of 1996, Netanyahu was already leading Peres in the polls, because the Israeli public would find that Clinton's "peace" process had an evil twin: Palestinian suicide attacks. When Netanyahu and his Likud Party spoke of security, the voters liked what they heard as opposed to the Labor Party's "peace" process that only led to more violence. Clinton, for his part, viewed the Likud Party and its leader, Netanyahu, as a Middle Eastern chapter of the Republican Party. Unfortunately, due to the Clinton administration's double-dealing and pressure, Netanyahu would not be able to deliver the security he had promised Israeli voters.

A few weeks before the elections, Rahm Emanuel, Clinton's senior advisor on internal affairs, arrived in Israel. Emanuel, by the way, comes from an Israeli family of former Irgun (the Israeli resistance movement of the 1940s) members. He came to hear assessments as to what could be expected in the elections and to coordinate with his staff the possibility of helping Peres's campaign. The American embassy in Tel Aviv invited a number of Israeli political experts, i.e., Yitzhak Herzog, Yaron Ha'ezrahi, Rafi Smith and others for a meeting with Emanual. Only one of those invited to the meeting dared disagree with the general consensus in the room, maintaining that the question was not if Benjamin Netanyahu would win the election, but rather by how much. Everyone laughed, including Emanuel.

That same individual bumped into Emanuel on a plane to Washington, where they had many hours to argue. "Get used to the idea that soon there will be a new sheriff in town," he told Clinton's top advisor, relating the policies that Netanyahu planned to introduce after the election, based on what Netanyahu wrote in his book, *A Place Among the Nations.* When the two parted company in Washington, Emanuel said, "Tell your friend that if he dares to act according to what you have described—we will kick him in the &ˆ$# so hard and he will be so miserable, that he won't know what hit him."[385]

Netanyahu, however, held the day and won the election. The confrontation between Clinton and Netanyahu on the personal-political level became immediately evident during Netanyahu's first state visit to Washington as prime minister in the summer of 1996. Clinton encountered a head of state standing beside him during a press conference whose sound bites were better than his and who gave a more impressive appearance. Telling the truth makes a difference; Clinton found it virtually intolerable.

American-Israeli relations in the mid-nineties should be viewed in the context of Clinton's overall policy, which may be defined as conciliatory towards terror and all potential aggressors. If Arafat wanted faster action or more concessions from Israel in their talks, all that had to happen was for violence to increase. Clinton could blame Netanyahu for moving too slowly. Arafat moved backwards, assured that Madeline Albright and the Clinton team would chastise the Israelis for any perceived failures. Clinton cared little about Israel's security and Palestinian violence—what he cared about was keeping the peace process going. It increased his approval ratings and diverted attention from his moral scandals. Clinton demonstrated laxness in the war against terror (as evidenced by his continually ignoring the growing threat of al Qaeda) and was largely responsible for creating an environment friendly to terror and the creation of destructive trends in the world. During his term, the

United States' systems and will to deter terrorism deteriorated. Clinton made only a weak gesture to respond to the Iraqi assassination attempt on former President George H.W. Bush in Kuwait in 1993. Clinton ordered the bombing of an empty Iraqi government building in the middle of the night, and as we will see later, paid virtually no attention to the first World Trade Center bombing that took place the same year. This was followed by a series of terror attacks peaking with the strike in Dhahran, Saudi Arabia, that killed nineteen Americans.

The year 1998 saw mass terror outbreaks in Kenya and Tanzania, in which 224 were killed and almost 5,000 injured as the US Embassies in Nairobi and Dar es Salaam (which, oddly enough, translates as "Haven of peace"). They were almost simultaneously attacked with truck bombs. Clinton responded by firing cruise missiles at insignificant targets in Sudan and an attack on an abandoned terrorist target in Afghanistan. (Poor judgment on Clinton's part led to bin Laden being tipped off about the attacks and escaping by minutes.) It sent the message that the Clinton administration only wanted to do enough to make it appear as though the president were taking action in order to keep the support of the public. Once US citizens went on with their lives thinking he was taking care of things, Clinton went back to his agenda and forgot about the terrorist threat. Subsequently, seventeen Americans were killed and thirty-seven injured aboard the *U.S.S. Cole* when a suicide bomber hit it on October 12, 2000 as it refueled at the dock in Aden, Yemen. It was the deadliest attack on a US warship since World War II. Clinton's continual weakness in the face of terrorists proclaimed an "open season" on Americans throughout the world.

In 1999, Clinton tried to restore the appearance of military strength during the war in Kosovo, but the massive air strike on the Serbians instead sent an unintended positive message to Yasser Arafat and a negative one to Israel. Arafat could see himself as part of the Kosovo Liberation Army among militants fighting to free Kosovo. Israel, on the other hand, found itself being falsely portrayed as a Serbian-type aggressor.

Israel's leaders also showed Clinton raw data proving that Arafat had given the green light to the renewal of terror attacks by Hamas. Israel had monitored the talks Arafat held with Hamas leaders in Gaza on March 12-19, 1997. Based on that information, the then-head of Israeli Military Intelligence, Moshe Ya'alon, determined that Arafat had indeed approved and sanctioned terror attacks on Israel. Clinton could have been expected to respond to this very harshly. However, he did nothing because he was unwilling to abandon Arafat, who was part of the Oslo legacy and peace process to which Clinton was committed.

In 1999, Clinton made even more blatant use of his special position as president in the eyes of the Israeli public. He attempted to undermine Netanyahu's standing and cause him to lose the election. Psychologically, Israel's unique relationship with the United States has always been one of the most important foundations of Israel's national security. The rationale was that if this relationship were to be viewed by the Israeli public as being shaken due to a particular individual, even if this had no objective basis in reality, it could result in serious public stress. Right at the start of the 1999 election campaign in Israel, Clinton sent a very clear message as to what he wanted: he again dispatched the team that had run both of his successful election campaigns to lead Ehud Barak's campaign. Composed of James Carville, Stanley Greenberg and Bob Shrum, this team was worth more than a million dollars, and regarding the activities for which the three were responsible, much more than that. Stanley Greenberg had already been involved in the process of figuring ways to win against Netanyahu back in 1998. He kept close contact with Barak. As the most prominent figure among the three, Greenberg did public opinion surveys and analyzed focus group data. While the general opinion in the US and Israeli press during 1998 was that Netanyahu would be in power for at least four more years, Greenberg found, and told Barak, that there was a way to beat Netanyahu. The method was to cross the security image threshold, and stick to the economy and social affairs—the same strategy Clinton had used to win his second term in office with the sleight-of-hand slogan "It's the economy, stupid!" It kept Americans focused on their wallets, and he did as he pleased while they weren't looking. That was the main input of the Americans, said Tal Silberstein, one of Barak's top advisors for the campaign. "They structured the research, they came with the insights, and we adapted it to Israel."[386]

Some of the top donors to Clinton and the Democratic Party were mobilized for Barak's campaign as though this were another election the Democrats must win.

Overall, the Labor Party spent between $50 and $80 million on its anti-Netanyahu contest, roughly ten times what Netanyahu's own Likud Party spent. In early 2000, the state comptroller of Israel produced a report that in doing so, the Labor Party had grossly violated strict Israeli campaign finance laws. The government fined the campaign an unprecedented $3.2 million.[387]

Clinton personally contributed to Ehud Barak by continuing his warm meetings with Arafat in the White House, while freezing out Prime Minister Netanyahu and receiving Barak and Yitzhak Mordechai, the two candidates running against Netanyahu in the election. "Clinton helped Barak more than he had to", says one of Barak's men.[388] The fact that Arafat had become the White House's most welcome official guest (he could have also been awarded the Blair House frequent-guest prize) was interpreted in the Israeli media to the detriment of Netanyahu rather than of the American president. The result of all those efforts was the collapse of the Israeli political center with six percent of Netanyahu's voters moving over to the other side, causing a change of government in Israel.

Clinton, now with his new Israeli Labor Party partner, continued his intensive race to curry favor with the most extreme leaders in the Arab world and attain a long sought-after peace. The timetable of the new Israeli prime minister in regard to the peace process on both fronts, the Palestinian and the Syrian, was now tied to that of the American president who had only one more year in office. It became evident with the Camp

David initiative of July 2000. Politically it was very risky for Barak to rush to Camp David, but the partnership with Clinton dictated a tight schedule. The results regarding both the Syrians and the Palestinians were disastrous.

The late Syrian President Hafiz al-Asad, although he had an Israeli agreement in his pocket to return to the June 4, 1967 lines, refused to sign it and negotiations began over parts of the Sea of Galilee and the Northern mountainous part of the Jordan River. Exactly the same thing happened with the Palestinians: they got everything they demanded, only to present new ultimatums backed by an onslaught of terror the likes of which had yet to be seen in the region. Of Clinton's appeasement policies, it has already been said that the road to hell is paved with good intentions. More than three months after the Palestinians began a Second *Intifada* against Israel (September 2000) with an increased wave of bloody suicide bombings, Arafat continued to be a welcome guest in Clinton's White House.

(35)

BILL CLINTON—REDUX

Those from among you Shall build the old waste places;
You shall raise up the foundations of many generations;
And you shall be called the Repairer of the Breach,
The Restorer of Streets to Dwell In.

PRESIDENT WILLIAM J. (BILL) CLINTON,
1997 INAUGURAL SCRIPTURE

On January 2, 2001—the lame-duck president was supposed to be getting ready to vacate the White House and make way for the about-to-be inaugurated President George W. Bush. This was about six months after Israel's prime minister had presented the most far-reaching concessions ever offered the Palestinians. President Clinton came up with yet another peace initiative, this one involving even more far-reaching Israeli concessions than those Prime Minister Ehud Barak had agreed to at Camp David; Arafat refused. The Second *Intifada* was having its desired effect.

Arafat landed at Andrews Air Force Base, and from there went to the Ritz-Carlton Hotel where he met with the ambassadors of Saudi Arabia and Egypt. They promised to back him if he agreed to the Clinton plan and warned him that he would receive no backing if he went back to war. When Arafat left the hotel for the White House and his meeting with Clinton, it was clear there were only two possible answers he could give: yes or no. Arafat was late returning. Clearly, the meeting was not going as planned. Clinton told Arafat: "It's five minutes to midnight, Mr. Chairman, and you are about to lose the only opportunity your people will ever have to solve their problem on satisfactory grounds by not being able to make a decision. . . . The Israelis accepted."[389]

The Saudi ambassador, Prince Bandar, knew that Arafat was responsible for causing the Clinton offer to fail and told him that missing the opportunity was not just a tragic mistake, but a crime also. Nevertheless, the next evening, a spokesperson representing Clinton said that Arafat had agreed to accept Clinton's proposals as the basis for new talks—in other words, he would not sign the agreement and expected yet more concessions to be made.

This pattern of willingness to negotiate endlessly with enemies, even when they were already shooting, was one of the trademarks of Clinton's presidency and in particular characterized his relations with Israel.

It was during President Clinton's early watch that the United States was rocked by a devastating attack planned by Osama bin Laden's organization: the February 26, 1993, truck bombing of the World Trade Center. While this first attack went relatively ignored, in it were seeds of the eventual September 11, 2001, attacks at the same location. Because our president at the time was more occupied with implementing his economic program than keeping America safe, no one else paid much attention to the bombing either. In his regular radio address the day after the bombing, President Clinton mentioned the "tragedy" (he never once used the words *bomb* or *terrorist* in the address) and never mentioned the incident in public again. Neither did he ever visit the site of the blast. The author of *Losing bin Laden*, Richard Miniter, addressed Clinton's inability to deal with bin Laden throughout his presidency:

> In 1993, bin Laden was a small-time funder of militant
> Muslim terrorists in Sudan, Yemen, and Afghanistan. By

the end of 2000, Clinton's last year in office, bin Laden's network was operating in more than fifty-five countries and already responsible for the deaths of thousands (including fifty-five Americans).

Clinton was tested by historic, global conflict, the first phase of America's war on terror. He was president when bin Laden declared war on America. He had many chances to defeat bin Laden; he simply did not take them. If, in the wake of the 1998 embassy bombings, Clinton had rallied the public and the Congress to fight bin Laden and smash terrorism, he might have been the Winston Churchill of his generation. But, instead, he chose the role of Neville Chamberlain (whose appeasements of Hitler in Munich in 1938 are credited with paving the way to the Nazi invasion of Poland that began World War II the next year).[390]

In September of that same year, Clinton held a celebration on the White House lawn for what he called "a brave gamble for peace," standing with his thumb actually pressed into the prime minister's back, and forced Rabin to shake hands with PLO Chairman Yasser Arafat over a blank sheet of paper that represented the Declaration of Principles, or Oslo Accords. The paper lay on the same table over which President Jimmy Carter had presided, as Menachem Begin and Anwar Sadat signed the peace treaty between Israel and Egypt in 1979. President Clinton later described it as one of "the highest moments" of his presidency as the two "shook hands for the first time in front of a billion people on television, it was an unbelievable day."[391]

One of Clinton's greatest hopes was to be the man who finally resolved the Arab–Israeli conflict in the Middle East. In order to do this, he used his tremendous aptitude of image transformation to change terrorist and murderer Yasser Arafat into a diplomat. It also seems likely that Arafat got some coaching from Clinton and his advisors on what to say, how to speak, and what to do to help in this metamorphosis.

Jewish actor and spokesman Theodore Bikel said of Arafat:

> Arafat turned out to be no partner for peace . . . he had never intended to be such a partner in the first place. Oslo and the handshake gave him the cachet of peacemaker; it also gave him half of a Nobel Peace Prize, which, if he had had any sense of shame, he would have returned. In truth, for him Oslo was nothing more than an opportunity to obfuscate and spin wheels. In all the summit meetings, he appeared to be pacific, conciliatory, and seemingly accommodating, yet he withdrew as soon as real concessions were required. . . . He never meant for the Oslo Agreement to be implemented.[392]

Bill Clinton and his obsession with going down in history as the author of peace in the Middle East caused an unremitting erosion of Israel's negotiating position with the Arab world in the 1990s. When Israel was forced to fight against terror, he did not give the country his full backing. As the Jewish state was the center of it all, it was also the focus of the president's pressure to force agreements. The fate of the Golan Heights was also a major issue, with these mountains providing a natural protective barrier from which to launch attacks, as Syria had done in the Six-Day War. Prime Minister Yitzhak Rabin, representing Israel, saw no mutual basis upon which Jerusalem could negotiate with Damascus.

What a joy it was for me to be in the White House when the prime minister conducted his first meeting with President Clinton. Years before, during one of my journeys to Israel, I first met Benjamin Netanyahu. I had gone to the home of his father, Benzion, to offer my condolences on the anniversary of the death of his son Jonathan, who was a fallen hero in the daring raid that freed the Israeli hostages being held by PLO terrorists in Entebbe, Uganda. Shortly after my arrival, Benjamin entered the room. After a few minutes of conversation, I asked if I could pray with him. He agreed, and I anointed him with oil and prophesied that he would serve as Israel's prime minister.

I thought of that encounter the morning on which he would be pressured to give up even more land for peace by my president. I called David Bar Ilan, Netanyahu's advisor and my friend, to tell him I had a word from God for Benjamin. David asked me what it was, and I responded:

> Tell him to be strong. President Clinton will pressure him to give more land to Arafat today. But this is Judgment day for President Clinton. There will be a major distraction in the meeting. What the distraction will be, I don't know. David, I only know that God said it, and it is as sure a word as when He told me more than twenty years ago that Bibi would be prime minister.[393]

Later, my phone rang. When I answered, David shouted: "You were right! A note was handed to the president and he ended the meeting. He told us he would have to meet later. He seemed very agitated. I just heard it has something to do with a lady named Monica Lewinsky. That name sounds Jewish. A story is going to break any minute now. It definitely looks like you were right about the distraction."[394]

Afterward, when Netanyahu spoke before Congress and received a standing ovation, especially from the Republican wing, Clinton began to treat the prime minister not as the person expressing the will of the Israeli people, but rather as if he were head of the opposition party in the United States. Moreover, Clinton seemingly made every effort to undermine Netanyahu while he was in office.

American–Israeli relations in the mid-nineties should be viewed in the context of Clinton's overall policy, which may be defined as conciliatory towards terror and all potential aggressors. If Arafat wanted faster action or more concessions from Israel in their talks, all he had to do was increase his violent tactics. Then Clinton could blame Netanyahu for moving too slowly, and Clinton's team and Secretary of State Madeleine Albright would start chastising the Israelis.

More than three months after the Palestinians began a Second Intifada against Israel (September 2000) with an increased wave of bloody suicide bombings, Arafat was still a welcome guest in Clinton's White House. According to columnist Charles Krauthammer, Arafat's intifada was designed to "demoralize Israel, destroy its economy, bring it to its knees and thus force it to withdraw and surrender to Palestinian demands, just as Israel withdrew in defeat from southern Lebanon in May 2000."[395]

President George W. Bush observed afterward that Clinton's final attempt at peace was the work of two "desperate people"—Clinton and Barak. One wanted to leave behind a legacy of peace in the Middle East when he completed his presidency (in addition to his need to clear his name after the sordid Lewinsky affair); the other needed a peace agreement in order to survive the next elections in Israel. On the eve of the 2001 elections, Eyal Arad, Ariel Sharon's strategic advisor, described Clinton and Barak as two children on a playground playing with a barrel of gunpowder.

Arab sources show that Clinton's extensive offer in July 2000 involved extraordinary concessions on Israel's part: It gave Arafat almost everything he wanted, including 98 percent of the territory of Judea, Samaria, and Gaza, all of East Jerusalem except for the Jewish and Armenian quarters, Palestinian sovereignty over the Temple Mount (conceding only the right of Jews to pray there), and a compensation fund of $30 billion. Incredibly, Arafat rejected the offer and walked out of the meeting. He did not want just part of Jerusalem and Israel, he wanted it all.

This pattern of willingness to negotiate endlessly with enemies, even when they continued senseless violence against innocent people, was one of the trademarks of Clinton's presidency. Personal, selfish motives characterized the whole of his relationship with Israel.

Bill Clinton was a president who could not stand being disliked, even by his enemies or those he had betrayed. Saudi Ambassador Bandar bin Sultan said of Clinton, "He gets excited by the possibility of talking to his enemy and changing him. If Clinton leaves office . . . and doesn't have a relationship with Cuba, North Korea, Iran, or Libya, he will feel internally that he has not accomplished his mission."[396]

As with the Obama administration, Clinton was, and apparently still is, incapable of grasping one basic fact: Palestinian leaders are not seeking statehood *alongside* Israel; they are seeking statehood with *no* Israel. This was again made patently obvious in an interview with a number of bloggers in early 2012. Clinton was in rare form as he castigated various Jewish groups for their refusal to negotiate with those who wished them dead:

> You've had all these immigrants coming in from the former Soviet Union, and they have no history in Israel proper, so the traditional claims of the Palestinians have less weight with them. The most pro-peace Israelis are the Arabs; second the Sabras, the Jewish Israelis that were born there; third, the Ashkenazi of long-standing, the European Jews who came there around the time of Israel's founding. The most anti-peace are the ultra-religious, who believe they're supposed to keep Judea and Samaria, and the settler groups, and what you might call the territorialists, the people who just showed up lately and they're not encumbered by the historical record.[397]

One of those detractors denounced by Mr. Clinton was none other than Natan Sharanksy, the Russian immigrant whose freedom was sought by Ronald Reagan. In riposte to Clinton's volley, Mr. Sharansky said: "I am particularly disappointed by the president's casual use of inappropriate stereotypes about Israelis, dividing their views on peace based on ethnic origins."[398]

It is ludicrous to believe that a man of Mr. Sharansky's stature, who spent years longing for the freedom Israel represents, would not fathom and embrace Israel's historical record. The obvious fact is that while he was president, Bill Clinton failed to recognize Israel's right to freedom from terror and for the Jewish people to be treated with human decency. He played jovial host to Yasser Arafat not once but thirteen times, and was seemingly eager to allow the despot to create a terrorist enclave.

It appears that Mr. Clinton was not content to blame Prime Minister Netanyahu for every perceived ill in the ongoing peace process; he drew God into the debate. He pondered: "The two great tragedies in modern Middle Eastern politics, which make you wonder if God wants Middle East peace or not, were Rabin's assassination and Sharon's stroke."[399]

Like many who have spent time occupying the chair in the Oval Office, Clinton allowed his ego to impede reality. He continues to refer to the deal rejected by Arafat in 2000 as "my deal." The inference is that he was more interested in securing his place in history than in negotiating a sure and lasting peace between Israel and her enemies. After all, a signed treaty would have been the jewel in the crown of his presidency—no matter the threat to Israel.

In September 2003, almost three years after leaving office, Clinton visited Israel to express his continued solidarity with Israel—even if it was only with a particular part of the Jewish state. He came to celebrate Shimon Peres' eightieth birthday.

I was in Jerusalem at the King David Hotel at the time to speak at a world summit on winning the war on terrorism through moral clarity. I spent the evening with dear friends, Benjamin and Sarah Netanyahu. Benjamin, the former prime minister, and at that time Minister of Finance, was also a keynote speaker.

He asked, "Are you going to the party in Tel Aviv?"

I said, "Not me. How about you?"

He replied, "Are you kidding? No chance."

I asked Benjamin, "Remember when Bill Clinton was pressuring you to give up more land to the PLO, and the meeting was cut short because the Monica Lewinsky scandal had broken?"

I added, "It just hit me! The date that report was submitted to Congress was September 11, 1998. Very interesting! By the way, I heard a rumor that Monica is in the air and on her way to Jerusalem. Is that true?"

Benjamin responded, "Yes, it is. President Clinton had better not stay too long."

However, that same evening we were speaking, there was another telling moment occurring across town that further reveals Bill Clinton's relativism and worldview. At a certain point in the celebrations for Peres' birthday, Clinton, clad in a tuxedo, got up on the stage and burst into John Lennon's 1971 hit, "Imagine," a theme song for moral relativists. He crooned, "Imagine there's no countries, It isn't hard to do, Nothing to kill or die for, No religion too . . ."[400]

GEORGE W. BUSH
BREAKS RANK

"A friend is always loyal, and a brother
is born to help in time of need,"
(Proverbs 17:17, NLT)

Only one other father and son had served as presidents of the United States before George Walker Bush was elected as the 43rd president of the United States: John Adams (2nd president) and John Quincy Adams (6th president). The elder Adams had apparently groomed his son to succeed him in the office of president; the elder Bush was quite shocked and surprised when George decided to run for governor of Texas and then tossed his Stetson in the ring for the 2000 presidential nomination.

George W. Bush, the son of George Herbert Walker Bush and Barbara Pierce, was born in New Haven, Connecticut. This transplanted Texan attended school in Midland, Texas, graduated from Yale, and then took a degree in business at Harvard, the only president at that time to have received an MBA. George then returned to Texas, where he cast his lot with the oil industry. It was there he met teacher and librarian Laura Welch at a friend's barbecue. She would have a dramatic impact on his life. He has said of Laura:

I saw an elegant, beautiful woman who turned out
not only to be elegant and beautiful, but very smart and
willing to put up with my rough edges, and I must confess
has smoothed them off over time.[401]

As presidential candidate and later chief executive, George would
become known as a pro-Israel, Christian Zionist president—unlike his
father before him. When George first met Israeli president Ariel Sharon,
he is said to have made it abundantly clear that he would not follow the
same path as his father. The elder Bush had been hard on Jewish leaders,
particularly on the issue of settlements, or what many refer to as the
"occupied lands." Sharon had been instrumental in the development of
those areas.

George first met Sharon when he was governor of Texas. On a visit
to Israel, the governor was accompanied by then-foreign minister Sharon
on a helicopter tour. Sharon, who preferred to meet in his office, was
advised by his aide, Raanan Gissin, that he should take Governor Bush on
a flying tour of Israel. Said Gissin:

> You're at your best when you explain in the air . . . Who
> knows? . . . the worst that could happen is that you gave a
> helicopter ride to one of the candidates. But the best that
> could happen [is] that one day this man could become
> president.[402]

When they next met it would be over tea in the Oval Office in March
2001. The president indicated to Mr. Sharon that he would strongly
support Israel. An anonymous source in attendance reported that Bush
indicated he would use force if necessary.[403]

Reportedly, Bush deviated from his father's policies primarily
because of his Evangelical ties—a resolute Republican group with strong
Zionist beliefs. Ideologically, he was cut more from the Reagan pro-Israel

cloth than that of his father. George was an adherent of Reagan's spiritual and emotional ties to Israel, seeing it as the land of the "good guys," who were working alongside the United States to battle fanatical evildoers.

The elder Bush had entered the White House with extended experience in diplomacy and a political worldview based not on theoretical aims but rather on a businesslike rationale—not with the dream of promoting democracy in the Arab world. He cast himself as a neutral player in Middle East politics. Whereas George the elder had courted the Middle Eastern monarchs, his son allied himself with Israel and God's Chosen People.

The father and son obviously had differing approaches in the ways they governed. According to William Kristol, a journalist who worked for the elder Bush:

> Bush the father was from a certain generation of political leaders and foreign policy establishment types. He had many years of dealings with leading Arab governments; he was close to the Saudi royal family. The son is less so. He's got much more affection for Israel, less affection for the House of Saud.[404]

In a speech delivered in Miami in 2006, Bush 43 delivered what some saw as a veiled criticism of his father's governing approach. He said:

> The current Middle East crisis between Israel and Hezbollah is part of a larger struggle between the forces of freedom and terror. For decades, the status quo in the Middle East permitted tyranny and terror to thrive. And as we saw on September the 11th, the status quo in the Middle East led to death and destruction in the United States, and it had to change.[405]

Perhaps Bush saw clearly what other chief executives before and after him had failed to grasp: The United States has an undeniable link with Israel. The Jewish state is clearly a democracy—the only one in that troubled region. The countries share the same values, enjoy free enterprise, embrace Judeo-Christian principles, cherish their freedoms, support an unrestricted press, and welcome a zest for life lived within fundamental parameters. The majority of Americans (more than 60 percent) are supportive of Israel; 56 percent consider Palestinians to be "extremists" and an "obstacle to peace," and 55 percent do not consider Palestinians to be "victims."[406]

Bush has been ridiculed because of his faith and castigated for his commitment to Jesus Christ as his Savior, but his beliefs are central to his support for the nation of Israel and in defining his worldview. He knows that Israel is the birthplace of the Christian religion and having many sites sacred to him and millions of Believers around the world—Golgotha, the Garden Tomb, the Via Dolorosa, and the Garden of Gethsemane, among others. He champions the preservation of the nation of Israel.

In the volatile Middle East of fanatical Muslims with a long history of infighting, it seems implausible that the peoples of two nations could be friendly simply due to shared beliefs and ethics. What possible good could come from such an alliance? The United States has no troops stationed in Israel. Neither exploits the other for the sake of oil, gold, diamonds, minerals, or industrial superiority. Arab leaders are unable to grasp the idea of anyone standing with the Jewish state and have concluded that there must be some Zionist conspiracy afoot.

Thanks to President Clinton's last-minute bungling, Bush entered office with Arafat's violent intifada in full swing. Reports of terror attacks infused the front-page headlines. There were over sixty such attacks— some major—before September 11, 2001. The new president worked to fulfill the role of peacemaker between the Israelis and Palestinians. Unlike Clinton, however, he closed the doors of the White House to Yasser Arafat. Bush stopped all contact with the godfather of terrorism in 2002, after a ship laden with weapons bound for the Palestinian Authority was intercepted. His dealings with Arafat also colored the way he dealt with Hezbollah and other terrorist organizations that still threaten Israel's existence today.

Bush ultimately assumed the role of intermediary and helped develop the Road Map for Peace, which was introduced in 2002. He seemed to be guided even in his peacemaking attempts by the events of 9/11. The president also recognized the inequity with which Israel is treated by other world powers. In an article for the *Jerusalem Post*, David Harris enumerated a number of ways that Israel is regarded differently from other countries:

» Israel is the only UN member state whose very right to exist is under constant challenge.

» Israel is the only UN member state that has been publicly targeted for annihilation by another UN member state.

» Israel is the only nation whose capital city, Jerusalem, is not recognized by other nations.

» Israel is the only country that has been censured by name not once, but nine times since the new UN Human Rights Council was established in June 2006. Astonishingly, or maybe not, this UN body has failed to adopt a single resolution critical of any real abuser of human rights.

» Israel is the only country that has won all its major wars for survival and self-defense, yet it's confronted by defeated adversaries who insist on dictating the terms of peace.[407]

History mandates that "to the victor goes the spoils," which includes decreeing the terms for peace with her enemies. This doesn't seem to apply to Israel, however. After defeating—nay, humiliating—her treacherous enemies in three successive wars (1948, 1967, 1973), Israel must fight for the right to keep what was hers in the beginning. She is frequently dragged to the bargaining table and forced to be nice to those who seek only her ultimate extermination.

Fundamental Islam's driving fanaticism to target not only the Jews in Israel but Americans in the United States stems from jealousy, according to Irwin N. Graulich:

> In addition, during that same period [1948–current], Israel totally embarrassed the entire Arab/Muslim world by defeating them economically, technologically, intellectually, culturally, religiously, medically, socially and morally. Since America's accomplishments are that much greater, it is no wonder that the Arab/Muslim nations feel totally frustrated. They subscribe to a religious belief that promises world greatness, strength and domination, while reality shows them trailing very far behind.[408]

Bush recognized the precarious position in which Israel reposes and vowed to give her his full support as president of the United States. In an address to the National Commemoration of the Days of Remembrance on April 19, 2001, he observed:

> Through centuries of struggle, Jews across the world have been witnesses not only against the crimes of men, but for faith in God, and God alone. Theirs is a story of defiance in oppression and patience in tribulation, reaching back to the exodus and their exile into the

diaspora. That story continued in the founding of the State of Israel. The story continues in the defense of the State of Israel.[409]

As the sands in the hourglass of his presidential era began to seep slowly to the bottom bulb, George Bush, like Carter and Clinton before him, began to seek a lasting Middle East peace. Unfortunately, he went back to play the appeasement card. Why? The first reason is that peace agreement signings play well to the home audience. Much of the American public had lost patience with protracted negotiations and endless rounds of international shuttle diplomacy. Many fail to understand the convoluted politics of the Middle East or to realize that it will take far more than signatures on a series of agreements, like the Hebron Agreement, the Oslo Accords, the Road Map Plan, and the Annapolis Summit, to usher in a lasting peace in the Middle East.

In an address of the American Jewish Committee in May of 2001, President Bush had these words to offer:

> We will speak up for our principles and we will stand up for our friends in the world. And one of our most important friends is the State of Israel. . . .
>
> Israel is a small country that has lived under threat throughout its existence. At the first meeting of my National Security Council, I told them a top foreign policy priority is the safety and security of Israel. My Administration will be steadfast in supporting Israel against terrorism and violence, and in seeking the peace for which all Israelis pray.[410]

On June 24, 2002, Bush made one of the most important speeches of his political career regarding Israel. His opening statement outlined conditions:

For too long, the citizens of the Middle East have lived in the midst of death and fear. The hatred of a few holds the hopes of many hostage. The forces of extremism and terror are attempting to kill progress and peace by killing the innocent. . . . For the sake of all humanity, things must change in the Middle East. It is untenable for Israeli citizens to live in terror. . . . Israeli citizens will continue to be victimized by terrorists, and so Israel will continue to defend herself.[411]

The president then outlined his dream for the region and the changes the Palestinian people and leaders would have to make in order to see this dream become a reality:

My vision is two states, living side by side in peace and security. There is simply no way to achieve that peace until all parties fight terror. Yet, at this critical moment, if all parties will break with the past and set out on a new path, we can overcome the darkness with the light of hope. Peace requires a new and different Palestinian leadership, so that a Palestinian state can be born. I call on the Palestinian people to elect new leaders, leaders not compromised by terror. I call upon them to build a practicing democracy, based on tolerance and liberty. If the Palestinian people actively pursue these goals, America and the world will actively support their efforts. If the Palestinian people meet these goals, they will be able to reach agreement with Israel and Egypt and Jordan on security and other arrangements for independence.[412]

Bush is, I am convinced, a religious man who loves God and loves his country. What then, I wonder, did he see when he looked outside his window during his visit to Jerusalem in 2008? Did he see the hatred for Jews that the Islamic world continues to clutch to its chest, as a drowning man would clasp a life preserver? Did President Bush see then the fanaticism that still today grips the Islamic world, one teaching its children that Jews are "monkeys and pigs"? Did he comprehend that determination not just to occupy half of Jerusalem but to literally push the Jews into the sea? Did he truly understand, as he stood in Jerusalem, that he was surrounded on all sides by terrorists that hate both the Jews and America with the same demonic passion? I'm afraid at that moment he was gripped by the desire to leave a legacy other than that of Iraq. He was determined that history would speak well of him and succumbed to the temptation to touch that which God has warned mankind not to touch: the apple of His eye (Zechariah 2:8).

While a two-state solution in the Middle East was a dream President Bush hoped to achieve, the reality was much uglier. When the president arrived in Jerusalem on Wednesday morning, January 9, 2008, he was met by Prime Minister Ehud Olmert. The two men have much in common: Both are fitness enthusiasts; neither could be proclaimed a "popular" leader, both had met terrorism head-on, and both tried to warn the world of the danger that exists from the threat of Islamic fanaticism. Yet both were also determined to hammer out some kind of agreement that would accomplish what other presidents and prime ministers before them had failed to do: create peace in the region.

The question still remains: How can any lasting peace be achieved in the Middle East when the nations surrounding Israel refuse to recognize her right to exist? The issue is not that her Arab neighbors want Israel to make land "concessions"; Israel's Arab neighbors want it all, minus any Jewish inhabitants. The Arab desire is not for a two-state solution, Israel and Palestine, the desired solution is for Israel to become another Arab state devoid of any Jewish population. It is worth noting here that Bush visited *Yad Vashem*, the Holocaust memorial and museum in Jerusalem. He called his visit "a sobering reminder that evil exists, and a call that when we find evil we must resist it."[413]

Even though he had detoured into "Legacyland," George Bush was otherwise ever the defender of Israel. In May 2008, he traveled to Israel to celebrate the 60th anniversary of the rebirth of the nation. He was welcomed with all the pomp and circumstance due the Jewish state's dearest ally. He visited the Holy Land amid rocket attacks launched from Hamas-controlled Gaza into Israel proper. In a speech delivered to a group in Jerusalem, Bush cited President Harry Truman:

> Because Harry Truman did what was right instead of following the conventional wisdom, we can say today that America is Israel's oldest and best friend in the world. America stands for peace and so does Israel. And as we stand in peace, we must understand the realities of the world in which we live. We must be steadfast. And we must be strong in the face of those who murder the innocent to achieve their objectives.[414]

As Bush's second term in office edged to a close, it became apparent that his successor would be Barack Hussein Obama, and with that election, Israel would lose her friend in the White House. It quickly became clear that the next chief executive had little regard for Israel. Perhaps Rabbi Steven Pruzansky put it most succinctly in his blog:

> Jews will have to cultivate warmer relations with the new Republican House and friendly Democratic congressmen, and bear in mind that Israel's base of support in America today is not in the White House, but in the Congress and, more importantly, with the American people. They are the ones who will resurrect and strengthen this relationship that reflects so well on both countries and can yet benefit all of mankind.[415]

Following the inauguration of Obama in January 2009, Bush returned to his beloved Texas. He and Laura purchased a home in a Dallas enclave and at this writing divide their time between there and their ranch in Crawford, Texas. When asked by Oprah Winfrey for a comment on his successor, the former president replied:

> I want to treat my successor the way I'd like to have been treated. I don't think it's good for a former president to be out there opining on every darned issue. He's got a plenty tough job. Trust me. And there's gonna be plenty of critics and he doesn't need me criticizing him. And I don't think it's good for the presidency. Other people have a different point of view.[416]

Many think Mr. Bush was referring to one of *his* harshest critics, Jimmy Carter. Even when given the opportunity, George Bush declined to name names. His courtliness had no effect on those in the new administration, who continued to blame him for every ill that has beset the country years after he left office. Although President Bush did make a few blunders in his presidency, one thing is certain: Israel would miss him in the days to come.

After leaving the White House, President Bush has maintained a low profile both at home and abroad. He and wife, Laura, strongly support humanitarian causes, and especially AIDS initiatives and cervical cancer prevention in Africa. According to the former president, he much prefers quiet leadership and hard work to being in the eye of a media storm.

(3 7)

BARACK OBAMA:
NO MIXED MESSAGE

*On that day, when all the nations of the earth are gathered
against her, I will make Jerusalem an immovable rock
for all the nations. All who try to move it will injure themselves,"*
(Zechariah 12:3, NIV)

As the days of the George W. Bush presidency wound down, the
country was faced with soon having a relative unknown in the White
House—Barack Hussein Obama. He had burst onto the political scene in
Illinois when he ran unsuccessfully for the House of Representatives in
2000. Four years later he was victorious in securing a US Senate seat. It
was during the Democratic National Convention in July 2004 that the
charismatic, mixed-race Obama grabbed national attention when he
delivered a stirring keynote address. Just three years later, he launched
his presidential campaign. After defeating Hillary Rodham Clinton
in the Democratic primaries in 2008, he won the nomination. He then
ran against and defeated Republican candidate John McCain and was
inaugurated on January 20, 2009.

Would that I could write Barack Obama is a Christian Zionist and tell
of his uncompromising support for the Jewish people; the opposite has

proven to be true. The appalling deterioration of the relationship between the United States and Israel has created a strain not apparent since the days of both George H. W. Bush and Bill Clinton. During his election campaign, Obama stated that one of his first goals as president would be to sit down and negotiate with the rogue leaders of such countries as Iran and Syria. The despotic heads of those countries and others like them search for any microscopic evidence of weakness on the part of an American president. When found, the tyrants historically make use of that toehold. To date, Syria is still in massive turmoil due to a bloody civil war, and Iranian leaders continue to thumb their collective noses at calls for a halt to their nuclear pursuits.

During his initial campaign, Obama surrounded himself with people whose anti-Israel leanings are sometimes known—sometimes suspect. One such individual is Robert Malley, whose Syrian-born father is said to have "loathed" Israel and who became a close confidant to Yasser Arafat. Malley has written a number of op-eds that are scathingly opposed to Israel. He often blames Israel for any perceived failure to reach a Middle East peace settlement with her enemies. Malley's rhetoric has proven to be rich fodder for the PA and anti-Israel militants worldwide.

Another man from whom Obama has sought advice is Joseph Cirincione, president of the Ploughshares Fund. Listed in "Discover the Networks," a guide to the Liberal Left, the Fund is defined as: "'a public grant-making foundation that supports initiatives to prevent the spread and use of nuclear, biological, and chemical weapons and other weapons of war, and to prevent conflicts that could lead to the use of weapons of mass destruction.' It also opposes America's development of a missile defense system."[417]

Cirincione, it has been said, has decidedly anti-Israel leanings. Ed Lasky, writer for *American Thinker*, concurs. He wrote that Cirincione is "another in a disconcertingly long line of Obama advisors who seemingly have an anti-Israel bias and who would be very willing to apply American pressure on our tiny ally to disarm itself in the face of its mortal enemies."[418]

Days before the 2008 election, the leader of one rogue state endorsed Obama, according to an AFP article in *YNetNews*:

> Iranian parliament Speaker Ali Larijani said Wednesday that Iran would prefer Democrat Barack Obama in the White House next year. Larijani also dismissed any idea that the US would attack Iran. "We are leaning more in favor of Barack Obama because he is more flexible and rational, even though we know American policy will not change that much," Larijani said at a press conference during a visit to Bahrain.[419]

Now, why do you suppose both a terrorist organization and a terrorist state would support one candidate over another? Could it have been the knowledge that one candidate was likely to be more left, more liberal, and more willing to sacrifice Israel than the other? And yet it is eerily apparent that despite his circle of anti-Israel advisors, the media and many voters continue to view Barack Obama as a staunch supporter of that tiny nation in the midst of a sea of detractors.

Shortly after taking office, Obama did his best to alienate American Jews and their Israeli counterparts. He made every effort to visit Muslim countries, including two trips to Indonesia and Afghanistan, and one each to Turkey, Iraq, Saudi Arabia (where he was caught on camera infamously bowing to King Abdullah), and Egypt. In an article for *Front Page Magazine*, Joseph Kline criticized Obama's treatment of Prime Minister Benjamin Netanyahu:

> Obama's latest blast at Netanyahu recalls his snub of Netanyahu during the prime minister's first visit to the Obama White House in March 2010. Obama presented Netanyahu with a list of demands, including a halt to all settlement construction in East Jerusalem. When

Netanyahu resisted Obama's charms, Obama picked up
his marbles. He stormed out of the meeting and declared,
"I'm going to the residential wing to have dinner with
Michelle and the girls." Obama also refused the normal
protocol of a joint photograph with the Israeli leader.[420]

During his first term in the White House, President Obama did more
to destroy Israel's legitimacy and weaken her already fragile place globally
than any president since Jimmy Carter. His tactic was elementary: He
simply became president with a world platform to demand that Israel halt
settlement construction as a prerequisite to peace talks. This includes
erecting homes for Jews in their own Jewish Quarter. Reportedly, his
first contact after becoming president was a telephone call to Palestinian
Authority President Mahmoud Abbas, not to the prime minister of Israel,
the chief US ally in the Middle East.

Less than six months after assuming office, Obama flew to Cairo
to deliver a major speech designed to impress the Muslim world.
During the speech he said, "Anti-Semitism in Europe culminated in an
unprecedented Holocaust."[421] He failed, however, to call attention to the
Arab anti-Semitism during World War II and its continuance in today's
Muslim world. He chose as his platform the country of the Grand Mufti
Haj Muhammed Amin al-Husseini, Hitler's frequent wartime guest in
Berlin, who was instrumental in helping the Führer advance the Final
Solution. Not one time did the president articulate the word *terrorism*.
But he did pander to the Palestinians present.

Anne Bayefsky, professor and Hudson Institute Fellow, wrote of
Obama's Egypt speech:

Obama [in the Cairo speech] analogized Palestinian
"daily humiliations . . . that come with occupation" to the
"humiliation of segregation" of black slaves in America
and the "moral authority" of "people from South Africa."

His Arab audience understood that the president of the
United States had just given a nod to the single most potent
defamation of the Jewish state today—the allegation that
Israel is a racist, apartheid state.[422]

In his speech, the president designated Israel as the "second major
source of tension" in the Middle East—following fanatical Muslim
terrorists. At the same time, he stated unequivocally that the United
States would not turn a blind eye to the desire of the Palestinians for
statehood. It seems that Mr. Obama was then, and still is, dedicated to
the proposition of a fifty-fourth Muslim country. With the creation of a
Palestinian state, Israel would be completely isolated—an island in a sea
of fanatical Muslim countries.

The truth is, no one—either at home or abroad—had any earthly idea
what Barack Obama would do when he arrived at 1600 Pennsylvania
Avenue. Even now after a second election, more questions than answers
remain: If there were a nuclear attack by Iran against Israel or the United
States, would Mr. Obama have the courage to open the briefcase and
enter the code for retaliation, or would he decline to become involved?
If fanatical Muslim terrorists were to again initiate an attack on US soil,
how would Mr. Obama respond? Would he jeopardize US allies in every
region of the world? Just what *is* his "backbone quotient"?

How did Barack Obama handle the challenges of his first term as 44th
president of the United States, in both domestic and foreign relations?
What will be the results of his second term? What will US foreign policy
look like in 2016? For an insightful glimpse, consider his treatment of our
ally Israel. Consider his inability to take a courageous stand against Iran's
nuclear ambitions. Consider his deferential behavior toward the world's
Muslim leaders. Consider his first post-election trip outside the United
States—to Cambodia, Thailand, and Myanmar, while Israel once again
faced an incoming barrage of missiles from Hamas, Iran's proxy in Gaza.

The question remains: When Iran reaches the threshold of nuclear weapons capabilities, will the United States stand with Israel, or remain on the sidelines, too fearful to act decisively? The 2012 election was a bitterly fought campaign for Mr. Obama. He won both the popular vote and the Electoral College, but nearly half the United States was disenfranchised by his victory. Like Presidents Clinton and Bush before him, he is a two-term president, but now as a lame duck head of state, there is little to indicate he will change his stance regarding the issues that plague Israel.

Just as Jimmy Carter gave away the Panama Canal and abandoned Iran to Islamic fundamentalists, will Obama give Israel away and then abandon the United States to her enemies? Has our nation become the frog in the pot of cold water? Have we elected and then re-elected a president so complacent, that when the Middle East fire is ignited, we will be forced to give in without a fight, turning a blind eye to Israel's plight, letting her perish without our support?

In July 2013, President Obama introduced his latest plan to resurrect talks between Israel and the Palestinian Authority. His proposal included granting freedom for over one hundred of terrorism's most heinous criminals. The men whose release has been given include the perpetrators of some of the most hideous acts of terror imaginable. Two of the terrorists in the group tossed Molotov cocktails into a bus traveling to Jerusalem. Rachel Weiss and her three children died, while IDF soldier David Delarosa was murdered trying to rescue them. Another duo, the men who invaded the home of David Dadi, stabbed him and his friend, Chaim Weitzman, to death and then cut off their ears as souvenirs.

Apparently the president has forgotten or perhaps never bothered to learn the origins of the PLO, which continues to hide under the banner of the Palestinian Authority. Masquerading as Abu Mazen, PLO chief financial officer, Mahmoud Abbas masterminded the Munich massacre during the 1972 Summer Olympics.

The PA/PLO has, over the years, been equally complicit in hijacking airplanes (TWA, Pan Am, and BOAC), attacking school buses filled with

Jewish children, and murdering, maiming, and mutilating the innocent. Its members have killed Americans abroad: Ambassador to the Sudan Cleo Noel and Leon Klinghoffer, a wheelchair-bound Jewish invalid, aboard the *Achille Lauro* cruise ship, to name just two of the many victims of the PLO.

The crisis facing President Barack Obama, and indeed, the world is a test of moral will and faith. Humanists make excuses for the evil of terrorists in the nations that surround Israel. At the worst, they refuse to confront terrorism by denying its existence. This only feeds the beast of evil. In truth, Israel's relationship with the United States is a unique *danse macabre*, and President Obama has embraced the role of dance master.

On October 1, 2013, Prime Minister Netanyahu spoke to the United Nations General Assembly. Just days before his address, President Barack Obama and Iran's President Hassan Rouhani who followed Mahmoud Ahmadinejad into office held the first direct talks between US and Iranian leaders since the 1979 Islamic revolution.

Exchanging pleasantries during a fifteen minute, have-a-nice-day telephone conversation, Obama communicated his "deep respects for the Iranian people," and congratulated Rouhani for his recent election. Mr. Obama also expressed his good wishes and hopes that he and the Iranian leader could resolve over the next few months the differences between the US and Iran.

For thirty-five years, Hassan Rouhani has served as an unswervingly loyal Islamic cleric and a close aide to the Ayatollah Khamenei. Despite the fact that President Obama congratulated him on his election, Rouhani was only one of six presidential candidates. After 678 had been disqualified by the regime as being ideologically unsound, Rouhani was the final choice. Obama had an opportunity to maintain moral clarity and keep the line of sanctions drawn in the sand. He had the chance to stand by the United States' greatest ally in the Middle East, Israel; instead, he played the appeasement card—that would only serve to devalue America's currency in the Middle East and embolden terror.

In his UN speech, Mr. Netanyahu called former Iranian President Mahmoud Ahmadinejad a "wolf in wolf's clothing", and made it clear that newly-elected Hassan Rouhani is unlike his predecessor. Instead, Netanyahu said, he was the more conventional wolf in sheep's clothing who thinks he can hoodwink the world at large. Said the prime minister, "I wish we could believe Rouhani's words, but we must focus on Iran's actions. And it's the brazen contrast, this extraordinary contradiction, between Rouhani's words and Iran's actions that is so startling. Rouhani stood at this very podium last week [September 28, 2013] and praised Iranian democracy...But the regime that he represents executes political dissidents by the hundreds and jails them by the thousands."[423]

Mr. Netanyahu then enumerated all the reasons why President Obama and others should not believe Iran's controlling clerics: One, all Iranian nuclear facilities are hidden deep underground to forestall attacks; two, facilities for uranium enrichment have been cloaked in secrecy; three, intercontinental ballistic missiles have been developed with the specific purpose of delivering nuclear warheads that would most certainly reach Israel, and could within years reach cities on the eastern seaboard of the United States; and four, Iran's leaders are prepared to subject the populace to crippling economic sanctions in order to keep International Atomic Energy Agency officials from scrutinizing the country's atomic operations. The prime minister had one answer: Iran's facilities are not for peaceful nuclear pursuits.

Apparently Rouhani's trite, but effective, hale-fellow-well-met strategy is one that works. The success of that falsely friendly approach was touted in his 2011 book when he wrote: "While we [the Iranians] were talking to the Europeans in Tehran, we were installing equipment in Isfahan." Mr. Netanyahu summed up that theory quite succinctly with "Rouhani thinks he can have his yellowcake and eat it too."[424]

Barack Obama, a lame duck president at this writing, is desperate and perhaps willing to do anything to create a legacy for which he will be long remembered. Israel, on the other hand, needs no reminder of what can happen when past lessons are buried under a barrage of bluster. Its people know the price that will be extracted if the fanatical regime in Tehran is allowed to arm itself with atomic weapons. Netanyahu reminded us, "We in Israel, we know all too well the cost of war. But history has taught us that to prevent war tomorrow, we must be firm today."[425]

President Obama's desire to negotiate no matter the cost gives rise to those in the West who have become unwilling cohorts of the jihadists. These individuals rationalize the presence of evil and the attacks by terrorists based on their perception of our past sins.

Time alone will provide an opportunity for his presidency to be properly evaluated. Will his imprint on the White House be similar to that of his idol, Abraham Lincoln, or will it be more like that of Jimmy Carter? What will be Obama's epitaph regarding the State of Israel? Will he ultimately be equated with the "Righteous Gentiles," or will his name be missing from the list of those who are "Friends of Israel"?

As we consider his track record so far with regard to the State of Israel, my best guess is that we will never find the name of Barack Obama in the Hall or Righteous Gentiles at *Yad Vashem*.

(3 8)

THE FIG TREE
BLOSSOMS

"For this is what the LORD Almighty says:
"After the Glorious One has sent me against the nations
that have plundered you—for whoever touches you
touches the apple of his eye—I will surely raise my hand
against them so that their slaves will plunder them.
Then you will know that the LORD Almighty has sent me,"
(Zechariah 2:8 NIV.)

The river of prophecy is filled with rocks, rapids, eddies, and undercurrents. It often has more to do with milestones we see along the way than it does in the details of how something that was foretold will be accomplished. Events tend to collide and conflict in the currents as prophecy is fulfilled. Sometimes it seems to move ahead briskly, other times it comes to a stagnant halt, flowing backwards for a time as its energy builds, or even disappearing from sight only to reemerge farther downstream. This often makes finding ourselves in the river rather confusing. It is easy to get lost unless progress is gauged relative to the bank, and this is why God gives us markers along the way to alert us to the next bend in the river. By understanding the flow of prophecy over the past few centuries, and seeing how those events relate to the patterns of today, we can begin to clearly see what effects Bible prophecy has on modern-day nations.

The US today is regarded as a world leader—and as such should have a presence in events that will shape the world during the final days of this earth. The key to the future is not buried in bureaucratic babble; it lies instead in understanding the Word of God and what God is doing and saying before the final confrontation that will be followed by a thousand years of peace.

Many look at prophecy and think because certain things are ordained it provides a reason to do nothing but sit and wait. As in the days of Noah, too many continue to eat and drink, marry and be given in marriage, while either disaster or deliverance is at the door.

While many may think the fulfillment of biblical prophecy is a sovereign act of God, the scriptures themselves indicate that we can choose on which side of prophecy we prefer to be—blessed or cursed. When God was about to destroy Sodom and Gomorrah, He asked, "Shall I hide from Abraham that thing which I do?" (Genesis 18:17, NIV.) God felt He should take no action of judgment without giving His friend Abraham the right to intercede on behalf of the inhabitants of the sinful cities.

Daniel, reading in the book of Jeremiah in his old age, came across a scripture that said, "After seventy years be accomplished at Babylon I will visit you, and perform my good word toward you, in causing you to return to this place," (Jeremiah 29:10, KJV.) Daniel did some hasty calculations: over seventy years had passed and Israel was still in captivity in Babylon! So he began to pray to Jehovah God. Thus was the heart of Babylonian King Cyrus changed and Nehemiah was given permission to return to Jerusalem and rebuild the Temple.

As Jesus said:

> You are my friends if you do what I command. I no
> longer call you servants, because a servant *does not know*

his master's business. Instead, I have called you friends,
for everything that I learned from my Father I have made
known to you, (John 15:14-15, NIV [emphasis added].)

As Jesus' followers, we should be informed as to what He's planning concerning events for our nation. We should be involved with praying about their fulfillment. As it was with Daniel, God needs someone to agree with Him, pray His promises into reality, and carry out His plan on earth.

In the parable of the fig tree (Matthew 24:32-44), Jesus warned His disciples that when we begin to see certain events unfold, they would be indications of the "season" of the end of this age. Just as new leaves on the fig tree would indicate that summer was coming, so the generation that saw these things would also see end time prophecy fulfilled. Look for a moment at what Jesus said would mark the final age and His return:

Many would come in His name setting themselves up
as Christ and establishing their own religions (Matthew
24:5, 11)

The twentieth century witnessed a dramatic decline in membership in mainline Protestant denominations. Not only has there been a decline in church membership and attendance, the last few decades have seen a departure from the historic faith. American studies show that two to five million young adults between the ages of eighteen and twenty-five are involved in approximately 2,000 to 5,000 cult groups today.[426]

Many churches and entire denominations have totally abandoned biblical truth. Openly gay men and women have been ordained in some of the older mainline churches. I have no doubt these clergyman and women are sincerely committed to the faith and want to help the people of their parish. The problem is a lifestyle that directly contradicts the clear teaching of Scripture. God does not hate gays—far from it—but does He want practicing homosexuals misleading His Church?

This is not a new problem, by the way. The church at Corinth had homosexuals, adulterers, and drunkards as members. The difference is that they had all given up their former lifestyles after accepting Christ as Savior:

> Do you not know that the unrighteous will not inherit the kingdom of God? Do not be deceived. Neither fornicators, nor idolaters, nor adulterers, nor homosexuals, nor sodomites, nor thieves, nor covetous, nor drunkards, nor revilers, nor extortioners will inherit the kingdom of God. *And such were some of you.* But you were washed, but you were sanctified, but you were justified in the name of the Lord Jesus and by the Spirit of our God, (1 Corinthians 6:9-11, KJV [emphasis added].)

There would be wars and rumors of wars; and nations will rise up against nations (Matthew 24:6-7.)

> All we need do is turn on any 24-hour radio or television news channel to hear of wars and rumors of wars worldwide, in countries such as Syria, Afghanistan, the Sudan, Egypt, and other locales. How long have 24-hour news channels been around? The first, CNN, began broadcasting in 1981. Now, terrorist strikes and the ongoing battle on terrorism are reported daily by that channel and several others.

There will be famines, epidemic diseases, and earthquakes all over the world (Matthew 24:7)

> An entire continent, Africa, is suffering from drought, war, poverty, and plagues. In recent years, parts of the

United States have suffered debilitating drought and wild changes in the weather—massive killer tornadoes, devastating hurricanes, and repeated historic floods are becoming commonplace.

Despite longer life expectancy, new diseases are being discovered regularly; AIDS and other sexually transmitted diseases are devastating entire continents. Viruses such as the West Nile and SARS, as well as a new strain of flesh-eating virus linked to strep have thrown many into panic. We have more knowledge than ever before about disease and better technology and techniques, yet at the same time we are seeing epidemic increases in cardiovascular disease, diabetes, and Alzheimer's.

Since 1900, the world has experienced more than a hundred different earthquakes where a thousand or more were killed, and of the twenty-one earthquakes in the history of the world where more than 50,000 were killed, over half of them have taken place in the last century.[427] In December of 2003 an earthquake hit Iran that killed as many as 30,000, injured another 30,000, and left more than 100,000 homeless. On that same day several other earthquakes over 5.0 on the Richter scale hit along the world's "ring of fire," all reported to be unrelated. In December 2004, an earthquake off the coast of Indonesia birthed a tsunami that killed as many as 300,000. In October 2005, an earthquake in Pakistan caused the deaths of as many as 100,000. In 2008 almost 70,000 died in an earthquake that hit Sichuan Province, China. The devastating earthquake that struck the Caribbean Island of Haiti in 2010 killed between 230,000 and 316,000. An earthquake and tsunami in Japan in 2011 left over 18,000 dead and thousands missing. In addition, there were hundreds of earthquakes with much lower death tolls felt worldwide.

Persecution shall increase (Matthew 24:8-10)

Over sixty-five percent of the nearly 69.5 million Christians who have died for their faith, died in the twentieth century. Today, an average of 435 Christians die for their faith *every day*.[428] In a 2011 article in the Church of England newspaper, it was reported that a Christian dies for his/her faith every five minutes, yet we hear little about this from the Liberal Left media worldwide.

Sin shall flourish and Christian love will grow cold (Matthew 24:12)

This prophesied "falling away" is quite evident today, and rapidly increasing. There is a modern disconnect between personal spirituality and the traditional church or synagogue. Polls consistently show that over ninety percent of Americans profess a belief in God, and more than sixty percent say religion is very important to their own lives; yet only forty-three percent attend church or synagogue on a regular basis.[429]

Liberals have used freedom of speech to legalize every form of perversion. What used to be unseen and spurned is now taking to the streets and growing. At the same time, Christians in the US seem less and less sure of themselves as the culture has turned against God. Christian expression is being increasingly and forcefully limited in our schools and society.

Meanwhile, our pews are filled with people who are

biblically illiterate. Why? Because many churches have abandoned Christian education in favor of a feel-good faith! We pay more attention to the music we sing than the gospel preached. Our marching orders are to go into the world and "make disciples . . . baptizing them . . . teaching them to observe all things," (Matthew 28:19-20) that God commanded. The goal is not converts; it is disciples; and discipleship requires more than a "don't-worry-be-happy" gospel; it requires faithful preaching of all of Scripture, including the parts that convict our hearts.

There shall also be an honored remnant of Believers who will not grow cold and indifferent, but will become more diligent. These disciples will see the gospel of God's kingdom preached in every nation (Matthew 24:13-14.)

While there are other signs of the end times foretold in the Bible, I think these are enough to cause us to see that the season Jesus spoke of is upon us. While we don't know the day or the hour, the leaves of the fig tree are definitely spouting and flourishing. It is time we understood the significance of today's events and our nation's precarious position between the two sons of Abraham, so that we know what to do in the days to come.

In order to do that, we must first know the milestones for which to watch. According to Bible prophecy as it has been interpreted by those who have dedicated much of their lives to studying and understanding it, here are the most significant biblical prophecies, past and present, with respect to the salvation of God's people:

- » Jesus' first coming (Isaiah 53; Psalm 41:9 55:12-14; Zechariah 9:9; 13:7)

- » Jesus' death on the cross and resurrection (Jeremiah 31:15; Psalm 22)

- » Jesus' ascension to the right hand of the Father and the gift of the Holy Spirit to the Church (John 20:17)

- » The destruction of the temple and Jerusalem (Matthew 24:1-2)

- » The scattering of the Jews to the nations of the earth (the Diaspora) (Genesis 49:7; Leviticus 26:33; Nehemiah 1:8)

- » The Reunification of the nation of Israel (Isaiah 11:1; 35:10; Jeremiah 31:10)

- » The Rapture (1 Corinthians 15:51-52; 1 Thessalonians 4:16; Luke 17:34)

- » The Antichrist's seven-year-peace pact with Israel (marking the beginning of the Tribulation) (Daniel 9:27)

- » The rebuilding of the Temple (Ezekiel 43:2-5; 44:4; Acts 15:13-17)

- » Gog and Magog (most commonly seen as representing Russia or a coalition of forces led by Russia or perhaps some of its former Soviet Republics) attack Israel, but are thwarted by a supernatural intervention of God (Revelation 20:8)

» The Temple's desecration by the Antichrist (marking the beginning of the three and a half years of Great Tribulation) (Daniel 9:27)

» The battle of Armageddon (Revelation 18)

» Jesus' Second Coming (1 Thessalonians 4:16-17; Acts 1:11; Matthew 24:30; 1 Peter 1:7; 4:13)

» The Millennium (Revelation 20:1-5)

» Satan again loosed for a season (Revelation 20:6-10)

» The Great White Throne Judgment (Revelation 20:11-15)

» Eternity

In looking at these prophetic mile markers, there are a couple of keys to notice—namely where we are in this series of events, and when and how they have occurred. One is that, since the destruction of the Temple and Jerusalem by the Romans in AD 70, the single most significant event of prophecy was the reunification of the nation of Israel on May 14, 1948.

A second is that the world sits on the threshold of one of the next two events: 1) The blessed hope, the Rapture, followed by 2) the hell of the Tribulation. If we are reading and interpreting the signs correctly, these are likely to happen soon, possibly within this generation. Though we have been told this to the point where its urgency has been lost for many, it is nevertheless true. Jesus said, "when you see all these things, know that it is near—at the door....This generation will by no means pass away till all these things take place," (Matthew 24:33-34.) It seems very likely that events currently seen in the Middle East are setting the stage for what will happen in the world during the Tribulation.

The spirit of Antichrist so active in the world today is, not surprisingly, rabidly anti-Semitic. While the twentieth century was the worst period of Christian persecution in the history of the world, it was also the time of the Holocaust and of pogroms designed to rid Germany and Russia of the Jewish populations. Today the cruelest persecution of Christians happens in fundamentalist Muslim countries under *Shariah* Law (the religious criminal code set forth by the Quran), and whose news media also promote Jew-hatred. These are the white-hot beds of coal that keep the fires of anti-Semitism and terrorism ablaze. If we interpret trends correctly, this spirit is also behind much of the Liberal Left's secular relativism trying to silence God's voice in the US today. Though this spirit has also infected the Church from time to time, turning it towards apostasy and anti-Semitism, we should not be confused. The true Church will always be the one following the Spirit of Christ, exhibiting His true fruit and gifts, not those who have turned to political correctness rather than the love of God as its rule of thumb.

While America is clearly in this river of prophecy, it is evident that nations such as Jordan (represented by the ancient peoples and lands of Ammon, Moab, and Edom), Egypt, Iran (biblical Persia), Iraq (biblical Babylon), the European Union (the reunited ten toes of the Roman Empire), Russia (Rosh), Saudi Arabia (Sheba and Dedan), among others, are specifically mentioned in the Bible. Some have also proposed that the United States is in prophecy disguised as the "tall and smooth-skinned" people who are "feared far and wide, an aggressive nation of strange speech, whose land is divided by rivers (Isaiah 19:2, NIV)" or as a young lion of Tarshish (see Ezekiel 3813, the "two wings of the great eagle," (Revelation 12:13-17, NIV) or even the spiritual Babylon of the end times. In fact, highly respected evangelical leaders such as the late Rev. David Wilkerson, pastor of Times Square Church in New York City, believed that the US, with New York City as its spiritual center, is the Babylon of Revelation 18. Look at how he described the nation that will be spiritual Babylon:

1. It is a nation of immigrants—Revelation 18:15

2. It is a cultural city—Revelation 18:22

3. It has a deep water port—Revelation 18:17-19

4. It has the wealth of the world—Revelation 18:15-19; Jeremiah 51:13

5. It is the last super power on the earth (Babylon the Great)—Revelation 17.

6. The world's leaders will assemble there—Jeremiah 51:44

7. It will be a world policeman—Jeremiah 50:23

8. It would seem to be connected to outer space—Jeremiah 51:53

9. It would have some amazing stealth-type technology—Isaiah 47:10-13[430]

However, while this may be a possibility, I believe the United States has another course. The Bible says, "Blessed is the nation whose God is the LORD," (Psalm 33:12, NIV) and "Righteousness exalts a nation, but sin is a disgrace," (Proverbs 14:34 NKJV.) Our politics and the course of our nation do not determine what is in our hearts. If God is to truly heal our land, it is not just a question of acceptable foreign and domestic policy; it is an issue of churches in the United States rejecting relativism and earnestly seeking God and His ways. The battle is not a conflict between Christian and secular *culture*, but between good and evil, between the Spirit of Christ and the spirit of Antichrist, between revealing Jesus to our world and being satisfied with complacency and lukewarm spirituality. America's roots were firmly established in the moral clarity of the Bible and prayer. If we call on God to heal our land, America might well be better aligned with Israel and aid in its revival in the end times, not engulfed by the spirit of the world that will place us on the wrong side during the battle of Armageddon.

While the Rapture of the church may not happen tomorrow, or perhaps for years, the Bible admonishes us to "Occupy till I come," (Luke 19:13.) There are things that can be done to have peace in our time, win the war on terrorism, and avoid abandoning Israel as other nations have done. With God's help, the US can accomplish what no other nation on earth could even hope to do, but not without a major course correction. It is time to realign our moral compass. The Church needs to be an eternal purpose-driven Body of Believers, determined to preach the truth from pulpits in America, determined to be salt and light to a dark and hopeless world.

We stand as Nineveh did after Jonah delivered a message from God: we must either choose to leave God behind and continue as we have in the past, or repent and experience revival. We are at a crossroads, but even more significantly, we are in the crosshairs of fanatics who hate Christians and Jews, and all things for which the United States and Israel stand. We must respond both spiritually and naturally with Christian love and compassion and with political wisdom based on clarity of vision and moral integrity. It is a worthy calling far more powerful than the suicide bombers' quest for martyrdom. Yet until we live with greater conviction than that for which they die, our generation will see nothing of God's plan and purpose.

Had the Church obeyed the Great Commission—to be a witness unto Him in Jerusalem, Judea and Samaria—Islamic fundamentalists such as Hamas, Hezbollah, Islamic Jihad, and others of that ilk would not have been able to corrupt the minds of Arab children with hatred for Jews and Christians. Instead, they would know the Word of God and more would become followers of Him, filled with love. Revival would be spreading across the Middle East and events of September 11 and the ensuing wars in Iraq and Afghanistan might never have occurred. The truth is: Palestinian *Christians* do not kill Jews.

Has the Church failed this nation and our Lord? Is the Church guiltier in the eyes of God than the apostates who have turned away from Him? Is it too late? No, it's not; but if ever the Church of Jesus Christ plans to repent and obey the Great Commission, rather than continuing to pursue the "Great Omission", it is now!

I pray that pastors will begin to preach on the Second Coming of the Lord. The Bible tells us that we are to "live soberly, righteously, and godly, in this present world," (Titus 2:12.) There has never been a time in history when God dwelt in a Church with an earthly perspective. It is time to proclaim this message. Why? The world has infiltrated the Church. Abortions, divorces, pornography, drugs, alcohol and even homosexuality are alive and well in the Church. Many pastors allow fear of retaliation to keep them from preaching against these matters.

God has placed one message on my heart to preach in this hour: Jesus is coming! The Bible says, "I know your deeds, that you are neither cold nor hot. I wish you were either one or the other! So, because you are lukewarm—neither hot nor cold—I am about to spit you out of my mouth," (Rev. 3:16, NIV.)

The Shepherd is calling for spiritual warriors—will you answer His call? If so, we need to understand the currents of American prophecy from our beginnings so that we know how to navigate the waters that lie ahead of us.

APPENDIX A:

AN INDEX *of* ANCIENT PROPHECIES

Israel is the nation mentioned most often in the Bible. Do you know what nation is second? It's Iraq! However, that is not the name used in the Bible. The names used in the Bible are: Babylon, Land of Shinar and Mesopotamia. The word "Mesopotamia" means "between two rivers"—more precisely, between the Tigris and Euphrates Rivers.

The name "Iraq" means "country with deep roots." Indeed, Iraq is a country with deep roots. That is very significant in the Bible. Here's why:

> No other nation, except Israel, has more history and
> prophecy associated with it than Iraq.

Prophecies: Curses on nations that reject God and His Word

Genesis 27:29	Malachi 1:14	Deuteronomy 30:1
Genesis 18:18	Genesis 22:18	Genesis 26:4
Psalm 72:17	Isaiah 61:9	Jeremiah 4:2
Malachi 3:12	Galatians 3:8	Deuteronomy 28:14-68
Joel 3:16		

Prophecies: God fighting against nations that reject His Word

Jeremiah 1:19	Jeremiah 15:20	Jeremiah 21:4
Jeremiah 21:5	Jeremiah 32:5	Jeremiah 34:1,7
Jeremiah 34:22	Daniel 10:20	Daniel 11:7,11
Zechariah 14:2, 3	Acts 5:39	Revelation 2:16
Genesis 12:1-3		

Prophecies: Curses on Nations that attempt to divide the land of Israel

Zechariah 7:3	II Samuel 7:10	Genesis 25:23
Genesis 17:4-9	Genesis 28:13	Zechariah 2:8
Jeremiah 12:14	Amos 9:14-15	

Prophecies: Nations that conspire together to divide the land of Israel
Psalm 83:1-18

Prophecies: Nations blessed for blessing Israel

Genesis 18:18	Genesis 22:15-18	Genesis 26:4
Genesis 27:29	Psalm 72:17	Isaiah 61:9
Jeremiah 4:2	Malachi 3:12	Galatians 3:8
Genesis 12:1-3	Isaiah 2:3	Isaiah 62:1-7
Psalm 128:5	Deuteronomy 28:10-13	

Prophecies: Curses on the nations that come against Jerusalem

Zechariah 12:1-6	Zechariah 2:8	Revelation 16:12-16

Prophecies: Specially chosen by God

2 Chronicles 6:6	Psalm 135:21	2 Chronicles 37:7

Prophecies: Protected by God

Isaiah 31:3	II Samuel 24:16	II Kings 19:34-34
Zechariah 2:5	Psalm 121:4-8	II Chronicles 12:7

Described as prophecies

Psalm 48:2	Jeremiah 22:8	Psalm 122:3
Psalm 46:4	Isaiah 60:14	Matthew 5:5
Isaiah 1:21, 26	Zechariah 8:3	Isaiah 62:12
Nehemiah 11:1	Jeremiah 3:17	Psalm 48:12
Isaiah 33:30	Zechariah 7:3	

Prophecies fulfilled

Jeremiah 20:5	Jeremiah 9:11	Jeremiah 26:18
Isaiah 64:10	Isaiah 44:26-28	Zechariah 9:9
Isaiah 2:3	Isaiah 40:9	Luke 19:42-44
I Kings 14:25, 26	II Kings 14:13, 14	II Chronicles 12:1-4
Isaiah 7:1	II Kings 16:5	II Kings 18:17
II Kings 19:1-37	II Kings 23:33-35	III Kings 24:10, 11
II Kings 25:1-30	Jeremiah 29:1-8	

Prophecies: Jerusalem and the nations

II Chronicles 32:23	Psalms 79:1	II Chronicles 33:9
Isaiah 66:20	Jeremiah 3:17	II Chronicles 34:14
Jeremiah 4:16	Ezekiel 5:5, 8	Ezekiel 26:2
Joel 3:1	Micah 4:2	Zechariah 8:22
Zechariah 9:10	Zechariah 12:3, 9	Zechariah 14:2, 12, 14, 16
Luke 21:24	Luke 24:47	Psalm 125:1-2

Future prophecies

Matthew 24:21, 29	Matthew 24:6-15	Revelation 2:12
Isaiah 2:3	Jeremiah 33:7-8	Revelation 21:1, 2, 10

Prophecies declaring the land and eternal covenant

Genesis 17:4-9	Genesis 15:18-21	II Chronicles 37:7
Psalm 89:28-37	Psalm 105:8-11	Genesis 13:14-15
Psalm 102:12-13	Isaiah 49:15	Amos 9:14-15
Jeremiah 30:3	Ezekiel 28:25-26	Ezekiel 36:24

Prophecies: The Messiah's return to Jerusalem
Psalm 102:15   Zechariah 14:1-3

Prophecies: The Rebirth of Israel in 1948
Isaiah 66:8-13

Prophecies: The Temple Site
Isaiah 14:12-15   Isaiah 2:2-4   Daniel 8:23-25

Prophecies: The return of the Jews to Israel

Isaiah 49:22	Isaiah 43:6	Ezekiel 11:1
Amos 9:14-15	Isaiah 11:12	Jeremiah 29:10-14

Prophecies: Babylon (Iraq)
Eden in Iraq: Genesis 2:10-14
Adam and Eve created: Genesis 2:7-8
Satan's first appearance: Genesis 3:1-6
Nimrod established Babylon: Genesis 10:8-9
Tower of Babel built: Genesis 11:1-4
Confusion of languages: Genesis 11:5-11
Abraham's hometown: Genesis 11:28-12:5, Acts 7:2-4
Isaac's bride from Iraq: Genesis 24:3-4, 10
Jacob in Iraq: Genesis 27:42-45, 31:38
First world empire: Daniel 1:1-2, 2:36-38
Daniel tested: 2 Kings 24; Daniel 2:49; 3:12-30; 6
Greatest revival in history: Jonah 3
Book of Esther: Esther
Book of Nahum: Nahum
Prophecies in Revelation: Revelation 17; 18; Revelation 9:13-16;
Revelation 16:16-19
Fall of Babylon: Daniel 14:8
Judgment: Ezekiel 37; 38; Isaiah 13:1,6, 19; Isaiah 14:22-23
Daniel's Prophecies: Isaiah 14:22-23; Daniel 2:44; Daniel 9:24–26;
Daniel 9:27; Daniel 11:31

Prophecies: The Promised Messiah
He will be born of a virgin: Isaiah 7:14
Place of His birth: Micah 5:2
Rachel weeps for her murdered children: Jeremiah 31:15
He will be called out of Egypt: Hosea 11:1
The Spirit's anointing: Isaiah 11:2

Triumphant entry into Jerusalem: Zechariah 9:9
Betrayed by His friend: Psalm 41:9; 55:12-14
Forsaken by His disciples: Zechariah 13:7
The price of His betrayal: Zechariah 11:12

Prophecies: The Returning Messiah

The Judge: Psalm 98:9
The Builder who appears in Glory: Psalm 102:16
Son of Man and Kingdom Claimer: Daniel 7:13
Glorious One from the Father: Matthew 16:26:27, Titus 2:11-15,
         Hebrews 9:24-28
Claims His throne: Matthew 19:28
Prophetic timeline of His appearing: Matthew 24, Mark 13, Luke 21
Bridegroom: Matthew 25:1-2
Judges His servants: Matthew 25:13-30, II Timothy 4:1
His appearing in the clouds: Matthew 26:64, Mark 14:62
Reward for denial: Mark 8:38, Luke 9:26, II Peter 3
Ready for His coming: Luke 12:35-48, Luke 17:20-37, 18:8
The ten talents: Luke 19:11-28
The promise of God's anointing: John 1:51
The promise of His return: John 14:3, John 14:18; John 14:28, Acts 1:10-11
Promised refreshing: Acts 3:19-21
Wait for His coming: I Corinthians 1:4-8, I Thessalonians 1:19
Judge not: I Corinthians 4:5
In Remembrance: I Corinthians 11:26
Behold, He comes: I Corinthians 15:23, 16:22, Philippians 3:10,
Revelation 16:15
Rejoice: II Corinthians 1:14
The Day of the Lord: Philippians 1:6-10
Watching for Him: Philippians 3:20-21, I Timothy 6:13-15, Hebrews 10:25
With Him: Colossians 3:3-5
The joy of His coming: I Thessalonians 2:19
Blameless: I Thessalonians 3:13, I Thessalonians 5:23, Hebrews 10:22
The Rapture: I Thessalonians 4:13-18, I Thessalonians 5:1-10, II John 7,
     Jude 14-15, Revelation 1:17, Revelation 2:25, Revelation 3:3,
     Revelation 14:14-16
The revelation: II Thessalonians 1:7-10, I Peter 4:13, I Peter 5:1-4
The reward: II Timothy 4:8
Satan defeated: II Thessalonians 2:1-8
Patience: Hebrews 10:35-37, James 5:7-8, I Peter 1:7, I Peter 1:13
Confidence: I John 2:28
Like Him: I John 2:2-3, I John 3:2-3,
Even so, come quickly: Revelation 22:20

At that time Michael shall stand up,
The great prince who stands watch over the sons of your people;
And there shall be a time of trouble,
Such as never was since there was a nation,
Even to that time.
And at that time your people shall be delivered,
Every one who is found written in the book.
And many of those who sleep in the dust of the earth shall awake,
Some to everlasting life,
Some to shame and everlasting contempt.
Those who are wise shall shine
Like the brightness of the firmament,
And those who turn many to righteousness
Like the stars forever and ever.
But you, Daniel, shut up the words,
and seal the book until the time of the end; many shall run to and
fro, and knowledge shall increase.

—Daniel 12:1–4 [italics added]

Behold, the nations are as a drop in a bucket,
And are counted as the small dust on the scales; . . .
All nations before Him are as nothing,
And they are counted by Him less than nothing and worthless. . . .
Even the youths shall faint and be weary,
And the young men shall utterly fall,
But those who wait on the LORD
Shall renew their strength;
They shall mount up with wings like eagles,
They shall run and not be weary,
They shall walk and not faint.

—Isaiah 40:15,17,30-31

And he carried me away in the Spirit to a mountain
great and high, and showed me the Holy City,
Jerusalem, coming down out of heaven from God.

—Revelation 21:10 NIV

The great dragon was hurled down—that ancient serpent
called the devil, or Satan, who leads the whole world astray.
He was hurled to the earth, and his angels with him.

—Revelation 12:9

ENDNOTES

1. Library of Congress website, "Bibles and Scripture Passages Used by Presidents in Taking the Oath of Office" Online at: http://memory.loc.gov/ammem/pihtml/pibible.html. Accessed: 5 January 2003.

2. Bowen, Clarence W. The History of the Centennial *Celebration of the Inauguration of George Washington, N.Y. 1892, 72, Illustration.*

3. Listed in the files of Legislative Reference Service, Library of Congress, source not given.

4. Wright, John. Historic Bibles in *America, N.Y. 1905, 46.*

5. List compiled by Clerk of the Supreme Court, 1939.

6. One source (The Chicago Daily Tribune, Sept. 23, 1881, p. 5) says that Garfield and Arthur used the same passage, but does *not indicate which one.*

7. Hutchins, Stilson. The National Capitol, Wa*shington, 1885, 276.*

8. Harper's Magazi*ne, August 1897.*

9. Senate Document 116, 65th Congress, 1st Session, 1917.

10. New York Times, Apr. 13, 1945, *1, col. 7.*

11. Facts on File, Jan. 16-2*2, 1949, 21.*

12. New York Times, Jan. *21, 1953, 19.*

13. New York Times, Jan. *22, 1957, 16.*

14. New York Times, Jan. 21, 196*1, 8, col. 1.*

15. Mooney, Booth. The L*yndon Johnson Story, 1.*

16. Office of the Clerk of the Supreme Court via phone July 1968.

17. Washington Post, Jan. *20, 1969, A1.*

18. New York Times, Aug. 10, *1974, p. A1.*

19. Washington Post, Jan. *21, 1977, A17.*

20. White House Curator's Office.

21. Washington Post, Jan. *21, 1997, A14.*

22. Inauguration staff. George W. Bush had hoped to use the Masonic Bible that had been used both by George Washington in 1789, and by the President's father, George H. W. Bush, in 1989. This historic Bible had been transported, under guard, from New York to Washington for the inauguration but, due to inclement weather, a family Bible was substituted instead.

23. Joby Warrick, "Nuclear Program in Iran Tied to Pakistan, *Washington Post,* December 21, 2003.

24. "The Role of Israeli Lobby in US Presidential Elections," http://ezinearticles.com/?The-Role-of-Israeli-Lobby-in-US-Presidential-Elections&id=1084134; accessed August 2013.

25. Tom Robbins, "The Lesson: Incident at the Towers, 1993," *New York Daily News,* December 9, 1998 in Richard Miniter, *Losing bin Laden: How Bill Clinton's Failure Unleashed Global Terror* (Washington, D.C.: Regnery Publishing, Inc., 2003), P. 19.

26. Miniter, Losing bin Laden, xvi, xix. (Insert added.)

27. Sheik Omar Abdel Rahman, speaking in Detroit in 1991, https://litigation-essentials.lexis-nexis.com/webcd/app?action=DocumentDisplay&crawlid=1&doctype=cite&docid=105+Yale+L.J.+1347&srctype=smi&srcid=3B15&key=4c30bebc9815da8a6077c0a42bb897ba; accessed August 2013.

28. Yossef Bodansky, *bin Laden: The Man who Declared War on America* (New York, NY: Random House, 1991) p. 57.

29. Martin Luther King, Jr. (1929-68), U.S. clergyman, civil rights leader. Strength to Love, Philadelphia, Fortress Press, pt. 4, ch. 3 (1963).

30. Yossef Bodansky, *The High Cost of Peace: How Washington's Middle East Policy Left America Vulnerable to Terrorism.* (Roseville, CA: Forum, 2002), 9-10.

31. "In Search of Truth: Historical Parallels as a Means of Understanding the Rise of Arab Nationalism," http://www.kesser.org/essays/arab-nationalism.html; accessed August 2013.

32. Thomas Jefferson, "Commerce between Master and Slave," 1782, http://douglassarchives.org/jeff_a51.htm

33. Holy Trinity Church v. United States. 143 U.S. 457, 465 (February 29, 1892).

34. Ibid, p. 471

35. David Barton, *The Bulletproof George Washington.* (Aledo, TX: Wallbuilders Press, 1990), 35, 44, 50, 57.

36. William F. Shirer, *The Rise and Fall of the Third Reich* (New York, NY: Simon & Schuster, 1960), p. 98.

37. Scholars today believe that Isaiah 18 refers to Cush—Egypt as we know it today. Though Pastor MacDonald may have misinterpreted this scripture, his call to action was still a godly one. It was the first step in the American conscience towards supporting the rebirth of the nation of Israel.

38. Peter Grose, *Israel in the Mind of America* (New York, NY: Knopf, 1984) p. 9.

39. John McDonald, *New Translation, Isaiah Chapter 18* (Albany: E. & E. Hosford, 1814), p. 23; http://olivercowdery.com/texts/1814McDn.htm; accessed September 2013.

40. Grose, p. 15.

41. Ibid, p. 23-4

42. Adolf Hitler, *Mein Kampf,* translated Ralph Manheim (Boston: Houghton Mifflin, 1943(, p. 161.

43. Shirer, The *Rise and Fall of the Third Reich*, p. 349.

44. Ibid, p. 77

45. Ibid, p. 1056

46. Ibid, p. 1069

47. Ronald Lewin, *Hitler's Mistakes* (New York, NY: Quill, William Morrow, 1948), pp. 15-16.

48. Abdulhak Adnan, La Science chez les Turcs ottoman (Paris: 1939), 87, 98-99 in Bernard Lewis, *What Went Wrong?: The Clash Between Islam and Modernity in the Middle* East (New York: Perennial, 2002), p. 7.

49. Lewis, What Went Wrong?, 9.

50. Albert Hourani, *Arabic Thought in the Liberal Age, 1798-1939* (Oxford: Oxford University Press, 1970), 37 in Dore Gold, Hatred's Kingdom: How Saudi Arabia Supports the New Global Terrorism (Washington DC: Regnery Publishing, Inc., 2003), 19.

51. Dore Gold, *Hatred's Kingdom: How Saudi Arabia Supports the New Global Terrorism* (Washington, DC: Regnery, 2003), p. 26-27.

52. Gold, *Hatred's Kingdom,* p. 13.

53. Nadav Safran, *Saudi Arabia: The Ceaseless Quest for Security* (Cambridge: Harvard University Press, 1985), 58 in Gold, *Hatred's Kingdom*, 60.

54. John Loftus and Mark Aarons, *The Secret War Against the Jews: How Western Espionage Betrayed the Jewish People* (New York: St. Martin's Griffin, 1994), p.71.

55. Sources: Gaeton Fonzi, *The Last Investigation* (Thunder's Mouth Press, 1994); Adam Lebor, *Hitler's Secret Bankers* (Birch Lane Press, 1997); John Loftus & Mark Aarons, *The Secret War Against The Jews* (St. Martins Press, 1994); Christopher Simpson, *Blowback* (Weidenfeld & Nicholson, 1988); Christopher Simpson, *The Splendid Blond Beast* (Grove Press, 1993).

56. Nawaf E. Obaid, "Improving U.S. Intelligence Analysis on the Saudi Arabian Decision-Making Process," (Master's Thesis, John F. Kennedy School of Government, Harvard University, 1998), 13 in Gold, *Hatred's Kingdom*, 60.

57. Nadav Safran, *Saudi Arabia: The Ceaseless Quest for Security* (Cambridge: Harvard University Press, 1985), p. 58; in Gold, *Hatred's Kingdom*, 60. Safran's source was the Saudi Arabian Ministry of Petroleum and Natural Resources.

58. The State Department's U.S. Commission on International Religious Freedom was the first government agency to step forward publicly and finger Saudi Wahhabism as a "strategic threat" to the United States. See Tom Carter's article, "Saudis' Strict Islam called a 'Threat,'" The *Washington Times* (November 19, 2003), http://www.washtimes.com/world/20031118-113127-4259r.htm; accessed November 2003.

59. Kenneth R. Timmerman, *Preachers of Hate: Islam and the War on America* (New York: Crown Forum, 2003), p. 66.

60. Safran, Saudi Arabia), p. 221 in Gold, *Hatred's Kingdom*, p. 119. Safran's source was the Saudi Arabian Ministry of Petroleum and Natural Resources.

61. Gold, *Hatred's Kingdom*, p. 126.

62. Blaine Hardin, "Saudis Seek U.S. Muslims for their Sect," *New York Times*, October 20, 2001 in Gold, *Hatred's Kingdom,* p. 126.

63. Reza F. Safa, Inside Islam (Orlando, FL: Creation House, 1997)

64. Cockburn, *Dangerous Liaison*, 194.

65. Gold, *Hatred's Kingdom*, 127.

66. Tom Carter, "Saudis; Strict Islam called a 'Threat,'" The Washington Times (November 19, 2003), http://www.washtimes.com/world/20031118-113127-4259r.htm; accessed November 2003.

67. IslamOnline.net, "Sudanese Islamist Group To Look For Office Abroad." http://www.islam-online.net/iol-english/dowalia/news-14-2-2000/topnews5.asp. Created: 14 February 2000; accessed November 2003.

68. Tom Robbins, "The Lesson: Incident at the Towers, 1993," *New York Daily News*, December 9, 1998 in Richard Miniter, *Losing bin Laden: How Bill Clinton's Failure Unleashed Global Terror* (Washington, D.C.: Regnery Publishing, Inc., 2003), p. 19.

69. Miniter, *Losing bin Laden*, xvi, xix. (Insert added.)

70. Joseph Grinstein, LexisNexis, Harvard Law Journal, March 1996, https://litigation-essentials.lexisnexis.com/webcd/app?action=DocumentDisplay&crawlid=1&doctype=cite&docid=105+Yale+L.J.+1347&srctype=smi&srcid=3B15&key=4c30bebc9815da8a6077c0a42bb897ba; accessed August 2013.

71. Congressional Budget Office, October 7, 2010, http://www.cbo.gov/publication/25107; accessed August 2013.

72. Gary Hart and Warren B. Rudman, *Roadmap for National Security: Imperative for Change* (Wilkes-Barre, PA: Kallisti Publishing, 2001), p.12.

73. Joel Mowbray, *Dangerous Diplomacy: How the State Department Threatens America's* Security (Washington DC: Regnery Publishing, Inc., 2003), p. 9-10.

74. Annual Report 2013, Saudi Arabia, http://www.amnesty.org/en/region/saudi-arabia/report-2013#page

75. http://christianactionforisrael.org/un/backs02.html; accessed August 2013.

76. Mortimer B. Zuckerman, "Graffiti on History's Walls," *U.S. News & World Report* vol. 135, no. 15 (November 3, 2003), p. 47-48.

77. Mike Evans' personal interview with Rudolph Giuliani

78. Jill and Leon Uris, *Jerusalem, Song of Songs* (New York: Doubleday, 1981), p. 9.

79. See Appendix C for more information on sales to these countries.

80. "Congressional report shows that arms exports tripled from previous year, with Gulf Arab states the main customers," http://www.aljazeera.com/video/americas/2012/08/20128273548544850.html; accessed August 2013.

81. Seymour Hersh, *The Samson Option: Israel's Nuclear Arsenal & American Foreign Policy* (New York, NY: Random House, 1991), p. 20.

82. Hersh, *The Samson Option*, p. 119.

83. Hersh, *The Samson Option*, p. 121.

84. Hersh, *The Samson Option*, p. 121.

85. Hersh, *The Samson Option*, p.9.

86. Yossef Bodansky, *The High Cost of Peace: How Washington's Middle East Policy Left American Vulnerable to Terrorism* (Rosehill, CA: Forum, 2002), p. 568.

87. Joby Warrick, "Dirty Bomb Cache Gone without a Trace, *The Washington Post,* October 13, 2003, http://www.smh.com.au/articles/2003/12/12/1071125654030.html; accessed August 2013.

88. George Santayana, *The Life of Reason*, Volume 1, 1905

89. Terminology that is often used to describe the Jews and their allies in the Islamist documents. See for example Dore Gold's Hatred's Kingdom, 231.

90. A convocation of world leaders was held in Jerusalem beginning on October 11, 2003. The purpose of the meeting was to discuss how to win the war on terrorism through moral clarity. Transcripts were made available of all addressed and are held by Dmitry Radyshevsky, executive director, The Michael Cherney Foundation. References to remarks offered during the summit are taken from these transcripts.

91. Ibid.

92. Ibid.

93. "The Jerusalem Embassy Relocation Act," The Jewish Virtual Library, http://www.us-israel.org/jsource/Peace/Jerusalem_Relocation_Act.html; accessed December 2003.

94. Mort Zuckerman, "Graffiti on History's Walls," *U.S. News & World Report,* 50.

95. Joseph Puder, "Dissolve the UNRWA," May 5, 2009, *FrontPage Magazine*, http://archive.frontpagemag.com/readArticle.aspx?ARTID=34682; accessed August 2013.

96. "Right of Return of Palestinian Refugees," http://www.zionism-israel.com/issues/return_detail.html; accessed August 2013.

97. Ibid.

98. Gold, *Hatred's Kingdom*, p. 246.

99. Paul Finkelman, "How The Proslavery Constitution Led To The Civil War" Rutgers Law Journal Volume 43 Fall/Winter 2013 Number 3, p. 405.

100. Thomas Jefferson, "Commerce between Master and Slave," 1782, http://douglassarchives. org/jeff_a51.htm. (Emphasis added.)

101. Abraham Lincoln, "Second Inauguration Address.," http://www.law.ou.edu/hist/lincoln2. html; accessed December 2003.

102. "Speech by Prime Minister Mahathir Mohamad of Malaysia to the Tenth Islamic Summit Conference, Putrajaya, Malaysia," (October 16, 2003). Complete text of the speech available online at: http://www.adl.org/Anti_semitism/malaysian.asp; accessed December 2003.

103. Der Parteitag der Arheit vom 6 bis 13 September 1937: Offizieller Bericht uber den Verlauf des Reichsparteitages mit samtlichen Kongressreden (Munich, 1938), p. 157, in Friedlander, Nazi Germany and the Jews, p. 184-185.

104. Ibid, p. 177

105. Gerald Fleming, Hitler and the Final Solution (Berkley: University of California Press, 1984), 17, in George Victor, Hitler: The Pathology of Evil (Dulles, VA: Brassey's, 1998), 123.

106. "Jerusalem on the Line," Messianic Times, July 17, 2013, http://www.messianictimes.com/ daily-news/israeli-news/1361-jerusalem-on-the-line-july-17-2013; accessed August 2013.

107. Phyllis Chesler, The New Anti-Semitism: The Current Crisis and What We Must Do About It (San Francisco, CA: Jossey-Bass, 2003), 218-223.

108. Sergei Trifkovic, "Islam's Nazi Connections," FrontPage Magazine, December 5, 2002, http://archive.frontpagemag.com/readArticle.aspx?ARTID=20831; accessed August 2013.

109. The Palestine Times No.114 (December 2000).

110. Associated Press (March 25, 2000).

111. Ahmad Abu Halabiya, "Friday sermon in Gaza mosque on October 13, 2000," broadcast live on Palestinian Authority TV.

112. Amos Nevo, "Hitler is a Youth Idol, Mein Kampf is a Bestseller," http://sitamnesty.word-press.com/2010/02/24/hitler-y-est-une-idole-des-jeunes-mein-kampf-un-bestseller/; accessed August 2013.

113. Ibid.

114. Daniel Pipes, "Locus of Euro-hate," December 10, 2003, The Jerusalem Post, http://www. danielpipes.org/1350/locus-of-euro-hate; accessed August 2013.

115. Manley Philips, February 20, 2002.

116. Courierra de la Sera (April 12, 2002).

117. Robert Wistrich, "Muslim Anti-Semitism, http://www.sullivan-county.com/id3/cairo.htm; accessed August 2013.

118. Inscribed on the Jefferson Memorial in Washington, DC.

119. John F. Walvoord, "Foreword" to William E. Blackstone, Jesus Is Coming: God's Hope for a Restless World, 3rd printing of an updated edition. (Grand Rapids, MI: Kregel Publications, 1989), p. 8.

120. William Blackstone, Jesus is Coming, (New York: Fleming Revell, 1908), p. 161.

121. Ibid, pp. 171, 175

122. Grose, Israel in the Mind of America (New York: Knopf, 1984), p. 45.

123. Elesha Coffman, "Zion Haste," Christianity Today, August 8, 2008, http://www.christianity-today.com/ch/news/2002/feb1.html?start=1; accessed September 2013.

124. William Eugene Blackstone, "The Blackstone Memorial, 1891," http://www.amfi.org/black-mem.htm; accessed October 2003.

125. Ibid.

126. Hilton Obenzinger, "In the Shadow of 'God's Sun-Dial': The Construction of American Christian Zionism and the Blackstone Memorial," http://www.stanford.edu/group/SHR/5-1/text/obenzinger.html. Last updated: February 1996; accessed October 2003.

127. Moshe Davis, "Reflections on Harry S. Truman and the State of Israel," in Allen Weinstien and Hoshe Ma'oz (eds.), *Truman and the American Commitment to Israel* (Jerusalem: The Magnes Press, 1981), p. 83.

128. Peter Grose, *Israel in the Mind of America* (New York: Alfred A Knopf, 1984), p. 41.

129. http://www.freerepublic.com/focus/f-news/2276917/posts; accessed August 2013.

130. "History of the Jews in the United States," Wikipedia; http://en.wikipedia.org/wiki/History_of_the_Jews_in_the_United_States; accessed October 2011.

131. "John Adams Embraces a Jewish Homeland," Chapter 33, American Jewish Historical Society; http://www.ajhs.org/scholarship/chapters/chapter.cfm?documentID=221; accessed October 2011.

132. "Judaism," Wikipedia: John Adams, in a letter to F. A. van der Kemp (February 16, 1809) as quoted in The Roots of American Order (1974) by Russel Kirk; http://en.wikiquote.org/wiki/Jews; accessed October 2011.

133. Reuben Finkh, Excerpting from an address by Woodrow Wilson on May 7, 1911, titled "The Bible and Progress"; http://www.sweetliberty.org/perspective/jewishpersecution12.htm; accessed October 2011.

134. "National Affairs: Abraham, Isaac, Jacob," *Time Magazine US*, May 11, 1925; http://www.time.com/time/magazine/article/0,9171,728422,00.html; accessed October 2011.

135. Ibid.

136. Charles Spencer Hart, *George Washington's Son of Israel* (Freeport, NY: Books for Libraries Press, 1937), p. 5.

137. Peter Grose, Israel in the Mind of America. (New York: Alfred A. Knopf, 1984), p. 5.

138. Bob Blythe, "Haym Salomon," National Park Service, U.S. Department of the Interior; http://www.nps.gov/revwar/about_the_revolution/haym_salomom.html; accessed June 2008.

139. Peter Wiernik, *History of the Jews in America* (New York: The Jewish Press Publishing Company, 1912), p. 95.

140. Dr. David Allen Lewis, "Haym Salomon: The Forgotten Patriot," Bridges for Peace International, Jerusalem, Israel, 1993, p. 35.

141. Jon Meacham, "God and Politics: From George Washington to Barack Obama," October 26, 2010; John C. Danforth Center on Religion and Politics; http://rap.wustl.edu/transcripts/transcript-jon-meacham-god-and-politics/; accessed November 17, 2011.

142. "John Adams Embraces a Jewish Homeland," http://www.jewishvirtuallibrary.org/jsource/US-Israel/adams.html; accessed July 2013.

143. "Judaic Treasures of the Library of Congress: The Author of the Declaration and the Architect of the Constitution," Jewish Virtual Library; http://www.jewishvirtuallibrary.org/jsource/loc/madison.html; accessed November 2011.

144. Thomas Jefferson, "Commerce between Master and Slave," 1782. http://douglassarchives.org/jeff_a51.htm

145. Thomas Jefferson Monticello; http://www.monticello.org/site/research-and-collections/no-nation-has-ever-yet-existed-or-been-governed-without-religionquotat; accessed November 2011.

146. Jefferson to Mordecai Noah, Qumsiyeh: A Human Rights Web; http://qumsiyeh.org/jeffersontomordechainoah/; accessed November 2011.

147. Thomas Jefferson, *Letter to Colonel Charles Yancey, January 6, 1816, The Writings of Thomas Jefferson, Vol. 11*, Paul L. Ford, ed. (New York and London: G. P. Putnam's Sons, 1904), p. 4.

148. "All my wishes end . . . at Montecello," Thomas Jefferson Monticello; http://www.monticello.org/site/jefferson/all-my-wishes-end-monticello; accessed March 2012.

149. President John F. Kennedy, remarks at a dinner honoring Nobel Prize winners of the Western Hemisphere, April 29, 1962. Public Papers of the Presidents of the United States: John F. Kennedy, 1962, p. 347. QuotationsBook; http://quotationsbook.com/quote/38431/; accessed November 2011.

150. Quoted by David G. Dalin and Alfred J. Kolatch in *The Presidents of the United States & The Jews* (Middle Village, NY: Jonathan David Publishers, 2000), p. 125.

151. Rabbi I. M. Wise, "On Colonization and Zionism," Chapter V, pp. 605–606. http://americanjewisharchives.org/wise/writings/5532/III_part_3-4.pdf; accessed February 2012.

152. Robert T. Carroll, "Protocols of the Elders of Zion," The Skeptic's Dictionary; http://www.skepdic.com/protocols.html; accessed July 2010.

153. Neil Baldwin, *Henry Ford and the Jews: The Mass Production of Hate* (Public Affairs, 2002), p. 99.

154. Ibid, p. 59

155. John Cunningham Wood, Michael C. Wood, *Henry Ford: Critical Evaluations in Business and Management* (London: Taylor and Francis, 2003), p. 130.

156. Fred Jerome, *Einstein on Israel and Zionism: His Provocative Ideas About the Middle East* (New York: McMillan, 2009), p. 11.

157. Termination of the Treaty of 1832 between the United States and Russia; Committee on Foreign Affairs, House of Representatives, Monday, December 11, 1911 (Washington, DC: Government Printing Office, 1911), p. 16.

158. "U.S. Presidents on Israel: Woodrow Wilson," Jewish Virtual Library; http://www.jewishvirtuallibrary.org/jsource/US-Israel/presquote.html#ford; accessed January 2012.

159. Louis Brandeis, "The Jewish Problem and How to Solve it," University of Louisville; http://www.law.louisville.edu/library/collections/brandeis/node/234; accessed March 2012.

160. Nomination of Louis D. Brandeis to the United States Supreme Court, 64th Congress, 1st Session, Document 409, Volume 2 (Washington, DC: Government Printing Office, 1916), p. 6.

161. Robert Merrill Bartlett, *They Did Something About It* (North Stratford, NH: Ayer Co. Publishing, 1939), p. 67.

162. Larry M. Roth, "The Many Lives of Louis Brandeis: Progressive Reformer, Supreme Court Justice, Avowed Zionist, and a Racist?" page 11; http://www.jlaw.com/Commentary/Louis-Brandeis.pdf; accessed February 2012.

163. Stephen J. Whitfield, *In Search of American Jewish Culture* (Lebanon, NH: UPNE, 2001), p. 34.

164. Ibid, p. 9

165. Wayne V. McIntosh and Cynthia L. Cates, *Judicial Entrepreneurship: The Role of the Judge in the Marketplace of Ideas* (Westport, CT: Greenwood Publishing Group, 1997), p. 23.

166. Herbert Levy, Henry Morgenthau, Jr., *The Remarkable Life of FDR's Secretary of the Treasury* (New York: Skyhorse Publishing, 2010), Footnote 81.

167. "Kaiser Wilhelm II," FirstWorldWar.com; http://www.firstworldwar.com/bio/wilhelmii.htm; accessed December 2011.

168. "Fourteen Points," Wikipedia; http://en.wikipedia.org/wiki/Fourteen_Points; accessed December 2011.

169. David G. Dalin and Alfred J. Kolatch, *The Presidents of the United States & The Jews* (Middle Village, NY: Jonathan David Publishers, 2000), p. 142.

170. "America Becomes a World Power: World War I; http://www.academicamerican.com/progressive/worldwar1/worldpower2.html; accessed December 2011.

171. Eli E. Hertz, "U.S. Presidents Support a Jewish National Home in Palestine — Eretz-Israel," Myths and Facts, May 25, 2011; www.mythsandfacts.com/article_view.asp?articleID=152; accessed December 2011.

172. Wayne Lutton, "Warren Harding: One of Our Most Accomplished Presidents?" Human Events, December 27, 2004, vol. 60, issue 44, p. 18.

173. Yitschak Ben Gad, *Politics, Lies, and Videotape: 3,000 Questions and Answers on the Mideast Crisis* (Jerusalem: SP Books, 1991), p. 160.

174. David Lanier Louis, *The Public Image of Henry Ford: An American Folk Hero and His Company* (Detroit, MI: Great Lakes Books, 1987), p. 146.

175. Theodor Herzl, *The Jewish State*, p. 140.

176. Lewis L. Strauss Papers, Scope and Content Note; http://www.ecommcode2.com/hoover/research/historicalmaterials/other/strauss/stramain.htm; accessed December 2011.

177. Ibid.

178. "Cardozo Is Named to Supreme Court," *The New York Times*, February 16, 1932; http://select.nytimes.com/gst/abstract.html?res=F40913FE355A16738DDDAF0994DA405B828FF1D3; accessed December 2011.

179. Herbert Hoover to Lewis L. Strauss, October 29, 1932; http://www.gilderlehrman.org/search/collection_pdfs/00/16/2/14/00162.14.pdf; accessed December 2011.

180. List compiled by Clerk of the Supreme Court, 1939.

181. James MacGregor Burns, *Roosevelt, Volume 1* (Norwalk, CT: Easton Press, 1956) p. 16.

182. NY: Random House, 204), pp. 27-28.

183. Frances Perkins and Adam Cohen, *The Roosevelt I Knew* (Westminster, London, England: Penguin Classics Reprint, 2011), pp. 135–136.

184. William D. Rubenstein, "The Historiography of Rescue," *The New York Times*; http://www.nytimes.com/books/first/r/rubinstein-myth.html; accessed December 2011.

185. Ibid.

186. Michael E. Parrish, "Frankfurter Without Tears," JSTOR; http://www.jstor.org/pss/2701566; accessed December 2011.

187. Michael Alexander, *Jazz Age Jews* (Princeton, NJ: Princeton University Press, 2001), pp. 77–78.

188. Robert A. Burt, *Two Jewish Justices: Outcasts in the Promised Land* (Berkeley: University of California Press, 1989), p. 40.

189. "Lyndon B. Johnson, Remarks With Under Secretary of State George W. Ball at the Presidential Medal of Freedom Awards, December 6, 1963," The American Presidency Project; http://www.presidency.ucsb.edu/ws/index.php?pid=26165#axzz1gXuAjKOi; accessed December 2011.

190. Robert Solomon Wistrich, *Who's Who in Nazi Germany* (Hove, East Sussex, UK: Psychology Press, 2002), p. 118.

191. William D. Hassett, *Off the Record with F.D.R. 1942–1945* (New Brunswick, NJ: Rutgers University Press, 1958), p. 209.

192. Michael Barak, e-mail to Renata Valar, February 22, 2002.

193. Parade Magazine, December 7, 2003, p. 6.

194. Jan Ciechanowski, *Defeat in Victory* (Garden City, NY: Doubleday, 1947), p. 182.

195. Transcript, "America and the Holocaust," American Experience; http://www.pbs.org/wgbh/amex/holocaust/filmmore/transcript/transcript1.html; accessed February 2012.

196. Transcript, "Eleanor Roosevelt," American Experience; http://www.pbs.org/wgbh/americanexperience/features/transcript/eleanor-transcript/; accessed February 2012.

197. Michael Soltys, "Holocaust blindness exposed," *Buenos Aires Herald*, June 28, 2001; http://www.raoulwallenberg.net/saviors/polish/karski/holocaust-blindness-exposed/; accessed December 2011.

198. "AJC Welcomes Presidential Medal of Freedom, Awarded Posthumously, for Jan Karski," *The Sacramento Bee*, May 29, 2012; www.sacbee.com/2012/05/29/4524166/ajc-welcomes-presidential-medal.hmtl; accessed June 2012.

199. Rabbi Yitschak Rudomin, "The Second World War and Jewish Education in America: The Fall and Rise of Orthodoxy," Chapter 5, Jewish Professional Institute; http://www.jpi.org/holocaust/hlchp5a.htm; accessed February 2012.

200. R. G. Price, "Fascism Part II: The Rise of American Fascism," May 15, 2004; http://rational-revolution.net/articles/rise_of_american_fascism.htm; accessed February 2012.

201. Quoted by Robert Bendiner in *The Riddle of the State Department* (New York: Farrar and Rinehart, 1942), pp. 100–101.

202. Moran, Brandon, "The Question of Refugees Fleeing Nazi Persecution: You're Not Welcome Here Either," November 12, 2009, http://voices.yahoo.com/the-question-refugees-fleeing-nazi-persecution-4851816.html?cat=37; accessed March 2012.

203. Walter Goodman, "Review/Television; How U.S. Barred Holocaust Refugees," *The New York Times*, April 6, 1994; http://www.nytimes.com/1994/04/06/movies/review-television-how-us-barred-holocaust-refugees.html; accessed March 2012.

204. Brandon Moran, "The Question of Refugees and Fleeing Nazi Persecution," Yahoo Voices; http://voices.yahoo.com/the-question-refugees-fleeing-nazi-persecution-4851816.html?cat=37; accessed February 2012.

205. "America and the Holocaust: Rabbi Stephen Wise (1874–1949)," American Experience; http://www.pbs.org/wgbh/amex/holocaust/peopleevents/pandeAMEX101.html; accessed February 2012.

206. "Jewish Organizations Press FDR to Act — Memorandum Submitted to the President of the United States," White House, December 8, 1942, Jewish Virtual Library; http://www.jewishvirtuallibrary.org/jsource/Holocaust/fdrmemo.html; accessed February 2012.

207. "State Department Instructs Swiss Mission to Stop Forwarding Reports from Jewish Organizations," February 10, 1943, Jewish Virtual Library; http://www.jewishvirtuallibrary.org/jsource/Holocaust/riegnercorrespond1.html; accessed February 2012.

208. Michael Beschloss, *The Conquerors: Roosevelt, Truman and the Destruction of Hitler's Germany*, 1941–1945 (New York: Simon & Schuster, 2002), p. 43.

209. Ibid, p. 53.

210. Ibid, p. 54.

211. Ruth Gruber, Haven: *The Dramatic Story of 1,000 World War II Refugees and How They Came to America* (New York: Three Rivers Press, 1983), p. 19.

212. Monty Noah Penkower, *Decision on Palestine Deferred: America, Britain, and Wartime Diplomacy 1939–1945* (Portland, OR: Frank Cass Publishers, 2002); http://www.meforum.org/1541/decision-on-palestine-deferred; accessed August 2012.

213. "Dr. Wise Dies at 75; Truman and Weizmann Mourn His Passing; Funeral to be Held Friday," Jewish News Archives; http://archive.jta.org/article/1949/04/20/3018752/dr-wise-dies-at-75-truman-and-weizmann-mourn-his-passing-funeral-to-be-held-friday; accessed February 2012.

214. "America and the Holocaust: 'Report to the Secretary on the Acquiescence of this Government in the Murder of the Jews,' initialed by Randolph Paul for the Foreign Funds Control Unit of the Treasury Department, January 13, 1944," American Experience; http://www.pbs.org/wgbh/amex/holocaust/filmmore/reference/primary/somereport.html; accessed February 2012.

215. "Operation Overlord," Wikipedia; http://en.wikipedia.org/wiki/Operation_Overlord#cite_note-FOOTNOTETamelanderZetterling2003341-70; accessed February 2012.

216. Doris Kearns Goodwin, *No Ordinary Time: Franklin and Eleanor Roosevelt, The Home Front in World War II* (New York: Simon and Shuster, 1994), p. 193.

217. Evan M. Wilson and William B. Quandt, *A Calculated Risk: The U.S. Decision to Recognize Israel* (Cincinnati, Ohio: Clerisy Press, 2008), p. 39.

218. Peter Grose, *Israel in the Mind of America*, p. 137.

219. Benjamin Cohen, National Archives RG59, Notter File, Box 56, P. Document 66, Palestine, September 4, 1942.

220. Robert Rockaway, "FDR: Move the Arabs out of Palestine," allBusiness.com; http://www.allbusiness.com/middle-east/israel/381693-1.html; accessed February 2012.

221. Peter Grose, *Israel in the Mind of America*, p. 141.

222. Edward R. Stettinius, *The Diaries of Edward R. Stettinius, Thomas M. Campbell and George C. Herring*, eds. (New York: New Viewpoints, 1975), p. 170.

223. Douglas Little, American Orientalism: The United States and the Middle East Since 1945 (New York: I. B. Tauris, 2003), p. 22.

224. Winberg Chai Ph.D., ed., *Saudi Arabia: A Modern Reader* (Indianapolis, IN: University of Indianapolis Press, 2006), p. 52.

225. Donald Neff, "Fallen Pillars: U.S. Policy towards Palestine and Israel since 1945," *The Washington Post*; http://www.washingtonpost.com/wp-srv/style/longterm/books/chap1/fallen-pillars.htm; accessed February 2012.

226. Frank Freidel, *Franklin D. Roosevelt: A Rendezvous with Destiny* (New York: Little, Brown, and Co., 1990), p. 594.

227. Howard Grief, *The Legal Foundation and Borders of Israel Under International Law* (Jerusalem: Mazo Publishers, 2008), p. 630.

228. Ibid

229. Monty Noam Penkower, *The Holocaust and Israel Reborn: From Catastrophe to Sovereignty* (Chicago, IL: University of Illinois Press, 1994), p. 279.

230. "Thoughts of a President, 1945," EyeWitness to History; http://www.eyewitnesstohistory.com/tru.htm; accessed December 2011.

231. David McCullough, *Truman* (New York: Simon and Schuster, 1992), pp. 37, 77, 1112.

232. Michael Joseph Cohen, Truman and Israel (Berkeley, CA: University of California Press, 1990), pp. 46–47.

233. Alan Brinkley and Davis Dyer, *The American Presidency* (Boston: Houghton Mifflin, 2004), pp. 365–380.

234. Michael T. Benson, *Harry S. Truman and the Founding of Israel* (Westport, CT: Greenwood Publishing Group, 1997), p. 20.

235. David McCullough, Truman, p. 336–337.

236. Paul C. Merkley, *The Politics of Christian Zionism*, 1891–1948, (London: Frank Cass, 1998), p. 167.

237. Walter Isaacson and Evan Thomas, The Wise Men (New York: Simon & Schuster, 1986), p. 452; quoted in A. F. K. Organski, The $36 Billion Bargain: Strategy and Politics in U.S. Assistance to Israel (New York: Columbia University Press, 1990), 26.

238. Michael Beschloss, The Conquerors: Roosevelt, Truman and the Destruction of Hitler's Germany, 1941–1945 (New York: Simon & Schuster, 2002), p. 224.

239. Margaret Truman, "Palestine Was One of Truman's Most Difficult Dilemmas," Sarasota Journal, December 14, 1972, Eleventh of Fourteen segments, p. 4; http://news.google. com/newspapers?nid=1798&dat=19721214&id=2XU0AAAAIBAJ&sjid=I40EAAAAIBAJ& pg=7314,3441247; accessed February 2012.

240. Joseph Marion Jones, The Fifteen Weeks, February 21–June 5, 1947 (New York: Viking, 1955) pp. 63–64.

241. James McDonald Report of Conversation with President Truman, July 27, 1946.

242. Alex Grobman, Daniel Landes, and Sybil Milton, Genocide: Critical Issues of the Holocaust (Springfield, NJ: Behrman House, Inc., 1983), p. 320.

243. Report of Earl G. Harrison, United States Holocaust Memorial Museum; http://www. ushmm.org/museum/exhibit/online/dp/resourc1.htm; accessed February 2012.

244. "Truman's Letter Regarding the Harrison Report on the Treatment of Displaced Jews," Jewish Virtual Library; http://www.jewishvirtuallibrary.org/jsource/Holocaust/truman_ on_harrison.html; accessed February 2012.

245. Clark Clifford, "Factors Influencing President Truman's Decision to Support Partition and Recognize the State of Israel," in Clark M. Clifford, Eugene V. Rostow, and Barbara W. Tuchman, The Palestine Question in American History (New York: Arno Press, 1978), p. 44.

246. "At War with the Experts," C-Span Video Library; http://www.c-spanvideo.org/program/197078-1; accessed December 2011.

247. Michael T. Benson, Harry S. Truman and the Founding of Israel, p. 121.

248. Barry E. Horner, Future Israel: Why Christian Anti-Judaism Must be Challenged (Nashville, TN: B&H Publishing Group, 2007), p. 124.

249. Frank Adler, "Margaret Truman Daniel's Harry S. Truman," Harry S. Truman Library, p. 4.

250. Frank Adler, Roots in a Moving Stream (Overland Park, KS: The Temple, Congregation B'nai Jehudah, 1972), p. 198.

251. James McDonald to B'nai B'rith's Frank Goldman, March 3, 1950, cited in Adler, Roots in a Moving Stream, p. 224.

252. Harry S. Truman to A. M. Levin, February 7, 1944, Truman Papers, Harry S. Truman Library.

253. Roosevelt to Ibn Saud, April 5, 1955. Cited in Department of State Bulletin, October 21, 1945, p. 623.

254. McCullough, Truman, p. 773.

255. King Saud to Harry S. Truman, July 9, 1946, OF 204-B; James Forrestal, The Forrestal Diaries, Walter Mills, ed. (New York: Viking, 1951), p. 180.

256. The New York Times, October 5, 1946, p. 2.

257. "Item 241: Message to the King of Saudi Arabia Concerning Palestine," Harry S. Truman Library and Museum, October 28, 1946; http://trumanlibrary.org/publicpapers/viewpapers. php?pid=1787; accessed December 2011.

258. Ibid.

259. Alfred Steinberg, Man from Missouri (New York: Putnam, 1962), p. 306.

260. "At War with the Experts," C-Span Video Library; http://www.c-spanvideo.org/program/197078-1; accessed December 2011.

261. "United States Department of State/Foreign Relations of the United States, 1947. The Near East and Africa," Vol. 5, p. 1081, University of Wisconsin Digital Collections; http://digicoll.library.wisc.edu/cgi-bin/FRUS/FRUS-idx?type=goto&id=FRUS. FRUS1947v05&isize=M&page=1081; accessed February 2012.

262. Ibid, p. 1054.

263. Peter Grose, "The Partition of Palestine 35 Years Ago," The New York Times, November 21, 1982; http://www.nytimes.com/1982/11/21/magazine/the-partition-of-palestine-35-years-ago.html; accessed March 2012.

264. Menachem Begin on the day partition of Palestine was approved, Wikiquote; http://en.wikiquote.org/wiki/Menachem_Begin; accessed March 2012.

265. Ami Isseroff, "President Harry S. Truman and US Support for Israeli Statehood," Copyright by MidEastWeb for Coexistence R.A.; http://www.mideastweb.org; All rights Reserved; accessed March 2012.

266. Ibid, pp. 2–4

267. Ibid, p. 5

268. The New York Times, March 20, 1948, p. 1.

269. Jonathan Daniels, Men of Independence (Columbia, MO: University of Missouri, 1998), Daniels' Research Notes, Harry S. Truman Library, p. 50.

270. Harry S. Truman, Off the Record (New York: Harper and Row: 1980), p. 127.

271. CBS Reports, "From Precinct to President," interview by Edward R. Murrow, February 2, 1958, Film Collection, HSTL.

272. McCullough, Truman, pp. 745–746.

273. Jacobson Papers, Harry S. Truman Library, pp. 8–9.

274. Walter Laqueur, A History of Zionism (London: Tauris Parke Paperbacks, 2003), p. 582.

275. James T. Patterson, Grand Expectations: The United States, 1945–1974 (New York, NY: Oxford University Press, 1997), p. 153.

276. John Acacia, Clark Clifford: The Wise Man of Washington (Lexington, KY: The University Press of Kentucky, 2009), p. 105.

277. Ambassador Richard Holbrooke, May 2008, Jerusalem Center for Public Affairs; http://www.jcpa.org/JCPA/Templates/ShowPage.asp?DRIT=2&DBID=1&LNGID=1&TMID=111&FID=376&PID=0&IID=2203&TTL=President_Truman%E2%80%99s_Decision_to_Recognize_Israel; accessed March 2012.

278. James Pfiffner, The Modern Presidency (Florence, KY: Cengage Learning, 2010), p. 60.

279. David Jeremiah, What in the World Is Going On? (Nashville, TN: Thomas Nelson, 2008), p. 21.

280. Richard H. Curtiss, "Truman Adviser Recalls May 14, 1948, US Decision to Recognize Israel," Information Clearing House; http://www.informationclearinghouse.info/article4077.htm; accessed March 2012.

281. "The Recognition of the State of Israel," Truman Library, Eliahu Epstein to Harry S. Truman with attachments re: recognition of Israel, May 14, 1948.

282. Ibid.

283. Clark Clifford, "Preserving the Free World," quoted in Kenneth W. Thompson, Portraits of American Presidents the Truman Presidency: Intimate Perspectives (New York: University Press of America, 1984), p. 18.

284. Judith Apter Klinghoffer, "Was the Recognition of Israel Contrary to U.S. National Interests?" George Mason University's History News Network; http://hnn.us/articles/24559.html; accessed December 2011.

285. Mitchell Geoffrey Bard, The Water's Edge and Beyond: Defining the Limits to Domestic Influence on United States Middle East Policy (Piscataway, NY: Transaction Publishers, 1991), p. 170.

286. Paul C. Merkley, The Politics of Christian Zionism 1891–1948, p. 191.

287. Harry Truman Quotes; Think Exist.com. http://en.thinkexist.com/quotation/i_had_faith_in_israel_before_it_was_established-i/344150.html

288. Margaret Truman, "After the Presidency," Life, December 1, 1972, p. 70.

289. "Liberators," A Teacher's Guide to the Holocaust; http://fcit.usf.edu/holocaust/people/liberato.htm; accessed January 2012.

290. "Ike and the Death Camps," Eisenhower stories, Dwight D. Eisenhower Memorial Commission; http://www.eisenhowermemorial.org/stories/death-camps.htm; accessed January 2012.

291. "Liberators: Lewis H. Weinstein, Lt. Col. and chief of the liaison section of General Eisenhower's staff, April 1945," A Teacher's Guide to the Holocaust; http://fcit.usf.edu/holocaust/people/liberato.htm; accessed January 2012.

292. "Holocaust Denial," Anti-Defamation League; http://www.adl.org/holocaust/introduction.asp; accessed January 2012.

293. "The Atom Spy Case," Federal Bureau of Investigation; http://www.fbi.gov/about-us/history/famous-cases/the-atom-spy-case; accessed January 2012.

294. "Suez Crisis," GlobalSecurity.org; http://www.globalsecurity.org/military/ops/suez.htm; accessed January 2012.

295. Colonel Richard Meinertzhagen, Middle East Diary, p. 332.

296. "Golda Meir 1898–1978," Israel and Judaism Studies; http://www.ijs.org.au/Golda-Meir/default.aspx; accessed January 2012.

297. Eric Rosenman, "Letter to the Editor: Israel entered Suez War for several reasons," The Washington Times; http://www.washingtontimes.com/news/2011/apr/6/israel-entered-suez-war-for-several-reasons/; accessed January 2012.

298. Peter Golden, Quiet Diplomat (London: Cornwall Books, 1992), p. 19.

299. David Geffen, "In appreciative memory of JFK," The Jerusalem Post, October 27, 2010; http://www.jpost.com/Features/InThespotlight/Article.aspx?id=193027; accessed January 2012.

300. Robert J. Donovan, PT-109: John F. Kennedy in WWII, 40th Anniversary Edition (Camden, ME: International Marine/Ragged Mountain Press, 2001), pp. 106–107, 119.

301. Ibid, p. 124

302. Ibid, pp. 125–126, 141–142, 162–164.

303. "John F. Kennedy and PT109," John F. Kennedy Presidential Library and Museum; http://www.jfklibrary.org/Historical+Resources/JFK+in+History/John+F.+Kennedy+and+PT109.htm; accessed January 2012.

304. Joseph P. Kennedy, Hostage to Fortune: The Letters of Joseph P. Kennedy, Amanda Smith, ed. (New York: Viking Press, 2001), p. 110.

305. Ibid, p.133

306. Arthur Hertzberg, A Jew in America (Harper Collins: New York, 2002), pp. 92–93.

307. John Fitzgerald Kennedy, Inaugural Address, January 20, 1961, http://www.yale.edu/lawweb/avalon/presiden/inaug/kennedy.htm; accessed November 2003.

308. Walter Eytan, *The First Ten Years: A Diplomatic History of Israel* (New York: Simon & Schuster, inc., 1958), 209ff in Schoenbaum, *The United States and the State of Israel*, 79.

309. Warren Bass, *Support Any Friend: Kennedy's Middle East and the Making of the U.S–Israel Alliance* (New York, NY: Oxford University Press, 2003), 144.

310. Herbert Druks, *John F. Kennedy and Israel* (Westport, CT: Greenwood Publishing Group, 2005), p. 34.

311. Ibid, p. 139

312. President John F. Kennedy, "Address Before the 18th General Assembly of the United Nations," September 20, 1963.

313. "JFK Assassination Coverage — Part 2: Lyndon B. Johnson Sworn in," Upi.com. 1963-11-22. http://www.upi.com/Audio/Year_in_Review/Events-of-1963/Lyndon-B.-Johnson-Sworn-in/12386108698633-4/; accessed January 2012.

314. Transcript, Lawrence F. O'Brien Oral History Interview XIII, 9/10/86, by Michael L. Gillette, Internet Copy, Johnson Library, p. 2.3.

315. "Abe Fortas," History of the Sixth Circuit, US Court of Appeals for the Sixth Circuit; http://www.ca6.uscourts.gov/lib_hist/Courts/supreme/judges/af-bio.html; accessed January 2012.

316. Paul C. Merkley, *American Presidents, Religion, and Israel: the Heirs of Cyrus* (Westport, CT: Greenwood Publishing Group, 2004), p. 58.

317. Zalmi Unsdorfer, "Young Winston Churchill — a true friend of our people," *The Jerusalem Post*, June 4, 2010; http://www.jpost.com/Opinion/Op-EdContributors/Article.aspx?id=172525; accessed March 2010.

318. "The Six-Day War," Committee for Accuracy in Middle East Reporting in America; http://www.sixdaywar.org/content/ReunificationJerusalem.asp; accessed January 2012.

319. Irwin Gellman, "The Richard Nixon vice presidency: Research without the Nixon manuscripts," as quoted in Melvin Small, *A Companion to Richard M. Nixon* (Oxford: Wiley-Blackwell, 2011), pp. 102–120.

320. Seymour Hersh, *The Samson Option: Israel's Nuclear Arsenal & American Foreign Policy* (New York, NY: Random House, 1991), pp. 224-226.

321. Ibid, p. 223

322. Seymour M. Hersh, *The Price of Power: Kissinger in the Nixon White House* (New York: Summit Books, 1983), p. 234.

323. Jason Maoz, "Nixon: The Anti-Semite who Saved Israel," *The Jewish Press*, August 5, 2005.

324. Keith Koffler, "Obama Wildly Cheered by Reform Jews," December 16, 2011, white house dossier; http://www.whitehousedossier.com/2011/12/16/obama-wildly-cheered-reform-jews/; accessed January 2012.

325. "Zionism, Nixon-style," *The Jerusalem Post* editorial, December 12, 2010; http://www.jpost.com/Opinion/Editorials/Article.aspx?id=199133&R=R6; accessed January 2012.

326. J. J. Goldberg, *Jewish Power: Inside the American Jewish Estate* (New York: Basic Books, 1997), p. 158.

327. Chaim Herzog, *Living History* (New York: Pantheon Books, 1996), p. 182.

328. "Ford Pardons Nixon: Address to the Nation," Watergate.info; http://watergate.info/ford/pardon.shtml; accessed January 2012.

329. Lewis Sorley, *Arms Transfers Under Nixon: A Policy Analysis* (Lexington, KY: University Press of Kentucky, 1983), pp. 193–194.

330. "U.S. Presidents On Israel: Gerald Ford," Jewish Virtual Library; http://www.jewishvirtuallibrary.org/jsource/US-Israel/presquote.html#ford; accessed January 2012.

331. Gerald R. Ford, "Section 925: The President's News Conference, October 20, 1976," Public Papers of the Presidents of the United States (Washington, D.C.: Government Printing Office, 1977), pp. 2592–2593.

332. Amy D. Goldstein, "response to a Letter to the Editor: Carter and Ford: an exchange," American Thinker, January 5, 2007; http://www.americanthinker.com/blog/2007/01/carter_and_ford_an_exchange.html; accessed January 2012.

333. "U.S. Presidents On Israel: Jimmy Carter (Jimmy Carter at the United Jewish Appeal National Young Leadership Conference, February 25, 1980)," Jewish Virtual Library; http://www.jewishvirtuallibrary.org/jsource/US-Israel/presquote.html#carter; accessed January 2012.

334. For a detailed study of Jimmy Carter, see Mike Evans, Jimmy Carter: the Liberal Left and World Chaos (Dallas, TX: TimeWorthy Books 2009).

335. Andrew Nelson Lytle, "The Hind Tit," I'll Take my Stand (New York: Harper & Bros., 1930), p. 205.

336. Steven F. Hayward, The Real Jimmy Carter (Washington, DC: Regnery Publishing, Inc., 2004), p. 14.

337. ThinkExist.com; http://thinkexist.com/quotation/sometimes_when_i_look_at_all_my_children-i_say_to/213661.html; accessed February 2008.

338. It seems that while fishing in a pond in Plains, the president encountered a rather berserk bunny. The Washington Post picked up the story under the headline, "President Attacked by Rabbit." The animal, a large swamp rabbit that Carter described as "making strange hissing noises and gnashing its teeth," seemed determined to climb into the president's dinghy. The president valiantly fought off the invading rabbit with his oar. The episode soon became known as the "attack of the killer rabbit."

339. One night in 1974, from a Cessna Citation aircraft, one of America's most famous citizens saw a UFO. There were four persons aboard the plane: pilot Bill Paynter, two security guards, and the governor of California, Ronald Reagan. As the airplane approached Bakersfield, California, the passengers called Paynter's attention to a strange object to their rear. "It appeared to be several hundred yards away," Paynter recalled. "It was a fairly steady light until it began to accelerate. Then it appeared to elongate. Then the light took off. It went up at a 45-degree angle — at a high rate of speed. Everyone on the plane was surprised . . . . The UFO went from a normal cruise speed to a fantastic speed instantly. If you give an airplane power, it will accelerate, but not like a hot rod, and that's what this was like." http://science.howstuffworks.com/ronald-reagan-ufo.htm; accessed August 2008.

340. Howard Norton and Bob Strosser, The Miracle of Jimmy Carter (Plainfield, NJ: Logos Books, 1976), p. 93.

341. Kenneth Morris, Jimmy Carter: American Moralist (Athens, GA: University of Georgia Press, 1996), p.169.

342. Dr. Evans' personal interview with Menachem Begin in Jerusalem, 1980.

343. Personal information given to Dr. Evans by Prime Minister Begin.

344. Kenneth W. Stein, "My Problem with Jimmy Carter's Book," The Middle East Quarterly, Spring 2007, pp. 3–15; http://www.meforum.org/pf.php?id=1633; accessed March 2012.

345. "Camp David Accords — Annex and Letters: September 17, 1978," Israel Ministry of Foreign Affairs; http://israelipalestinian.procon.org/view.background-resource.php?resourceID=1541; accessed March 2012.

346. "Carter Meets Arafat in Paris, Praises Him as Peacemaker," The New York Times, April 5, 1990; http://query.nytimes.com/gst/fullpage.html?res=9C0CE2DB133AF936A35757C0A966958260; accessed March 2008.

347. Noel Sheppard, "Jimmy Carter on Al-Jazeera: 'I Wasn't Equating the Palestinian Missiles with Terrorism,'" NewsBusters; http://www.newsbusters.org/node/10199; accessed March 2008.

348. Jay Nordlinger, "Jimmy Carter, Apologist for Arafat," *National Review*, October 16, 2002; http://frontpagemag.com/Articles/Read.aspx?GUID=5A1AEC45-2FFD-456B-9CD9-0D50BF0F2F43; accessed March 2008.

349. "Quotes: Arab Leaders," Serious Games Interactive; http://learning.seriousgames.dk/quotes.aspx; accessed March 2008.

350. Toby Klein Greenwald, "Jimmy Carter, an unwilling Bilaam," *The Jerusalem Post*, January 12, 2012; http://www.jpost.com/LandedPages/PrintArticle.aspx?id=145861; accessed January 2012.

351. Malkah, Fleisher, "Jimmy Carter: I Repent for Stigma I Created Against Israel," December 22, 2009, http://www.israelnationalnews.com/News/News.aspx/135149; accessed January 2011.

352. The roadmap for peace is a plan to resolve the Israeli–Palestinian conflict proposed by a quartet of international entities: the U.S., the EU, Russia, and the UN.

353. Jimmy Carter, *Palestine: Peace Not Apartheid* (New York: Simon and Schuster, 2006), p. 213.

354. See: Mike Evans, *Jimmy Carter: the Liberal Left and World Chaos.*

355. "If My people who are called by My name will humble themselves, and pray and seek My face, and turn from their wicked ways, then I will hear from heaven, and will forgive their sin and heal their land" (2 Chronicles 7:14 nkjv).

356. Personal conversation: Dr. Mike Evans, Reuven Hecht, and Isser Harel, 1980.

357. Donald Wagner, "Bible and Sword: US Christian Zionists Discover Israel," Information Clearing House, October 10, 2003; http://www.informationclearinghouse.info/article4950.htm; accessed March 2012.

358. Donald Wagner, "Evangelicals and Israel: Theological Roots of a Political Alliance," *The Christian Century*, November 4, 1998, pp. 1020–1026.

359. David Schribman, "Reagan, all-American, dies at 93," *The Boston Globe*, June 6, 2004; http://www.boston.com/news/nation/articles/2004/06/06/reagan_all_american_dies_at_93/.; accessed January 2012.

360. Paul Kengor, *God and Ronald Reagan: A Spiritual Life* (New York: Harper, 2004), p. 15.

361. Michael Beschloss, Presidential Courage: Brave Leaders and How they Changed America 1789–1989 (New York: Simon & Schuster, 2008), p. 296.

362. Gore Vidal, *Imperial America: Reflections on the United States of Amnesia* (New York: Nation Books, 2005), p. 72.

363. "U.S. Presidents On Israel: Remarks at a White House Meeting with Jewish Leaders, February 2, 1983; http://www.jewishvirtuallibrary.org/jsource/US-Israel/presquote.html#4; accessed January 2012.

364. Ibid, (Remarks at the Welcoming Ceremony for President Chaim Herzog of Israel, November 10, 1987.)

365. Elizabeth Stephens, *US Policy Towards Israel: The Role of Political Culture in Defining the 'Special Relationship'* (East Sussex, UK: Sussex Academic, 2006), p. 201.

366. "Reagan," Free Republic; http://www.freerepublic.com/focus/f-bloggers/2669552/posts#reagan; accessed January 2012.

367. The Iran-Contra Affair was a clandestine action not approved by the United States Congress. It began in 1985, when President Ronald Reagan's administration supplied weapons to Iran — a sworn enemy — in hopes of securing the release of American hostages held in Lebanon by Hezbollah terrorists loyal to the Ayatollah Khomeini, Iran's leader.

368. Jon E. Dougherty, "Reagan: A Staunch Friend of Israel," NewsMax.com; June 9, 2004; http://archive.newsmax.com/archives/articles/2004/6/8/172342.shtml; accessed January 2012.

369. Statement on Signing the United States–Israel Free Trade Area Implementation Act of 1985, June 11, 1985; http://www.sice.oas.org/tpd/usa_isr/uslaw1985_e.pdf; accessed January 2012.

370. Elizabeth Stephens, *US Policy Towards Israel: The Role of Political Culture in Defining the 'Special Relationship,'* p. 201.

371. "U.S. Presidents On Israel: Remarks at a White House Meeting with Jewish Leaders, February 2, 1983; http://www.jewishvirtuallibrary.org/jsource/US-Israel/presquote.html#4; accessed January 2012.

372. "Reagan Quotes: November 5, 1994," American Experience; http://www.pbs.org/wgbh/americanexperience/features/general-article/reagan-quotes/; accessed January 2012.

373. "Ronald Reagan Library Opening," Plan B Productions, November 4, 1991; http://www.planbproductions.com/postnobills/reagan1.html; accessed January 2012.

374. "Lieutenant Junior Grade George Bush, USNR," Naval History and Heritage Command, April 6, 2001; http://www.history.navy.mil/faqs/faq10-1.htm; accessed January 2012.

375. "Israel, Ignoring Bush, Presses for Loan Guarantees,"Thomas Friedman, *The New York Times,* September 7, 1991, http://www.nytimes.com/1991/09/07/world/israel-ignoring-bush-presses-for-loan-guarantees.html; accessed July 2013.

376. Yedinot Aharonot, Tel Aviv, January 16,1996. Quoted in Samuel Segev, "The Arab-Israeli Conflict under President Bush," p. 127.

377. Marshal Breger, "Bush, George Herbert Walker," Jewish Virtual Library; http://www.jewishvirtuallibrary.org/jsource/judaica/ejud_0002_0004_0_03769.html; accessed January 2012.

378. "Address by US President Bill Clinton to the Knesset," October 27, 1994, http://www.mfa.gov.il/mfa/go.asp?MFAH0bz20; accessed November 2003, and "Remarks by President and Prime Minister Netanyahu in Exchange of Toast," December 13, 1998. Online at: http://clinton3.nara.gov/WH/New/mideast/19981214-14375.html; accessed November 2003. President Clinton quoted this on many different occasions to audiences concerned with the future of Israel, but at times interchanged the word "forget" for "abandon." I have used abandoned here because it seems the more commonly used in the quotation than "forget."

379. See Luke 2.

380. Simon Tisdall, "Symbolic gesture seals hopes to end blood and tears" *Guardian Unlimited* (September 14, 1993), http://www.guardiancentury.co.uk/1990-1999/Story/0,6051,112648,00.html; accessed November 2003.

381. Ambassador Dore Gold, an interview with Amnon Lord, October 2003.

382. Elliot Engel, address during the Jerusalem Summit: Building Peace on Truth, October 12-14, 2003.

383. Alan M. Dershowitz, *Why Terrorism Works: Understanding the Threat, Responding to the Challenge* (New Haven and London: Yale University Press, 2002), p. 2.

384. Dr. David R. Reagan, "Yitzhak Rabin," http://www.raptureforums.com/IsraelMiddleEast/yitzhakrabin.cfm. Accessed September 2013.

385. Yoram Etinger, an interview with Amnon Lord, Oct. 25, 2003.

386. Tal Silberstein, an interview with Amnon Lord, Nov.2, 2003.

387. Yossef Bodansky, *The High Cost of Peace: How Washington's Middle East Policy Left America Vulnerable to Terrorism* (Roseville, CA: Forum, 2002), p. 223.

388. Tal Silberstein, an interview with Amnon Lord, Nov.2, 2003.

389. *The New Yorker* (March 24, 2003).

390. Richard Miniter, *Losing bin Laden: How Bill Clinton's Failures Unleashed Global Terror* (Washington, DC: Regnery Publishing, Inc., 2003), pp. xvi, xix. (Insert added.)

391. White House Report, "Clinton on Life, Career, Decisions," August 11, 2000; http://wfile.ait.org.tw/wf-archive/2000/000811/epf501.htm; accessed November 2003.

392. Alan Dershowitz, *What Israel Means to Me* (Hoboken, New Jersey: John Wiley & Sons, Inc., 2006), p. 53.

393. Private conversation between Dr. Evans and David Bar Ilan.

394. Ibid.

395. Charles Krauthammer, "The failure of Arafat's intifada," *The Seattle Times,* June 21, 2004; http://community.seattletimes.nwsource.com/archive/?date=20040621&slug=krauthammer21; accessed January 2012.

396. Ibid.

397. Elliott Abrams, "Clinton Reinvents Israel," Council on Foreign Relations, September 22, 2011; http://www.cfr.org/israel/clinton-reinvents-israel/p26017; accessed January 2012.

398. Ibid.

399. Ibid.

400. http://www.lyrics007.com/John%20Lennon%20Lyrics/Imagine%20Lyrics.html; accessed August 2013.

401. "Read her lips: Literacy efforts on first lady's agenda," People in the News, April 8, 2001; http://www.cnn.com/CNN/Programs/people/shows/bush/profile.html; accessed January 2012.

402. Mark Matthews, *The Lost Years: Bush, Sharon, and Failure in the Middle East* (New York: Nation Books, 2007), p. 20.

403. Sheryl Gay Stolberg, "Bush and Israel — Unlike his father," *The New York Times*; February 8, 2006; http://www.nytimes.com/2006/08/02/world/americas/02iht-bush.2363483.html?pagewanted=all; accessed January 2012.

404. Ibid.

405. Steven Donald Smith, "Bush Calls for Lasting Middle East Cease-Fire, End of Status Quo," American Forces Press Service, U.S. Department of Defense, July 31, 2006; http://www.defense.gov/news/newsarticle.aspx?id=310; accessed January 2012.

406. Rebecca Ann Stoil, "Poll: American voters' support for Israel rising," *The Jerusalem Post,* November 11, 2011; http://www.jpost.com/International/Article.aspx?id=245193; accessed January 2012.

407. David A. Harris, "Ten Ways Israel is Treated Differently," *The Jerusalem Post*, (no date given); http://www.aish.com/jw/me/ten_ways_israel_is_treated_differently.html; accessed January 2012.

408. Irwin N. Graulich, "Why America Supports Israel," FrontPageMag.com, December 20, 2002; http://archive.frontpagemag.com/readArticle.aspx?ARTID=20579; accessed January 2012.

409. Mitchell G. Bard, "Deconstructing George W. Bush's Middle East Strategy," Jewish Virtual Library; http://www.jewishvirtuallibrary.org/jsource/US-Israel/deconstruct.html; accessed January 2012.

410. Speech to American Jewish Committee, (May 3, 2001).

411. President George W. Bush, "Speech on the Middle East," Council on Foreign Relations, June 24, 2002; http://www.cfr.org/publication.html?id=4746&issue=26; accessed January 2012.

412. Ibid.

413. "President Bush Visits Yad Vashem," The White House: President George W. Bush, January 11, 2008; http://georgewbush-whitehouse.archives.gov/news/releases/2008/01/20080111.html; accessed January 2012.

414. "As Bush celebrates Israel's 60th birthday, rocket attack hurts dozens," *New York Daily News*, May 15, 2008; http://articles.nydailynews.com/2008-05-15/news/17897335_1_popular-resistance-committees-mideast-peace-rocket-attacks; accessed January 2012.

415. "Why Obama 'hates' Israel," Rabbi Pruzansky's Blog, November 23, 2010; http://rabbipruzansky.com/2010/11/23/why-obama-%E2%80%9Chates%E2%80%9D-israel/; accessed January 2012.

416. David Jackson, "Bush won't critique Obama (or Palin)," *USA Today*, November 5, 2010; http://content.usatoday.com/communities/theoval/post/2010/11/bush-wont-critique-obama/1; accessed January 2012.

417. "Ploughshares Fund," DiscovertheNetworks.org; http://www.discoverthenetworks.org/groupprofile.asp?grpid=7156&category=79; accessed January 2012.

418. Ed Lasky, "Obama Keeps Hiring Anti-Israeli Advisors," *American Thinker*, April 25, 2008; http://www.americanthinker.com/blog/2008/04/obama_keeps_hiring_antiisraeli.html; accessed January 2012.

419. "Larijani, Iran Prefers Obama," *YNetNews.com*, October 22, 2008; http://www.ynetnews.com/articles/0,7340,L-3611840,00.html; accessed October 2008.

420. Joseph Klein, "Obama, Sarkozy's Contempt for Netanyahu Exposed," *Front Page Magazine*, November 9, 2011; http://frontpagemag.com/2011/11/09/obama-sarkozys-contempt-for-netanyahu-exposed/; accessed January 2012.

421. Joshua Rolnick, "Obama's Speech: First Take," National Jewish Democratic Council, June 4, 2009; http://www.njdc.org/blog/post/obamas_speech_first_take; accessed March 2012.

422. "Obama and Israel," DiscovertheNetworks.org, November 11, 2011; http://www.discoverthenetworks.org/viewSubCategory.asp?id=1521; accessed January 2012.

423. "Full Text of Prime Minister Netanyahu's speech before the United Nations General Assembly 2013," October 1, 2013, *Times of Israel*, http://www.timesofisrael.com/full-text-netanyahus-2013-speech-to-the-un-general-assembly/; accessed October 2013.

424. Ibid.

425. Ibid.

426. Robinson, Frye, and Bradley 1997.

427. United States Geological Survey, "Earthquakes with 1,000 or More Deaths from 1900," http://neic.usgs.gov/neis/eqlists/eqsmajr.html. Last updated: 23 October 2003; accessed January 2004; and USGS, "Most Destructive Known Earthquakes on Record in the World: Earthquakes with 50,000 or More Deaths," http://neic.usgs.gov/neis/eqlists/eqsmosde.html. Last updated: 23 October 2003; accessed January 2004.

428. David B. Barrett and Todd M. Johnson, *World Christian Trends a.d. 30–a.d. 2200: Interpreting the Annual Christian Megacensus* (Pasadena, CA: William Carey Library, 2001), 229.

429. www.pollingreport.com/religion.html; accessed November 2003.

430. This list is from Mark Hitchcock, *Is America in Bible Prophecy?* (Sisters, OR: Multnomah Publishers, 2002), pp. 27-28, though I have changed some of the scripture references to verses that more clearly represent his points.

BOOKS BY: MIKE EVANS

Israel: America's Key to Survival

Save Jerusalem

The Return

Jerusalem D.C.

Purity and Peace of Mind

Who Cries for the Hurting?

Living Fear Free

I Shall Not Want

Let My People Go

Jerusalem Betrayed

Seven Years of Shaking: A Vision

The Nuclear Bomb of Islam

Jerusalem Prophecies

Pray For Peace of Jerusalem

America's War: The Beginning of the End

The Jerusalem Scroll

The Prayer of David

The Unanswered Prayers of Jesus

God Wrestling

Why Christians Should Support Israel

The American Prophecies

Beyond Iraq: The Next Move

The Final Move beyond Iraq

Showdown with Nuclear Iran

Jimmy Carter: The Liberal Left and World Chaos

Atomic Iran

Cursed

Betrayed

The Light

Corrie's Reflections & Meditations (booklet)

GAMECHANGER SERIES:
GameChanger
Samson Option
The Four Horsemen

THE PROTOCOLS SERIES:
The Protocols
The Candidate

The Revolution

The Final Generation

Seven Days

The Locket

Living in the F.O.G.

Persia: The Final Jihad

Jerusalem

The History of Christian Zionism

Countdown

Ten Boom: Betsie, Promise of God

Commanded Blessing

Born Again: 1948

Presidents in Prophecy

COMING SOON:

Born Again: 1967

Stand with Israel: Friends of Zion

Christopher Columbus

To purchase, contact: orders@timeworthybooks.com

P. O. Box 30000, Phoenix, AZ 85046